GENESIS

GENESIS

TRUMAN, AMERICAN JEWS, AND THE ORIGINS OF THE ARAB/ISRAELI CONFLICT

JOHN B. JUDIS

FARRAR, STRAUS AND GIROUX   NEW YORK

Farrar, Straus and Giroux
18 West 18th Street, New York 10011

Copyright © 2014 by John B. Judis
Printed in the United States of America
First edition, 2014

The maps on pages xi–xiii are courtesy of the University of Texas Libraries,
the University of Texas at Austin.

Library of Congress Cataloging-in-Publication Data
Judis, John B., author,
    Genesis : Truman, American Jews, and the origins of the Arab/Israeli conflict / John
B. Judis. — First edition.
       p.   cm.
    Includes index.
    ISBN 978-0-374-16109-5 (hardback)
    1. Arab-Israeli conflict—Causes.   2. Arab-Israeli conflict—Moral and ethical
aspects.   3. United States—Foreign relations—Israel.   4. Israel—Foreign relations—
United States.   5. United States—Politics and government—1945–1953.   6. Truman,
Harry S., 1884–1972—Relations with Jews.   7. Zionism—United States—History—
20th century.   I. Title.

DS119.6 .J83 2014
327.7305694009'044—dc23

2013036637

Designed by Abby Kagan

Farrar, Straus and Giroux books may be purchased for educational, business, or
promotional use. For information on bulk purchases, please contact the Macmillan
Corporate and Premium Sales Department at 1-800-221-7945, extension 5442,
or write to specialmarkets@macmillan.com.

www.fsgbooks.com
www.twitter.com/fsgbooks • www.facebook.com/fsgbooks

1   3   5   7   9   10   8   6   4   2

For my colleagues, past and present, at *The New Republic*

Are ye not as children of the Ethiopians unto me, O children of Israel? saith the Lord. Have not I brought up Israel out of the land of Egypt? and the Philistines from Caphtor, and the Syrians from Kir?

—AMOS 9:7

CONTENTS

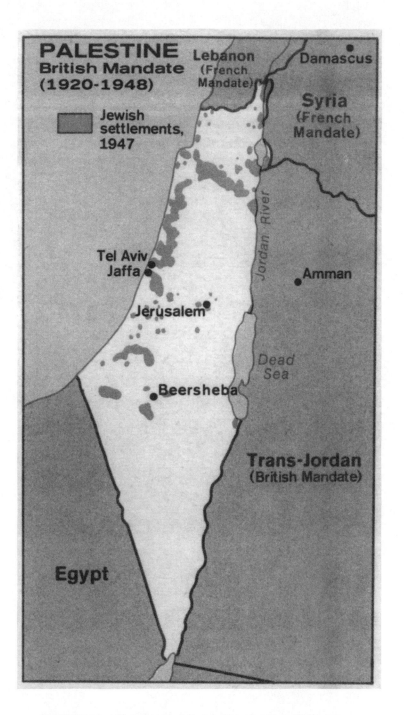

PALESTINE BEFORE THE UNITED NATIONS PLAN FOR PARTITION, 1947

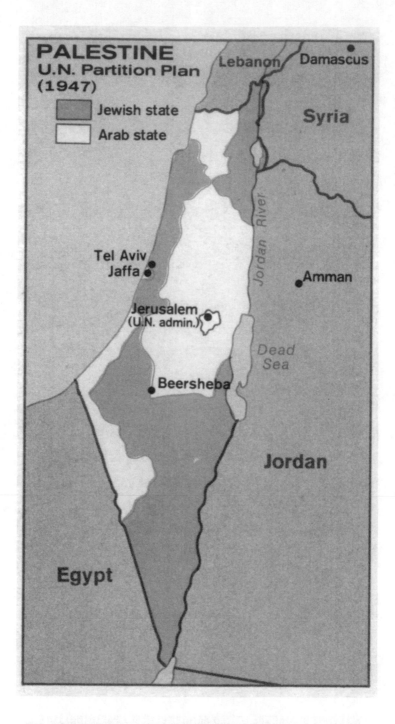

THE UNITED NATIONS PLAN FOR PARTITIONING PALESTINE INTO A JEWISH
AND AN ARAB STATE, NOVEMBER 1947

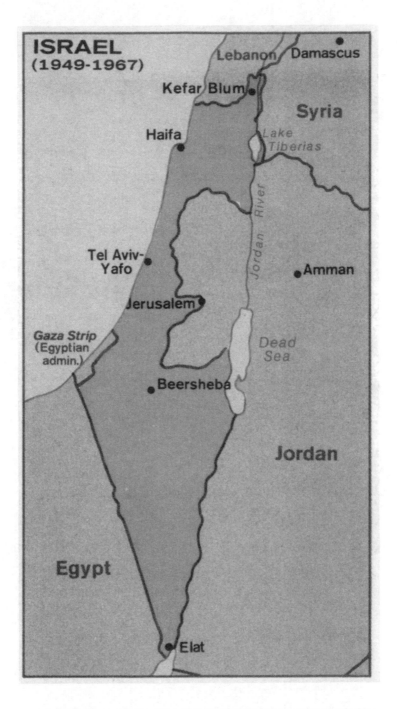

THE NEW STATE OF ISRAEL AFTER THE 1948 WAR AND THE 1949 ARMISTICE

GENESIS

INTRODUCTION: TRUMAN'S QUALMS

On Wednesday, September 8, 1948, Harry Truman was in a sea of troubles. He was in the middle of an election he was expected to lose; the Soviet Union was blockading Berlin; and, in the Middle East, Israel and five of its Arab neighbors were at war. That morning, Truman's first visitors in the White House were a delegation from the Jewish War Veterans of America, headed by Brigadier General Julius Klein.

It was supposed to be a routine fifteen-minute visit—a chance for the war veterans to invite Truman to their National Encampment in Monticello the next week—but Klein surprised the president by presenting him with a long list of demands related to the new state of Israel. They included ending the arms embargo that the United States had imposed on all the combatants, granting Israel a $100 million loan to help it settle immigrants from Europe's displaced persons camps, and championing Israel's membership in the United Nations.[1]

Truman was taken aback. As Klein later recounted, the president said, defensively, that he was "the best friend the Jews had in America." And then he said something that clearly shocked Klein and the delegation. He complained to the Jewish War Veterans that he and British foreign secretary Ernest Bevin "had agreed on the best possible solution for Palestine, and it was the Zionists who killed that plan by their opposition."

Truman was referring to the recommendations of the Anglo-American Committee, which came out in the spring of 1946, and to the plan negotiated by the American Henry Grady and the British official Herbert Morrison for implementing the recommendations. The committee called for allowing 100,000 Jewish survivors of Hitler's final solution, who were marooned in displaced persons camps, into Palestine. But it also recommended organizing Palestine into a federated state that would be neither Arab nor Jewish.

Klein reportedly left the meeting looking glum. One thing that must have bothered him was that, just four months before, Truman had recognized the new Jewish state of Israel. Now he was saying that the "best possible solution" had not been a Jewish state but a state that was jointly administered by Jew and Arab. And he was blaming America's Zionists for blocking this solution.

Truman has sometimes been portrayed as a Christian Zionist whose decision to recognize Israel was in line with his own deepest convictions.[2] But that is not reflected in his comment to Klein. Truman was a Jeffersonian Democrat who rejected the idea of a state religion—state religions were what had caused centuries of war in Europe. He didn't think that a nation should be defined by a particular people or race or religion. Far from being a Christian Zionist, Truman was deeply skeptical about the Zionist project of founding a Jewish state, as he repeatedly told Jewish leaders during his first year in office. He had personally overseen Henry Grady's work in developing the recommendations for a federated Palestine.

Truman backed down in October 1946 and supported a Jewish state in a part of Palestine. He did so to some extent, as he told Klein, because of political pressure from Zionist organizations. In the upcoming November elections, Truman feared that the Democrats could lose key races if the Jews, in response to attacks on Truman from the Zionist groups, voted for the Republicans. He also backed down because, with the Cold War beginning, he could not use American forces to help impose the kind of solution he and Bevin favored. After October 1946, Truman's wishes for a federated or binational Palestine found expression only in repeated private complaints to people like Klein.

Was Truman right in the first place to advocate a federated or binational Palestine? Truman was not insensitive to the plight of European Jews, who had lost 6 million to Hitler's final solution, and who had been, and still were, blocked from emigrating to Western Europe or the United States by draconian immigration laws. Truman had infuriated the British and Palestinian Arabs by insisting that the survivors of the Holocaust be allowed to emigrate to Palestine. But Truman also understood that Europe's Zionist movement, beginning in the late nineteenth century, had been seeking to create a Jewish state in a land where another people had lived and made up the overwhelming majority for 1,400 years. Truman didn't know all the details of this history, but he knew enough of it to fear that establishing a state where either Jews or Arabs dominated would likely lead to war and injustice, so he sought to create a state with a federal arrangement that might satisfy the aspirations of both peoples.

After he gave up trying to impose a federated state, Truman continued to press for an equitable resolution to the conflict between the Arabs and Jews. His concern was partly strategic. He was worried, as was his State Department and Pentagon, about taking the side of the Zionists and alienating the region's Arabs at a time when the United States and its allies might need Arab oil to fight a war against the Soviet Union. But Truman's foreign policy views were grounded in personal morality. He saw the world divided between good guys and bad guys and between underdogs and bullies. He worried about fairness. He was outraged by what had been done to the Jews in Europe, but he was worried about a settlement that was unfair to Palestine's Arabs.

In October 1947, when the United Nations was debating partition, Truman favored a division of Palestine that would give the Arabs, who still made up two-thirds of the population, a proportionate majority of the lands. After the wars of 1948, he favored a peace agreement between Israel and the Arab states that would at least restore the 40 percent of Palestine that the UN had earlier allotted to the Arabs and would allow many of the 700,000 Arab refugees displaced by the war to return to their homes. But Truman was beaten back in each instance by a powerful American Zionist movement working in tandem with the

Jewish Agency in Palestine and later the Israeli government. In the end, the new Jewish state took up almost 80 percent of Palestine, and Palestine's Arabs were dispersed and deprived of a state of their own. Europe's Jews had been given their due, but it was at the expense of Palestine's Arabs.

Should American Zionists have been expected to fight tooth and nail for their Jewish brethren overseas? Yes and no. The American Zionist movement was led in its first decades by liberals and progressives like Louis Brandeis, Stephen Wise, Felix Frankfurter, David Dubinsky, and Horace Kallen. Zionism also attracted the enthusiastic support of Christian liberals, including Reinhold Niebuhr, Henry Wallace, and Eleanor Roosevelt, and of the country's most liberal media, including *The Nation*, *The New Republic*, the *New York Post* (in its earlier incarnation), and the daily *PM*, which featured I. F. Stone's journalism.

These liberals and progressives supported labor rights, civil rights, and the first amendment. Wise was a founder of the American Civil Liberties Union and the National Association for the Advancement of Colored People. Many of them had also backed Wilson's call for the self-determination of colonial peoples. But when it came to Palestine, they were oblivious to the rights of Palestine's Arabs. In the movement's first decades, American Zionists averred that the Jews were emigrating to a largely unoccupied wasteland or desert; later, when it became clear that Arabs already lived there, they insisted that these Arabs, who could trace their lineage in Palestine to 638 C.E., could easily pick up and move to Jordan, Iraq, or Syria. After the 1948 wars, they contended that the Palestinian refugees had either fled of their own accord or were induced to flee by Arab leaders.

As liberals and progressives, they might have been expected to help Truman fashion a compromise that recognized the rights of Jews and Arabs, but they did nothing of the kind. They excoriated Truman for doing what in any other context they would have condoned and supported. In 1948, Henry Wallace's Progressive Party targeted Jewish voters unhappy with Truman's attempts to reach a compromise between Jew and Arab with pamphlets warning that "a vote for Truman is a vote to rebuild Nazi Germany."[3] These liberals seemed to be willfully ignorant of what was actually going on in Palestine.

Truman was a genuine liberal who had moral qualms about Zionism. He was also the last president to express them. But almost every American president since Truman has tried to find a way to improve the lot of Palestinian Arabs—through trying to get Israel to allow refugees to return and later by trying to persuade the Israelis to leave the occupied West Bank and permit the Palestinian Arabs a state of their own. Yet Truman's successors have, as a rule, suffered the same fate as he did. They began with a moral and strategic conviction that something had to be done to right the situation of the Palestinians, but under relentless pressure from supporters of Israel (and after 1948 from the Israeli government itself), they gave up.

That's what happened to Barack Obama during his first term. When he took office, he declared that Israel had to stop expanding into the West Bank and agree to the existence of a Palestinian state. "The United States does not accept the legitimacy of continued Israeli settlements," Obama declared. "It is time for these settlements to stop."[4] But at odds with Israeli prime minister Benjamin Netanyahu and facing sharp opposition from his supporters in Washington, Obama eventually backed down. By the end of his first term, he was heeding Israel's wishes to focus on the threat from Iran rather than on settlements, and was opposing a Palestinian effort to win recognition at the United Nations.

This pattern of surrender to Israel and its supporters began in the Truman years. The actors have changed—the Zionist movement now calls itself the "pro-Israel" movement—and the issue itself is no longer whether there should be a Jewish state, but whether there should also be a Palestinian state and, if so, whether it should constitute more than a few barren hills carved up by checkpoints and security barriers. But the underlying problem remains the same: whether an American president and the American people can forthrightly address the conflict of Jew and Arab in the Middle East, or whether they must bow to the demands of a powerful pro-Israel lobby and an increasingly rightward-leaning Israeli government.

I started out some years ago to write a book about Truman's attempt to resolve the conflict between Jew and Arab because I thought that his failure to do so established a pattern that plagued his successors. That remains the subject of this book. But I found that while I could adequately tell the story of what happened in the Truman years, I could not adequately address the moral dimension of what had happened. And that is as important to me as it was to Truman.

In the years right after World War II, revelations about Nazi genocide against the Jews loomed very large in the debate over a Jewish state, making it difficult for many Americans to understand, or take seriously, Arab opposition to the state of Israel, and later to Israeli policies toward the Palestinians. And, remarkably, that is still the case, and maybe even more so.[5] To understand how Palestinian Arabs felt then, and even to assess what should be done now, it is necessary to revisit the beginnings of Zionism in Europe, of Arab nationalism in Palestine, and of Zionism in the United States.

This book tells the story of the Truman years, but it begins in the 1890s with the first Zionist émigrés to Palestine from Russia's Pale of Settlement and with the founding in 1898 of the Federation of American Zionists. And it takes the story of European and American Zionism and of Palestinian Arab nationalism up to April 1945 when Truman finds himself thrust into the presidency by Franklin Roosevelt's death.

When I was beginning this project, friends questioned why I didn't write a book criticizing what the American and Israeli governments are doing now and propose alternative policies. I don't doubt such a book would be useful, but I am not the one to write it. That's a task for a journalist or a political scientist who is thoroughly acquainted with the current actors. But I also believe that one reason why debate over American policy has been so fruitless is because Americans lack a historical perspective in addressing the conflict between the Jews and Arabs.

Discussions about the Israeli-Palestinian conflict are sometimes mired in "he said–she said" debates about the present: Did Hamas fire the rocket before or after Israel assassinated one of its leaders? Did Ariel Sharon or Yasir Arafat precipitate the Second Intifada? But many discussions are also framed in a kind of timeless history that begins well in the past and then jumps directly into the present. Defenders of Israel base their arguments either on what the Bible says happened several millennia ago, or by reminding critics of the Holocaust. Arab critics of Israel begin with the Crusades or with the massacre at Deir Yassin in April 1948. It is important to approach the subject from when the conflict actually began and to carry it forward consecutively from there.

This book is primarily about what *Americans* can learn from the failure of the Truman administration to resolve the conflict between Zionism and Arab nationalism. I am not writing this book from the standpoint of or primarily for the benefit of the Jewish community. But I have asked myself why someone who had written principally about American political and intellectual history and who is Jewish, but has no religious allegiance to Judaism, was spending so much time writing about Truman, American Zionists, and the Israeli-Palestinian conflict.

I became interested in Israel out of disillusionment with my own country during the sixties and the Vietnam War, and when the Six-Day War began in 1967, I contacted the Israeli consulate in San Francisco to volunteer. (It was too late.) But I began to wonder about Israel's direction after it occupied and began to colonize the West Bank. I began to wonder, too, about American policy, when, some years later, as a reporter covering Capitol Hill, I discovered how scared politicians were to buck Israel's powerful lobby.

There are also inevitable connections between my being Jewish and my writing this book. As a Jew, I do worry more about American policy toward Israel, and about how the Israelis are conducting themselves, than I worry or care about American policy toward Brazil and about how the Brazilians are acting. I am also more upset and offended by Israel's occupation of the West Bank than I am about China's occupation of Tibet, although I think that on some objective scale of injustice, they are about equal.

Prior to writing this book, I knew much more about the history of Protestantism than of Judaism. But in researching this book I discovered that there was an American Jewish political tradition that I could identify with—that of the Reform Jews in the late nineteenth century. These Jews were close politically to the proponents of the Protestant Social Gospel, about whom I knew considerably more. Some of them, like Stephen Wise, became Zionists, but others opposed Theodor Herzl's idea of a Jewish state. These Reform Jews from Isaac Mayer Wise to Obama's Chicago neighbor Arnold Wolf believed that the role of Jews was not to favor Jews at the expense of other people but to bring the light of ethical prophecy to bear upon the welfare of all peoples.

I can't claim to be fulfilling the role of ethical prophet, but what I took from this Reform tradition was the idea that an American Jew should be as concerned about the rights of a Palestinian Arab as he is about the rights of an Israeli Jew. That's not a view you'll find today at many of the so-called pro-Israel organizations, or at the evangelical churches that call for the Jewish conquest of Judea and Samaria, but it's my view, and it's the one that informs this history.

PART ONE

TWO PEOPLES
AND
ONE LAND

How men are to live together and be governed is a spiritual question with far-reaching implications. The fact remains that Palestine is small and is not empty.

—Judah L. Magnes

1

THE ORIGINS OF ZIONISM: HERZL, AHAD HA'AM, AND GORDON

If you had been alive in the mid-nineteenth century and visited the land that would become Palestine and then Israel, you would have found few signs of the conflict that would later tear the country apart. You would have heard references to "Palestine," but you wouldn't have found a nation with its own laws and government that corresponded to Palestine or Israel. The Turks, who ruled the region, divided the land into three parts for purposes of collecting taxes. The West Bank was part of the province of Syria; northern Palestine was part of the province of Beirut; and Jerusalem and its environs had their own district.

According to one estimate, the area corresponding to Palestine had about 340,000 people, of whom 300,000, or 88 percent, were Muslims or Druze, 27,000, or 8 percent, Christians, and 13,000, or 4 percent, Jews.[1] Many of these Jews lived in Jerusalem, Nablus, and Hebron. A few were well-to-do descendants of Sephardic émigrés from Spain, but many were more recent émigrés from Europe who devoted themselves to religious study and prayer and survived off donations from abroad.

The Jews of Palestine suffered religious persecution, but no different from that inflicted on Christians in a society dominated by Muslims. For instance, both Jews and Christians were officially prohibited from building new houses of worship, but both groups were able to use bribes to get around the law. There was nothing like the wave of anti-Semitism that would sweep Europe during the late nineteenth century. "Jews enjoyed a higher standing in Muslim society and enjoyed a greater affinity with the culture of their surroundings than the Jews in Eastern Europe," wrote the historian Yosef Gorny.[2]

There was also little of a Western presence in the region. Americans were preoccupied with the Civil War and its aftermath. The great powers of Europe were just beginning to divide up Asia and Africa. The British had an interest in allying themselves with the Turks against the Russians, they were about to gain a foothold in Egypt, and they had begun to consider Palestine and its environs as a path eastward, but they had not done anything about it, and would not do so for the rest of the century.

There were rabbis and some notable Christians in Europe and the United States who thought the Jews should return to Palestine. The Christians were called "restorationists," and in Britain they were able to attract support for their views among high officials who saw a Jewish Palestine in commercial or imperial terms. But most Jews accepted the Diaspora as an enduring condition. The Orthodox thought that the Jews would eventually return to Zion, but by a Messianic act of God rather than by an organized mass migration. Jews declared "Next year in Jerusalem" annually during Passover dinners, but few took these words literally.

Then, over the next forty years—from the 1880s to the end of World War I and the early 1920s—the region was utterly transformed. The Ottoman Empire was dissolved, a casualty of Turkey's alliance with Germany during World War I. Through a League of Nations mandate, Britain assumed control of Palestine, an area that initially included what became Transjordan and later Jordan, but it administered the two areas separately. As a result, the western part of the mandate, administered through Jerusalem, became known again as Palestine, the name the Romans had originally given the country, but that also had a more ancient root in the seafaring Philistines who were contemporaries of the Old Testament Jews.

By 1922, according to a British census, Palestine's population had grown to 752,048, of which Jews accounted for 83,900, or 11 percent. The sevenfold increase in the Jewish population had been spurred by the development of a Zionist movement in Europe, particularly in the Russian Pale of Settlement, which was in response to the simultaneous growth of nationalism and anti-Semitism in Central and Western Europe. Zionism was Jewish nationalism, but unlike German or Romanian nationalism, it was not centered on an existing homeland but on one that Jews had once inhabited and now wanted to return to.

The outward logic of Zionism was impeccable. The nations of Europe, where Jews had dwelt for hundreds of years, were treating them as a nation in their midst. Nationalist politicians and intellectuals in Central and Eastern Europe called for purging their countries of this alien nation. In response, Jews wanted a genuine nation of their own where they could be secure from persecution and oppression. The trouble came when Zionists specified where that nation should be. Two thousand years before, most Jews had lived in Palestine, and a few thousand still did. But other peoples had also inhabited Palestine over the millennia, and Arabs had lived there for 1,400 years. If Zionism's objective was to establish a Jewish state in Palestine, that meant ruling over or driving out the Arabs who already lived there.

In justifying their attempt to colonize Palestine, some Zionists—who cited the influence of the Russian Zionist Ahad Ha'am—tried to come to terms with the Arab presence in Palestine. But many Zionists, following the example of Theodor Herzl, the Viennese author of *The Jewish State*, fell back on the same kind of rationalizations that the great powers had advanced in attempting to extend their reach over Asia and Africa, and that Christian Europe, and that Christian restorationists, and even before them, the Crusaders, had used to justify the conquest of Palestine. They promised to reclaim Palestine for the religion of the Bible, to civilize the Arabs, and to revive the land that, they claimed, the Arabs had allowed to become a desolate wasteland. Most American Zionist leaders would trace their lineage back to Herzl rather than to Ahad Ha'am and would adopt a distorted understanding of Palestine and its Arab inhabitants.

Anti-Semitism and Zionism

The idea of a Jewish return to Zion (which originally referred to Jerusalem) goes back to the Babylonian captivity in the sixth century B.C.E. and was promoted over the centuries by a succession of Jewish rabbis and mystics. The English Puritans, including those who settled in New

England, believed on biblical grounds in a Jewish return to the region of Palestine. Napoleon advocated a Jewish state during his eastern campaign in 1799. And in the early nineteenth century, British officials, led by the Christian revivalist Lord Shaftesbury, called on Britain to promote a Jewish return to the Holy Land.

By midcentury, there was some stirring among Jewish intellectuals. In the 1860s, the German Socialist Moses Hess, a former comrade of Karl Marx, and the Polish rabbi Zvi Hirsch Kalischer, both of whom were deeply impressed by the Italian movement for national unification, Il Risorgimento, advocated the gradual creation of a Jewish state. But the birth of a Zionist movement—and the beginning of emigration—had to wait until the 1880s, till the outbreak of anti-Semitism in Russia and Eastern Europe and its spread westward. This turned Jewish Zionism from a religious fantasy into a political movement.

Jews, of course, had suffered persecution for centuries, but much though not all of it was based on their beliefs and what they were reputed to have done to Jesus Christ. It was religious persecution. By contrast, nineteenth- and early-twentieth-century anti-Semitism was primarily a toxic blend of nationalism, racism, and imperialism directed at Jews as an alien national group within nations or empires rather than as a religious group among other religions. It coincided with the rise throughout Europe of the unified nation state and of national rebellions against empires.

In the nineteenth century, Italians and Hungarians sought to free themselves from the Austro-Hungarian Empire; Romanians and other Balkan peoples from the Ottoman Empire; the Poles from the Russian Empire; and Germans from the Hapsburgs and from the legacy of defeat in the Napoleonic wars. They defined their national aspirations along ethnic and quasi-racial lines that led them to see Jews as an alien nation. Johann Gottlieb Fichte, a father of German nationalism, described Germans as a race that nature "joined to each other in a multitude of invisible bonds" and Jews as "a state within a state." Fichte infamously declared that he could only imagine granting civil rights to Jews if one were "to cut off all their heads in one night, and to set new ones on their shoulders, which should contain not a single Jewish idea."[3]

In Austria and Russia, defenders of the empire invoked their own brand of nationalism against the secessionists and against Jews, whom they blamed for the unrest. In Austria, George Ritter von Schönerer built a pan-German movement based on the premise that Austria had to rid itself of Jewish influence.[4] In Russia, the Black Hundreds swore loyalty to the czar and Russian absolutism while leading violent assaults against Jews.

This fusion of religious intolerance, national chauvinism, and what the Russian Zionist Leo Pinsker called "demonopathy" inspired new laws threatening Jews' livelihood and led to a succession of violent pogroms in Russia and the Russian Pale of Settlement—the western edge of the Russian empire to which the czarist regime restricted Jews. In the spring of 1881, massive anti-Jewish riots took place in response to false rumors that the Jews had assassinated Alexander II. These riots, in which Jews were killed and homes and synagogues destroyed, spread to 160 cities and villages in the Pale and recurred over the next four decades. The American ambassador wrote, "The acts which have been committed are more worthy of the Dark Ages than of the present century."[5]

In Eastern and Southern Europe, nationalist movements, seeking to throw off Austrian or Turkish rule, turned violently against the Jews. In Central and Western Europe, where Jews were no longer confined to ghettos, anti-Semitic movements and parties, typified by Karl Lueger's Austrian Christian Social party and Adolf Stoecker's party of the same name in Germany, directed their ire at the least and most successful Jews. They stirred fear that poverty-stricken Jewish immigrants from Russia and Eastern Europe were creating new ghettos while at the same time they excoriated wealthy, successful Jews who had lived in Germany and Austria for generations and who were assuming high positions in the professions, government, and the media. These parties called for restricting immigration and setting quotas for Jews in professions and universities. In France, an upsurge in anti-Semitism in the 1880s and '90s culminated in the frame-up, trial, and conviction of the Jewish army captain Alfred Dreyfus for treason.

By stigmatizing Jews as an alien nation rather than as a religious group, the new anti-Semitism inspired Jews to consider whether, if they were a national group, they needed a land-based nation of their own. And the pogroms lent urgency to the task. While the first great Zionist tract, Hess's *Rome and Jerusalem*, was ignored during his lifetime, the Russian Zionists of the 1880s, writing in the wake of the pogroms, were able to parlay their readership into an organized following.

The first two prominent Russian Zionists, Moshe Leib Lilienblum and Leo Pinsker, became Zionists in the wake of the pogroms. Lilienblum was a Talmudic scholar who, after breaking with the rabbinical orthodoxy, fled to Odessa, the capital of Jewish modernism. Pinsker was born in Russian Poland, the son of a distinguished Hebrew scholar. He was trained as a physician at the University of Moscow. He practiced in Odessa and was honored by Czar Nicholas I for his treatment of soldiers during the Crimean War.

Pinsker initially advocated Jewish assimilation, or "Russification" through the use of the Russian language and education in Russian culture. He was a leading member of the Society for the Spread of Culture among the Jews of Russia. But the pogroms turned him to Zionism. He resigned from the Society for the Spread of Culture and in 1882 published *Auto-Emancipation*, which helped inspire the Zionist movement in Russia. According to Pinsker, the Jews' problem was that "among the nations under which they dwell," they were the "ghost" of a nation rather than a real nation. Even after leaving Palestine, "they lived on spiritually as a nation," but "they lack a certain distinctive national character, inherent in all other nations, which is formed by common residence in a single state."[6] That accounted for what Pinsker called "Judeophobia." "If the fear of ghosts is something inborn, and has a certain justification in the psychic life of mankind," he wrote, "why be surprised as the effect produced by this dead but still living nation."[7]

Pinsker was convinced that Judeophobia was unavoidable as long as Jews were scattered as foreign bodies in the midst of other nations. "As a psychic aberration it is hereditary," he wrote, "and as a disease transmitted for two thousand years, it is incurable." Lilienblum, writing in 1883, was similarly pessimistic: "Civilization, which could virtually deliver us from those persecutions which have a religious basis, can do nothing at all for us against those persecutions that have a nationalistic basis."[8]

Pinsker's solution was not to fight Judeophobia. "We must give up contending against these hostile impulses as we must against every other inherited predisposition," he wrote.[9] Instead, Jews must eliminate the ghosts by establishing a real nation of their own. "Grant us our independence, allow us to take care of ourselves, give us but a little strip of land like that of the Serbians and Romanians, give us a chance to lead a national existence and then prate about our lacking manly virtues."[10]

Pinsker thought that Palestine was the likely site of a Jewish state, but he didn't claim Jewish title on biblical grounds. "The goal of our present endeavors must be not the 'Holy Land,' but a land of our own," he wrote.[11] Lilienblum was more willing to evoke past ownership. "Why should we be strangers in Gentile countries," he asked, "while the land of our fathers has not yet disappeared from the face of the earth, is still desolate, and can, along with its neighboring environs, incorporate our people?"[12]

Lilienblum's question, which was really an assertion, lay at the heart of early arguments for Zionism. While a few secular Jews like Pinsker eschewed biblical claims to Palestine, most Zionists did not—and that included secular Zionists like the young Pole David Ben-Gurion. Zionists regarded Palestine as the Jews' home from which they had been unjustly expelled by the Romans in the first and second centuries C.E., and to which they were fully entitled to return and to lay claim as their own.

This conception of Zionism, rooted in the Old Testament, rested on a mythic version of Palestine. In fact, the land from "Dan to Beersheba" that the Jews briefly ruled was home to many different peoples and tribes.[13] The area was also a "land of passage" in the Middle East through which different peoples entered and left—some voluntarily, some forcibly. In historical terms, the Zionist claim to Palestine had no more validity than the claim by some radical Islamists to a new caliphate. Nevertheless, this argument for Zionism, based on the Old Testament, carried great weight.

It was reinforced by Christian Zionism and its conception of Palestine as a "holy land" that had been despoiled by Islamic infidels. That idea went back to the Crusades, but it had been reshaped by the Christian Restorationists in the nineteenth century who called for a Jewish return to Palestine. It was as if Palestine had fallen out of history when the Muslims came during the sixth century and that its history would only resume when the Jews returned and reclaimed the land that was theirs.

Lilienblum, who had never set eyes on Palestine, assumed that if the Jews were to reclaim Palestine, they would discover a "desolate" land that was "desolated." The term "desolate" has had two meanings: that Palestine was largely uninhabited (and therefore open for colonization), and that those who inhabited it had desolated it (and therefore didn't deserve to inhabit or own title to it). Lilienblum seemed to use the term "desolate" primarily to imply a lack of inhabitants, even though in 1880 Palestine had about 500,000 inhabitants.[14] This idea of a desolate Palestine would permeate early Zionist thought. The historian Anita Shapira writes, "The conception of return was closely related to another, namely, that the land was desolate, pining away in expectation for Jews to come and settle there."[15]

This kind of thinking was common among Europeans who set out to colonize lands where the inhabitants were not Christian and at a lower level of economic development. In the seventeenth and eighteenth centuries, English colonists and would-be colonists described North America as a "wasteland."[16] In 1702, the Puritan Cotton Mather described the migration into New England as "some thousands of Reformers [sailing] into the Retirements of an American Desert."[17] The English saw Africa and the West Indies as "barren" and therefore open to Western exploitation.

As applied to the "holy land" of Palestine, the concept of desolation rendered the Arab inhabitants virtually invisible. That was the thrust of what Christian Zionists, biblical scholars, and travel writers wrote about Palestine in the early nineteenth century. One English scholar, for instance, wrote of Palestine in 1838 that "the cup of wrath and desolation from the Almighty has been poured out upon her to the dregs; and she sits sad and solitary in darkness and dust."[18] Fifty years later, an emerging Zionist movement would echo these conceptions, promising to bring happiness and light to a forsaken and deserted land.

Ahad Ha'am and the Lovers of Zion

In 1884, Pinsker summoned thirty-four delegates to Kattowitz in German-controlled Silesia (and out of the czar's reach) to the founding conference of the Lovers of Zion. About a score of Russian Jews had already made their way to Palestine; and the new organization was intended to send more. Although Pinsker was a secular Jew, the organization attracted the religiously devout who viewed the return to Zion in biblical terms. The Lovers of Zion established chapters across Europe and even a support group in the United States. But after initial reports of hardship, it had difficulty inducing Jews to emigrate to Palestine.

That changed somewhat after Baron Edmund James de Rothschild began investing—about $6 million from 1884 to 1890—in colonies in Palestine. In 1890 the Lovers of Zion was also able to win recognition from Russian authorities by defining itself specifically as a support group for émigré families; the Russians were happy to permit a group that encouraged Jews to leave. And in 1890–91, three thousand Russian and Romanian Jews left for Palestine.

As the Lovers of Zion was organizing, Russian Zionism acquired a new intellectual voice. Ahad Ha'am (meaning "one of the people") was the pen name of Asher Ginsberg, who shunned publicity and who, as a result, has become known by his pen name rather than his given name. Ahad Ha'am articulated better than anyone before or after Zionism's spiritual and emotional bonds with Palestine. And unlike many of his fellow Zionists, he also recognized the pitfalls of colonizing a country where people of a different nationality (and two different religions) already lived.

Ahad Ha'am, who was born in 1856, grew up in a rural estate in Ukraine that his father, a well-to-do farmer, rented from a Russian landowner. He even had his own bedroom and a separate study. His parents were members of the Hasidic religious cult that had sprung up in Poland during the eighteenth century. Hasidism was comparable to the Christian awakenings that date from the Reformation. It rejected an emphasis on textual interpretation and rote recitation in favor of emotional affirmation through faith and prayer. But it was also opposed to the Jewish enlightenment, which welcomed European science and culture. The precocious Asher Ginsberg was chastised for trying to learn algebra and Russian. Possessed of omnivorous curiosity, he eventually broke with Hasidism and acquired the learning and languages of a European intellectual. But in his conception of Zionism, he retained something of the emotional and cultural kernel of Hasidism.

Like other Russian Zionists, Ahad Ha'am seems to have come to Zionism in reaction to the pogroms of the early 1880s. When they occurred, he was, he wrote later, "like a man stunned . . . my world began to totter."[19] In 1884, while staying in Odessa, he joined Pinsker's Lovers of Zion. In 1886, after the czar forbade Ahad Ha'am's father and other Jews from leasing land, Ahad Ha'am and his family moved to Odessa, where he and his father went into business, and where Ahad Ha'am became a regular in Zionist political circles. In 1888 he penned his first major essay, "The Wrong Way," a critique of the Lovers of Zion's colonization strategy. Introverted, bookish, with short legs, a large head, and piercing eyes, he tried to stay out of the leadership of political groups, but he was possessed of strong and controversial opinions that he expressed in a lucid Hebrew that quickly made him famous among Russia's Zionists.

While Ahad Ha'am was driven to Zionism by czarist repression, he did not see Zionism as a means of combating anti-Semitism; nor did he envisage Palestine as (in Pinsker's words) a "safe retreat" from the pogroms of the Pale. He saw Zionism as a means of reviving Judaism rather than rescuing Jews. His Zionism was a mixture of nineteenth-century nationalism and of the Hasidism whose overt practices he had discarded. He saw the return of Jews to Palestine as a way of restoring the Jewish nation. He didn't see the nation necessarily as a state but as a spiritual entity defined by a common culture and purpose. In Palestine, Jews would speak Hebrew and practice their religion openly and seek to live according to the Prophets. They would become a "people" again.

In current American terms, Ahad Ha'am was a communitarian rather than an individualist, but his was a hyper-communitarianism that derived from Hasidism and European nationalism. He associated individualism and the pursuit of self-interest with the decadent West and with the Reform Jews of Germany and France who were bent on assimilation. By settling in Palestine, Jews would not necessarily become prosperous, but they would contribute toward a national revival. Ahad Ha'am traced his nationalism back to the Law of Moses. "All the laws and ordinances, all the blessings and curses of the Law of Moses have but one unvarying object: the well-being of the nation as a whole in the land of its inheritance—the happiness of the individual is not regarded," he wrote in "The Wrong Way." "The individual Israelite is treated as standing to the people of Israel in the relation of a single limb to the whole body: the actions of the individual have their reward in the good of the community."[20]

In his essay, Ahad Ha'am traced the embrace of individualism back to the fall of the First Temple, the growing popularity of otherworldly messianism, and the idea of an afterlife as a reward to the individual.

But Ahad Ha'am's more immediate target was the colonization appeals made by the Lovers of Zion. With America beckoning many Jews from the Pale, the Russian Zionists promised equal, if not greater, happiness and prosperity to Jews who would move instead to Palestine. When these emigrants often found poverty and malaria, they returned disillusioned. Ahad Ha'am argued that for colonization to succeed, the Zionists should stop appealing to self-interest. They "ought to have made it our first object to bring about a revival—to inspire men with a deeper attachment to the national life, and a more ardent desire for the national well-being."[21]

Ahad Ha'am described the "nation" that he hoped to build as a "spiritual center" rather than a "state." It would radiate outward to the Diaspora, reviving Judaism there as well as in Palestine. In an essay in 1891 in memory of Pinsker, he spelled out what he meant by spiritual center:

> What we lack above all is a fixed spot to serve as a "national, spiritual center," a "safe retreat," not for the Jews, but for Judaism, for the spirit of our people . . . The establishing and development of such a center is to be the limited work of all the members of our nation wherever they may be scattered. Their common efforts are to effect the mutual approximation of those hitherto separated in space and spirit, and the visible center created by their limited striving is in turn to exert an influence upon every point at the periphery of the circle reviving the national spirit in all hearts, and strengthening the feeling of national kinship.[22]

Ahad Ha'am's concept of a spiritual center has been compared to that of a Jewish Vatican, but his spiritual center was not strictly religious or theocratic. It was cultural and ethnic. Ahad Ha'am thought the Jewish religion was integral to the Jewish nation, but he didn't think that every individual in the nation had to practice the religion. "It is possible to be a Jew in the national sense without accepting many things in which religion requires belief," he wrote to the prominent New York Rabbi Judah L. Magnes.[23]

At various times, when Ahad Ha'am was accused of not being a genuine Zionist, he would insist that he saw a Jewish state, based on a Jewish majority, evolving eventually from the establishment of a Jewish spiritual center. But Ahad Ha'am's references to Jewish statehood are few and almost always eclipsed by his discussion of Palestine as a "spiritual center." One reason for that is that he saw the establishment of a spiritual center as the prerequisite for the establishment of a Jewish state. If Jews were to establish a state without creating the spiritual basis for it, the Jews, he wrote, "shall simply create a 'problem of the Jews' in a country in which it has not hitherto existed—in our ancestral land."[24]

Unlike other early Zionists, Ahad Ha'am also recognized that in colonizing Palestine, the Jews would have to coexist with the existing non-Jewish inhabitants. In 1891, the Lovers of Zion sent Ahad Ha'am to observe conditions there. What he discovered contradicted the prevailing assumptions about Palestine. He wrote about his trip:

> From abroad, we are accustomed to believe that Eretz Israel is presently almost totally desolate, an uncultivated desert, and that anyone wishing to buy land there can come and buy all he wants. But in truth it is not so. In the entire land, it is hard to find tillable land that is not already tilled . . . If the time comes when the life of our people in Eretz Israel develops to the point of encroaching upon the native population, they will not easily yield their place.[25]

Ahad Ha'am's awareness that Arabs already dwelt in Palestine—and could covet a nation of their own—contributed to his emphasis of building a spiritual center not a state. As the Jewish settlements grew—and as the Arabs in Palestine reacted angrily, and then violently, to the prospect that a Jewish state would subordinate them—Ahad Ha'am would try to create a Zionism that could accommodate Arab nationalism. He would advocate a country where two nationalities, Jewish and Arab, could live side by side. That position would be taken up by Palestine's first high commissioner, Herbert Samuel, and by a small group of eminent émigrés, including Martin Buber and Magnes, who would emigrate to Palestine and found the Hebrew University. But most Zionist leaders would reject it out of hand.

Herzl and the Jewish state

In 1893, when Ahad Ha'am visited Palestine for the second time, the Zionist settlements still only amounted to a few dots on a map. If the Zionist experiment had ended then, Walter Laqueur wrote, "it would now be remembered as one of the less important sectarian-Utopian movements which sprouted during the second half of the nineteenth century, an unsuccessful attempt at a Jewish Risorgimento, trying to graft the ideas of the Enlightenment on to the Jewish religious tradition."[26] It took a Viennese Jew, Theodor Herzl, to put Zionism in the forefront of European politics. Herzl did it by fitting Zionism into the prevailing framework of European imperialist politics.

Herzl was the son of a well-to-do Hungarian clothing merchant. His parents moved to Vienna when he was eighteen, and Herzl entered the University of Vienna, where he immersed himself in German culture and in the post-Enlightenment politics of Austria's Liberal Party, which had championed Jewish emancipation.[27] Herzl got a law degree, but he aspired to be a writer. A dandy and aesthete—elegantly attired, with a long beard—he wrote plays and freelance journalism. In 1891, he got hired by Vienna's foremost Liberal newspaper, the *Neue Freie Presse,* as its Paris correspondent.

Growing up in Budapest and Vienna, Herzl had every reason to believe that he would be accepted as a Jew. The Jews of Central and Western Europe enjoyed far more social and economic freedom than did the Jews of the Russian Pale. No longer confined to ghettos, and to trade and usury, they could aspire to high ranks in the professions or in business. In Great Britain, Benjamin Disraeli, who was descended from Sephardic Jews, became prime minister. In Austria, Germany, France, and Great Britain, Jews defined their national identity as Austrian, German, French, or British rather than Jewish. Judaism, they insisted, was a religion, not a nationality.

In Vienna during the mid-1880s, however, Herzl began to feel the ill wind of anti-Semitism blowing in from the east. Von Schönerer campaigned for restricting Jewish immigration from Russia and Poland into Austria. Lueger's Austrian Christian Social Party, following von Schönerer's lead, took an anti-Semitic turn in the late 1880s. Herzl says in his diaries that he was alarmed by Eugen Duehring's anti-Semitic book, *The Jewish Question,* which appeared in 1881. "In the course of succeeding years, the question gnawed and tugged at me," he wrote.[28] But when Herzl moved to Paris in 1891, he believed that he wouldn't encounter the kind of anti-Semitism that had begun to stir in Central Europe.

European Jews had held up France as the vanguard of emancipation.

In *Rome and Jerusalem*, Moses Hess had predicted that "France, beloved friend, is the savior who will restore our people to its place in universal history."[29] Herzl discovered, however, that France was not immune to the anti-Semitic infection. Soon after Herzl arrived to take his post, French newspapers began headlining a corruption scandal surrounding the construction of the Panama Canal. Two German Jews were marginally involved, but got the brunt of the blame. That was followed by the Dreyfus case, during which Herzl witnessed street demonstrators shouting "Death to the Jews."

Of course, what Herzl experienced in Central and Western Europe didn't compare in severity to the Russian pogroms that Pinsker, Lilienblum, and Ahad Ha'am had witnessed. But Russian Jews were inured to a far greater level of anti-Semitism than Herzl. The French scandals, along with the spread of anti-Semitism to Central Europe, challenged Herzl's most basic assumptions about his place as a Jew in European society. Herzl initially responded by advocating assimilation on a grand scale, proposing that, in exchange for the pope's repudiation of anti-Semitism, Jews convert en masse to Christianity. But that passing fancy gave way to Zionism.

Herzl turned to the establishment of a Jewish state as a refuge from anti-Semitism and not as an affirmation of Judaism. The historian Carl Schorske wrote of Herzl, "The very model of a cultivated liberal, he generated his highly creative approach to the Jewish question not out of immersion in the Jewish tradition but out of his vain efforts to leave it behind."[30] In 1895, Herzl penned an "address" to the family council of the Rothschilds asking for help in founding a Jewish state. The next year, he converted the address into a short book, *The Jewish State*, which became the manifesto of the new Zionist movement. And the next year, using it as his platform, he convened the first congress of the World Zionist Organization in Basel.

When he wrote *The Jewish State*, Herzl had not yet read Moses Hess and Leo Pinsker, but, like they did, he based his argument for a Jewish state on the growth and persistence of anti-Semitism, which he attributed to the existence of unassimilable Jewish minorities within nations striving for homogeneous ethnic identity. The "Jewish question," Herzl wrote, is a "national question," the solution of which was for Jews to establish a nation of their own outside of Europe.[31] That would not only create a country devoid of anti-Semitism but it would undercut the basis of anti-Semitism in Europe, which, he argued, was based entirely on fear of an alien nation inside other nations. The new Jewish state "means the end of anti-Semitism," Herzl wrote.[32]

Herzl's vision of the Jewish state was very different from that of the Russian Zionists. He was a nineteenth-century European bourgeois liberal (as opposed to an American New Deal liberal). In *The Jewish State*, Herzl envisioned an "aristocratic republic" dominated like liberal Vienna by the educated upper classes.[33] It would be ruled by Jews, but would not be dominated by the Jewish culture that Ahad Ha'am esteemed. Church and state would be separate. Immigrants would speak the language of their native lands. "Who amongst us has a sufficient knowledge of Hebrew to ask for a railway ticket?"[34] Herzl asked. All faiths would be welcome. Herzl's vision of Palestine, Schorske remarked, was "not a Jewish utopia but a Liberal one."[35]

Herzl's predecessors in the Lovers of Zion believed that Jews should establish a foothold in Palestine through gradual migration and settlement. By contrast, Herzl advocated buying or leasing Palestine as a colony before settling there. He wanted Jews to form a private company like Britain's East India or South Africa Company that could buy title to land from a reigning imperial power. (Herzl admired the imperialist Cecil Rhodes, whom he described as "a visionary politician or a practical visionary," and to whom he periodically appealed for help in founding a new Jewish state in Palestine.)[36] The company could also buy out the native inhabitants and, if possible, convince them to emigrate. Following this strategy, Herzl tried to interest the Ottoman sultan in ceding Palestine and Britain's colonial secretary in providing adjacent lands in the Sinai.

Herzl wanted the Jews to buy into the imperial system that had arisen over five centuries, and whose growth had accelerated since the 1870s as the great powers of Europe, joined later by Japan and the United States, sought to carve up the world into colonies and client states.[37] The new Jewish state would become a junior partner in the British or the Ottoman Empires. To the Turks, Herzl proposed offering Jewish financial management of their imperial affairs. When it became clear they weren't interested, he turned to the British, who had gained control of the Suez Canal and were looking for a buffer between the Turks and British-controlled Egypt. When his overtures to the British stalled, he looked to imperial Germany and even to Russia, courting Russia's notorious minister of the interior Vyacheslav von Plehve, who had been a promoter of Russia's pogroms.

Herzl's appeal was geopolitical but also cultural, reflecting the widespread European justification of imperialism as an instrument of civilization.[38] The new state, he promised, "should there form a part of a wall of defense for Europe in Asia, an outpost of civilization against barbarism."[39] The writer Max Nordau, who would become Herzl's second-in-command in the Zionist movement, agreed. "We will endeavor to do in the Near East what the English did in India. It is our intention to come to Palestine as the representatives of culture and to take the moral borders of Europe to the Euphrates."[40]

In *The Jewish State*, which he wrote before visiting the Near East, Herzl did not mention the Arabs by name. He also described the region as a "desert."[41] But Herzl knew there were people living in Palestine. Dismissing the evolutionary approach of the Lovers of Zion, Herzl asked, "What is achieved by transporting a few thousand Jews to another country? Either they come to grief at once, or, if they prosper, their prosperity gives rise to anti-Semitism."[42] A gradual infiltration, Herzl wrote, "is bound to end badly. It continues until the inevitable moment when the native population feels itself threatened, and forces the government to stop a further influx of Jews." But if Jews had the "sovereign right"—if they controlled the state—then they could permit immigration to continue.[43]

That would seem to give rise to an even more virulent anti-Semitism, but Herzl thought that the Jews could eventually win over the natives by making them prosperous. We "could build new roads for traffic . . . and many other things," Herzl wrote.[44] He spelled out this vision in *Altneuland* (*Old-Newland*), a utopian novel set in the Palestine of 1923, which he wrote in 1902. In the novel, the Zionists gain possession of the new land through a financial deal with the Turks. The local Arabs are initially wary, but they are won over when the Jews bring prosperity to the country and to them. "The Jews have enriched us. Why should we be angry with them?" Reschid Bey, one of the Arab leaders, explains. "They dwell among us like brothers. Why should we not love them?"[45]

Herzl also had a darker vision of how the new Jewish state would deal with its Arab inhabitants. In his *Diaries*, Herzl considered the possibility of getting rid of the natives by paying very high prices for their lands. He also envisioned Arabs as day laborers to drain the country's malarial swamps—exactly the kind of employment to which imperial powers often consigned the natives they ruled.

Herzl's motives in *The Jewish State* were not ignoble. He saw himself as rescuing his own people from persecution. And his vision of a Jewish Palestine was not inconsistent with a multinational, multiethnic society that tolerated differences in religion. But, like other Europeans during this age of imperialism, he viewed the natives in Asia, Africa, and Latin America as lesser beings who could be bought off—and, if that failed, subjugated. While he argued for a Jewish nationalism on a par with other European nationalisms, he couldn't conceive of an Arab nationalism that would not be content with new roads and high land prices. Herzl's achievement was to accommodate Zionism and Jewish nationalism to Great Power imperialism and to define Zionism as the quest for a Jewish state, but by doing so, he also set the stage for the century-long conflict between Jew and Arab.

A year after *The Jewish State* appeared, Herzl organized the first World Zionist Congress in Basel. It was attended by 197 delegates from all over Europe. Herzl had hoped to attract the Jewish upper crust, but many of the delegates from the Russian Pale had to scrape together the rail fare. "I stand in command of striplings, beggars, and sensation mongers," Herzl complained in his diary. But he added, "Nevertheless, even this army would do the job if success were in sight."[46] The congresses became regular events and attracted a growing following. They gave rise to the Zionist Organization, headquartered in Berlin, and to a newspaper, *Die Welt*.

Together, these institutions established Zionism as a Western movement that commanded the attention of governments in Berlin, London, Paris, Moscow, and Washington. They also established Herzl as the movement's leader. At the first congress, the British author Israel Zangwill, best known for his play *The Melting Pot*, described Herzl as "a majestic Oriental figure [who] stands dominating the assembly with eyes that brood and glow—you would say one of the Assyrian kings, whose sculptured heads adorn our museums, the very profile of Tiglath Pileser."[47]

At the first Congress, the delegates came together around the goal Herzl had outlined in his book of establishing a Jewish state rather than the spiritual center that Ahad Ha'am had described. Establishing a Jewish state would remain the underlying aim of the Zionist movement. But it would also rarely be stated for fear of inflaming the opposition to a Jewish state. At the time, the delegates were worried about provoking the Turks, so they used euphemisms to describe their objective, calling for a "publicly recognized, legally secured home in Palestine for the Jewish people" rather than calling explicitly for a Jewish state.[48] But everyone understood what was really involved. Writing in his diary after the first Congress, Herzl remarked, "Were I to sum up the Basel Congress in a word—which I shall guard against pronouncing publicly—it would be this: At Basel I founded the Jewish State."[49]

Herzl had invited Ahad Ha'am, who had consented to attend, but as a visitor rather than as a voting delegate. Ahad Ha'am, already filled with misgivings, was sorely disappointed and even, it seems, enraged by the proceedings. He believed—and, as it turned out, with justification— that Herzl was deceiving the delegates by holding out the hope of being able to lease Palestine from the Ottomans. And he thought the basic premise of Herzl's political Zionism was wrong. "The salvation of Israel will be achieved by prophets not diplomats," he remarked in a note he published afterward.[50]

A year later, Ahad Ha'am expounded his differences with Herzl at greater length in an essay, "The Jewish State and Jewish Problem." Even if by some miracle the political Zionists were able to acquire a Jewish state of Palestine, Ahad Ha'am argued, it would not "provide a remedy for poverty, complete tranquility and national glory." Zionists, Ahad Ha'am wrote, should look to a Jewish homeland to provide only a "secure refuge for Judaism and a cultural bond of unity for our nation." Herzl's Zionism, Ahad Ha'am warned, "begins its work with political propaganda; the Lovers of Zion begins with national culture, because only through the national culture and for its sake can a Jewish State be established in such a way as to correspond with the will and the needs of the Jewish people."[51]

At the third Zionist Congress in 1899, a debate broke out between the pro-Herzl "Politicals," who favored winning title to a new Jewish state before encouraging large-scale immigration, and the "Practicals," led by the Eastern European Zionists, who were influenced by Ahad

Ha'am. Following Ahad Ha'am, they favored creating a Hebrew-speaking Jewish community in Palestine through gradual immigration that could become the basis for a Jewish state; but, in line with Herzl, they unambiguously backed the creation of a Jewish state. At the fifth congress in 1901, the Practicals formed a faction to resist the Politicals, and after Herzl's death in 1904 they shared leadership with the Politicals.

Part of the debate revolved around the strategy for securing a Jewish state. Should the Zionist movement emphasize high-level diplomacy and deal making, as Herzl favored, or gradual immigration and evolution? The Practicals won that debate after Herzl died in 1904 without having made any headway in securing an imperial sponsor, and after a new wave of Jewish immigration to Palestine, a "Second Aliyah," sparked by Russian pogroms. But the debate also touched the nature of the Jewish state. Should it primarily be a cosmopolitan, polyglot, multinational, and secular refuge for European Jews, as Herzl described in *Altneuland*, or a center for Hebrew and Judaic revival, as Ahad Ha'am proposed in his essays? The Practicals won that debate, too, as delegates decided to press ahead with establishing schools that would make Hebrew the official language of the new settlers. And their position was reinforced and redefined by the emergence, as a result of the Second Aliyah, of a new Labor Zionism that emphasized the primacy of land and labor in the creation of a Jewish nation.

Gordon and Labor Zionism

Labor Zionism was initially composed of two different and sometimes conflicting political tendencies—a Tolstoyan blend of nationalism associated with Aaron David Gordon and a socialist Zionism identified with Ber Borochov, Berl Katznelson, and David Ben-Gurion—but in the broader sweep of history the two tendencies were like people who spoke in different dialects but made the same point. And they were united in the late 1920s in the political party Mapai and in a politics called Labor Zionism that dominated the early years of the Zionist movement in Palestine. The key philosophical figure was Gordon, who is best known as the father of the kibbutz, the Jewish communal settlement.

Gordon was born in western Ukraine in 1856, the same year as Ahad

Ha'am. Like Ahad Ha'am, he was from a well-to-do family that managed an estate and observed Hasidic Judaism. Sickly as a youth, he was educated by private tutors. When he was fourteen, he went to work managing the estate leased by a wealthy cousin, but in 1904 at age forty-eight, after the lease on the estate expired, he left for Palestine, where his wife and his children joined him three years later. Gordon had joined the Lovers of Zion. Influenced by Ahad Ha'am, he saw in Palestine a chance for the "national rebirth" of the Jewish people, who had been dispersed and degraded during their long exile.[52]

Gordon, like Ahad Ha'am, did not avidly practice the Jewish religion. Instead, he looked to Palestine for a cultural and ethnic rebirth of the Jewish people. But his sense of culture was different from the conventional understanding: he saw it not as "entirely as matter of ideas and ideology" but in "whatever life creates for living purposes. Farming, building and road-making—any work, any craft, any productive activity—is part of culture and is indeed the foundation and stuff of culture."[53] Under the influence of Leo Tolstoy, and perhaps as a result of his own unhappiness as a white-collar worker, Gordon exalted the role not just of any work but of manual labor as the key to the redemption of Eastern Europe's Jews, who have "been completely cut off from nature and imprisoned within city walls. Only by making Labor, for its own sake, our national ideal shall we be able to cure ourselves of the plague that has affected us for many generations and mend the rent between ourselves and nature."[54]

Just as Ahad Ha'am had regarded the Jewish return to Palestine as being devoid of meaning without a reaffirmation of Jewish culture, Gordon insisted that it had to be coupled with a return to the land and to labor. "We come to our Homeland in order to be planted in our natural soil from which we have been uprooted, to strike our roots deep into its life-giving substances, and to stretch out our branches in the sustaining and creating air and sunlight of the Homeland . . . Here, in Palestine, is the force attracting all the scattered cells of the people to unite into one living national organism."[55]

After arriving in Palestine, Gordon worked for five years at a Jewish agricultural settlement that used Arab labor in its vineyards. But in 1906, Gordon helped inspire the founding of Hapoel Hatzair, a party devoted not only to the revival of Jewish culture through the use of Hebrew but to the Jewish commitment to labor on their own land. Hapoel

Hatzair started one of the first kibbutzim, on which Gordon, who never formally joined the party, remained until his death in 1923. Balding, with a huge head and a long, flowing white beard, Gordon became the patriarch to his younger followers.

Gordon's vision of a Jewish nation was influenced by, but different from, that of Ahad Ha'am. Gordon envisaged a nation of laborers; Ahad Ha'am envisaged a nation of scholars and rabbis. Ahad Ha'am's years in business had not soured him on white-collar work the way that Gordon's had. They also differed in their very concept of a Jewish nation. When Ahad Ha'am wrote of a Jewish nation, he often included implicitly the Jews of Palestine and the Diaspora. Palestine was to be the spiritual center of the larger Jewish nation. Gordon saw the Jewish nation as existing only in Palestine and as the foundation of whatever Jewish state came into existence. The Diaspora was irrelevant.

Gordon was, in this sense, a more typical nineteenth-century European nationalist—the heir of Rousseau and Herder—than Ahad Ha'am was. He saw the individual with his "ethnic self" being able to realize his true nature only through membership in an ethnic nation. In the Diaspora, Jews could possess a "historical" but not a transcendental ethnic identity. That could only be achieved by the return to Palestine. "We come to our homeland in order to be planted in our natural soil from which we have been uprooted," Gordon wrote.[56]

The "foundation stones" for this "new national spirituality" were to be laid through what the members of Hapoel Hatzair, drawing directly upon Gordon's ideas, called the "conquest of labor" and the "conquest of land." Many of the colonists, who had been sponsored by Baron Edmond Rothschild, Baron Maurice de Hirsch, and the Jewish Colonization Association, had hired Arabs to do the manual work. But according to Gordon, Jews should employ only Jewish labor, whether on farms or later in offices and factories. "We must ourselves do all the work," Gordon wrote, "from the least strenuous, cleanest and most sophisticated, to the dirtiest and most difficult . . . Only then shall we have a culture of our own."[57]

The conquest of land meant that Jews could no longer rent their land from other nationalities, as Ahad Ha'am's parents had done, but must own it and prevent its transfer to other peoples. In 1901, before Gordon's arrival, the Practicals at the World Zionist Congress set up the Jewish National Fund to purchase land in Palestine that would be leased only to Jews and on which they would employ Jewish labor. Gordon provided an abiding rationale for its practices.

Gordon's vision of a Jewish nation and state could be described as an ethnocracy. It excluded not only Arab labor but the Arab people themselves. Gordon acknowledged that Arabs had "a historical right to the country, just as we do," but he claimed that the Jewish right "is undoubtedly greater." "And what did the Arabs produce in all the years they lived in the country?" he asked. "Such creations, or even the creation of the Bible alone, give us a perpetual right over the land in which we were so creative, especially since the people that came after us did not create such works in this country, or did not create anything at all."[58] Gordon added: "Some hold that when we come to Palestine to settle upon the land, we are dispossessing Arabs who are its natural masters. But what does this term mean? If mastery of the land implies political mastery, then the Arabs have long ago forfeited their title."[59] Ahad Ha'am's vision of Palestine left an opening for compromise with its existing inhabitants. Gordon's did not; and Gordon's vision of nationhood eventually superseded that of Ahad Ha'am.

Ben-Gurion, Katznelson, and the socialist Zionists who arrived during the Second Aliyah still gave some adherence to international socialism, but they subordinated the dictates of the international class struggle to the attempt to create a Jewish state. Zeev Sternhell calls them "nationalist socialists."[60] Within nationalist socialism, there was still room for concern about Arab workers and their fate; and at intervals over their first thirty years in Palestine, some of the socialists would voice support for a more democratic or binational Palestine.

But while the socialist Zionists didn't necessarily share Gordon's mystic notions of nationhood, their views of the importance of labor in building the Jewish state jibed perfectly with his. They would extend Gordon's ideas from the kibbutz to the factory and office. Gordon justified his exclusion of Arab labor on Tolstoyan grounds of national rejuvenation through labor; the socialist Zionists did so on more pragmatic grounds—the new Jewish immigrants who were eventually going to constitute a majority in Palestine needed work. But they also invoked a quasi-socialist argument that by excluding Arab labor, they were avoiding the kind of exploitation that other colonists had inflicted on native populations. In 1934, Ben-Gurion told the Palestinian Arab intellectual Musa al-Alami, "We do not want to create a situation like that which exists in South Africa, where the whites are the owners and rulers, and the blacks are the workers. If we do not do all kinds of work, easy and hard, skilled and unskilled, if we become merely landlords, then this will not be our homeland."[61]

Ben-Gurion and the socialist Zionists wanted to avoid being seen as colonialists, but they ended up replacing the colonialism of the European settler in Africa who exploited the native laborers with the colonialism of the European settler in North America who displaced rather than employed the Native Americans who lived on the lands they coveted. Moreover, in justifying their displacement of Arab labor, the Zionists invoked the same arguments that European settler colonialists had used in Australia, Africa, and North America: they were putting to good use lands the Arabs had desolated.

The Labor Zionists who came out of Gordon's ethnocratic nationalism and Ben-Gurion's nationalist socialism rejected Herzl's strategy for creating a state, and his reliance on imperial philanthropy, but they accepted his elementary commitment to establishing a Jewish state, and borrowed many of their justifications for doing so from arguments that he had made. They also accepted Ahad Ha'am's emphasis on gradually building a Zionist culture that could undergird a Zionist state, but they defined "state" and "nation" in such a way as to exclude Palestine's Arabs.

In these early years, some Zionists questioned the prevailing view of Jewish-Arab relations. At a meeting in Basel during the Seventh Zionist Congress in 1905, Yitzhak Epstein, a teacher who had migrated to Palestine, raised what he called the "Hidden Question." "Among the difficult problems associated with the idea of the renewal of life of our people in its land, there is one question that outweighs all the others, namely, the question of our attitude to the Arabs," Epstein said. "We have overlooked a rather 'marginal' fact—that in our beloved land there lives an entire people that has been dwelling there for many centuries and has never considered leaving it."[62]

In a subsequent debate that took place over several years in Zionist publications, a few people took Epstein's side. Hillel Zeitlin, who wrote in Hebrew and Yiddish, charged that Zionists "forget, mistakenly or maliciously . . . that Palestine belongs to others, and it is totally settled."[63]

But the bulk of the comments wished the problem away. Many Zionists, echoing Herzl in *Altneuland*, argued that the Jews' superior culture and knowledge would eventually win out over the native population. Yosef Klausner, a Lithuanian émigré and Hebrew scholar, wrote, "All our hope that someday we will be the masters of the land of our forefathers is not founded on the sword or the fist, but, rather, on the cultural advantage that we enjoy over the Arabs and the Turks, an advantage due to which our influence in the land will slowly increase. Ultimately the inhabitants there will subject themselves to this cultural influence, since they will find it brings benefit and blessing even for them."[64]

Klausner's views, even though sharply at odds with the reality of Palestine, would persist in those first decades among Zionists, especially those in the Diaspora, who would insist that large-scale Jewish immigration—and the eventual establishment of a Jewish state—would not or should not worry the native Arabs because of the economic benefits it would confer upon a desolate underpopulated land. These were rationalizations by which the early Zionists justified their conquest of the lands on which another people lived. They laid the basis for a Zionism that, while justifiable in the abstract, committed in practice many of the sins that Western European countries had visited upon native populations and that led to national rebellions.

2

THE ORIGINS OF PALESTINIAN NATIONALISM

In the early 1840s, a Christian Restorationist in Britain, Alexander Keith, described the Jews as "a people without a country even as their own land . . . is in a great measure a country without a people."[1] The Earl of Shaftesbury put Keith's dream of a Jewish return to Palestine in catchier terms as "a land without a people for a people without a land," and Shaftesbury's statement, repeated by Israel Zangwill in 1901, became a mantra for the Zionist movement in Palestine.[2]

The statement itself was ambiguous. "A land without a people" could mean a land that was "desolate without inhabitant," in Keith's words, but it could also mean—and this is, perhaps, what Shaftesbury had in mind—a land that didn't house a distinct *people* like the Jews or the French or the English. The early Zionists in Europe or the United States, looking at Palestine from afar, interpreted the slogan in the first sense— as referring to an empty land that Jews could populate and revive without incurring the wrath of inhabitants.

But that illusion was ruled out for the Zionists who actually migrated to Palestine and found hundreds of thousands of Arabs already there, many of whom viewed the new settlers suspiciously. These Zionists insisted that the current inhabitants had no religious or historical claim upon the land. They acknowledged that the people who lived in Palestine were Arabs, but they took that to mean that they could as easily move to and live in another Arab country the way an Englishman could move from London to Birmingham without losing his national identity. They claimed that "there was no such thing as Palestinians," as Israeli prime minister Golda Meir was saying to the London *Sunday Times* as late as 1969.³ Variations on that charge have continued to be echoed, most recently by former House speaker and Republican presidential candidate Newt Gingrich.⁴

Like the claim that Palestine was "desolate," this one was superficially plausible. From 1880 to 1919, maps did not show a place called "Palestine." The country's Arabs were subjects of the Ottoman Empire and of greater Syria—Arabs (by language), predominately Muslim, but also Christian—yet inhabitants of a place that was still thought of as Palestine or as the "Holy Land." They had overlapping identities as had many peoples, including Eastern European Jews.

That changed rapidly in the early twentieth century. The increase of Jewish settlers committed to establishing a Jewish state, along with the breakup of the Ottoman Empire, spurred the rapid development of a militant Arab nationalism in Palestine. After the British claimed Palestine, the Arabs of Palestine became Palestinians, and after the French took over Syria, the Arab nationalism in the region became Palestinian nationalism. To be sure, the Arabs of Palestine *constructed* and had constructed for them an identity. But so did the Jews of Europe, the Poles, the Serbs, the Americans of 1776, and many of the other people who found themselves embroiled in conflict with imperial powers or rival nationalities.

The Holy Land

Some of the Arabs who resided in Palestine in the late nineteenth century may be as likely to have descended from Palestine's original inhabitants as the Jews who came to Palestine from Europe. From what archaeologists have been able to reconstruct, there were at least two groups of people in ancient Palestine—the Canaanites and the Philistines—from whom some Palestinian Arabs may have descended. But little is certain. If the ancient history of the Jews is shrouded in myth, the ancient history of Palestine's other inhabitants has had to be gleaned primarily from the shards of pots.

What's known is that Palestine has always been a "land of passage" through which travelers passed on their way to Damascus, Beirut, Mecca, and Cairo and through which peoples, including Jews, have migrated, whether forcibly or voluntarily. In the first centuries after the birth of Christ, it was inhabited by Greeks, Egyptians, Phoenicians (descended from the Philistines), Bedouins, and Jews.[5] It got the name "Palestine" after the Romans put down another Jewish revolt in 132 C.E. The Romans designated the land that the Maccabees ruled from 167 B.C.E. to 63 B.C.E. and that the Old Testament described as going "from Dan [in the north] to Beersheba [in the south]" as "Syria Palaestina."[6]

Over the next thousand years, Palestine became known to Jews, Christians, and Muslims as the "holy land." It went through different religious incarnations after the pagan Romans ousted the Maccabees. In 400 C.E., when the Roman emperor Theodosius made Christianity the official state religion, the majority of its citizens became Christian. In 638, Muslim armies invaded and made Palestine part of the Umayyad caliphate. During the next century, Muslims erected the Dome of the Rock and al-Aqsa Mosque in Jerusalem. But in 1099, Christian Crusaders took back Palestine from the Muslims. In Jerusalem alone, the Crusaders killed seventy thousand Muslims and Jews, including thirty thousand Muslims who had sought sanctuary in the al-Aqsa Mosque.

The Kurdish Muslim warrior Saladin drove the Crusaders out of Jerusalem in 1187; and the Muslim armies of the Cairo-based Mamluk dynasty ousted the Crusaders from all of Palestine in 1291. Then, in 1516, the Istanbul-based Ottomans seized power and ruled Palestine until the end of World War I. The Mamluk and Ottoman sultans were both temporal rulers and Muslim caliphs, and their empires were caliphates. That was important for ensuring the loyalty of their Muslim subjects.

Palestine from Dan to Beersheba remained relatively intact through the role of the Romans, the Umayyad caliphate, the Crusaders, and the Mamluk caliphate. But when the Turks took over, they divided Palestine into two provinces that included Syria and Lebanon. Later, in the nineteenth century, aware of Jerusalem's special religious significance as the third-holiest site in Islam, as well as a holy city for Jews and Christians, the Ottomans made it and neighboring towns a separate district answerable directly to Istanbul.

During the Ottoman reign, Muslims, Christians, and Jews retained a distinct notion of Palestine as the "Holy Land." Geographically, the memory of Palestine endured the same way that the geography of Armenia endured even after it was absorbed by various empires. Indeed, Ottoman court records regularly referred to "Palestine" as a separate region.[7] And in the nineteenth century, American representatives in Constantinople likewise referred to "Palestine" in their dispatches to Washington.[8]

For Muslims, Palestine was a place to be defended against Western crusades. For centuries, the memory of the Crusades had haunted the Muslim Middle East. When an Ottoman Sultan violated a ban on visits by foreign emissaries to Jerusalem by allowing a French consul to visit Jerusalem in 1701, more than eighty Muslim notables issued a statement warning that "this holy land" could be "occupied as a result of this, as has happened repeatedly in earlier times."[9] That understanding of the "Holy Land" would carry over to the Arab and Muslim reaction to Zionism. In the fall of 2007, Khaled Meshal, the leader of the Palestinian group Hamas, told a visiting journalist that his bedside reading included Ibn Kathir's biography of Saladin.[10]

During the first centuries of Ottoman rule, Palestine suffered from neglect. The Turks looked to Southern Europe and the Balkans as their more valuable properties. Palestine was an imperial backwater. Illiteracy, disease, and banditry were rife. It had no cities: Jerusalem, the largest town, had only 10,000 people, while by comparison Damascus had 100,000 and Istanbul 350,000.[11] It subsisted on a peasant economy centered in the hilly, relatively infertile, and often inaccessible areas of the West Bank. (Many peasants kept their villages inaccessible to discourage tax collection.) The only easily passable roads were the north–south roads from Damascus through Jerusalem, but travelers on these roads were likely to encounter Bedouin bandits.

In the mid-nineteenth century, the Ottomans suffered a series of setbacks: Greece and several Balkan states declared their independence, Russia attacked from the north, and Egyptian forces occupied Palestine and Syria during the 1830s. In response, the Ottoman rulers decided to initiate reforms in Palestine that would strengthen its economy and tie its citizens closer to the empire, making tax collection easier. Istanbul initiated what are called the Tanzimat reforms. Roads, schools, and hospitals were built. Infant mortality was sharply reduced, and the population grew from about 275,000 in 1800 to about 575,000 in 1880, on the eve of Zionist immigration.[12]

Tax collection was centralized. Formerly the responsibility of village sheiks, it was now put in the hands of urban notables directly accountable to Ottoman officials. The Ottomans also changed the land law in 1858 to permit people to buy up lands that had been held in common and "owned," in effect, by whatever family was farming it. Peasants, fearful of conscription and of being forced to pay taxes, didn't want to register the land in their names or were deeply in debt, so they sold their holdings to notables in Palestinian towns and to wealthy merchants in Beirut and Damascus. That included some of the best farmland near the coast or in the Galilee.

The change in land ownership encouraged the growth of larger-scale agriculture, including the production of exportable grains and citrus. One British traveler reported in 1883 that "readers will be surprised to learn that almost every acre of the Esdraelon [just east of Haifa] is at this moment in the highest state of cultivation; that it is perfectly safe to ride across it unarmed in any direction."[13] While some peasants remained in the hilly, less fertile east, the locus of agriculture and of population growth began to shift westward toward the coast and toward the growing port cities of Jaffa and Haifa.

Left to their own devices, the Palestinian Arabs might have developed a viable export economy through the port cities on the Mediterranean and a tourist economy around Jerusalem and the other holy sites. It might have even come to rival Lebanon as an Arab financial center and Syria as an oil pipeline route. But the natural development of Arab Palestine was cut short and diverted by the onset of Zionist immigration in the late nineteenth century.

The Arab Awakening

As Zionist immigration began in the early 1880s, the first public signs of Arab dissatisfaction came from intellectuals, including clerics, who were in a position to be aware of the numbers involved. In 1891, when eight thousand Zionist immigrants arrived from the Pale (roughly equivalent in 2008 to 4 million immigrants to the United States in a year), five hundred Arab notables in Jerusalem sent a petition to the sultan demanding that Jewish immigration be halted.[14]

Yusuf Diya al-Khalidi, the son of a Jerusalem official, who was educated in the West, had served as a member of the Ottoman parliament until the Sultan, Abd al-Hamid, eager to silence his critics, disbanded it in 1878. In March 1899, al-Khalidi wrote a letter to Theodor Herzl warning that if the Zionists tried to "demand" Palestine "for themselves," they would have to use "the force of cannons and warships" to take it over. "For the sake of God, leave Palestine in peace," al-Khalidi pleaded.[15] To his credit, Herzl replied, but he ignored al-Khalidi's central point about Zionists taking over Palestine. Instead, invoking the promise of Zionist colonialism, he insisted that the Arabs had "nothing to fear" from Jewish immigration—that the Jews were a "completely peaceful element" and that their arrival would benefit "the well-being of the entire country." "Do you think," Herzl asked, "that an Arab who owns land or a house in Palestine worth three or four thousand francs will be very angry to see the price of his land rise . . . five or ten times in value perhaps in a few months?"[16]

In 1905, Negib Azoury, a former Ottoman official in Jerusalem who had to flee to France to escape the sultan's wrath, published *Le Reveil de la Nation Arabe* (The Awakening of the Arab Nation), in which he, too, warned of Arab resistance to Zionism. Wrote Azoury:

> Two important developments, similar in nature yet opposite, which have not yet drawn attention, have appeared at this moment in Ottoman Asia: they are the awakening of the Arab nation and the growing effort of the Jews to reestablish on a large scale the ancient monarchy of Israel. These two movements are destined to clash continuously until one conquers the other . . . It is not the first time, either, that the interests of Europe in the Mediterranean have caused a stir in the Arab lands . . . [17]

Azoury's comment is notable for identifying Zionism with previous European attempts at conquest—a reference to British and French incursions in North Africa and to the Crusades. But these comments—Azoury was living in Paris and Yusuf Diya al-Khalidi in Istanbul when they wrote—were detached from any protest that was occurring in Palestine. Except for sporadic violence, the first real protests began to occur around the turn of the century. And they were focused primarily on Arab land sales to Zionists.

The Zionists who settled in Palestine during the first "Aliyah" of the 1880s and early 1890s and who acquired land through the Jewish Colonization Association hired Arab laborers because they were cheaper and were readily available. While some Arab intellectuals complained about these Jewish land purchases, the peasants, who had found themselves landless after the 1858 land law, often didn't distinguish Arab from Jewish absentee landlords. But when the next generation of Jewish settlers, who often acquired land from the Jewish National Fund, began kicking Arabs off the land and replacing them with Jews, the Arabs resisted.

The historians Baruch Kimmerling and Joel Migdal summed up the political effect of the Zionist land purchases: "The Jews were establishing an economy based largely on the exclusion of Arabs from land they farmed and from the Jewish labor market. Slowly, the most fertile lands in the northern valleys and in the coastal plain passed to Jewish hands, with jobs and higher wages going to the Jewish newcomers. The logical conclusion of this process was the separate development of the Arab and Jewish economies and, eventually, the creation of two separate nationalist movements."[18]

The Arab rebellion against Zionism began at the turn of the century over these land purchases and the expropriation of Arab peasants. Only several thousand peasants and settlers were involved, but the events crystallized fears among Arab peasants that the Zionists were going to take away their lands and their country. Of a number of incidents, one stood out.

In 1910, at the nearby village of al-Fula, the Jewish National Fund bought 2,500 acres of prime agricultural land from a Beirut merchant family. The local Arab official refused to give the deed to the Jewish National Fund, prompting an order to complete the sale from his Ottoman superior in Beirut. The local official, Shukri al-Asali, still refused, sending troops to prevent the Zionist paramilitary force from occupying the lands. Al-Asali's superior finally countered with troops of his own and drove out the peasants, but the peasants then began armed attacks on the settlers.

In 1911, al-Asali got elected to the Ottoman parliament on an anti-Zionist platform. In a speech that year, he charged that the Zionists would do to Palestine what it had done to al-Fula. The Zionists, he explained, wanted "to create a strong state, for after taking possession of the land they will expel the inhabitants either by force or by the use of wealth."[19] Al-Asali, a journalist as well as a politician, described the al-Fula incidents for the newspaper *al-Ittihad al-Uthmani* in Beirut. In the first of these articles, al-Asali reminded readers that the land the Zionists purchased included an old Crusader castle that Saladin had captured in 1187—drawing a comparison between the Crusader onslaught and that of the Zionists.

Arab newspapers, which had sprung up in the Palestine-Lebanon-Syria area after the Young Turks overthrew the sultan in 1908, became the voice of opposition to the land sales and to Zionism.[20] Among the new publications were *Filastin* out of Jaffa, *al-Karmil* from Haifa, and *al-Mufid* from the Beirut district, which included northern Palestine. Each of them characterized Zionism as a Western European movement aimed at colonizing Palestine. *Al-Karmil* reprinted al-Asali's reports on al-Fula as well as covering the Zionist movement in great detail, including the congresses of the Zionist Organization.

In 1911, *al-Karmil* published one hundred issues that included seventy-three articles on Zionism. These included lengthy histories of the Zionist movement. The editor of *al-Karmil*, Najib Nassar, held up Saladin as an example for the opponents of Zionism to follow.[21] *Filastin*, a biweekly, published an article on Zionism in each issue in 1912. *Al-Mufid* carried fifty-two articles and twenty-two editorials criticizing Zionism in 1911. For nine months, it carried an article in each issue opposing land sales to the Zionists.[22]

Initially, most Palestinian Arabs who protested Zionism supported the Ottoman Empire. Many backed the Young Turks, who appeared to be reviving the empire and who in their first year banned Zionist immigration and colonization. Ruhi al-Khalidi, who was elected to parliament from Jerusalem in 1908, called on the Zionists to renounce their national ambition and to "acquire Ottoman nationality."[23] In spite of its name, *Filastin* advocated a unified Ottoman state with full equality for all citizens. It argued that the Turks' centralized leadership would help the Arabs hold off Zionism.[24]

But even before World War I and the collapse of the empire, support for the Young Turks was diminishing, particularly among Palestinian intellectuals. The empire under the Turks suffered defeats in Libya in 1911–12 and in the Balkans in 1912–13. The Young Turks alienated Arabs by launching a campaign of "Turkification," making Turkish the official language throughout the empire. And, eager for Zionist and European support in the Balkan Wars, they backed off their opposition to Zionist immigration and colonization.[25]

In 1914, the Ottoman government shut down *Filastin*, which had protested the Young Turks' unwillingness to confront Zionism. In their closing issue, the editors wrote, "Dear Readers, it seems we have done something serious in the view of the central government in warning the Palestinian nation of the danger which threatens it from the Zionist current."[26] *Filastin*'s appeal to the "Palestinian nation" foreshadowed the rise of Palestinian nationalism in the 1920s, but it would take World War I, the division of the region between the French and British, and the British support for Zionism to push Palestine's Arabs into becoming "Palestinian" nationalists.

3

CHAIM WEIZMANN AND THE BALFOUR DECLARATION

In the years before the outbreak of World War I in August 1914, Europe's imperial powers displayed only passing interest in Palestine. Britain had assumed control over the Suez Canal in 1888, using it as a gateway to India. That meant thwarting any attack on the canal from the north that could go through Palestine. In 1911 a British company discovered oil in Persia, and there was speculation about oil in Mesopotamia, and an east–west oil route that would possibly pass through Palestine to the Mediterranean—made more urgent by Britain's decision to convert its navy from coal to oil. And Britain's chief rival, Germany, had begun to build a railway that would connect Berlin with Baghdad and the port cities on the Persian Gulf and through them to its colonies in Africa. Nonetheless, on the eve of war, Palestine remained a sleepy, little-noticed backwater that was part of the decaying Ottoman Empire.

Within Palestine, there were local spats between Zionist Jews and Arabs over land, but—except in the minds of the region's intellectuals—these did not yet rise to the level of a national conflict over statehood. Jews, even after the second wave of immigration in the early 1900s, made up less than a tenth of Palestine's citizenry.[1] But World War I utterly transformed the relations between Jews and Arabs. Britain entered the region in earnest, and the Zionist movement found in the British the imperial sponsor that Herzl had sought.

When the British threw their weight behind the Jews by issuing the

Balfour Declaration, the Zionists realized Herzl's dream. But they also confirmed the Arab nightmare, going back to the Crusades, of agents from the West seeking to rob Arabs and Muslims of their birthright. Defenders of a Jewish state would later deride this perception as if it had no validity—to their mind, Jews were a stateless people, free of complicity with Western imperialism, who, in the face of persecution, were seeking to reclaim their ancient home—but the perception of Western conquest was firmly rooted in the role that Britain, eager to preserve their empire, would play.

Weizmann and Samuel

On the eve of the Great War, few European leaders expected that a world war would soon erupt. The conventional wisdom, articulated in Norman Angell's *The Great Illusion*, was that imperialism was laying the groundwork for peace rather than war by creating an interdependent world economy. When war did break out on the European continent in August 1914, it quickly spread to the Middle East, as Turkey, once seen as a British ally, threw in its lot with Germany and the Central countries against Britain, France, and Russia. Many Arabs from the region around Palestine followed suit and backed Germany.

The Zionist Organization, which was headquartered in Berlin but which had significant outposts in London and New York, was officially neutral, but it was no secret that many Zionists in Europe, the United States, and Palestine were rooting for Germany out of opposition to Czarist Russia. Britain's tolerance of its Jewish citizens took second place in their minds to Russia's state-sponsored pogroms. In Palestine, David Ben-Gurion and another Labor Zionist, Yitzhak Ben-Zvi, even tried unsuccessfully to win Turkish approval for a Jewish legion to defend Jerusalem against Allied forces. Turkish authorities, fearing that the two Russian Jews were secretly working for Russia, deported them.

But wars have a way of undermining alliances and redrawing maps. In the Middle East, the main impetus for change came from Great Britain, which, after Turkey allied with Germany, began considering how it could protect the Suez Canal from a Turkish and German assault from the north. To do that required Britain gaining a foothold in the area between Turkey and the canal—and that meant Palestine. In December 1914, Ronald Storrs, the oriental secretary and later governor of Jerusalem, wrote a memorandum about the need for a "buffer state," but he dismissed the idea that "the Jewish State is in theory an attractive idea . . . [T]he Jews," he wrote, "are very much a minority in Palestine generally and form indeed a bare sixth of the whole population."[2]

Britain's Liberal prime minister Herbert Asquith was also cool on the idea of the Jewish state, but a group of British Zionists began to make the case for a Jewish Palestine as a British imperial protectorate. The leading British Zionist was Chaim Weizmann. Weizmann had been raised in Motol and Pinsk, two towns in what is now Belarus. The son of a struggling timber merchant, Weizmann was drawn to Zionism by the writings of Ahad Ha'am, of whom he wrote later, "He was, I might say, what Gandhi had been to the Indians, what Mazzini was to Young Italy a century ago."[3] After getting his undergraduate degree in Berlin, Weizmann obtained a doctorate in chemistry from the University of Fribourg in Switzerland. In 1904, he became a lecturer at the University of Manchester.

In 1901, Weizmann had been part of the Practicals at the World Zionist Congress; and he was one of the most vocal dissenters when Herzl tried to interest the congress in August 1903 in accepting British colonial secretary Joseph Chamberlain's offer of Uganda as a temporary home. But unlike some of the Practicals, Weizmann was not against lobbying the Great Powers for a Jewish state. At the congress in 1907, he introduced and won passage of a resolution on "Synthetic Zionism" that combined the approach of the Practicals and the Politicals. And Weizmann was a more effective lobbyist than Herzl—or anyone, for that matter—in the Zionist movement.

Weizmann, bald and sporting a goatee, had an unmatched talent for diplomacy. Storrs described him as having an "almost feminine charm."[4] Weizmann was able to insert himself into the highest circles of foreign governments—from the British war cabinets during the First World War to the Truman White House during the debate over the recognition of Israel in 1948. In January 1906, only two years after arriving in England, he was already engaging in private talks with Conservative prime minister Arthur Balfour.

Weizmann excelled at persuasion. Balfour himself later acknowledged that, in their first conversation, Weizmann had convinced him that the Jews must be given Palestine rather than Uganda.[6] Weizmann had asked Balfour, "Mr. Balfour, supposing I were to offer you Paris instead of London, would you take it?" Balfour replied, "But, Dr. Weizmann, we have London." To which Weizmann replied, "That is true. But we had Jerusalem when London was a marsh."[7]

German Zionist Nahum Goldmann, who would later work closely with Weizmann, wrote that he had a "quite uncanny instinct for adapting himself to a situation or an opponent. He talked to lords like a lord, to labor leaders like a labor leader, and to Frenchmen like a Frenchman."[5] The diplomat and historian Charles Webster would later echo this opinion: "With unerring skill he adapted his arguments to the special circumstances of each statesman."[8] That was a polite way of saying that Weizmann could fit his arguments perfectly to his interlocutor's preconceptions, even at the expense of disguising or disclaiming his own convictions. To take the most important example—Weizmann's objective was to establish a Jewish state, but when he believed that saying so would enflame the opposition, he dissimulated by practicing what he called "safe statesmanship."[9]

Weizmann had first met Ahad Ha'am in Berlin, where the Zionist thinker, whose business in Odessa had failed, had taken a job representing a Russian tea company owned by a wealthy Jewish admirer. The two men were reunited after Ahad Ha'am was transferred to London in 1908, and Ahad Ha'am became as much as anyone Weizmann's mentor. When war broke out between Britain and Germany, Weizmann and Ahad Ha'am were alone among British Zionists in believing that the British would eventually win the war and that the Ottoman Empire would be a casualty of Germany's defeat.

Ahad Ha'am still took an evolutionary view of Zionism, but he saw an opportunity for unrestricted Jewish immigration and industry if the British took over Palestine from the Turks. After Turkey entered the war on Germany's side on October 29, 1914, Ahad Ha'am wrote Weizmann that "the great historic hour for the Jews and for Palestine has struck."[10] With Ahad Ha'am advising him, Weizmann set out to convince the British of the strategic importance of having a Jewish Palestine as part of the British Empire.

Weizmann charmed his way up the ladder of authority until he reached the top. At a tea party in November 1914, he met C. P. Scott, the powerful editor of *The Manchester Guardian*, the leading Liberal Party newspaper. Scott found Weizmann "extraordinarily interesting" and admired "his perfectly clear conception of Jewish nationalism."[11] Weizmann assured Scott that if the British were to annex Palestine and encourage Jewish settlement, the new settlers could "form a very effective guard for the Suez Canal."[12]

Scott provided Weizmann with an introduction to Postmaster General Herbert Samuel, the first Jew in a British cabinet. (Benjamin Disraeli had been of Jewish ancestry but was raised as an Anglican.) Weizmann was wary of Britain's upper-class Jews—who, like their German or American counterparts, generally regarded Judaism as a religion and not a nationality and Zionism as a threat to their hopes for assimilation—and put off a visit to him. But when Weizmann met Samuel a month later, he discovered, to his amazement, that the postmaster general was an ardent Zionist.

Samuel, who would eventually play almost as important a role in the history of Zionism as Weizmann, was the son of a prominent banker. After he lost his father when he was only six, his uncle Samuel Montagu (originally named "Montagu Samuel"), the founder of the London firm Montagu and Samuel, became his guardian and entrée into British Liberal politics. Besides being one of Britain's foremost financiers, Montagu represented the heavily Jewish district of Whitechapel in Parliament. Herbert Samuel, after graduating from Oxford, began a long career as a Liberal Party politician. He was a founder of the "new Liberalism" that emphasized government intervention to right the wrongs of capitalism.

Samuel's contemporaries and subordinates regarded him, with his carefully clipped moustache and penchant for formal attire, as cold, austere, and passionless, but there was one cause that roused him. Zionism, his biographer Bernard Wasserstein writes, "was the one political passion of a singularly passionless career."[13] Samuel had abandoned any religious commitment to Judaism while he was studying at Oxford in 1893, but Zionism became—as it did for a contemporary, the American Louis Brandeis—the expression of his commitment to Judaism.

Along with his uncle, Samuel had read and admired Herzl's *The Jewish State*. But while Montagu gave up on Zionism after Herzl's death, Samuel retained his connection to the movement through a family friend, Rabbi Moses Gaster, who was close to Weizmann. After Turkey's entry into the war against Britain, and Asquith's statement at a cabinet meeting that Britain must abandon "Ottoman integrity," Samuel had seen an opening for a Jewish state, and had tried to make the case for Zionism to Foreign Secretary Edward Grey.

Samuel told Grey that "if a Jewish State were established in Palestine, it might become the center of a new culture." Samuel envisaged the Jewish Palestine as a neutral state, but he maintained that "British influence ought to play a considerable part in the formation of such a state because the geographical situation of Palestine, and especially its proximity to Egypt, would render its goodwill to England a matter of importance to the British Empire."[14]

Through Gaster, Samuel had earlier helped Weizmann become a British citizen, but he had never met him until that December. He was instantly charmed. He wrote his son the next year, "I never see him without being more and more impressed by his breadth of view and sound judgment, and by—a rare combination—his union of those qualities with a passionate fervor and enthusiasm."[15] Weizmann was equally impressed with Samuel. After their meeting, Weizmann wrote his wife, "Messianic times have really come. It turns out that he knows a great deal about Zionism, even about Ahad Ha'amism."[16]

Ahad Ha'am had advised Weizmann to temper his demands in meetings with British officials. "I think we should be moderate in our claims and content ourselves with the right of colonization and cultural activity . . . under the aegis of English," he wrote to Weizmann.[17] In line with this advice, Weizmann implored Samuel to consider the desirability of a place where Jews "formed the important part of the population" and had a university of their own, but the postmaster general, who was still thinking about a Jewish state, chided him that his demands were "too modest."[18]

After the meeting, Samuel continued to confer with Weizmann, and in January he arranged for him and Weizmann, accompanied by Scott, to take their plan for a Jewish state to David Lloyd George, the chancellor of the exchequer. Samuel expected Lloyd George to be receptive. The

Welshman's grandfather and uncle had been Baptist preachers, and he had grown up, he said, knowing "far more about the history of the Jews than about the history of my own land."[19] Lloyd George's sentimental attachment to ancient Jewry extended to Zionism. As a London lawyer, he had represented Herzl and the Zionist Organization in negotiations in 1903 with Chamberlain.[20] But his support for Jewish Palestine rested equally, if not more, on the importance of a Jewish protectorate to British holdings in the Near East. Lloyd George saw a Jewish Palestine as a part of the British Empire.

As a result of his discussions with Weizmann and meeting with Lloyd George, Samuel abandoned his idea of a neutral Jewish state. In a memo to Grey and Asquith, he urged that the British conquer Palestine in order to "civilize" it and to "add luster to the British crown."[21] Faced with the British official's question of what a Jewish state would mean for Palestine's Arab inhabitants, Samuel also gave up the idea that the British could establish a Jewish state. He now moved toward an evolutionary Zionism more in line with Ahad Ha'am's advice to Weizmann.

In this memo, Samuel wrote, "The time is not ripe for the establishment there of an independent, autonomous Jewish state. If the attempt were made to place the 400,000 or 500,000 Mohammedans of Arab race under a Government which rested upon the support for 90,000 or 100,000 Jewish inhabitants, there can be no assurance that such a Government . . . would be able to command obedience. The dream of a Jewish state, prosperous, progressive, and the home of a brilliant civilization, might vanish in a series of squalid conflicts with the Arab population . . . To attempt to realize the aspiration of a Jewish state one century too soon might throw back its actual realization for many centuries more."[22]

In his memo, and his conversations with Weizmann, Grey, and Lloyd George, Samuel had laid out most of the arguments, and dealt with most of the difficulties—including the "400,000 or 500,000 Mohammedans"—that would figure in the British decision to back Zionism and would later haunt the British occupation; and Samuel himself would play a key role in British Palestine; but in 1915 his memo failed to sway Asquith, who was, he lamented, "not attracted by this proposed addition to our responsibilities." Asquith noted that "it is a curious illustration of Dizzy's [Disraeli's] favorite maxim that 'race is everything' to find this almost lyrical outburst proceeding from the well-ordered and methodical brain of H.S."[23]

Wartime Diplomacy

European diplomacy had a long history of secret wartime agreements that countries used to build alliances against their foes. Asquith's goal in the Near East was to win Arab support against Turkey and Germany. That became even more urgent after the British and French failure at Gallipoli to capture Constantinople from the Turks and Germans. In October 1915, Henry McMahon, the British high commissioner in Egypt, on instructions from London, wrote to the sharif Hussein bin Ali, the titular head of Saudi Arabia, promising that if he were to mobilize Arab forces on behalf of the British, the British would support "the independence of the Arabs in all the regions within the limits demanded by the Sharif of Mecca."[24]

That was a generous offer, and the only limits the British explicitly set were "districts" west of Damascus and around Basra and Baghdad. McMahon believed his words were sufficiently ambiguous "to tempt the Arab people in the right path" without "bind[ing] our hands."[25] Foreign Secretary Edward Grey thought that insofar as Hussein was unlikely to keep his end of the bargain, the British promise "was a castle in the air which would never materialize."[26] But the sharif, and succeeding generations of Arab leaders, believed he had secured a British promise for the independence of what would be Syria, Jordan, and Palestine.

Asquith also wanted to include Britain's French allies in any postwar plans for the region, and he negotiated terms with them and the Russians that contradicted those with Hussein. In May 1916 the British, French, and Russians secretly signed the Sykes-Picot Treaty dividing up Palestine, Lebanon, Syria, Mesopotamia, and Turkey. The French were to get Syria and Lebanon; most of Palestine was to be under joint Allied control; the British were to control what became Jordan, part of Iraq, and the ports of Haifa and Acre; and Russia was to get parts of Turkey, including Istanbul and the Straits of Bosporus. These agreements set the stage for postwar charges of betrayal, and complicated Weizmann and Samuel's efforts to secure British support for Zionism.

Balfour, Sykes, and Lloyd George

In December 1916, the Liberal Party split over the conduct of the war, and Lloyd George replaced Asquith as prime minister in a coalition cabinet. He appointed the Tory Balfour, whom Weizmann had wooed for a decade, as foreign secretary. Samuel, who had been an Asquith protégé, was out of the government, but Lloyd George and Balfour were ready to make the case for Britain backing Zionism, even if that meant repudiating or ignoring the agreements with both Sharif Hussein and the French.

Balfour, like Lloyd George, had a biblical attachment to Zionism. Raised as a devout Scottish Presbyterian, he accepted from Weizmann in 1906 the Zionist argument that the Jews had a right to reclaim their ancient land and would repeat it for the rest of his life. He also thought of anti-Semitism as a "great evil" that "has been the cause of the most abominable crimes wherever it has prevailed."[27] Earlier, he had maintained Dreyfus's innocence and protested the exclusionary policies of British clubs. He said he considered Jews to be the most gifted peoples since the ancient Greeks.

But Balfour, Lloyd George, and other British officials held views of the Jews that had been influenced by anti-Semitic mythology. They thought of Jews as a kind of superrace that secretly pulled the levers of power. Balfour termed Jews "exceedingly clever."[28] Balfour's deputy Robert Cecil declared, "I do not think it is easy to exaggerate the international power of the Jews."[29] Like Lloyd George, much of Balfour's support for Zionism would rest on his desire to buttress the British Empire with what he imagined to be the enormous behind-the-scenes power of international Jewry.

Weizmann and other British Zionists would do what they could to reinforce these illusions. Afterward, Harry Sacher, who was close to Weizmann and who worked for Scott at *The Manchester Guardian*, wrote that the officials "have a residual belief in the power and the unity of Jewry. We suffer for it, but it is not wholly without its compensations . . . To exploit it delicately and deftly belongs to the art of the Jewish diplomat."[30]

Balfour and other British officials also supported Zionism as an alternative to Jewish immigration to Britain. In 1905, when he was prime minister, Balfour had championed the Aliens Act that was intended to restrict Jewish immigration by allowing British port inspectors to turn back "undesirable aliens." Balfour's contorted argument on the bill's behalf appeared to denounce anti-Semitism to justify anti-Semitism. He argued that if more Jews were admitted to Britain, Britain could follow the "evil example set by some other countries" of anti-Semitism.[31] He deplored "the undoubted evils which have fallen upon parts of the country from an alien immigration which was largely Jewish."[32]

Balfour seems to have seen Zionism as a means of diverting the flow of Eastern European Jewish immigrants from Britain to Palestine. When he was roundly criticized for backing the Aliens Act by MP Stuart Samuel, Herbert Samuel's brother, Balfour cited his government's offer of Uganda to the Zionists. His government, he said, "had offered to the Jewish race a great tract of fertile land in a British possession in order that they might, if they so desired it, find an asylum from persecutors at home."[33] In other words, Zionism was Balfour's cure for anti-Semitism.

In making their case for a Jewish Palestine under British rule, Lloyd George and Balfour were seconded by a third key player in the drama, Mark Sykes, whom Lloyd George promoted to be an assistant secretary to the war cabinet with principal responsibility for policy in the Middle East. Although Sykes had helped negotiate the agreement with the French that bore his name, he had been talking regularly for over a year with Aaron Aaronsohn, a Palestinian Jew who worked as a spy for the British. Aaronsohn, a legendary figure who had already helped win the American Louis Brandeis over to Zionism, convinced Sykes to favor a Jewish Palestine under British rule.

Sykes was persuaded to back Zionism largely on geopolitical grounds, and convinced his assistant, Leopold Amery. "Sykes soon persuaded me," Amery recalled, "that, for the purely British point of view, a prosperous Jewish population in Palestine, owing its inception and opportunity of development to British policy, might be an invaluable asset as a defense of the Suez Canal against attack from the North and as a station on the future air-routes to the East."

Sykes and Amery saw Zionism as an agent of Western civilization. The Jews, they believed, would have a "regenerating . . . influence" on "the whole Middle Eastern region."[34] And of Palestine itself, Sykes shared the early Zionist presumption that no one really lived there. "If the Zionists do not go there, no one will. Nature abhors a vacuum," he declared.[35] Finally, like Lloyd George, Balfour, and Cecil, Sykes ascribed magical powers to international Jewry. "Believe me when I say that this race, despised and weak, is universal, is all powerful and cannot be put down," he wrote to an Arab ruler. Jews were to be found "in the councils of every state, in every bank, in every business, in every enterprise."[36]

In sum, Lloyd George, Balfour, and Sykes's support for Zionism was compounded of biblical convictions—which were strong in the case of Lloyd George and Balfour—geopolitical considerations, the imperial ideology of civilization, paranoia and wishful thinking about Jewish international influence, and the fear that if Eastern European Jews couldn't emigrate to Palestine, they would flock to Britain. It was hard to say which of these considerations predominated, but when the British officials made the case to skeptics, they stressed the geopolitical benefit that Zionism would bring to the British Empire and to the current war effort. They did not dwell on the moral argument for Zionism.

To gain control over Palestine, the British had to renege on the Sykes-Picot agreement. In February 1917, Sykes held a meeting with Weizmann, Moses Gaster, Nahum Sokolow, and Walter Rothschild, the leaders of the English Zionist Federation. Samuel was also present. Sykes wanted to use the Zionists to convince the French to cede any claim over Palestine. When Sykes had raised the possibility of French control of Palestine without revealing that the British had signed the Sykes-Picot treaty, Weizmann and Sokolow had rejected the idea and sharply rebuked him for even raising it. That's exactly what Sykes wanted to hear. The next day he took Sokolow to meet with Sykes's French counterpart, François Georges-Picot. Sokolow expressed the Zionist preference for British control of Palestine. When Picot questioned Sokolow about native resistance to Zionism, Sokolow claimed that the Arabs were more interested in controlling other parts of the region.[37]

The next step was to win American president Woodrow Wilson's support. In May 1917, Balfour went to Washington to sound out the Americans about Britain turning Palestine into a British protectorate. Balfour, Lloyd George, and Sykes feared that the Wilson administration, which was on record against imperialism, would oppose a British takeover of Palestine. They hoped to win Wilson over by portraying Britain as the guardian of the Jewish people's right to national self-determination. And with American support, they hoped to discourage the French from claiming part of Palestine. Sykes outlined the strategy to a fellow cabinet official:

> As regards purely British interests it is, I think, desirable . . . without in any way showing any desire to annex Palestine or to establish a Protectorate over it, to so order our policy, that when the time comes to choose a Mandatory power for its control, by the consensus of opinion and the desire of the inhabitants, we shall be the most likely candidacy.[38]

Balfour visited Brandeis, a confidant of Wilson's whom the president had appointed to the Supreme Court. Brandeis told Balfour that Wilson would support a British protectorate. He also learned from Wilson's advisor Colonel Edward House that the United States would oppose the secret Sykes-Picot Treaty. Balfour and Lloyd George decided to ditch the French and go ahead with British plans for backing Zionism. The foreign minister gave the go-ahead to Weizmann and his colleagues to draw up a draft of a letter that Balfour would send declaring Britain's support for a Jewish Palestine.

Balfour's Letter

Weizmann warned the members of the English Zionist Federation that they must practice "safe statesmanship" by not stating publicly that they back a Jewish state even though it was their "final ideal."[39] Weizmann asked Henry Sacher to draft a statement that Balfour could issue. But with Weizmann out of the country trying on Britain's behalf to scuttle an American initiative toward Turkey, Sacher didn't heed his warning. His draft put the British government on record as supporting "the reconstitution of Palestine as a Jewish state and as the national home of the Jewish People."[40] Sokolow and Ahad Ha'am, however, echoed Weizmann's concerns. With Ahad Ha'am's backing, Sokolow countered with a draft that called for "recognizing Palestine as the national home of the Jewish people."

The two sides went back and forth and finally compromised on a draft that pledged the British government to the principle that "Palestine should be reconstituted as the national home of the Jewish people."

It said that the government would use "their best endeavors to secure the achievement of this object." Walter Rothschild, acting for the committee, sent the draft to Balfour and the Foreign Office.

Over the next three months, the Foreign Office and war cabinet discussed different drafts of the statement. Those Foreign Office officials who were less sanguine about Zionism wanted to remove any hint that Britain was going to transform Palestine into a Jewish *state*. They were also concerned that the statement didn't mention Palestine's Arab majority. Lord Milner, a member of the war cabinet, assured the House of Lords that the government was not interested in establishing "a Jewish government of Palestine, but a Jewish home there, which will receive as many Jews as the country can reasonably support . . . while at the same time taking care . . . that the interests of the Arab population do not suffer."[41]

The government drafters dropped the idea of "reconstituting Palestine as the national home of the Jewish people," which could be taken to imply Jewish ownership of Palestine based on prior residence. Instead, they said the government "views with favor the establishment in Palestine of a national home for the Jewish people." The establishment of a national home "in" Palestine could consist of the kind of Jewish Vatican that Ahad Ha'am proposed. The drafters also replaced a government commitment to "secure" this objective with a weaker commitment to "facilitate" it.

The government added a new pledge that "nothing shall be done which may prejudice the civil and religious rights of existing non-Jewish communities in Palestine." That was supposed to refer to the Arab inhabitants of Palestine, but by specifically referring to Jews and not to Arabs in the statement, the British gave precedence to Palestine's Jews over its Arabs. By omitting *political* rights for non-Jews, the wording suggested that in spite of using terms like "home," the British were committed to a Jewish state.

In October, the British war cabinet and foreign ministry officials debated whether the government should issue the statement. Lord Curzon, who was the House of Lords' representative in the war cabinet and who would succeed Balfour as foreign secretary in 1919, took the lead in opposing the statement. Curzon, who had served as viceroy in India and had traveled extensively in the Middle East and Asia, charged that the term "national home" was dangerously ambiguous and would commit Britain to creating a Jewish state in a land that "already has an indigenous population of its own of a different race." The Arabs who lived there already, Curzon warned, would "not be content either to be expropriated for Jewish immigrants or to act merely as hewers of wood and drawers of water for the latter."[42]

But Curzon failed to carry the day. Cabinet officials had repeatedly heard from Weizmann and other British Zionists that the Germans were making overtures to the Zionists. These rumors were largely baseless, but Lloyd George warned the cabinet that if Britain didn't step forward, Germany would gain the upper hand in Palestine. Lloyd George and Balfour also repeated Weizmann's dubious contention (which was meant to appeal to stereotypes of international Jewry) that if Britain committed itself to Zionism, then Russia's Jews would prevent the Bolsheviks from abandoning the war and American Jews would use their influence in Britain's favor after the war. Balfour told the cabinet meeting, "The vast majority of Jews in Russia and America . . . now appear to be favorable to Zionism. If we could make a declaration favorable to such an ideal, we should be able to carry on extremely useful propaganda both in Russia and America."[43] (Balfour even believed that Lenin was Jewish.)[44] Lloyd George added that "the Zionist leaders gave us a definite promise that, if the Allies committed themselves to giving facilities for the establishment of a National Home for the Jews in Palestine, they would do their best to rally to the Allied cause."[45]

When the cabinet approved the Balfour Declaration, Sykes rushed outside to congratulate Weizmann. "Dr. Weizmann, it's a boy," he exclaimed.[46] But Weizmann didn't like the final statement, which he believed had diluted the British commitment to a Jewish state. He objected to the inclusion of a statement about "non-Jewish communities" because, he wrote later, it could be taken "to impute possible oppressive intentions to the Jews."[47] Rothschild also disliked that clause, which, he charged, was "a slur on Zionism, as it presupposes the possibility of a danger to non-Zionists, which I deny."[48]

Of the British Zionists, only Ahad Ha'am actually preferred the objective of a "home" over a "state," and welcomed the inclusion of the Palestinian Arabs. Ahad Ha'am wrote in praise of the declaration:

> The Balfour Declaration does not affect the right of the other inhabitants who are entitled to invoke the right of actual dwelling. Palestinian

Arabs, too, have the right to a National Home, have the right to develop national forces to the extent of their ability . . . In such circumstances it is no longer possible that the national home of one of them
could be total. The management of the whole has to be directed in
agreement with the interests of all.[49]

In the end, though, the ambiguities and nuances of the declaration,
which alternatively maddened Weizmann and delighted Ahad Ha'am,
eluded the media and the general public. The document was taken as a
straightforward endorsement of a Jewish state. In Britain, the *Daily
Express* headlined their story, "A State for the Jews," while the London
Times and *The Morning Post* headlined their stories "Palestine for the
Jews." And the British Department of Information did its part, drop-
ping leaflets to Jews in German, Austrian, and Russian territory saying,
"The Allies are giving the Land of Israel to the people of Israel."[50]

Predictably, the nuances also eluded Jews and Arabs in Palestine. The
Jews rejoiced. Recalled Gad Frumkin, a member of Palestine's supreme
court during the British mandate, "The word passed in the camp of
Israel and the nations that the Balfour Declaration was like unto the
creation of the state of Israel."[51] The Arabs mourned, believing that
they had been betrayed by the British. When Weizmann organized a
celebration in Jerusalem on the first anniversary of the declaration,
two Arab protestors grabbed a banner and beat up one of the celebrants.
The next day, a delegation headed by Jerusalem's mayor handed Britain's military governor a petition protesting Britain's intention to give
Palestine to the Jews. This was, to be sure, a relatively tame protest, but
riot and rebellion would soon follow.

Curzon and British officials like Gertrude Bell who were familiar
with the Middle East recognized that the declaration would spark a
conflict between Jew and Arab. But it seems that Balfour—persuaded,
perhaps, by Weizmann's assurances of an amicable transition to a Jewish state, and by a dubious promise Weizmann made in 1918 of 5 million
Jews ready to emigrate—never worried about this. According to George
Kidston, who served in the Middle East division of the Foreign Office,
Balfour promised Palestine to Zionists "irrespective of the wishes of
the great bulk of the population, because it is historically right and politically expedient that [Britain] should do so. The idea that carrying out

of these programs will entail bloodshed and military repression never seems to have occurred to him."[52]

If the measure of responsible decision making in politics is carefully assessing the consequences of your actions before acting, Balfour and Lloyd George acted irresponsibly or at least naively in pressing for the Balfour Declaration. And by denying that the Arabs would oppose the declaration and by encouraging British officials to believe that the declaration would keep the Bolsheviks in the war and increase America's role, Weizmann, Sokolow, and other British Zionists encouraged Balfour and Lloyd George to act blindly.

Some British officials thought of the Balfour Declaration as merely another wartime expediency—like the McMahon letter—that could be disregarded or seriously modified once the war was over. But the Jews had different ideas. For them, it was the parting of the waters. And historically, of course, that judgment proved correct. From their standpoint, the Balfour Declaration turned what might have been a noble failure into a rousing success. From the standpoint of Palestinian Arabs, however, it turned what might have been a historical nuisance— the cause of strife, but not war, and perhaps in the end a benefit, as Jews came to constitute a vibrant minority within an Arab Palestine—into a challenge to their very identity and self-determination.

■ 4 ■

HERBERT SAMUEL AND THE BRITISH MANDATE

Until 1917, the conflict between the Jews and Arabs in Palestine was limited to local skirmishes over land purchases and polemics in Arab and Zionist publications. As long as Turkey controlled Palestine, there was no prospect of a Jewish or an Arab state. There was a simmering moral argument between Jew and Arab, but it was largely confined to the intelligentsia. The Zionists sought a land that had as yet no definite borders and that was still controlled by a power unfriendly to Zionist aims. The Arabs of Palestine lacked a national identity. But in December 1917 the British changed all that.

The Balfour Declaration and the British conquest of Palestine emboldened the political Zionists who insisted on a new Jewish state, and marginalized cultural Zionists like Ahad Ha'am who were content with building a Jewish community in a binational Palestine. From then on, the main Zionist organizations were determined to plant the Jewish flag over Palestine, even if that meant ruling an Arab majority. They continued to invoke imperial justifications for Zionist rule. And secular as well as religious Zionists cited the Jews' biblical right to reestablish their homeland.

The region's Arabs were inspired by the British promise to Sharif Hussein, the ouster of the Turks, and Wilson's advocacy of national self-determination to seek states of their own. Palestine's Arabs initially imagined a Greater Syria, including the Holy Land, under Arab control, but when the British ceded control of Syria to France and created a border between Palestine and Syria, the country's Arabs focused on an Arab-controlled Palestine. They protested the Balfour Declaration as a betrayal of the McMahon letter, and they hoped that their superior numbers and the acknowledgment of national self-determination would sway the British. When that did not happen, the stage was set for civil war.

British leaders were largely oblivious to the prospects for war and rebellion. They were determined to use Palestine as a strategic buffer state, and they thought they were doing a good deed in championing Zionism. Zionism, Balfour wrote Curzon, "is rooted in age-long traditions, in present needs, in future hopes, of far profounder import than the desires and prejudices of the 700,000 Arabs who now inhabit that ancient land."[1]

To the extent that they acknowledged discontent among Palestine's Arabs, they believed that it could be eased by the prosperity that Jewish immigration would bring. Except for those officials who were actually familiar with the Middle East, the British were taken entirely by surprise when violent conflicts broke out between Zionism and Arab nationalism in 1920.

By the early 1920s, in response to the Arab rebellions, many British leaders had lost their enthusiasm for the Balfour Declaration and the mandate and begun to seek ways to reach some accommodation between the Jews and Arabs. The first of these efforts took place after the Jaffa riots of 1921 and involved Herbert Samuel, who had become the high commissioner of Palestine. To the consternation of Palestine's Jewish leadership, Samuel tried to work out a genuine compromise that recognized that the Arabs as well as the Jews had a right to a national homeland. But Samuel couldn't overcome the momentum toward conflict that Britain's diplomacy had already created.

The British Mandate

British troops under General Edmund Allenby entered Jerusalem in December 1917, and took control of the rest of Palestine from the Turks over the next year. In London, Lloyd George, Balfour, and Sykes prepared the groundwork for incorporating Palestine into the British Empire and for carrying out the Balfour Declaration. But they faced the problem of justifying an extension of the British Empire at a time when imperialism had fallen into disrepute—blamed by Wilson and Lenin, as well as by the labor and social democratic parties of Europe, for World War I—and when the principle of national self-determination had become wildly popular among colonized peoples.[2]

To avoid the charge of imperialism, the British agreed to the idea, formulated by the South African Jan Smuts and endorsed by Wilson, that the victorious Allies should receive "mandates" to oversee the transition of former Ottoman or German colonies to self-government. In Wilson's mind, these mandates were to go to countries like Sweden that had no stake in becoming colonial powers, but Britain, France, Italy, and Japan saw the mandates as a means of expanding their holdings without incurring the charge of imperialism. That ruse became easier to pull off after Wilson, the main foe of imperialism, became incapacitated, and after the U.S. Senate refused to ratify the League of Nations treaty. So Britain set out to broaden its holdings in the Middle East by securing the mandate for Palestine.

In line with the principle of self-determination, the postwar peace conference at Versailles established three classes of mandates. The former territories of the Ottoman Empire were said to belong to "Class A," former German territories "Class B," and territories to be annexed "Class C." Class A territories had "reached a stage of development where their existence as independent nations can be provisionally recognized subject to the rendering of administrative advice and assistance by a Mandatory until such time as they are able to stand alone. The wishes of these communities must be a principal consideration in the selection of the Mandatory."

But what about former Ottoman Palestine? The British recognized that their occupation of Palestine could not meet these conditions. "The weak point of our position of course is that in the case of Palestine we deliberately and rightly decline to accept the principle of self-determination," Balfour wrote Lloyd George in 1919. "If the present inhabitants were consulted they would unquestionably give an anti-Jewish verdict."[3] To bypass the present inhabitants, the British decided to write the Balfour Declaration into the mandate for Palestine.

To advise the British delegation at the peace conference, Weizmann set up a committee, chaired by Samuel, to draft language on the declaration. At that point Samuel, inspired by the Balfour Declaration, had forgotten his earlier qualms and was bent on turning Palestine into a Jewish state as quickly as possible regardless of what Palestine's other inhabitants desired. His committee's draft pledged the British to developing "the country of Palestine . . . into a Jewish commonwealth."[4] Under the British, the Jews would have the majority on Palestine's executive and legislative councils. Samuel's committee also submitted a map of Palestine that included most of Jordan and chunks of southern Lebanon and Syria.

The Zionist draft revived the controversy in the British government over the initial drafts of the Balfour Declaration. Curzon, who had succeeded Balfour as foreign minister in 1919, strenuously objected to the idea of a Jewish commonwealth, which he called "a euphemism for a Jewish state."[5] The Foreign Office also objected to the map and to the plan for a Jewish-dominated administration. As a result, British officials threw out the language recommended by Samuel's committee and adopted the ambiguous language of the original Balfour Declaration calling for a "national home" rather than a "commonwealth." That concession was supposed to quiet Arab protests, but, like the Balfour Declaration, the proposal denied the Arabs political rights, merely noting that "nothing shall be done which may prejudice the civil and religious rights of existing non-Jewish communities in Palestine." To make matters worse, the British barred an Arab delegation from the peace talks, and British officials privately assured Weizmann and other prominent Zionists, including Brandeis, that they backed a Jewish state.

Weizmann and Sokolow played a double game of their own. They urged that the British put the Jews in charge in Palestine to prepare them for statehood. Weizmann even complained to Balfour that the British had permitted a play at an orphanage that called on "the Arab nation to wake from its torpor."[6] At the same time, Weizmann urged members of the Zionist Commission to avoid any mention of a Jewish state in their visits to Palestine. British officials and the Zionist leaders had, however, little control over the Zionist settlers in Palestine or over Zionists in the United States and Eastern Europe, most of whom had little compunction in proclaiming their commitment to a Jewish state.

Palestine's Zionists

In the wake of the Balfour Declaration, Zionist publications around the world celebrated the fulfillment of Herzl's dream of a Jewish state. A young David Ben-Gurion, who had spent part of the war in New York, praised the Balfour Declaration in the newspaper of the Zionist labor organization Poale Zion. Britain, he wrote, "has recognized our existence as a political entity and has endorsed our right to the country."[7] In Palestine, the local newspaper, *Palestine*, printed articles in the fall of 1918 calling for a Jewish state that would extend north to Beirut and encompass Jordan. At meetings, speakers regularly called for "a system of the future ruling of Palestine by the Jews."[8]

The Zionists in Palestine backed a British takeover of the country as a way of preparing imminently for a Jewish Palestine that would be part of the British Commonwealth along with Canada, South Africa, and Australia. In December 1918, about a hundred prominent Zionists, including representatives from the Zionist Commission—a group chaired by Weizmann to advise the British—gathered in Jaffa to draft a constitution for the new Palestine, which they planned to present to the peace conference in Paris. The provisions they adopted show the extent to which the Balfour Declaration had emboldened Palestine's Zionists and led them either to overlook or belittle the Arab cause.[9]

The participants at the meeting rejected a draft, proposed by the Zionist Commission, that would have called for Palestine to become the "national home" for the Jews. Instead, they called upon the peace conference to recognize "the claim of the Jewish people that Palestine should become again a Jewish commonwealth." The new Palestine would display the Zionist flag and it would be called "Eretz Israel," the land of Israel. In all respects, except its British administration at the very top, it would be a Jewish state.

The participants supported Britain becoming the trustee responsible for the "building up of the Jewish commonwealth." And a governor-general appointed by Britain was to govern through a six-person executive council drawn from the departments of the government. But Palestine's Jews were to be the de facto rulers. The Zionist Commission would appoint a permanent undersecretary for Palestine, who would serve directly under the governor-general. The undersecretary would provide the governor-general with a list of acceptable candidates for the executive council.

The Zionist Commission would be in charge of immigration; it would assume control of all state lands, including those taken from the Turks, and would have the sole right to "exploit all underground, or other natural resources and forces." The Arabs would get a single representative, a minister of Arab affairs, on the executive council, who would be chosen from recommendations by the Zionist permanent undersecretary. In short, the Arabs would have no independent representation in the new government of Palestine. They would have civil and religious but not political rights.

The Zionists in Palestine knew they were a minority—about 10 percent of the population—but at the conference they tried to bypass the problem through fanciful proposals. Delegates suggested that some of the difference could be made up quickly by Jewish immigration, or by the transfer of Arabs to Arab-controlled states, or by means of the dubious conception that the world's Jews were to be regarded as "citizens in potentia" of Palestine.[10]

Two of the three members of the plan's drafting committee, Vladimir Jabotinsky, later the leader of a breakaway faction in the Zionist movement, and the agronomist Yitzhak Wilansky, urged participants to be realistic about the opposition they were going to face from the Arabs. But instead of calling on the settlers to take a more conciliatory posture, they proposed that the delegates recognize and accept the fact that they were imposing their will on the Arabs. Jabotinsky and Wilansky argued, in effect, that Zionists should not concern themselves with the morality of their position.

Both of them recognized that the Arabs would not willingly accept Jewish rule. Would the Arabs who had been "living in the country for 2000 years," Jabotinsky asked, agree that "another people come and multiply in it?" Wilansky described the Zionists as a "foreign body" entering "into the midst of the Arab nation." But instead of conceding that the Jews should respect Arab rights, they advocated running roughshod over them while accepting the consequences in conflict and in conscience. Jabotinsky warned that the Zionists should not give ground on their contention "that the government should be entirely ours."[11] Wilansky warned against allowing "supreme righteousness and morality" toward the Arabs to dictate Zionist policy. "When you enter into the midst of the Arab nation and do not allow it to unite, here too you are taking its life." "One must be an extremist," Wilansky advised, meaning that one must put moral considerations aside in justifying Zionism.[12]

Zionist calls for transferring power to themselves alarmed Palestinian Arabs. Statements in favor of a Jewish Palestine were widely reported in the Arab press and, as a British commission later discovered, were even circulated in the countryside where many of the villagers were illiterate. These statements upset Balfour and Sykes. Balfour wrote Samuel in June 1919, "May I take this opportunity of stating frankly that the position in Palestine is giving me considerable anxiety. Reports are reaching me from unbiased sources that the Zionists there are behaving in a way which is alienating the sympathies of all the other elements of the population."[13] Balfour wrote in a similar vein to Weizmann, who refused to acknowledge that Palestine's Zionists were promoting a Jewish state. Instead, he blamed the French press for spreading rumors about a "Jewish state."[14] But Weizmann himself would do more than any of Palestine's Zionists to alarm Palestine's Arabs about Jewish intentions.

At Versailles, where Weizmann headed the Zionist delegation, he carefully resorted to the formula of a "national home" to describe the movement's aims. Yet when the American secretary of state Robert Lansing asked him what was meant by a "Jewish national home," he let down his guard and responded famously that "there should ultimately be such conditions that Palestine should be just as Jewish as America is American and England is English."[15] Weizmann's statement, which was widely reported, became a mantra of hope for Zionists and of fear for Arab nationalists. For the former, it summed up what they wanted to accomplish; for the latter, what they wanted at all costs to prevent.

Arab Protest

As Allenby was entering Jerusalem, the sharif Hussein's son, Faisal, with T. E. Lawrence in tow, was setting out with 3,500 Arab irregulars to aid the British against the Germans and Turks. Faisal was keeping his father's side of the bargain with McMahon. In September 1918, Faisal and his forces entered Damascus with the Allies, and Faisal became the head of a provisional Syrian government. The Ottoman Empire crumbled. Faisal's success, combined with the collapse of the Ottoman Empire and Woodrow Wilson's promise of self-determination, led to the "Arab awakening" that Azoury had predicted in 1905. In Syria, Lebanon, Mesopotamia, and Palestine, Arab leaders clamored for independence.

During the war, the Ottoman regime had banned all political activity in Palestine, but with the collapse of the empire, Arab newspapers began publishing again, older literary and cultural clubs from the Young Turk period reconvened, and new political organizations sprung up. These included the Muslim-Christian Associations, the Literary Forum, and the Arab Club. By 1919, the Muslim-Christian Associations claimed a membership of about three thousand in Palestine. The Literary Forum and Arab Club claimed about five hundred members each, but were more politically militant. Once pro-Ottoman, the members of these groups now identified themselves primarily as Arabs. "We live and die in the name of the Arabs," the Literary Forum announced.[16]

In the spring of 1919, a group of prominent Arab Muslims and Christians sent a petition to the peace conference that expressed their anger, and apprehension, about Zionism:

> The principles of justice and equity cannot admit of the crushing of a nation by an influx of a greater number of another foreign nation that will assimilate her . . . The country is ours and has been so of old. We have lived in it longer than they did, and have worked in it more than they did. Our historical and religious relations with it, we Moslems and Christians, far exceed those of the Jews. Therefore, their claim to their ancient historical rights in the country do not give them the right of appropriating it, in as much as in our historical rights we Arabs cannot justify our claims in Spain, our old home, where our rule and glory flourished for eight centuries and thus gave birth to the modern civilization of Europe . . . Does justice then allow of the violation of the rights of the majority?[17]

The Muslim-Christian Associations organized meetings and protests in villages and towns. In May 1919 a meeting in Jaffa drew five hundred participants who adopted a statement promising equality for the country's Jews but opposing further Jewish immigration. "We do not at all oppose the Jews. We only oppose Zionism. That is not the same thing. Zionism has no roots at all in Moses' law. It is an invention of Herzl's."[18]

W. F. Stirling, a British military official stationed in Jaffa, later wrote that the Balfour Declaration, "coupled with the attitude of the Jews, caused the Arabs to fear an eventual Jewish domination; for while it stated that the British government favored the creation of a Jewish national home in Palestine, the Jewish interpretation of it, which was openly preached, suggested that we favored the conversion of the whole country into a national home for them. The Arabs, not unnaturally, took alarm . . . This fear of Jewish domination . . . became the prevailing consideration."[19]

The protests themselves became more heated and violent. Arabs attacked Zionist settlements at Tel Hai and Kfar Giladi, both of which were subsequently evacuated. They staged large demonstrations in Jerusalem. On the first anniversary of the Balfour Declaration in 1918, Arab demonstrators had marched peacefully through the city. But in February and March 1920, violent clashes took place in Jerusalem after the British announcement that it was putting the Balfour Declaration into effect.

Weizmann had tried to assure Balfour that the demonstrations, which he blamed on French "misrepresentation," were inconsequential, but in Palestine the British administrators knew better.[20] In August 1919, Major General H. D. Watson, who had become part of the military administration in Jerusalem, wrote the Foreign Office:

> The antagonism to Zionism of the majority of the population is deeply rooted—it is fast leading to hatred of the British—and will result, if the Zionist program is forced upon them, in an outbreak of a very serious character necessitating the employment of a much larger number of troops than at present located in the territory.[21]

And that outbreak occurred. In April 1920, at the annual Nebi Musa parade in Jerusalem celebrating the shrine of Moses (whom Muslims honor as a prophet), Arab politicians called for a greater Syria ruled by Faisal. The parade quickly degenerated into a full-scale anti-Zionist riot that spread outward and lasted several days. Four Jews were killed and more than two hundred were wounded.[22]

Palestinian Nationalism

The call for a greater Syria reflected the prevailing sentiment among Palestine's Arab intellectuals. Some notables who were active in the Muslim-Christian Associations wanted an Arab Palestine within the British Empire, but many of the activists and intellectuals, inspired by Faisal's success, envisaged Palestine as "Southern Syria." In September 1919, a new newspaper appeared called *Suriyaa al-Janubiyya*, or *Southern Syria*. "We are residents of southern Syria," the paper declared. "We do not want partition, we want an independent Syria, and we are against Zionist immigration."[23]

There was a good geographical as well as political argument for greater Syria. As subsequent events would reveal, Palestine lacked natural boundaries, especially in the north and south. There were looming disputes over water rights that could be avoided by combining Palestine and Syria. The Christian Arab George Antonius wrote of greater Syria in *The Arab Awakening*, "In spite of the great diversity of its physical features, it was geographically one and formed a self-contained unit enclosed by well-defined natural frontiers."[24]

General Syrian congresses were held in Damascus in July 1919 and April 1920 that brought delegates from eastern (Syria proper), western (Lebanon), and southern (Palestine) Syria. They declared their support for "a constitutional monarchy based on the principle of democratic and broadly decentralized rule." They placed their hope on the "lofty principles proclaimed by President Wilson" and rejected "the claims of the Zionists for the establishment of a Jewish commonwealth in that part of Southern Syria which is known as Palestine."[25] At the April 1920 demonstrations, demonstrators waved pictures of Faisal and banners saying, "Palestine is part of Syria." Amin al-Husseini, who had moved to Damascus to work for greater Syria and would later become Jerusalem's grand mufti, displayed a picture of Faisal while shouting to the crowd, "This is your king."[26]

But Southern Syria was not to be. After Faisal had entered Damascus, the British entertained the idea of keeping their promise to his father at the expense of the Sykes-Picot Treaty, which had given Syria and Lebanon to France. Faced with a rebellious Arab population in Palestine and in Iraq, however, the British decided at the San Remo Conference in April 1920 to let the French have their way in Syria in exchange for French support for British mandates in Palestine and Iraq. "We had not been honest with either French or Arab," Balfour later admitted. "It was preferable to quarrel with the Arab rather than the French."[27]

The British, fearful that the movement for a greater Syria would undercut their hold over Palestine, encouraged Palestine's Arabs to think of themselves as Palestinian. Undersecretary of State Charles Hardinge wrote to Curzon in 1919, "It would on the whole, I believe, be advantageous to us to use the cry 'Palestine for the Palestinians' and 'Mesopotamia for the Mesopotamians.'"[28] In response, Curzon promised to advise his French counterparts to do the same. So, in the interest of quelling the disorder in Syria, the British encouraged the emergence of Palestinian Arab nationalism.

In July 1920, three months after the last Syrian congress had declared Southern Syria independent and Faisal its king, French troops moved in and deposed and exiled Faisal, installing their own military regime and quashing any hopes of greater Syria. The British gave Faisal the new state of Iraq as a consolation prize. Two years later the British, to the consternation of Weizmann and other Zionists, split Transjordan off from Palestine and gave it to Faisal's brother Abdullah to rule. The sharif Hussein's sons had done all right, but the Arab nationalists in Syria and Palestine who rested their hopes on the McMahon letter were sorely disappointed.

In Palestine, the same Arab nationalists who had advocated a greater Syria now talked only of an Arab Palestine. The successor to the Syrian Congress was called the Arab National Congress, and it was held in Haifa in December 1920. It identified Palestine as a separate nation. "It made 'Palestine' Palestine," the historian David Lesch remarked.[29] *Suriyaa al-Janubiyya* closed its doors, but its successor *al-Sabah* called Jerusalem rather than Damascus the capital of Palestine.[30] In March 1920, *Filastin* resumed publishing. Once a voice of Ottoman aspirations, it now spoke modestly of "Palestine and its sister Syria," making clear they were separate countries.[31]

Arab nationalists and Zionists now aspired to control exactly the same land, and the British—who were able to obtain a mandate from the League of Nations to administer Palestine—had exacerbated the conflict by fueling Zionist ambitions to conquer and not merely live in Palestine. Both the Jews and Arabs initially expected the British to side with them: Palestine's Jews assumed that the British would honor what they believed was the Balfour Declaration's commitment to Jewish statehood; and Palestine's Arabs thought the British would eventually see the error of their ways and settle for an Arab Palestine within the British Empire. In the end, both Jew and Arab would be disappointed, and so would the British, as they realized that Curzon had been right when he predicted that the Arabs would not "be content either to be expropriated for Jewish immigrants or to act merely as hewers of wood and drawers of water for the latter."

Samuel Appointed

In the wake of the Nebi Musa riots in April 1920, Menachem Ussishkin, the chairman of the Zionist Commission, accused Ronald Storrs, the first military governor of Jerusalem, of permitting a "pogrom."[32] In Britain, Weizmann and members of the Zionist Commission demanded that the military government be replaced by civilians sympathetic to Zionism. Lloyd George and Balfour, who believed that the authorities could have stopped the riots by rounding up a few troublemakers, acceded to the Zionists' wishes and decided to replace the military authorities—some of whom were not sympathetic to Zionism—with civilian officials who were.

At the San Remo Conference, Lloyd George asked Herbert Samuel, who was attending the conference along with Weizmann and Sokolow, to be the high commissioner of Palestine. Britain's Zionists had been lobbying for Samuel's appointment, and Weizmann was overjoyed. "Well, my darling," he wrote his wife, "our trials have come to an end."[33] In Palestine, Jewish leaders in Haifa issued a statement: "Could there be anything better than to have one of our own at the head of the Palestine Government? A Nehemiah! A liberator!"[34]

Palestine's Zionists thought they were getting an unabashed supporter of Jewish statehood, but Samuel was beset by conflicting priorities. He was a Zionist but, having been influenced by Ahad Ha'am as well as Herzl, he was willing to reconsider what that meant. In the brief time between his service as chair of the committee that drafted language for the Versailles peace conference and his departure for Palestine, he moved back toward a more evolutionary Zionism. He foresaw a Jewish state, but only after decades of immigration had created a Jewish majority. On the eve of leaving for Jerusalem to assume his post, he wrote a friend:

> What is practicable in Palestine now is one thing. What the present measures will lead to—and are designed to lead to in the future—is another. For the time being there will be no Jewish state, there will be restricted immigration; there will be cautious colonization. In five years, the pace will probably be accelerated and will grow after that progressively in speed. In fifty years there may be a Jewish majority in the population. Then the Government will be predominately Jewish, and in the generation after that there may be that which might properly be called a Jewish country with a Jewish state.[35]

He had come to reject any hint of an immediate Jewish government in Palestine. "The immediate establishment of a complete and purely Jewish state in Palestine would mean placing a majority under the rule of a minority," he said in a speech in London on the second anniversary of the Balfour Declaration. "It would therefore be contrary to the first principles of democracy, and would undoubtedly be disapproved by the public opinion of the world."[36]

Samuel's view of Palestine was also shaped by the fact that he was a British official—whose first loyalty was to his government at home—and a prominent member of the left-leaning Liberal Party. Unlike his Liberal colleague John Hobson, he did not oppose the British Empire but envisioned the empire as a commonwealth of self-governing nations. He didn't subscribe to the view of empire as an instrument of subduing and civilizing barbarous peoples. And that influenced how he viewed the Arabs of Palestine.

Samuel was a creature of his times, but for the most part he refused to treat Palestine's Arabs as inferior beings with lesser rights. That was evident before he arrived in Jerusalem by his attitude toward the question of population transfer. Many Zionists would not concede that the Arabs of Palestine had any special rights to the land. There was wide support for the idea that the Arabs, who collectively were about to inherit a wide swath of lands including Saudi Arabia, Iraq, and Syria, should not begrudge the Jews what Balfour called a "small niche" of Palestine.[37] If the Arabs proved unwilling to move out of Palestine voluntarily, then they should be transferred out.

That proposal was aired in the meeting at Jaffa, and in an article by the prominent Zionist Israel Zangwill, and was discussed in the Palestine Advisory Committee that the Foreign Office set up after the peace conference.[38] At the meeting in Jaffa, Wilansky had rejected population transfer as impractical, but refused to rule it out because it was immoral. "If it were possible," he declared, "I would commit an injustice towards the Arabs."[39]

When it had been raised at a meeting of the Palestine advisory committee in 1919, Samuel rejected the proposal for involuntary transfer on moral grounds. "Any movement of that kind," he said, "must be absolutely voluntary and conducted without any form of pressure . . . There will be the most equitable and sympathetic treatment of the Arab populations of that country. If we were to go to Palestine to oppress other people it would be an unspeakable disgrace."[40] Samuel later summed up his approach:

> Some thought . . . that a National Home for the Jews must mean subordination, possibly spoliation, for the Arabs. I did not share that view. If I had, it would have been impossible for me to accept the office of High Commissioner. All my life a convinced Liberal, for ten years a minister in a Liberal government, steeped in British principles of administration, I was the last man to take a hand in any policy of oppression.[41]

That approach, the product of Samuel's liberalism and of his commitment to Britain, would lead to conflict between him and the Zionist leadership in Britain and Palestine.

Samuel arrived in Jerusalem in July 1920 to assume his post. To ease tensions, he granted amnesty to Arabs and Jews imprisoned for their role in the Nebi Musa riots. These included Amin al-Husseini, who had fled to Jordan after being sentenced to ten years for incitement to riot, and Jabotinsky, who had organized a self-defense force and was arrested and sentenced to fifteen years for possessing weapons. Samuel also made a point of visiting Arab villages and conferring with Christians and Muslims as well as Jews. For his first months Samuel was rewarded with relative calm, but it was probably due more to the shock created by the French takeover of Syria than to anything that Samuel did.

Samuel assumed, however, that he was making progress. He reported to Lloyd George in October that "the mass of the population are quite contented."[42] In a December letter to Curzon, who had replaced Balfour as foreign minister, he dismissed the significance of that month's Arab National Congress in Haifa. "It was attended by about 25 persons," he wrote, who "need not be taken seriously in themselves, although undoubtedly they stand for a considerable body of opinion latent in the country."[43] But what Samuel assumed to be latent had already begun to surface.

At the December congress in Haifa, Arab leaders had elected an executive committee headed by Musa Kazim al-Husseini, the president of the congress, whom the British had deposed as mayor of Jerusalem after the Nebi Musa riots. The committee began organizing new protests against the Zionists. The first took place in Nablus in January. Others were planned for late March, when the new colonial secretary Winston Churchill was to visit Palestine, but the British stepped in to prevent them from occurring. The executive committee was allowed, however, to present its grievances to Churchill.

In the statement it presented, the executive committee insisted that it bore no ill will toward the Jews as such. "Had Zionists come to Palestine simply as visitors, or had matters remained as before the war, there would be no question of Jew or non-Jew. It is the idea of transforming Palestine into a home for the Jews that Arabs resent and fight against." The committee's statement complained that while the British had "recognized Zionist congresses, congratulated them, encouraged them, and wished them good luck," it had ignored the December congress in Haifa. And it noted that the British had appointed a Jew rather than an Arab as high commissioner. "We have no say in the government, no representative parliament," the statement declared. It called for revocation of the Balfour Declaration, the cessation of Jewish immigration, and the creation of a representative government.

The committee's statement also revealed the extent to which the Palestinian Arabs, looking to buttress their case against Zionism, had begun importing anti-Semitic conspiracy theories from Eastern Europe. "We have seen a book entitled *The Jewish Peril*," the statement declared. "It is a collection of the minutes of a secret society of prominent Jews who meet from time to time to discuss world affairs in relation to Judaism."[44] The Arab opposition was to Zionism, not Judaism, but anti-Semitic theories became a persistent undercurrent in this opposition, creating even greater distance between Arab and Jew.

Churchill, like Balfour and Lloyd George, was personally sympathetic to Zionism and had been an avid supporter of the Balfour Declaration.[45] He gave short shrift to the Arab complaints. He reasserted his support for the Balfour Declaration. Creation of a Jewish national home, he said, "will be good for the world, good for the Jews and good for the British Empire. But we also think it will be good for the Arab, and we intend that it shall be good for him." Echoing the older argument of Herzl's *Altneuland* and of Weizmann, he claimed that the creation of a Jewish national home would lead to "general diffusion of wealth and well-being . . . and by an advance in the social, scientific and cultural life of the people as a whole."

Churchill also chided Arabs for ignoring the content of the Balfour Declaration, which, he said, promises "to the inhabitants of Palestine the fullest protection of their civil and political rights."[46] (In fact, the declaration promised to protect the "civil and religious" but not the "political" rights of the "non-Jewish communities.") Echoing Churchill, Samuel reaffirmed the colonial secretary's statement that the Arabs' fears of a Jewish takeover were "unfounded."[47] Samuel, like Churchill, was insisting that the Arabs ignore what was before their eyes: the Zionist commitment to a Jewish state.

Churchill's visit left Palestine's Jews overjoyed, and its Arabs bitter. Captain C. D. Brunton of British Intelligence summed up the Arab response:

Ever since our occupation of the country the inhabitants have disliked the policy of founding a national home for the Jews in Palestine. This feeling has gradually developed into nothing short of bitter and widespread hostility, and the Arab population has come to regard the

Zionists with hatred and the British with resentment . . . Mr. Churchill's visit put the final touch to the picture. He upheld the Zionist cause and treated the Arab demands like those of a negligible opposition to be put off by a few political phrases and treated like bad children.[48]

That hostility would explode the next month in Jaffa.

The May Day Riots

On May Day in Jaffa, a town of about fifty thousand with between fifteen thousand and twenty thousand Jewish residents, the Jewish Communist Party held a parade calling for a Soviet Union of Palestine, which was attacked by Jewish Labor Party demonstrators. The police came and chased the Communists into Arab districts, where they got into a fight with Arab men. An Arab riot against Jews, fueled by opposition to Zionism, began. Jewish pedestrians were attacked, homes destroyed, and stores looted.

As the riot spread outward, Samuel called for two destroyers to be sent to Jaffa and used the air force to bomb Arab rioters. Jews also retaliated. Stirling, who was serving in Jaffa at the time, described the mayhem. "Jews were shot and stabbed in the narrow lanes . . . and Arab women joined in the attacks on Jewish colonies," he wrote. "Atrocities were committed by both sides, and some Arab women lying wounded in the fields were seen to have their breasts scythed off by Jewish colonists." All in all, forty-seven Jews, including the writer Josef Chaim Brenner, were killed, and forty-eight Arabs.

Initially, some officials in Jerusalem blamed the riots on provocation from the Jewish Bolsheviks, but it soon became clear that the cause was Arab hostility toward Zionism. In its report back to the State Department, the American consulate declared that "the underlying cause of all the political unrest in Palestine is and will continue to be the very direct and unmistakable antagonism which the majority Arab population of the country bears against Zionism and its aims."[49] This had been exacerbated in Jaffa by the "growth of ill-feeling between the Jewish and Moslem workmen at Jaffa. The latter have always controlled the stevedoring business at that port and the immigrant Jewish workmen have been attempting to supersede them by various means."[50]

The riots jolted Samuel out of his complacency. They challenged his assumption that Palestine's Arabs could be won over to the prospect of a Jewish state by the promise of economic progress while denying them any kind of national self-determination. Afterward, Samuel told Sokolow, who was visiting Jerusalem, "This is a war of the Arab nation against the Hebrew nation."[51] Samuel wrote Churchill that "a serious attempt must be made to arrive at an understanding with the opposition to the Zionist policy, even at the cost of considerable sacrifices. The only alternative is a policy of coercion which is wrong in principle and likely to prove unsuccessful in practice."[52]

After the violence subsided, Samuel suspended Jewish immigration into Palestine. He quickly moved toward a reevaluation of the Balfour Declaration and of his own Zionism. On June 3, Samuel used the occasion of King George V's birthday to give a speech in Jerusalem. Samuel said that "the British government . . . has never consented and will never consent . . . to a Jewish government being set to rule over the Moslem and Christian majority." The Balfour Declaration meant, Samuel said, "that the Jews . . . should be enabled to find here their home, and that some among them within the limits that are fixed by their numbers and the interests of the present population should come to Palestine in order to help by their resources and efforts to develop the country to the advantage of all its inhabitants."[53]

By suggesting that only "some" of the world's Jews would find their way to Palestine and that their numbers would be limited by the "interests of the present population," Samuel was moving closer to Ahad Ha'am's understanding of Zionism and away from that of the Zionist leaders in Palestine. In a government white paper he drafted, he echoed Ahad Ha'amism, declaring that the British wanted to facilitate a "center . . . in which the Jewish people as a whole . . . may take pride." It would be "founded *in Palestine*," but "Palestine as a whole" would not "be converted into a Jewish national home."[54]

Samuel, along with his second-in-command Wyndham Deedes, who was a Christian Zionist, wrote to Churchill suggesting the Zionist Commission formally renounce the objective of making Palestine a Jewish state. And he proposed a legislative council in which Arabs would constitute ten of twenty-three positions, with Jews occupying three positions and the British the remainder. And at Curzon's suggestion he proposed an Arab Agency that would parallel the Jewish Agency (the successor to the Zionist Commission and the Zionist Executive) in representing Palestine's Arabs.

Samuel sought to co-opt the Arab rebellion by elevating one of their spokesmen to a leadership position. Samuel chose the recently pardoned Amin al-Husseini to fill the recently vacated post of mufti (now dubbed "grand mufti"), which oversaw Muslim religious observance in Palestine. Samuel also created the British-funded Supreme Muslim Council with al-Husseini at the head, which was to be responsible for mosques, Muslim schools, clinics, and orphanages. That would prove to be a fateful step.

Al-Husseini, who was born in 1895, had studied theology at Cairo's al-Azhar University, where he had fallen under the spell of Syria-born Rashid Rida, who would later inspire Egypt's Muslim Brotherhood. Rida had warned as early as 1898 that Zionists were transforming the region's "masters into wage-laborers and [its] affluent men into paupers."[55] Al-Husseini had become an advocate of a greater Syria and briefly worked in Damascus, but after the French overthrew Faisal, he returned to Jerusalem, where he advocated an Arab Palestine and organized demonstrations against the Balfour Declaration. But Samuel was confident of his choice, having privately extracted from al-Husseini a promise to cooperate with the British administration.

Samuel Repudiated

British Zionists in Britain and Palestine reacted sharply to Samuel's speech and to the white paper and to his attempts to appease the Arabs. Weizmann called his speech "timid and apologetic."[56] When the Colonial Office asked Weizmann about Samuel's and Deedes's proposal to forswear a Jewish state of Palestine, he shot it down immediately. "What else are we striving for?" Weizmann wrote Deedes. "What other meaning is there in the 'National Home'?"[57]

Frederick Kisch, an aide to Weizmann who would become the head of the Zionist Commission in 1923, described Samuel as having "a sort of fifty-fifty attitude as between Jews and Arabs."[58] David Eder, a member of the Zionist Commission, called Samuel a "Judas." Arthur Ruppin, a founder of the city of Tel Aviv and later a professor at Hebrew University, wrote on June 4 that "Herbert Samuel, who was sort of a god to the Jews in Palestine only yesterday, had now become a traitor to the Jewish cause in their eyes."[59]

The Va'ad Leumi, the elected Jewish assembly in Palestine, rejected Samuel's interpretation of the Balfour Declaration. Its "true contents," the body declared, do "not allow for any of numbers or incidental interests of the present population of the country to affect the life and the historic aspirations of the Jewish people, whose return to the land of its fathers had been decided by historic justice and by the decision of the Nations."[60] The assembly rejected a conciliatory posture toward Palestine's Arabs, whom one member described as "half-savage masses."[61]

British Zionists took a condescending view of Samuel's efforts. Harry Sacher summed up the prevailing opinion. "One may guess that his somewhat old-fashioned Liberalism is peculiarly sensitive to the appeal of a majority," Sacher wrote. "There has probably always been within him something of a conflict between the Jew desirous to help in the creation of the National Home and the Liberal haunted by the phrase 'self-determination.'"[62] Sacher was, in effect, writing off Samuel's attempt to adhere to the principles of democracy as old-fashioned.

A Zionist publication in Britain, *The Jewish Chronicle*, put Samuel's efforts in a starker context. "Imagine the wild animals in a zoological garden springing out of their cages and killing a number of spectators, and a commission appointed to enquire into the causes of the disaster reporting first and foremost that the animals were discontented with and hostile to the visitors who had come to see them! As if it were not the first business of the keepers to know the habits and disposition of the animals, and to be sure that the cages were secure."[63]

Within the British government, the reaction to the Jaffa riots reopened the debate about the Balfour Declaration. The cabinet's Committee of Imperial Defence raised questions about the strategic necessity of occupying Palestine. In Palestine, many of the British officials urged abandoning the Balfour Declaration. "If the policy is not modified, the outbreaks of today may become a revolution tomorrow," C. D. Brunton wrote from Jaffa.[64] Charles Robert Ashbee, who was an advisor to the mandate, wrote, "The policy of the Balfour Declaration is an unjust policy. Palestine is emphatically a land of tribes. The idea that it can ever belong to one nation, even though this were the Jews, is contrary to both nature and the Scripture."[65]

The British Haycraft Commission of Inquiry, chaired by Sir Thomas

Haycraft, the chief justice of the Supreme Court of Palestine, rejected Zionist contentions that the riots were premeditated and motivated by anti-Semitism, that is, an irrational hatred of Jews as Jews. Instead, the commission found that "the fundamental cause of the Jaffa riots and the subsequent acts of violence was a feeling among the Arabs of discontent with, and hostility to, the Jews, due to political and economic causes, and connected with Jewish immigration, and with their conception of Zionist policy as derived from Jewish exponents."[66]

But as Zionist protests to the commission report and to Samuel's proposals rose, Lloyd George, Balfour, and Churchill worked both sides of the aisle. They endorsed the white paper, which Churchill introduced. But privately they assured Zionists that they still backed a Jewish state. At a meeting with Weizmann after Samuel's June speech, the three assured him that Britain was still committed to the most expansive interpretation of the Balfour doctrine. "We meant a Jewish state," Lloyd George told Weizmann. The prime minister told Weizmann that he thought that Samuel was "very weak and has funked the position."[67] Their support emboldened Weizmann and the Zionist Commission to oppose Samuel's initiatives.

Samuel's views did get some support. Ahad Ha'am, who moved to Palestine in 1922, continued to advocate giving Palestine's Arabs their due. "We think that the Arabs are all savages who live like animals and do not understand what is happening around them," Ahad Ha'am wrote in a letter to Ha'aretz in 1922. "This is, however, a great error . . . What do our brethren do in Palestine? . . . Serfs they were in the lands of the Diaspora and suddenly they find themselves in freedom, and this change has awakened in them an inclination to despotism. They treat the Arabs with hostility and cruelty, and even boast of these deeds; and nobody among us opposes this despicable and dangerous inclination."[68]

Y. H. Castel, who was head of the Zionist Commission's press bureau, made a similar argument. "So long as we insist upon the principle 'Palestine for the Jews as England for Englishmen,' our schemes for a peaceful settlement will be of no avail; but, on the other hand, if we come to the logical conclusion that 'Palestine cannot be built up except of the basis of a Common State for our two Nationalities,' like Belgium, Switzerland etc., then we may succeed in realizing the Balfour Declaration," he wrote.[69] But Ahad Ha'am and Castel were drowned out by those who refused to brook Samuel's compromise with the original Zionist aim of a Jewish Palestine.

In a pattern that would recur over the next eight decades, Palestine's Arab leadership peremptorily rejected Samuel's proposal. They charged that the proposals didn't recognize Arab political rights. In Samuel's legislative council, the Zionists and British could constitute a majority to block any attempt to abandon the Balfour Declaration. The Palestinian Arab opposition was on firmer ground in rejecting his plan for an Arab agency. While Samuel had called for an Arab agency that would hold consultative powers similar to those of the Zionist Commission, he proposed that British officials appoint its members—reflecting, perhaps, his unwitting adherence to an imperial view of the Palestinian Arabs. That was in stark contrast to the Jewish Agency, which was elected by the Zionist Organization. In retrospect, though, Samuel's proposals represented a genuine effort to recognize Arab rights.

In the end, Samuel, lacking support in London and under fire from Palestine's Zionists and Arabs, abandoned his own proposals. The status quo prevailed. There was no legislative council, but the Zionists were represented globally and in Palestine by the Jewish Agency that the League of Nations' mandate had designated to advise the British, while the only Arab organization with any clout was the Supreme Muslim Council, which was merely supposed to handle religious affairs of Palestine's Muslims, and which was entirely dependent on British financial support. The resulting absence of any secular body representing Palestine's Arabs elevated the political role of religion.

Geographically, the division between Jew and Arab grew. One outgrowth of the Jaffa riots was the creation of Tel Aviv as an independent Jewish town in what had been the suburbs of Jaffa. Thousands of Jews from Jaffa fled to Tel Aviv after the riots. Jewish towns and villages generally had their own police force, while Arab towns and villages remained under British supervision. The Zionist exclusion of Arab labor—which a British government investigation blamed in part for the Jaffa riots—continued apace, as did Jewish purchases of Arab lands.

Samuel took pride in the fact that in the final years of his five-year tenure in Palestine, there were no major disturbances like those in Jerusalem in 1920 or Jaffa in 1921. He was also heartened by the development of Jewish institutions within Palestine, culminating in the opening of the Hebrew University in 1925. But he left behind an even more deeply divided Palestine than had existed before his arrival—one that, under British rule, continued to favor the Jews over the Arabs. His failure was the failure of a Zionism that drew upon Ahad Ha'am's support for a binational Palestine. In the wake of the Balfour Declaration and the League of Nations mandate, the great majority of Palestine's Jews were committed to nothing less than a Jewish state, even if that meant depriving Palestine's Arabs of their right to self-determination.

Samuel had tried and failed to reconcile the Balfour Declaration and Zionism with "the first principles of democracy" and of justice, which would have recognized the rights of the Arab majority not to be subject to the rule of a Jewish minority. That was also behind the efforts of Ahad Ha'am, whose background was in ethnic Odessa rather than liberal London, and of Ahad Ha'am's followers, who would join the faculty of the new Hebrew University. But for most Zionists in Palestine, as well as in Europe and the United States, the goal of establishing a Jewish state took precedence over any adherence to democracy and even to social justice. In Jaffa in 1918, Wilansky had proposed simply abandoning morality as a criterion for action. But most Zionists would instead seek to redefine the place of democracy and justice in Palestine to fit their ultimate objectives. Samuel knew better, but he failed.

5

THE FAILURE OF THE "DOUBLE UNDERTAKING"

After the Jaffa riots, there was an outward calm in Palestine, which convinced Samuel and his successors, Herbert Plumer and John Chancellor, that the British were on their way to pacifying the country. Palestine's Arab leaders even proposed a compromise with the Jews over a legislative council. But the outward calm concealed a simmering conflict fueled by Zionist attempts to create a nation within a nation in Palestine, and by the British attempt to divide Arab Muslims and Christians by encouraging an Islamic nationalism.

In 1929 the conflict burst into the open in a new wave of rioting. This time, the British government in London made an effort to forge a compromise in Palestine. This was perhaps the last and only time under British rule—before the Nazi rise to power in the 1930s—when a compromise might have been possible. What happened, however, established a pattern of futility that would later haunt American efforts to reach a compromise after World War II.

Ben-Gurion and Labor Zionism

After the Jaffa riots and the British white paper, the main Zionist leaders did not abandon their quest for a Jewish state, but they softened their rhetoric. Weizmann took the lead again in practicing "safe statesman-ship." At the Zionist Congress that met at Carlsbad in the summer of 1921, Weizmann said he looked forward to "a future in which Jew and Arab will live side by side in Palestine and work conjointly for the prosperity of the country."[1] But privately Weizmann was seeking as-surance from Balfour, Lloyd George, and Churchill that they backed a Jewish state.

In the wake of the riots, Zionist leaders did abandon their attempt to seek immediately a Jewish state or Jewish administration of a British colony. Weizmann, Ben-Gurion, and other leaders now advocated what the historian Anita Shapira called "evolutionary Zionism," encapsulated in the slogan "One more acre, one more goat."[2] In 1923, Weizmann told a meeting in Palestine, "After the Mandate there will be no political suc-cesses for years; those political successes that you want you will have to gain by your own work in the Emeq, the Valley of Jezreel, in the marshes and the hills, not in the offices of Downing Street."[3] It was Ahad Ha'am's old strategy, but with an unbending goal of political statehood and with tactics that furthered conflict with Palestine's Arabs.

The Zionists sought to create a nation within the nation in Palestine—with their own exclusive schools, factories, farms, offices, parties, and legislature from which Arabs were barred. In 1918, at Jaffa, the Zionists had established a general assembly and a higher body, the Va'ad Leumi, chosen from within it; in 1920, Ben-Gurion and other Labor Zionists had established the labor organization Histadrut. And the Jewish National Fund continued to buy up Arab lands for exclusive use by Jewish settlers. The Arabs had no comparable institutions.

Ben-Gurion was the principal architect of the evolutionary strategy. Born in a small Polish village in 1886, he joined the Warsaw branch of the Poale Zion in 1904, which under Ber Borochov was straining in 1904 to combine Zionism and Marxist socialism. But Ben-Gurion does not seem to have been a Marxist. He put the creation of a Jewish na-tion above the creation of socialism. After moving to Palestine two years later, he helped organize a moderate faction within Poale Zion. "The comrades have the wrong idea," he said at the time. "They think they have to show us how to organize a socialist society, but what they must show us is how to create a Jewish society in Eretz Israel."[4]

Ben-Gurion was short of stature, with an outsized head topped in his youth by an unruly mass of hair. Like Weizmann, he had a finely honed sense of strategy that led him sometimes to mince words and to accept compromise without wavering from the ultimate goal of building a Jewish state. While the suave Weizmann was Zionism's diplomat, Ben-Gurion was the master apparatchik and movement leader who would eventually oust Weizmann as the leader of international Zionism and become Israel's first prime minister.

Ben-Gurion's crowning achievement in the 1920s was the Histadrut. The organization functioned partly like a union or guild. It ran a labor exchange for its members, assigning them to jobs on factories, on farms, or in offices that only employed Jews. It was not opposed to private industry, but it fought private employers who tried to hire workers that were not from the Histadrut—or, even more so, who were not Jews. It also ran schools, hospitals (including a health insurance system), and the nation's largest construction firm, as well as a host of other businesses. It solicited funds for business investment. It took the funds raised by the Zionist Organization and Jewish Agency and distributed them as social welfare to the indigent and unemployed.

During the 1920s, Ben-Gurion's focus and that of most of the Labor Zionists was inward and not outward. They were interested not in reaching an accommodation with the Arabs but in laying the basis for a Jewish state. And they rejected any proposal, including those for binational assemblies, that might legitimate an Arab claim to Palestine. That, along with the evolution of pro-state institutions, inflamed the Arab opposition. Wrote the historian Howard Sachar, "The moderation of the Left was one of theory more than of practice. While carefully avoiding so much as mentioning ultimate Jewish statehood, its leadership devoted little thought or effort to a rapprochement with the Arabs. In fact, no group was more intent than the Laborites in building a totally self-sufficient economy and community amid the Arab majority."[5]

Brit Shalom

On the Zionist left, there was one notable exception to Labor's outlook. In 1925, several prominent intellectuals—most of them émigrés from Central Europe who were teaching at the new Hebrew University in Jerusalem—formed Brit Shalom (Covenant of Peace). As much a discussion club as a political group, Brit Shalom backed a binational state of Arabs and Jews. The group's members looked to Ahad Ha'am rather than Herzl as their mentor. They rejected the attempt to impose a Jewish state on Palestine's Arabs as politically impossible without the use of force, and they saw doing this as contrary to the ethical principles of Zionism. Their objective, the sociologist Arthur Ruppin, the chairman of the group, said, was "to settle the Jews, as a second people, in a country already inhabited by another people, and to accomplish this peacefully."[6]

There were Labor Zionists who thought that the Jews would eventually reach an accommodation with the Arabs, but only after they had created a majority that would allow them to rule Palestine democratically. The members of Brit Shalom rejected the evolutionary strategy. "A program like that orients itself toward the distant future in order to avoid dealing with the burning problem of the present," the philosopher Hugo Bergmann wrote.[7]

There were at best about a hundred members of Brit Shalom, but what they lacked in numbers they made up for in reputation. Judah Magnes, the chancellor of the Hebrew University, sympathized with its objectives. Outside Palestine, Brit Shalom enjoyed the sympathy of Albert Einstein, Martin Buber (who later migrated to Palestine), and Herbert Samuel. But it failed to attract a popular following among Palestine's Jews or Arabs. Among Palestine's Jews, the principal challenge to Labor Zionism would come from the right, not the left.

Revisionism

The main challenge to Weizmann and Ben-Gurion's evolutionary strategy came from Vladimir Jabotinsky's Revisionist Party. Jabotinsky was born in 1880 in Odessa, the intellectual capital of Russian Zionism. He spent his youth immersed in Russian literature, but when he was eighteen, he was sent to Rome as a correspondent for a Russian newspaper and became enamored with the nationalism of the Italian Risorgimento. He returned to Odessa in time for the massacre at Kishinev in 1903. Just as the pogroms of the early 1880s had turned Pinsker into a Zionist, the pogroms of the early 1900s made a committed Zionist of Jabotinsky.

———

In 1904, Jabotinsky attended the Sixth Zionist Congress, where he met and was deeply impressed by Herzl. Like Herzl, Jabotinsky believed that the creation of a Jewish state took precedence over anything else. Herzl was willing to negotiate with Russia's arch anti-Semite Plehve and Jabotinsky with Ukraine's ousted regime, which, when it had been in power during World War I, had been responsible for the death of about thirty thousand Jews. Jabotinsky, like Herzl, had little interest in evolutionary Zionism or in the cultural notions of Ahad Ha'am or A. D. Gordon. But while Herzl had wanted to establish a Jewish state by purchasing it from one of the imperial powers, Jabotinsky became convinced that Jews would have to fight for a Jewish state.

During World War I, Jabotinsky organized a Jewish legion from Palestinian émigrés in Egypt that fought briefly alongside the British; after the war, he was one of the founders of the Haganah, the Jewish self-defense force. During the 1920 riots, the British sentenced him to jail for leading a self-defense force in Jerusalem, but Samuel pardoned him when he became high commissioner. Jabotinsky, who excelled as an orator, became a hero in the Zionist movement. In June 1920, Meer Grossman profiled him in *The Maccabean*, the publication of the Zionist Organization of America. "Jabotinsky is a perfect specimen of the virile, self-contained, combative and creative type," he wrote. "He is a strong-willed fighter with clear, elemental concepts, an endless belief in his own powers, an unquenchable confidence in the strength of his speech and his pen."[8]

In 1921, Jabotinsky was invited to join the Zionist Executive, the successor to the Zionist Commission and the chief link that the Balfour Declaration established between international Zionism and the British in Palestine. He quickly became a critic of the British lack of support for the declaration. In 1922 he signed off on the white paper because he felt it was his "duty to share with my colleagues the shame of defeat."[9] But he rejected the British redefinition of the Balfour Declaration and the removal of Transjordan from Palestine. In 1923, Jabotinsky quit the Zionist Executive. In 1925 he founded the Revisionist Party, named for its rejection of the British exclusion of Transjordan from Palestine. He also founded a paramilitary youth organization, Betar, which grew steadily under his leadership. For the new generation of Zionists, Jabotinsky said, the most important thing was "learning how to shoot."[10]

Jabotinsky's militarism stemmed in part from his having a more realistic view of the conflict between Zionism and Arab nationalism. While Weizmann believed that the Arabs could be bought off, and Ben-Gurion and other Labor Zionists drew a specious distinction between the Arab effendis, whom they believed to be the source of opposition to Zionism, and the Arab proletariat, whom they believed to be potential comrades, Jabotinsky insisted that Arab nationalism was real and that the Jews would succeed in gaining Palestine only by defeating, or intimidating, the Arabs militarily. He candidly compared Palestine's Arabs to the Aztecs of Mexico or the Indians of the United States who were determined to fight off colonial invaders. "There was no misunderstanding between Jew and Arab, but a natural conflict," he wrote.[11]

Jabotinsky thought the Jews in Palestine should put a greater priority on establishing a large defense force than on "building up the land." "That military force should create an impregnable iron wall that the Palestinian Arabs could not breach," Jabotinsky wrote in 1923. "Zionist colonization, even the most restricted, must either be terminated or carried out in defiance of the will of the native [Palestinian] population. This colonization can, therefore, continue and develop under the protection of a force independent of the local population—an iron wall which the native [Palestinian] population cannot break through."[12] Or as Jabotinsky would later write, "The messiah will not come in the figure of a poor man riding on a donkey. The messiah will come, like all messiahs, riding on a tank, delivering his orations to the people."[13]

In Jaffa in December 1918, Wilansky, who was allied with Jabotinsky, had suggested that Zionists had to put aside questions of morality in considering whether and how to found a Jewish state. Jabotinsky didn't brush aside questions of morality. In an essay published in 1923, "The Ethics of the Iron Wall," Jabotinsky attempted to justify Zionism without disguising its motives or fostering illusions about its adversaries. Unlike Weizmann or the Labor Zionists, Jabotinsky acknowledged that "we are seeking to colonize a country against the wishes of its inhabitants, in other words, by force." That fact, Jabotinsky wrote, was the basis of the contention that Zionism itself was "immoral." But Jabotinsky argued that what seemed immoral was in this case justified.

When Jews, who amounted to "15 million people scattered through the world," sought to create a homeland, any attempt to do so—whether in Palestine or Uganda—would involve displacing another people. "The whole earth has been allocated," Jabotinsky wrote. But in the case of Palestine, Jews would be displacing a people who number 38 million and already "inhabit Morocco, Algeria, Tunisia, Tripoli, Egypt, Syria, Arabia and Iraq—an area that apart from desert equals the size of half of Europe." The Jews, who had no land, would be displacing a people who had more than enough. "The soil does not belong to those who possess land in excess but to those who do not possess any," Jabotinsky wrote. It was right and just for Jews to demand a share of these lands and, if necessary, to go to war against the native inhabitants in order to obtain it. "If such a landowning nation resists what is perfectly natural, it must be made to comply by compulsion. Justice that is enforced does not cease to be justice."[14]

Jabotinsky's argument rested on the assumption that self-determination did not apply to Arabs in Palestine but only to Arabs in general—that Arabs were a fungible people who could easily change their national home. An Arab in Ramallah or Bethlehem could as easily live in Tikrit or Riyadh. But the term "Arab" denoted a common language, rather than a single nation, of which there were member states, like the member states of federal Germany or the United States. In effect, Jabotinsky was consigning Palestine's Arabs to the same fate as Eastern and Central European Jews. An Arab in Palestine was not really a Palestinian just as a Jew in Poland was not really Polish.

Labor Zionists and General Zionists—the term Weizmann gave to his less avowedly socialist party—adopted Jabotinsky's argument to justify giving Jews precedence over Arabs in Palestine. Where Jabotinsky differed from Ben-Gurion and Weizmann was in his call to arms to achieve a Jewish state and in his immediate objective of securing Transjordan as well as Palestine for the new state. There were also underlying ideological differences. Jabotinsky's opponents regularly accused him of being a fascist, but he claimed that he was, like Herzl, a nineteenth-century liberal. Historian Eran Kaplan makes a good case, however, that in denying charges of authoritarian or fascist leanings, Jabotinsky was practicing his own brand of "safe statesmanship."[15] He praised Benito Mussolini's regime, and his attitude toward democracy was at best instrumental. As he had made clear in Jaffa in 1918, what mattered was achieving a Jewish state. It didn't matter what Jews had to do to get there or what kind of state was eventually established.

Some of Jabotinsky's most important followers were less reticent about fascist ideas and methods. Abba Ahimeir, who called Jabotinsky "Duce" and eventually supplanted him as an active leader of the Revisionists in Palestine, penned a series of articles in 1928 called "From a Diary of a Fascist." Ahimeir dismissed the "liberal rubbish of the middle of the nineteenth century." He extolled the twentieth century as "the century of dictatorship, enthusiasm and the cult of the fist that was formed amid the fumes of tanks."[16] Together, Jabotinsky, Ahimeir, and the young Revisionists in Betar would undermine any efforts by Weizmann or Ben-Gurion to soften the Zionist message. They would confirm the Arab population's worst fears about Zionist intentions.

Tribal Rivalries

Unlike their Zionist counterparts, Palestine's Arabs did not attempt to build a nation within a nation. And unlike their Arab neighbors, they didn't participate in a national parliament, even one that had little effect on policy, but that might still have prepared them to act collectively.[17] Worse still, the leadership of Palestine's Arabs was afflicted by tribal rivalries among notables, making it impossible for any leader to speak clearly on behalf of the country's Arabs.

There were two main political families—the Husseinis and the Nashashibis—that had divided up power in Palestine. The British and the Zionists, who wanted to keep the Palestinian Arabs at bay, reinforced these divisions. After the Nebi Musa riots in 1920, the British removed Jerusalem mayor Musa Kazim al-Husseini and replaced him with Raghib al-Nashashibi. As a counter to the Nashashibis, the British made Kamil al-Husseini grand mufti and then after his death in 1921 appointed his half brother Haj Amin al-Husseini to succeed him and to rule over the new Supreme Muslim Council, which was in charge of local Sharia courts and religious property and observances.

Similar divisions were replicated in Arab political movements. At the December 1920 Arab Congress in Haifa, the delegates set up an Arab executive committee chaired by Musa Kazim al-Husseini that was monopolized by Husseini relatives and allies. In response, Raghib al-Nashashibi established the Palestine Arab National Party, which became known as the "oppositionists." Zionists helped fund the Nashashibi effort on the presumption that it would be more accommodating than the Arab Executive Committee, but when the founding congress met in Jerusalem in November 1923, the delegates denounced Zionism. "Rather than tempering their demands, they sought to outbid the Arab Executive," the historian Ann Mosely Lesch concludes.[18] That meant that Palestinian Arabs had rival organizations distinguished primarily by their family ties rather than their programs.

By 1928, both groups were losing adherents and decided to come together at the Arab Congress that year. At the congress, the Arab leaders accepted the proposal that Samuel had made earlier for a binational legislative council in which Arabs would have more representatives than Jews (reflecting their proportion of the population) but where the British and Jews could still theoretically outvote them. They altered their position largely, it seems, because they were no longer worried about being outvoted on Jewish immigration. The previous year, with the worldwide depression looming, more Jews had emigrated from Palestine than had immigrated to it.

The British were interested in the Arabs' proposal, and if the Zionists had been willing to negotiate, it might have led to a compromise that would have kept the peace in Palestine. But the Zionists were unwilling to agree to a council in which they were a minority. They turned the Arabs down flat. That ended efforts to achieve a binational government in Palestine and sent to the Arabs a clear message that the Zionists were only interested in creating a Jewish state, which in turn set the stage for the riots of 1929. These riots would initially take the form of dispute over religion, not politics.

Muslims Versus Jews

To prevent an Arab rebellion, the British, aided by the Zionists, tried to drive a wedge between Palestine's Muslims and Christians. Muslims constituted about 90 percent of Palestine's Arabs, but the Christians, who were more urban and educated, made up a disproportionate part of the anti-Zionist leadership. The Muslim-Christian Associations provided much of the political base for the Arab Congress and Arab Executive Committee. To undermine them, the Zionists funded Muslim associations. Similarly, the British encouraged the Supreme

Muslim Council to act as a principal governing organization for Muslim Arabs.

But the attempt to stoke sectarian division had unintended consequences. Instead of heightening the conflict between Muslims and Christians, it heightened the conflict between Muslims and Jews. At the uneasy center of the conflict was the mufti. Haj Amin al-Husseini had promised the British to ride herd on militant anti-Zionism and prevent any recurrence of the 1920–21 riots. In exchange, the British financed his endeavors as mufti and head of the Supreme Muslim Council. Through most of the 1920s the mufti kept his word: the Nebi Musa riots did not recur. But as mufti he built up the Muslim presence in Jerusalem.

With funds from Muslims in other Arab countries, al-Husseini refurbished the al-Aqsa Mosque and the Dome of the Rock in Jerusalem and organized international conferences of Muslims in Jerusalem. His objective was to restore Jerusalem's reputation as the third holiest place in Islam. To enlist support for his efforts and gain an advantage over the Nashashibis, the mufti fueled fears that the Zionists were targeting Jerusalem's holy sites. Al-Husseini was not trying to start protests, and certainly not a riot, but when Jerusalem's Jews objected to his plan to refurbish the area around the Wailing or Western Wall, and when Zionist groups began to claim that the wall was theirs, Palestine's Arabs took to the streets.

The wall, which stands in the old city of Jerusalem, is what remains of the temple that was reputedly (according to the Bible) built by Solomon but then razed by the Babylonians in 586 B.C.E., rebuilt in 516 B.C.E., expanded by Herod, and finally destroyed by the Romans in 70 C.E. The wall is Judaism's holiest site. But it is also a Muslim holy site, where Muhammad is said to have parked his steed, Buraq, during his night journey to the heavens, and is part of the foundation on which the al-Aqsa Mosque and the Dome of the Rock—which together make up Islam's third-holiest site—were built.

The Muslim endowment, or Waqf, owned the area, including the wall. By an arrangement dating back to the Ottoman Empire, Jews were allowed to file through the narrow alley separating the wall from a Muslim living quarters, but they were not supposed to build permanent structures or bring imposing temporary ones into the alley with them. The rules on temporary structures were not always enforced, but when Orthodox Jews on Yom Kippur of 1928 brought a large screen to separate men from women worshippers, Muslim authorities complained to the British administration. The British ordered the screen taken down, and when the Orthodox beadle in charge didn't comply, British police came and destroyed the screen. That unleashed a series of protests and counterprotests that continued over the next eleven months.

Zionists had been calling for years for the British government to "hand over the Wall to Jews."[19] During Yom Kippur in 1925, Jews brought in benches in violation of the agreement. That year, *Ha'aretz* urged people "to arrange protest meetings in each town, village and settlement and appeal to the League of Nations for the restoration of the Wailing Wall to the Jewish people," while *Davar* called for the British authorities to "hand over the Wall to the Jews."[20] When the police removed the screen, the Zionists organized demonstrations against the police for taking the screen down, and Zionist publications proclaimed the need to "reclaim our homeland." Revisionists called for protests until "the wall is restored to us" and organized the Committee for the Western Wall.[21]

On the other side, the mufti, who had promoted Jerusalem as a holy site and was fund-raising to repair the mosque and the Dome of the Rock, warned of a Zionist takeover of the holy sites. He convened an international conference of Arab Muslims in November 1928 that established a Society for the Protection of the al-Aqsa Mosque and the Islamic Holy Sites, including the wall. He also helped organize the Committee for the Defense of the Noble Buraq Wall.

Both sides in the controversy saw it as a struggle not merely over the right to worship but over control of Palestine. Zionists saw the new Muslim focus on Jerusalem as a threat to their future state. Muslims believed that the Jews wanted to take over the wall and destroy the al-Aqsa Mosque and the Dome of the Rock and rebuild the ancient temple on the site. In fact Weizmann had tried earlier, but failed, to purchase it from the Muslim Waqf.

There was sporadic violence against worshippers, but the Zionist leadership advocated a cautious response. On August 15, however, several hundred members of the Revisionist youth militia Betar, shouting "The wall is ours!" and carrying the Zionist flag, marched to the mufti's home, where they held a large demonstration. That set off a succession of Arab demonstrations that degenerated into large-scale riots. The central office of the Zionist Organization released a statement in the London *Times* blaming the British administration for not safeguarding Jewish rights of assembly. "The demonstration was in no way intended as an act of hostility against the government," the release said.[22] But David Ben-Gurion blamed the Revisionists for the subsequent riot. Had the Revisionists shown some restraint, he wrote in 1936, "the entire history of 1929 might have been different."[23]

In Jerusalem, seventeen Jews were killed by crowds, but the worst violence took place in neighboring Hebron and Safed, where for centuries Orthodox Jews, many of them opposed to Zionism, had lived peacefully with Arabs. In Hebron, Arab mobs killed between 65 and 70 Jews and in Safed 18 Jews were killed. Overall, 123 Jews were killed and 116 Arabs—the latter primarily by British police.

An Opening for Compromise

Zionist leaders confident about evolution of a Jewish state were shaken. Some, including Ben-Gurion, began to consider an accommodation with the Arabs. In October, Ben-Gurion met with the leaders of Brit Shalom to discuss a binational or federated state. Ruppin told Ben-Gurion that it would take thirty years to create a Jewish majority. "Can we reasonably expect to rely for thirty years . . . upon British support for us against the Arabs?" he asked. Ruppin proposed "two nations with equal rights in Palestine" on the model of Switzerland's or Canada's binational constitutionals. Ben-Gurion demurred, but within a month had begun to promote a plan of his own for a federated Palestine.[24]

In the wake of the riots, Judah Magnes, who had previously avoided public politics, came out in favor of negotiating a binational Palestine. Magnes was an American, born in San Francisco in 1877, who had courted controversy as the rabbi of the citadel of Reform Judaism, New York's Temple Emanu-El, and as a leader of the Federation of American Zionists. His views on religion proved too traditional for his Reform congregants and his views on Zionism too moderate for the federation.

Magnes migrated to Palestine in 1923, where he helped found the Hebrew University. In 1925 he became its chief administrator and fund-raiser and in 1935 would become its president. After the 1929 riots, he became a vocal proponent of compromise between the Jews and Arabs. "We, the great democrats of the world, are trying to find every kind of reason to justify the denial of even the beginning of democracy to ourselves and others," Magnes wrote in December.[25]

Like the founders of Brit Shalom, which he had privately supported but never joined, Magnes was a disciple of Ahad Ha'am. His vision of Palestine, he wrote, was "of the kind that Ahad Ha'am pictured, a spiritual and intellectual Center for Judaism and the Jewish people, rooted in agriculture, industry and all kinds of labor." Magnes called on the Jew to say to the Arab, "We want no political domination by any one," and the Arab to say to the Jew, "We recognize the Jew's full right to be here." He favored a "bi-national government, a Palestine Government, in which the word Palestine includes all three religions equally."

Magnes was under no illusions that Palestine's Arabs, rent by division and largely illiterate, were ready for self-government, but he wanted the mandatory power to prepare them for self-government by initiating the transition toward a binational state. "I am not unmindful of the risks of such an experiment particularly because of the political immaturity of large parts of the country, and the low state of morals and education," he wrote.[26] But he thought the alternative was worse. "If as a minority we insist upon keeping the other man from achieving just aims, and if we keep him from this with the aid of bayonets, we must not be surprised if we are attacked and, what is worse, if moral degeneration sets in among us."[27]

Magnes's views attracted attention partly because of who he was, and also because in those months after the riots there appeared to be a slight opening—even amidst the incredible bitterness and hatred caused by the riots—for some kind of rapprochement between Zionism and Arab nationalism. And the British were determined, as they had been after the Jaffa riots, to take advantage of this opportunity.

The Passfield White Paper

The riots frightened the British, who, before the Wailing Wall controversy, had believed that their attempts at co-optation and divide and rule were working. Colonel Frederick Peake, who had tried to quell the rioters, wrote a memo to John Chancellor, who had become high commissioner the year before, that rejected the assumption that had underlain British support for Zionism in Palestine. "It is a fallacy," Peake wrote, "to think the Oriental content with high wages and no power. If the Indian, to whose country we have made untold improvements, would throw off European control were it possible, how much sooner would the Arab of Palestine do so . . . Nationalism is a very real thing, which cannot be neglected nor abolished."[28] Chancellor believed the Balfour Declaration a "colossal blunder."[29]

In London the new Labor government of Ramsay MacDonald and its colonial secretary Lord Passfield (the Fabian Socialist Sidney Webb) called on Sir Walter Shaw, a prominent London jurist, to investigate the riots. Shaw's report, which appeared in April 1930, condemned "a vicious attack by Arabs on Jews accompanied by wanton destruction of Jewish property." But, like the Haycraft Commission's finding on the Jaffa riots, the report concluded that the ultimate cause of the violence was the Palestinian Arab reaction to Zionism rather than, as some Zionists claimed, irrational anti-Semitism.

The report noted that while there had been "serious attacks . . . by Arabs on Jews," the attacks had begun in 1920 and not in the centuries before and were the result of Arabs seeing "in the Jewish immigrant not only a menace to their livelihood but a possible overlord of the future." The report recommended that the British regulate immigration and Zionist land purchases to safeguard "the rights of non-Jewish communities." It warned that the "tendency towards the eviction of peasant cultivators from the land should be checked." And it called for the British to develop government institutions that included Palestine's Arabs.[30]

The British report made sense, but in Palestine, opinion had already moved away from reconciliation. The main Zionist organization denounced the report. Declared the Va'ad Leumi, "The Jewish people of Palestine regard the Report of the Inquiry Commission as one of the most unjust documents which our people have had to face in the course of 2000 years of persecution. Even the enquiries instituted after Jewish pogroms in Czarist Russia displayed more respect for fairness and justice than three of the commissioners of His Majesty's Government have evinced in their report."[31] The Va'ad Leumi reaction typified the overkill with which Zionist organizations greeted attempts to reconcile Arabs and Jews in Palestine.

But the British government was not deterred. It appointed another commission, chaired by Sir John Hope Simpson, a Liberal member of Parliament, to investigate Palestine's economic conditions. Simpson's report, which he submitted at the end of August, complemented the findings of the Shaw Commission. It concluded that the Zionists' exclusionary labor policies were largely responsible for the conflict. "The present position, precluding any employment of Arabs in the Zionist colonies, is undesirable from the point of view both of justice and of the good government of the country," the report said. "It is impossible to view with equanimity the extension of an enclave in Palestine from which all Arabs are excluded."[32]

On October 1, 1930, Lord Passfield issued his own white paper based on the Shaw and Simpson reports.[33] Like these, it singled out the Jewish National Fund and Histadrut's policies of excluding Arab labor and called for taking Arab unemployment into consideration in gauging policies on immigration and land use. Passfield also urged developing the "constitutional means" to allow Palestinian Arabs to put "their view on social and economic matters before the government."

Passfield went beyond even the 1922 white paper's interpretation of the Balfour Declaration. His paper didn't simply clarify Lord Balfour's words but subtly repudiated them. Citing a speech by Prime Minister Ramsay MacDonald in which he had called for "a double undertaking . . . to the Jewish people on the one hand and to the non-Jewish population of Palestine on the other," Passfield's white paper rejected the idea that the mandate's obligation to Palestine's Arabs should be seen as "secondary" to its obligation to the country's Jews. According to the white paper, "the obligations laid down by the mandate in regard to the two sections of the population are of equal weight" and "are in no sense irreconcilable." The white paper backed what it called a "double undertaking" in Palestine. That was, in effect, an endorsement of binationalism.

The report called for Arabs and Jews to compromise. It called upon Arabs to recognize the contribution that Jews were making to the country's prosperity. That meant accepting continued Jewish immigration (regulated by the government) and participating in legislative bodies with Jews. And it called upon Jews to include Arabs in the country's economic, social, and political development. "Jewish leaders," the statement said, "needed to make some concessions on their side in regard to the independent and separatist ideals which have been developed in some quarters in connection with the Jewish National Home" and accept that "the general development of the country shall be carried out in such a way that the interests of the Arabs and Jews may each receive adequate consideration."

The Passfield report outlined the principles of a bi-national state. Encouraged by the British approach, the Arab Executive Committee sent a delegation to London that year that included the mufti and his uncle, Arab Executive Committee head Musa Kazim al-Husseini, to discuss a new legislative council and the regulation of land sales from Arabs to Jews. The Arab leaders adamantly opposed Zionism, but not the mandate per se—some of them like the Mufti depended on the British for their living. To make that clear, Amin's cousin and political representative, Jamal al-Husseini, had circulated a letter to British members of Parliament saying they hoped to gain their aspirations "through the friendship and assistance of Great Britain."[34]

But the Zionists in Britain, Palestine, and the United States rejected any compromise between the Zionists and Arabs. Even before the white paper was published, Weizmann, who had an advanced copy, complained bitterly to Passfield that it went far toward "denying the right and sterilizing the hopes of the Jewish people in regard to the Jewish National Home in Palestine."[35] After it appeared, Weizmann resigned from the Jewish Agency in "emphatic protest against a one-sided and unjust criticism of our work, and my refusal to accept a policy which is in direct contradiction to the solemn promise of the British Nation and the text of the Mandate."[36] Lord Melchett, a leading British industrialist, the banker-philanthropist Edmond de Rothschild, and the American banker Felix Warburg also resigned from the Jewish Agency in protest.

British Zionists wanted Passfield replaced. Labor Party intellectual Harold Laski and Pinhas Rutenberg wrote a revealing memo that they circulated among Zionist groups describing a discussion they had with Lord Reading, the historian Lewis Namier, and the mathematician Selig Brodetsky. The men described Passfield as "hostile" to Zionism. "He worked for the 'under-dog' all his life and postulates that the poor Arabs have to be helped against the powerful and wealthy Jews," they explained.

"He assumed office with the intention to give to the Arabs the benefit of representative government . . . he now again seems to be keen on it."[37] Laski, of course, was a well-known Socialist on the Labor Party's left who had shared the same urge to help the underdog and spread democracy, but he could not countenance this urge being extended to Palestine's Arabs. His commitment to political Zionism blinded him to the inconsistency.

The Va'ad Leumi announced that it would refuse to participate in the legislative council outlined in the white paper. And the Jewish Agency, which had incorporated the Zionist Executive, attacked the white paper. "The White Paper is conceived in a spirit which is not that of a government seriously interested in the establishment of the Jewish National Home," it charged.[38] And it dismissed the white paper's call for a "double undertaking" toward Jews and Arabs, arguing that the two groups were unequal.

According to the Zionists, when the Balfour Declaration and the mandate referred to the Jews, and to a Jewish national home, it was referring to "the Jewish people as a whole" and not simply to the Jews currently living in Palestine, whereas when the declaration referred to "non-Jewish population," it was referring specifically to non-Jews currently living in Palestine. So Passfield was offering a "distorted interpretation" in saying that it was "a question of balancing the interests of one section of the population of Palestine as against another." It was a question of a people spread across the world against a non-Jewish group in Palestine—the white paper, the Jewish Agency noted (inaccurately), did not even refer specifically to Arabs. Accordingly, the British obligation to the two groups was unequal.[39]

Labor Party stalwarts and Ernest Bevin, the country's main trade union leader, warned MacDonald that their party would face political repercussions in Whitechapel, a suburb of London where a special parliamentary election was under way to fill the seat of a Labor MP who had died. The party wanted to elect someone who had just been appointed to MacDonald's cabinet, but MacDonald was told that the district contained seven thousand Jewish voters who were up in arms over the white paper.

MacDonald also faced an outcry from leading politicians, including Lloyd George, former prime minister Stanley Baldwin, and Winston Churchill. In addition, MacDonald heard from prominent Americans, including Rabbi Stephen Wise and the Harvard law professor Felix Frankfurter. A chastened MacDonald asked the Jewish Agency to send representatives to a special cabinet committee on Palestine chaired by Foreign Secretary Arthur Henderson. Laski, who sat on the committee, drafted a letter that MacDonald read to Parliament. The letter ostensibly claimed to supplement the white paper, but in fact it repudiated it.[40]

In the letter, MacDonald accepted the heart of the Jewish Agency's criticism. "The undertaking of the Mandate is an undertaking to the Jewish people, and not only to the Jewish people of Palestine," he said. He rejected any criticism of the Jewish National Fund and Histadrut's exclusionary labor policies. The Jewish Agency, he wrote, is "entitled to affirm . . . exclusive employment of Jewish labor by Jewish organizations." He also rejected considering Arab welfare in restricting Zionist immigration or land use. "The obligation to facilitate Jewish immigration and to encourage close settlement by Jews on the lands remains a positive obligation of the Mandate and it can be fulfilled without prejudice to the rights and position of other sections of the population of Palestine."[41]

Weizmann announced that MacDonald's letter had "reestablished the basis for that cooperation with the Mandatory Power on which our policy is founded."[42] The letter was also accompanied by the withdrawal of legislation that would have made it possible for the high commissioner to block Arab land sales to Jews.[43] Weizmann and other Zionist leaders rejoined the Jewish Agency.

The Arabs were infuriated by MacDonald's letter, which they dubbed "the black letter" and which they saw as a betrayal by the British. After they returned home, some of them began organizing against the British occupation as well as against the Zionists.[44] The British had hoped to resolve the conflict, but they had once again succeeded in exacerbating it. Moreover, they soon would become targets in the war between the Zionists and the Palestinian Arab nationalists.

If the British had acted on the Shaw and Hope-Simpson commissions and the Passfield white paper, they might have reduced or resolved the conflict between the Arabs and Jews. But that would have required defying the Zionists in Palestine, Great Britain, and the United States. The British did that when they separated Transjordan from

Palestine in 1922—and after an interval the Zionists accepted Britain's decision. But the MacDonald government, which already was suffering politically from the Great Depression, couldn't withstand the pressure from the Zionists and their allies.

The failure of the Passfield white paper ended the initial phase of conflict between the Zionists and Arab nationalists. Although it has become obscured by later controversies and overshadowed by the Nazi genocide that followed it, the moral contours of that early history are remarkably clear. From the 1890s, when Zionists first settled in Palestine with the express purpose of creating a Jewish state where Arabs had lived for centuries, until the early 1930s, the responsibility for the conflict lay primarily with the Zionists. They initiated it by migrating to Palestine with a purpose of establishing a Jewish state that would rule the native Arab population.

The British had done their part to exacerbate the conflict through the Balfour Declaration and their own unwillingness to modify its terms when faced with Arab rebellion. But when they tried to modify the terms of the declaration, and recognize the political rights of Palestine's Arabs, they were blocked by Zionists in the United States, Great Britain, and Palestine. The moral balance in Palestine—and the case for a Jewish state—would change over the next decade as a new global conflict became superimposed upon that which was taking place in Palestine, but the Palestinian Arabs could still look back in anger at the rank injustice of these first decades.

6

THE IRREPRESSIBLE CONFLICT

In the nineteenth century, anti-Semitism flourished in Germany. It arose initially in reaction to the Germans' defeat at the hands of Napoleon, who emancipated the Jews in the German states. Germany's defeat also sparked nationalist movements that became fused with anti-Semitism. By the late nineteenth century, anti-Semitic parties in Germany were attracting several hundred thousand voters. But Germany did not have the kind of state-sponsored violence against Jews that occurred in Eastern Europe and the Pale of Settlement. Nor were Jews ghettoized. On the contrary, they enjoyed in Germany, as in Austria, prominent positions in the professions, finance, and in liberal and social democratic politics. But the resentments and recriminations spawned by Germany's defeat in World War I, the harsh terms of the Versailles Treaty, and the economic hardship of the 1920s, which peaked during the beginning of the Great Depression, sowed the seeds for a much more violent and virulent anti-Semitism and for the stratospheric rise of Adolf Hitler and the National Socialist, or Nazi, Party.

Hitler was an Austrian who moved to Munich and served in the German army in World War I. He was influenced by Karl Lueger and Austrian anti-Semitism, but became critical of Lueger because, he wrote in *Mein Kampf*, his anti-Semitism was "based on religious ideas instead of racial knowledge"—in other words, on a difference with the Jewish religion rather than a rejection of the Jewish race.[1] There was also a fundamental difference between the place of anti-Semitism in Lueger's and Hitler's politics. Lueger's anti-Semitism was opportunistic; Hitler's was integral to his worldview. Hitler thought Jews were a viral menace poisoning the Aryan bloodstream and that by removing them from Germany he would revive the defeated nation. When Hitler and the Nazis took power in 1933, he began that effort by adopting more than four hundred measures that were designed not just to scapegoat Jews but to force them to emigrate; the "final solution" of genocide would come during World War II. Jews were banned from professions and the government; their businesses were boycotted and auctioned off; they were denied citizenship and barred from marrying or even having sexual relations with non-Jews. And they were subject to arbitrary acts of violence by Nazi storm troopers and inflamed mobs.

In the past, when faced with this kind of violence and discrimination, European Jews had emigrated westward, primarily to the United States. Of the 2.5 million Jews who left Russia before World War I, 2 million went to the United States. Only 30,000 migrated to Palestine. But in 1924 the United States passed laws severely restricting immigration. Great Britain, another possible destination, had adopted similar limits in 1905 under Balfour and in 1933, when German refugees began arriving, imposed new limits. In 1937, Brazil and South Africa, two desirable destinations for Central European Jews, closed off immigration, followed by Italy in 1938. Some Jews went to France and other neighboring countries, but Palestine became a principal place to which German Jews could flee—and the Nazis, before they became worried about alienating the Arabs, encouraged Jewish emigration to Palestine. Jewish emigration rose from 9,500 in 1932 to over 30,000 in 1933, the year Hitler took power. In 1936, it was a record of 66,000, and by 1936 the number of Jews in Palestine had nearly doubled over three years to just under 400,000 and now made up 30 percent of the population. One and a half times more Jews had emigrated in those years than in all of the 1920s.

Many of the new arrivals came from Germany, but also from Poland, Romania, Austria, and Czechoslovakia, where the Nazis' rise had emboldened anti-Semitic parties. These Jews were refugees from anti-Semitism rather than committed Zionists. One joke from 1933 had immigrants to Palestine being asked, "Are you coming from conviction or from Germany?"[2] But through their skills and the capital they brought with them, they contributed to a business boom in Jewish Palestine. From 1931 to 1935, Jewish lands more than doubled, much of them devoted to citrus growing for export. The number of industrial firms increased from six thousand in 1930 to fourteen thousand in 1937, and the Histadrut's campaign for Jewish labor reached its peak in those years in order to justify employment for the new Jewish immigrants.

The rise of Hitler and the restrictions on Jewish immigration to the West altered the moral balance between Zionism and Palestinian Arab nationalism. The Jewish right to rule Palestine's Arabs was as tenuous as ever, but the right of Europe's Jews to seek refuge in Palestine had been strengthened. It was a matter of sheer survival rather than religious rebirth. Compromise should have been in order, but it was not.

The new wave of Jewish immigration to Palestine sparked diametrically opposed reactions. Palestine's Zionists, who had expected to reach a majority sometime by the end of the twentieth century, suddenly realized that a state was within reach and, with the Nazi assault against the Jews accelerating, were more determined than ever to achieve one. Palestinian Arabs, already furious at the MacDonald letter, felt renewed fear of a Jewish takeover of Palestine. "If Jewish immigration continues, we shall be in a position of being a minority," Emile Ghouri, a key advisor to the mufti, lamented.[3] Both sides became more certain of the rightness of their cause. Compromise became even less likely, and riot and rebellion more.

Armed Struggle

There had been a lull between 1923 and 1929 in the conflict between the Palestinian Arabs and the Zionists, but there was no similar hiatus after the 1929 riots and demonstrations. Demonstrations, along with guerrilla raids and other armed assaults, continued throughout the early thirties, climaxing in a country-wide armed rebellion and general strike in 1936. In the process, the Palestinian movement acquired features—a resort to sectarian and self-destructive violence, lack of effective leadership, subordination of politics to religion—that would plague it for the rest of the century. There is direct line between the mufti and Palestinian leader Yasir Arafat and between the Islamic guerrilla movement that arose in the 1930s and Hamas and the Palestinian Islamic Jihad.

In the London talks after the riots at the Wailing Wall, the Arab Executive Committee, led by Musa Kazim al-Husseini and dominated by the Husseini family, including the mufti, negotiated on behalf of the Palestinian Arabs. The AEC remained active in the early 1930s, organizing large demonstrations in Jaffa and Jerusalem in 1933 against Jewish immigration. But the AEC was eclipsed by newer organizations and by a younger generation of militants. They joined organizations like the Young Men's Muslim Association (which, at a conference in 1931, called for armed struggle against Zionism), the Arab Young Men's Association, and the National Congress of Arab Youth. These groups were generally headquartered outside Jerusalem to avoid the squabbling between the Husseinis and Nashashibis.

After the MacDonald letter, the new groups saw the British as the enemy and Zionism as an arm of British imperialism. Kimmerling and Migdal write, "The young nationalist now argued that British support of Zionism was not simply a delusion, to be corrected. Rather, Zionism was part and parcel of Western imperialism in the Middle East, and only the eradication of the latter could halt the advance of the former."[4] The new groups scorned the mufti and the older Arab leadership as British collaborators.

In 1932, Awni Abd al-Hadi, a French-educated lawyer who had served as Faisal's private secretary during Versailles and later became the lawyer for the Supreme Muslim Council, founded the Istiqlal (Independence) Party. Awni Abd al-Hadi had also been part of the fateful delegation to London in 1930. The party's "Manifesto to the Arab World" demanded "complete independence for the Arab countries."[5] The Istiqlal Party, which was heavily influenced by the anti-imperialism of the Indian National Congress, called for Arabs to withhold their taxes from the British administration. In 1933 it organized several protests against Zionism and British imperialism. It was the first Arab political group that aspired to be a mass organization for the independence of Arab Palestine. It was also secular nationalist rather than Islamic.

The Istiqlal Party only lasted several years. The mufti, jealous of the party's influence and secular example, undermined it. He fired Awni

Abd al-Hadi and other Istiqlal members from their positions with the Supreme Muslim Council (upon which they depended for their livelihood) and planted rumors in the press that the Istiqlal leadership was collaborating with the Zionists.[6] In its place rose smaller armed cadre organizations held together by radical Islam, anti-Zionism, and anti-imperialism. These groups proved a much greater threat to civic order, but unlike Istiqlal they didn't help prepare the Palestinian Arabs for self-government. Instead, they were instruments of armed struggle and sectarian conflict.

In 1931, Izz ad-Din al-Qassam, the imam of a mosque in Haifa, began organizing guerrilla bands that would conduct armed struggle against the British and the Jews. Al-Qassam was born in 1882 in Syria and educated at al-Azhar University in Cairo. Qassam, like the mufti, had fallen under the spell of Rashid Rida's blend of anti-Zionism, Arab nationalism, and radical Islam.[7] He was an adherent of the Salafiyya reform movement, which advocated a purer Islam, but he was also committed to social reform and anti-imperial armed struggle. In Haifa, he called for the "bootblack to exchange his shoe brush for a revolver and to shoot the Englishman rather than polish his shoes."[8] Ad-Din al-Qassam appealed to a new political base, the former peasants who, having lost their land, had migrated to the cities on the coast, where they lived in shantytowns—in Jaffa they slept in tin huts or out in the open.

In 1933, after a series of raids, Qassam tried to convince the mufti to join him, but the mufti wouldn't break with the British. The mufti still preferred political action. After being rejected by the mufti, Qassam convinced a Syrian sheikh to bestow his blessing on his efforts, and by 1935 Qassam had assembled several hundred militants organized into cells of five or less. He told his followers, "This is Jihad, victory or martyrdom."[9] In November 1935, after a cache of arms destined for the Haganah was seized by authorities in Jaffa, Qassam and his followers set out to Jenin to recruit fellahin. He was ambushed and killed by the British on November 20, 1935. Thousands attended his funeral. Many of his followers stuck together in small armed groups. Some of them gravitated to the Holy War organization that Musa Kazim al-Husseini's son Abd al-Qadir al-Husseini had established. This and other groups would play a critical role in igniting the full-scale rebellion that would break out in April 1936.

Rise of Revisionism

After the riots of 1929, a few Zionist leaders thought the Jews should negotiate with the Arabs, but most of the leaders, and the rank and file, were even less willing to deal with Palestine's Arabs. They were more convinced than ever that they were dealing with savages and barbarians who didn't deserve their own land and could easily live elsewhere. The riots had reinforced this imperial/social Darwinian mind-set. This attitude is typified by the Labor Zionist Eliezer Yaffe, who was a founder of the moshav, a cooperative community similar to the kibbutz. The historian Anita Shapira summarizes a parable that Yaffe published that was supposed to illustrate Jewish-Arab relations in Palestine:

> A man who flees to his home because of predatory animals has the right to break into that house even if a stranger is currently dwelling there. He does not wish to drive the stranger out and even brings him benefit. And that stranger is already rich, an owner of many lands. [And he says to the stranger,] "You trampled my peace for many generations, as savages of the desert, who live by the sword, by robbery."[10]

There was no room for compromise between attitudes like these and those of the militant Palestinian Arabs. The prevalence of these views even on the Zionist left helps explain the growing appeal of the Revisionist movement.

During the early thirties, Jabotinsky's Revisionists became a significant minority within the movement. With Jabotinsky prohibited from returning to Palestine by British authorities, leadership of the movement passed to people like Ahimeir who were less compromising and who identified with the methods of Europe's fascists. Some Revisionists even praised Hitler's methods. "Were it not for Hitler's anti-Semitism, we would not oppose his ideology," one revisionist declared.[11]

The Revisionists tried to break up Histadrut strikes and called for outlawing Brit Shalom. In 1932 they were widely believed to have been responsible for the assassination of a prominent Labor Zionist official. In 1935 the Revisionists broke from the World Zionist Congress and established their own National Zionist Organization. At their first congress, delegates claimed to represent 713,000 members worldwide. In contrast to Jabotinsky, who dreamed of the new Jewish state being part of the British Commonwealth, the new Revisionist leaders, who included a young Menachem Begin, touted armed struggle against both the British and the Arabs. They were the Zionist counterpart to Qassam and the Palestinian Arab guerrillas.

Magnes and Ben-Gurion

The new British high commissioner, Arthur Wauchope, who was appointed in 1931, sought to avert greater conflict. His plan was to allow Jewish immigration to rise in the 1930s until Jews constituted 35 to 40 percent of the population. At that point, Wauchope reasoned, the Arabs would feel forced to negotiate with the Jews, and a binational legislature could be created that would be the basis of a binational state.

Wauchope befriended Ben-Gurion, who would become the leader not only of the Histadrut but also the Jewish Agency, and Musa al-Alami, a Cambridge-educated lawyer from a prominent Palestinian family who was also related by marriage to the Husseinis. Wauchope appointed Alami as his aide and he became his link to the Palestinian Arab leadership. He encouraged Ben-Gurion and Alami to hold talks.

Magnes set up the talks. He got Ben-Gurion and Moshe Sharett, the head of the political section of the Jewish Agency, to meet with Musa al-Alami and Istiqlal founder Awni Abd al-Hadi to see whether there was any basis for accommodation between the Jews and Arabs. But the meetings failed.

The Nazi seizure of power strengthened Ben-Gurion's commitment to establishing a Jewish state in Palestine that was large enough to accommodate all the Jews from Central Europe—a state that would include Transjordan. In January 1934 he warned the members of Mapai, the Labor Zionist political party he had helped found, that "Hitler's rule places the entire Jewish people in danger."[12] And he saw increasing immigration as "the chief task of the Zionist movement."[13] As Jews began fleeing Central Europe, he told Mapai members that they should "initiate a policy leading to the Jewish state."[14] As he prepared to meet the Arab leaders, he told Magnes, "The difference between you and me is that you are ready to sacrifice immigration for peace, while I am not, though peace is dear to me. And even if I was prepared to make a concession, the Jews of Poland and Germany would not be, because they have no other option. For them immigration comes before peace."[15]

But Ben-Gurion was still willing to meet his adversaries. In his first meeting with Alami, at Sharett's house, Ben-Gurion set forth what he thought was an equitable deal. As Ben-Gurion later recalled the conversation, he asked Alami, "Is there any possibility at all of reaching an understanding with regard to the establishment of a Jewish state in Palestine, including Transjordan? We would agree to the establishment of an Arab Federation in the neighboring countries and an alliance of the Jewish state with that federation, so that the Arabs in Palestine, even if they constituted a minority in that country, would not hold a minority position, since they would be linked with millions of Arabs in neighboring countries."[16]

Ben-Gurion couldn't accept that the Palestinian Arabs had any stake in Palestine. Echoing arguments that Jabotinsky had made in 1923, he envisaged Arabs as a fungible people whose home was regional rather than local. Al-Alami appears to have been polite in his response—he and Ben-Gurion were to meet once more—but when Ben-Gurion made the same proposal to Awni Abd al-Hadi, the Istiqlal founder terminated the meeting. After an unsuccessful meeting with two Syrians who published the influential *La Nation Arabe*, Ben-Gurion gave up trying to win over Arab leaders. While he continued to meet with Arabs, including George Antonius, as a tactical gesture, and to discern Arabs' thinking, he decided that he needed British acquiescence to immigration of 100,000 to 200,000 Jews a year.

Ben-Gurion told a Mapai meeting in early 1936, "There is no chance for an understanding with the Arabs unless we first reach an understanding with the English, by which we will become a preponderate force in Palestine. What can drive the Arabs to a mutual understanding with us? . . . *Facts* . . . Only after we manage to establish a *great Jewish fact* in this country . . . only then will the precondition for discussion with the Arabs be met."[17] He wrote Magnes, "For only after the total despair on the party of the Arabs, despair that will come not only from the failure of the disturbances and attempt at rebellion, but as a consequence of our growth in the country, may the Arabs finally acquiesce in a Jewish Eretz Israel."[18]

Ben-Gurion shared the Revisionists' objective of a greater Israel; he also shared their pessimism about reaching any agreement with the

Arabs until the latter despaired of having a state of their own. His strategy for establishing "facts" was his own version of Jabotinsky's "iron wall" and would become the hallmark of Zionist and then Israeli strategy toward the Palestinian Arabs. But, unlike the Revisionists, Ben-Gurion still believed in the evolution of a Jewish state through immigration.

In 1935, Wauchope, with the Jewish population hovering around 30 percent, reintroduced the proposal for a joint legislative council that Arabs had backed earlier. It was to have eleven Muslims, seven Jews, and three Christians, along with British representatives. At a December 1935 meeting, the Palestinian Arab parties indicated they would consider it seriously, but Zionists in Palestine and London succeeded in killing it in a parliamentary vote in March 1936. Wauchope lamented being outmaneuvered in London by Weizmann. "The thing is I have never met the PM [prime minister] and I don't suppose I ever shall. Weizmann can go in there when he wants to."[19] That was the last time that Arab leaders offered a compromise solution. One month later, a massive Arab rebellion began.

General Strike

On April 15, 1936, Palestinian Arabs who may have been followers of Qassam ambushed a bus and killed two Jewish passengers. The next night the Haganah retaliated by killing two Arabs. The funeral for the two Jewish passengers mushroomed into anti-Arab demonstrations, which led to anti-Zionist Arab demonstrations and the spontaneous formation of local Arab committees that called for Arab workers to strike Jewish and British businesses and boycott Jewish and British products.

There was no single cause of the rebellion. It was in reaction to the rejection of the legislative council, the ambush and killing of Qassam, and—on a positive note—the success of Arab movements in Iraq, Syria, and Egypt in securing at least nominal independence for their countries. But the enduring cause was the increase in Jewish immigration and land sales that portended the creation of a Jewish state.

On April 25, after Arab workers had begun striking, Arab notables formed the Arab Higher Committee to coordinate the rebellion. It included the different factions, including the Husseinis and Nashashibis, with the mufti as head. The committee issued a manifesto calling for a complete halt to Jewish immigration, prohibition of the transfer of Arab lands, and a national government responsive to a proportionately representative legislative council. And it called for a general strike of Palestinian Arab workers, which took hold throughout the country.

The Husseinis and Nashashibis were still hoping that the pressure of the strike would persuade the British to grant Palestine's Arabs the same self-government neighboring Arabs had won, but younger militants, dismissive of peaceful protest, took the initiative in pressing the case for an Arab Palestine. Over the next six months, Arab groups attacked the Jews and the British. The oil pipeline from Iraq to Haifa, which had opened in 1935, was sabotaged. British police stations and railways were targeted. Forests planted by the Jewish National Fund were burned down. About eighty Jews were killed.

The British imposed press censorship, suppressed demonstrations, and bulldozed areas suspected of housing rebels, including the Arab section of Jaffa, one of the places where the rebellion had begun. But Wauchope, still hoping to achieve a settlement, vetoed even harsher measures such as bombing villages. And while Revisionists called for fighting the Arabs, Ben-Gurion and the Zionist leadership opted for a defensive strategy that put the responsibility for quashing the rebellion onto the British.

The general strike proved devastating to the Arabs and a boon to the Jews. Due to Zionist labor policy, only 5 percent of Arabs were working for Jewish farms and businesses. Arab businesses were far more dependent on Jewish customers than Jewish businesses on Arab customers. Strikes among Arab dockworkers led to Tel Aviv displacing Jaffa as Palestine's main port city, and the loss of jobs to Tel Aviv's Jewish dockworkers. It was a self-defeating strategy.

The mufti recognized the problem. That summer, Amin al-Husseini, along with British officials, induced the Arab leaders of Transjordan, Egypt, and Iraq to intervene. This was the first time Palestine had become a pan-Arab issue. In October, with encouragement from other Arab leaders, the Arab Higher Committee worked out an agreement with the British to end the strike. For their part, the British agreed to appoint a new commission, headed by William Robert Wellesley Peel, Earl Peel, to address the issues raised by the rebellion.

The Case for Partition

After holding hearings among Zionists and Palestinian Arab leaders, the Peel Commission came out with a report in July 1937. Twenty years too late, the commission acknowledged that in issuing the Balfour Declaration, the British had failed to take account of the Arabs' interest in, and right to, a Palestinian homeland. The commission's report warned that the declaration, and the mandate, had barred "the way to the attainment by the Arabs of Palestine of the same national status as that attained or soon to be attained, by all the other Arabs of Asia."[20]

The report also acknowledged that there was "an irrepressible conflict . . . between two national communities within the narrow bounds of one small country . . . There is no common ground between them."[21] The mandate and declaration, the report declared, had helped make the conflict irrepressible. "It is manifest that the Mandate cannot be fully or honorably implemented unless by some means or other the antagonism between Arabs and Jews can be composed. But it is the Mandate which created that antagonism and keeps it alive and as long as the Mandate exists we cannot honestly hold out the expectation that Arabs or Jews will be able to set aide their national hopes or fears or sink their differences in the common service of Palestine."[22]

The commission's solution was to divide the two peoples by partitioning Palestine, including Transjordan, into a Jewish nation on the east coast and the Galilee; an Arab nation in Transjordan, the West Bank, and the Negev; and a British-controlled strip from Jaffa to Jerusalem that would include common religious sites. In theory, the solution was just. It recognized the right of Palestine's Arabs as well as Jews to a homeland. It also acknowledged implicitly that the mandate had created the conflict between Arabs and Jews by encouraging Zionists to build a Jewish state in Arab Palestine. And it recognized that as the antagonism between the two peoples had grown, there was little possibility of a binational state.

The actual plan, however, was fatally flawed. The Arab state would make up 70 percent of the land only if Jordan were included in the Palestinian nation. The smaller Jewish state would include the most fertile lands; and while negligible numbers of Jews would live within the Arab state, 225,000 Arabs would reside in the Jewish area. The commission proposed "the most strenuous efforts" to transfer the Jewish population to the Jewish state and the Arabs to the Arab state, but those transferred in this case would overwhelmingly be Arabs rather than Jews.

The mufti and Awni Abd al-Hadi refused to accept the existence of a Jewish state of any size. Both men even called for deporting recent Jewish arrivals to Palestine. "Frankly speaking, we object to the existence of 400,000 Jews in the country," Abd al-Hadi told the commission.[23] They were as blind and indifferent to the Jews' plight as the Zionists were to theirs. Only George Antonius, while rejecting partition, acknowledged the plight of the Jews. But Antonius refused to accept their need for a Palestinian safe haven. "The treatment meted out to Jews in Germany and other European countries is a disgrace to its authors and to modern civilization but . . . the cure for the eviction of the Jews from Germany is not to be sought in the eviction of the Arabs from their homeland; and the relief of Jewish distress may not be accomplished at the cost of inflicting a corresponding distress upon an innocent and peaceful population," Antonius wrote.[24]

The Zionist reaction was also negative. A solid bloc of delegates to the Zionist Congress, including many from the United States, rejected any plan that precluded Jewish control of all of Palestine. Menachem Ussishkin, the chairman of the Jewish National Fund and an outspoken proponent of removing Arabs from Palestine, contended that a Jewish Zionist state could not start "with half the population being Arab."[25] Ussishkin and the Mizrachi, an organization of religious Zionists formed in Lithuania in 1902, also reiterated biblical claims for a Jewish Palestine. At the other side of the political spectrum, the left-wing Hashomer Hatzair rejected partition on the chimerical grounds that it precluded the unity of Jewish and Arab workers against their Jewish and Arab bosses in a unified Palestine.[26]

But Weizmann and Ben-Gurion, the leaders of international Zionism, saw partition as a victory for Zionism. "The Jews would be fools not to accept it even if [a state] were the size of a tablecloth," Weizmann exclaimed.[27] Both men believed that if the Jews rejected the plan, they would face restrictions on immigration; and they argued that even if the Jewish Palestine was undersized, it could still admit at least 100,000 new immigrants who might otherwise be barred entry. And both men were particularly pleased with the Peel Commission's proposal to transfer Arabs from one area to another.

The idea of transferring Arabs out of a Jewish state had been broached periodically since the beginning of the century. It was the ultimate solution to creating a Jewish state in a country in which Jews would otherwise remain a minority, even after decades of immigration. But the idea was deemed too provocative to be voiced publicly. The Peel Commission's proposal removed the moral stigma from it. For Zionists, it complemented the idea that Arabs were a fungible people who could be equally "at home" in Syria or Iraq as in Palestine.

At the time, Ben-Gurion wrote in his diary, "The compulsory transfer of the Arabs . . . could give us something which we never had . . . This is national consolidation in an independent homeland."[28] And he declared at the congress, "Transfer is what will make possible a comprehensive settlement program. Thankfully, the Arab people have vast empty areas. Jewish power, which grows steadily, will also increase our possibilities to carry out the transfer on a large scale. You must remember, that this system embodies an important human and Zionist idea, to transfer parts of a people to their country and to settle empty lands."[29] Weizmann was equally enthusiastic about transfer but predictably circumspect about proposing it publicly.[30]

But there were also differences between the two men. Ben-Gurion was for accepting the Peel proposal, perhaps in the hope that sometime in the future the Jewish boundaries could be widened.[31] Weizmann gave only qualified support to the Peel Commission's partition proposal. He favored neither accepting nor rejecting it, but calling for further negotiations on the boundaries. The congress would eventually adopt a negative version of Weizmann's proposal; it turned down the Peel recommendation but expressed willingness to negotiate a different partition.

There was also a subtle difference in the way the two men viewed Palestine's Arabs and the revolt. Weizmann continued to view the Arabs through the lens of Western imperialism. He said of the Arab revolt, "On one side, the forces of destruction, the forces of the desert, have risen, and on the other side stand firm the forces of civilization and building. It is the old war of the desert against civilization, but we will not be stopped."[32] By contrast, Ben-Gurion saw the Arab uprising as evidence that Jews would have to contend with an Arab nationalism that was as deeply rooted and difficult to dismiss as Zionism.

For David Ben-Gurion, al-Qassam's life had discredited the perception, common among Zionist leaders, that the Arab resistance was led by wealthy and corrupt landowners who could eventually be bought off. Ben-Gurion compared al-Qassam to the Zionist martyr Josef Trumpeldor, a veteran of the Zionist Mule Corps who fought for the Allies during World War I, and who died in defending the isolated Zionist outpost of Tel-Hai during the 1920 riots. Ben-Gurion described the ambush of al-Qassam's guerrillas as "their Tel-Hai."[33]

Ben-Gurion had come to a better understanding after talking to Antonius in April 1936. "There is a conflict, a great conflict. There is a fundamental conflict. We and they want the same thing: We both want Palestine," he told a Jewish Agency meeting the next month.[34] After the rebellion began, he concluded that the Arabs were no longer "a wild and fractured mob, aspiring to robbery and looting," but "an organized and disciplined community, demonstrating its national will with political maturity and a capacity for self-evaluation."[35]

In September 1936, he told a Mapai meeting that the Arabs were "fighting against dispossession . . . The fear is not of losing land, but of losing the homeland of the Arab people, which others want to turn into a homeland for the Jewish people. The Arab is fighting a war that cannot be ignored. He goes out on strike, he is killed, he makes great sacrifices."[36] In a later speech he said, "I want to destroy first of all the illusion among our comrades that the terror is a matter of a few gangs financed from abroad . . . From the time of Sheikh Izz ad-Din al-Qassam it was clear to me that we were facing a new phenomenon among the Arabs. This is not Nashashibi, not the mufti, not a matter of a political career or money . . . And politically we are the aggressors and they defend themselves. Militarily, it is we who are on the defensive who have the upper hand . . . but in the political sphere they are superior."[37] Ben-Gurion would later return to his earlier jaundiced view of Arab nationalism, but—facing the Arab revolt in the latter half of the 1930s—he grasped the moral and political dimensions of the conflict between Jew and Arab in Palestine.

Rebellion Crushed

Unable to win Arab or unequivocal Zionist support, the British appointed still another commission. This one, chaired by Sir John Woodhead, was tasked with drawing up a plan to implement partition. But even before the commission arrived in Palestine for hearings, the rebellion reignited. In September 1937, followers of Qassam assassinated Lewis Andrews, the district commissioner of the Galilee. That prompted Wauchope to disband the Arab Higher Committee. When he ordered the mufti's arrest, Amin al-Husseini fled to Lebanon. The other Arab notables on the committee were exiled to the Seychelles, an island group off the southeast coast of Africa.

That didn't end the rebellion, however. With the older leaders exiled, younger, local militants, many of them radical Islamists who followed Qassam's lead, stepped forward. In their own villages, they imposed Islamic customs, including forcing women to wear veils. They targeted Christian Arabs and Druze. When they raided Jewish villages, they killed indiscriminately. In Tiberias, rebels killed nineteen Jews, including eleven children, who appear to have been burned alive.[38] By early 1938 these rebels, who numbered at their height about 10,000, controlled much of the countryside and had forced the British to evacuate Jericho and other towns. The British military commander in Palestine wrote in August 1938 that "the situation was such that civil administration of the country was, to all practical purposes, nonexistent."[39]

At this point, the British took brutal actions to quash the rebellion. The conciliatory Wauchope was replaced by Harold MacMichael, a bureaucrat without sentimental attachments to the Jews or the Arabs. Two counterinsurgency experts, Charles Tegart and Orde Wingate, were brought in. Tegart imported Doberman dogs from South Africa to intimidate prisoners and established a training center in Jerusalem to instruct British soldiers in torture. He instituted waterboarding, beatings, and other brutal methods against Arab prisoners, who at one point numbered more than 9,000. Tegart also used a Histadrut company to build a barbed-wire fence blocking Syrian recruits from crossing the border into Palestine.

Wingate's special responsibility was protecting the Haifa oil pipeline, which began in Iraq, from sabotage. To accomplish that, he engaged in collective punishment. Convinced that a village was harboring rebels, he lined up and randomly shot villagers. Villagers were herded into pens outside and left to die of heat, thirst, and starvation. Wingate, a Christian Zionist, took Haganah members on his nighttime raids; and British commanders permitted Haganah members to arm for self-defense. The British paid for about 2,000 to be trained and the Haganah for 12,000 more soldiers or constables.

After the British signed the Munich Agreement in September 1938 in order, they hoped, to postpone war in Europe, they brought in 25,000 more troops into Palestine under the command of Major General Bernard Montgomery, who would make his name in World War II. The British campaign against the rebels was the largest since the end of World War I, and by early 1939 they had pretty much pacified the country. The rebellion was over. About 5,000 Arabs, 2,000 Jews, and 600 British had been killed. By Rashid Khalidi's estimate, over 10 percent of the adult male Arab population were either killed, wounded, imprisoned, or exiled.[40] Some of the methods that the British used to quash the rebellion—collective punishment, bulldozing homes, and even torture—were later adopted by the Israelis against Palestinian rebellions.

Balfour Declaration Repudiated

While the Colonial Office was pursuing partition, there was opposition to it in the Foreign Office and War Office. Officials there increasingly saw the conflict in Palestine through the prism of the gathering storm in Europe, and were worried about Arab support during a war against Germany and Italy. In March 1936, fascist Italy had completed its conquest of Ethiopia on the Red Sea. The next year Italy left the League of Nations and joined Germany and Imperial Japan in the Axis alliance. Control of Ethiopia gave the Axis powers a potential platform from which to block the British and their allies from using the Suez Canal to ship goods and troops. If the bulk of British troops were involved on the European continent, then the defense of the canal would rest on a small Middle East reserve force that was presently bogged down in Palestine.

In the event of a European war, Palestine was an important crossroads. If the canal was blocked and the British wanted to get troops from India to North Africa, these troops would have to go through Palestine. And, of course, the British obtained oil from Iraq through the pipeline that ended in Haifa. So the British had a special interest in pacifying Palestine. But it was important how they did it. Britain was particularly worried about securing the cooperation of the Arab leaders of Saudi Arabia, Egypt, Iraq, and Jordan in the event of war. In January 1939 the Middle Eastern Subcommittee of the Committee of Imperial Defence reported:

> [A] strong feeling . . . exists in all Arab States in connection with British policy in Palestine. It is evident that by far the most important measure which could be taken to influence the Arab States in favor of the United Kingdom would be our Palestine policy . . . If we fail thus to retain Arab goodwill at the outset of a war, no other measures which we can recommend will serve to influence the Arab States in favor of this country.[41]

Earlier in a letter to Foreign Secretary Anthony Eden, Sir Miles Lampson, the influential ambassador to Egypt, suggested how the British could obtain Arab goodwill. "While I do not suggest that we should swallow whole the Arabic case against Zionism," Lampson wrote, "it is essential that it shouldn't appear to the Arab and Egyptian governments . . . that our weight is definitely on the Zionist side."[42] Neville Chamberlain, who became prime minister in May 1937, put it this way: "If we must offend one side, let us offend the Jews rather than the Arabs."[43] That was, of course, a reversal of British officialdom's attitude after World War I. Just as the British had swept aside the rights of Palestinian Arabs after World War I, they were now ignoring the nightmare of European Jewry.

By the fall of 1937, the Foreign Office began opposing partition on the grounds that it would alienate the Arab leaders. In early August 1938, the new colonial secretary, Malcolm MacDonald, visited Palestine to discuss partition with MacMichael, the high commissioner, and other officials. MacDonald came away convinced it wouldn't work—not only because of opposition from the Arab states, but because the Arab population wasn't ready for self-government. The rebellion, he decided, was being led by "bandits" who lacked any political significance.[44] The Woodhead Commission admitted failure at devising a new plan of partition.

The Chamberlain government invited Palestinian Jews and Arabs, along with Arab state leaders, to London for a conference in February 1939 at St. James's Palace. The British didn't expect to reach an agreement at the conference—they assumed the Zionists would oppose any plan that didn't include a state and that also sharply restricted immigration and land sales—but they wanted to show the Arab state leaders that they had made an effort to support their brethren in Palestine by blocking the formation of a Jewish state.

To appease the Arab state leaders, the British cabinet acceded to the Arab states' proposal to allow only 75,000 immigrants for the next five years, after which the Palestinian Arab population would have a veto on further immigration. Jews would amount to no more than a third of the population. Land sales from Arabs to Jews would be restricted. Both Arabs and Jews would participate in government according to their population—in other words, Arabs would enjoy a political majority. And after ten years Palestine would become an independent binational state.

As the British had hoped, the leaders of the Arab states backed the proposals. And as they had expected, the Zionists walked out of the conference. The British published the proposals in a white paper in early May. Ben-Gurion said of the white paper, "A more evil, foolish, and short-sighted policy could not be imagined."[45] In Jerusalem, Jewish demonstrators stoned British police, and one policeman was killed. Banners in demonstrations compared MacDonald to Hitler. A Polish Jewish student at Oxford told Moshe Shertok, the head of the Jewish Agency's political department, that she was willing to kill Chamberlain and then herself. An oath was read in Palestine's synagogues that "this treacherous policy will not be tolerated . . . No power in the world can destroy the natural right of our brethren to enter the ancestral land."[46]

The Palestinian Arab leaders had been expected to back the British proposals, which nearly met the demands of the Arab Higher Committee. Former Jerusalem mayor Raghib Nashashibi's representatives, and two people close to the mufti, supported them. So did Istiqlal founder Abd al-Hadi. But the mufti, acting through his cousin, Jamal al-Husseini, manipulated the delegation into turning the proposals down. It issued a statement: "The ultimate decision as to the fate of a virile people depends on its own will, not on White or Black papers. Palestine will be independent within the Arab union and will remain Arab forever."[47]

Kimmerling and Migdal, as well as the mufti's biographer Philip Mattar, contend that Amin al-Husseini acted out of pique at the British for barring him from London. Rashid Khalidi argues that the mufti was worried about losing support from the remaining militants within Palestine, who opposed any concession to the Zionists and who had issued a statement calling for independence and warning the delegates not to listen "to the Nashashibis or to the Husseinis, nor to the Arab kings, who were ruling by the grace of Britain."[48] Michael Cohen says a majority of the Palestinian Arabs wanted independence within three years as the Iraqis had been promised.[49] Whatever the cause—and each of these explanations make sense—the mufti and the delegation's rejection of the white paper's proposals set a precedent for feckless leadership.

The white paper ended British commitment to the Balfour Declaration—at least as it had been originally understood by Balfour himself, Lloyd George, Churchill, Weizmann, Samuel, and the Zionists in Palestine, Europe, and the United States. The white paper stated that "his Majesty's Government now declare unequivocally that it is not part of their policy that Palestine should become a Jewish state."[50] The British retained the mandate, but it was only a matter of time—eight years, as it turned out—before they gave up trying to administer Palestine. Their policy had been an abysmal failure. What they had hoped would be a short courtship culminating in a happy marriage with a loyal Jewish state resulted in two decades of strife culminating in a nasty divorce.

Over the two decades, the British had helped raise the standard of living for both Arabs and Jews. The British established a unified postal system, paved roads, and introduced the telegraph. (The telephone and home electricity were still limited to the few cities.) Literacy and life expectancy also increased during the mandate. But the British occupation helped ensure that the region would suffer from continuing strife through the rest of the century. At the very least, the mandate had merely postponed an inevitable conflict between Arab and Jew; more likely, it helped create the basis for it, exacerbated it, and made any resolution difficult if not impossible.

In its account of the British occupation of Palestine and of the effect of the Balfour Declaration, the Peel Commission's report achieved a moment of moral and political clarity about the conflict between the Zionists and the Palestinian Arabs. The circumstances created by the occupation and the declaration had already ruled out any resolution to the conflict, but the proposals, and their rationale, would be revived after World War II and would become the basis of the United Nations plan to partition Palestine.

Palestine After the Rebellion

With the white paper's publication, Palestine's Arabs had seemingly won the diplomatic battle, but they had lost in every other respect. The rebellion of 1936–39 had had a devastating impact on Palestinian Arab politics. Most of the indigenous leadership was exiled or killed. And much of what remained, Rashid Khalidi writes, "had become envenomed."[51] In the last years of the rebellions, the Husseinis and Nashashibis were busy ordering assassinations of each other's supporters. And as MacDonald discovered, the younger militants had little capacity to govern. Their rebellion was conducted with a political fanaticism and religious sectarianism that would plague the Palestinian movement for years to come.

In reaction to Zionism, Palestine's Arabs fell prey to the worst of European anti-Semitism. Arab shops featured pictures of Hitler, and swastikas were commonly displayed on walls. Arab magazines adopted Nazi slogans. And *The Protocols of the Elders of Zion* was widely circulated among literate Arabs. During the Shaw Commission hearings in Palestine in late 1929, the mufti had conspicuously perused *The Protocols* during the sessions and discussed their thesis during his testimony.[52]

The mufti's political trajectory is indicative of what happened to the Palestinian leadership. An opponent of Zionism but an ally of the British and a moderate in the Arab world, he began to solicit the Nazis' help against Zionism soon after they took power in 1933. Facing exile, he looked to the German counsel for help in 1936. And after a sojourn in Lebanon and Iraq, he spent World War II in Berlin trying to help Hitler conquer Palestine. Between the mufti, ensconced in Berlin, and the radical Islamists of the village, the Palestinians emerged from the British mandate without the kind of leadership that could be the basis for self-government.

The Palestinian economy also came out of the interwar mandate without the rudiments of a nation in embryo. During the two decades, Jews acquired from Arabs much of the most fertile land. Many landless Arab peasants showed up in Jaffa and Haifa looking for laboring jobs that didn't exist, or from which they were excluded by Jewish employers. The peasants still tilling their land were beset by high taxes that took between 25 and 50 percent of their income. There was very little Arab industrial growth—only about thirty to thirty-five enterprises that had thirty or more workers by the mandate's end. By 1939, about 5,000 Arabs were engaged in industrial enterprises.[53] Culturally, the mandate years created a shared Palestinian identity, but the political, social, and economic foundation of that identity had eroded. As Kimmerling and Migdal wrote of the rebellion of the 1930s, "The revolt helped to create a nation—even while crippling its social and political basis."[54]

By contrast, the Jews in Palestine built their own nation within Palestine during the mandate years. The Jewish Agency, which the mandate had authorized to advise the occupying forces, became the de facto Jewish government with which the British government negotiated and cooperated. In the early 1930s the Haganah, which was created as a self-defense force, was barely functioning, but by the decade's end it had become the basis of the army—with almost 15,000 trained soldiers under arms—and would win the battle in 1948 for the Jewish state.

The Jewish economy, largely separate from the Arab, had prospered in the 1930s and would rapidly expand during World War II. Jewish Palestine had 2,000 factories in 1939 and would have 6,000 by the war's end, when Jewish industry would be producing 80 percent of Palestine's output.[55] From 1931 to 1939, the Jewish-owned Palestine Electric Company increased its output to industry sevenfold. The first Zionist émigrés had worked on the land, but the émigrés after World

War I flocked into the cities. By 1939 one in three Jews in Palestine lived in Tel Aviv. And during the rebellion Tel Aviv had displaced Jaffa as the country's main port.

The Zionist movement remained divided among the Labor Zionists on the left, the Revisionists on the right, and Weizmann's General Zionists in the center, but the three political organizations shared the single objective of establishing a Jewish state in opposition to the Arabs and the British. While a small faction within the Revisionists broke off during World War II to fight the British, Ben-Gurion held the rest of Jewish Palestine together in the war against Hitler even as the British were turning back refugee ships. The Jews, he advised, should "support the British as if there is no White Paper and oppose the White Paper as if there is no war."[56] The Palestinian Arabs were virtually leaderless. Writes the historian Gudrun Krämer, "What counted in the long run was the decisive weakening of Arab leadership at a time when the Jewish *yishuv* [community] was growing daily stronger . . . The imbalance with regard to economic performance, social cohesion, political organization, and not least military capacity would become evident after World War II."[57]

The Dissenters

A very small group of Zionists—the successors of Brit Shalom—believed that Palestine's Arabs had a right to self-determination and that Palestine's Jews should accept being a minority in a binational state. They were under no illusion about the sorry state of Arab leadership, but they believed that the responsibility of the mandatory power—which it exercised for better or worse in surrounding Arab countries—was to prepare a country's people for self-government. The British had failed to do that with Palestine's Arabs, so it would take time to develop a fully functioning binational state.

Magnes was the leader of the group, but it included Einstein, Buber, Hannah Arendt, and other eminent Jews. Baltimore-born Henrietta Szold, the founder of Hadassah, the main American women's Zionist organization, favored a binational solution. Like Magnes, Szold was deeply influenced by Ahad Ha'am's benign vision of Palestine as a Jewish spiritual center. She had migrated to Palestine in 1933 to oversee

Hadassah's relief and medical work among Jews and Arabs. Herbert Samuel, who had given up hope of establishing a Jewish state without violently suppressing the Arab majority, now favored a binational state in which Jews would be limited to 40 percent of the population. Norman Bentwich, who served as Palestine's attorney general under Samuel, favored a binational state.

It's hard to say why *these* men and women came to that conclusion, but it may be because (at least in the case of Magnes, Szold, Samuel, and Bentwich) they were deeply familiar with Palestine—they knew Arabs lived there—and were part of the international Zionist movement, yet retained a certain distance from it. Magnes and Szold had emigrated to Palestine to fulfill a dream rather than to escape persecution; they had independent sources of income (Magnes married into money). Samuel and Bentwich were well-to-do members of Britain's political establishment with divided loyalties to Britain and Jewish Palestine.

Their views attracted considerable attention in the United States and Great Britain. Magnes always got his opinions aired in the non-Zionist *New York Times*. But they never attracted a large following within the Zionist movement in Palestine, the United States, or Great Britain. And even though they were among the few Zionists who took the Palestinian Arab case for self-determination seriously, they were ignored except by Musa al-Alami, George Antonius, and a handful of Arab intellectuals. They understood the pitfalls of Zionism but their proposals for reconciling Jews and Arabs proved to be utopian.

Liberation and Oppression

By the end of the 1930s the Jews and Arabs in Palestine were irreconcilable. With European Jewry in peril, Zionist leaders no longer backed any form of partition. Instead, they shared the Revisionist objective of a greater Israel that could accommodate the immigrants from Central Europe. The Arab rebellion had also confirmed their imperial view of the country's Arabs as savages and barbarians who did not merit political rights. In the Jewish Palestinian press of the late 1930s, Anita Shapira recounts, Arabs were described repeatedly as "highway robbers," "treacherous murderers," "barbarian, savage, and shedders of blood," and "bloodthirsty savages who perpetuate their deeds in darkness, and all their courage is from ambush."[58]

Some Labor Zionists had worried in the 1920s about the movement being an arm of British imperialism. But by the late 1930s the Arabs' and the mufti's identification with Hitler's Germany had allowed these Zionists to reframe their own role in Palestine and on the world stage to avoid any taint of imperialism or settler colonialism. Labor Zionists began to see their struggle against the Arabs as part of the democratic front against fascism and Nazism.

"We see our mission here as combined and interwoven with the Great War being waged along the entire front of civilized humanity," one leaflet from Mapai, the Labor Zionist party, declared.[59] The Labor Zionist Yitzhak Tabenkin said, "The swastika that has been unfurled over Hitlerite Germany, and the green flag, the Arab 'national' flag, hoisted now by the reactionary leadership of the Arabs in Palestine—these flags are one and the same; the banners of hatred between peoples."[60] Faced with an Arab challenge, backed up by Europe's fascists and Nazis, Labor Zionists declared themselves victims of a "feudalist-imperialist" coalition.[61] The Arab "savages" were now part of this "feudalist-imperialist" coalition led by Nazi Germany.

Over the next decades, even after the Allied victory in World War II and the collapse of Western colonialism in the Middle East, Asia, and Africa, Zionists and later Israelis would continue to view their conflict with the Arabs through this twin prism of higher versus lower races and democracy against fascism and Nazism. They continued to describe Arabs as savages and barbarians, and their leaders as the heirs of Hitler. That included the mufti after World War II, Egypt's Gamal Abdel Nasser, PLO leader Yasir Arafat, and Hamas's Khaled Meshal. Such a view highlighted Zionism as a national liberation movement for oppressed Jewry and ally of the world's advanced democracies and obscured its role as a settler-colonial movement that had displaced or driven out a native population.

Palestine's Arabs—defeated, demoralized, torn by internal distrust, consumed by fear of higher powers conspiring against them—had begun even by the early 1920s to display attitudes toward their oppressors that could be found among Africans colonized by English, French, or Portuguese settlers or, for that matter, among America's Native Americans after being driven off their lands by settlers from abroad.

And that, too, would continue well after World War II, confirming Zionists' view that Arabs were their cultural inferiors.

There had been a period before World War I when one could have imagined Palestine evolving somewhat differently—perhaps along the lines Ahad Ha'am and later Magnes had advocated as a majority Arab state with a vibrant Jewish minority. Such a nation would not have been free of conflict, but it might have nurtured the strengths of both peoples instead of putting them irrepressibly at odds. Any chance of doing that was probably dashed by the issuance of the Balfour Declaration in 1917. And much of what the British did in the interwar period—most notably, encouraging religious division between Arab Christians and Muslims and thereby laying the basis for an Islamic politics—made things worse. There was one period where they might have forged a compromise between Jew and Arab—after the Wailing Wall riots—but Zionists in Palestine, Great Britain, and the United States dashed any hopes of accommodation.

Most of the Zionist leaders believed after 1917 that whatever chance they had of securing a Jewish Palestine rested with British sponsorship of their efforts. Jabotinsky was typically the most candid in describing the relationship, complaining at the Peel Commission hearings in 1937 that the British had failed to treat the Jews in Palestine as well as they had treated the British colonial settlers in Kenya.[62] But after the British white paper in 1939, Zionist leaders—with the exception of the Anglophile Weizmann—began to lose faith in Britain's support for their efforts.

Palestine's Jews were not ready to step out on their own or reverse course entirely, as Hannah Arendt had advocated, and seek an alliance with the Arabs against Western imperialism.[63] Outnumbered by Palestine's Arabs and surrounded by Arab states, Zionist leaders knew they needed a champion among the Great Powers to replace Great Britain. And that's when Palestine's Zionists began to turn their attention to the United States, which already had the largest and most powerful Zionist movement outside of Palestine, and which had almost single-handedly bankrolled the Jewish Agency in the interwar years. After the British issued the white paper, David Ben-Gurion wrote, "I turned to the United States. I saw that nothing good would come from England anymore."[64]

PART TWO

THE PARADOX

OF

AMERICAN ZIONISM

The situation reminds me of that in America, when the settlers who founded the Massachusetts Bay Colony had to protect themselves against the Indians.
—Louis Brandeis, November 1929

7

THE ORIGINS OF AMERICAN ZIONISM

In the nineteenth century, before the rise of an organized Zionist movement, there were Christian and Jewish Restorationists in the United States just as there were in Great Britain. They saw the Jewish return to Palestine not as a needed response to growing anti-Semitism but as the culmination of biblical prophecy. Warder Cresson, from a prominent Philadelphia family, converted to Judaism after having been successively a Quaker, a Shaker, and a Mormon. In 1844 he talked Secretary of State John C. Calhoun into appointing him counsel in Jerusalem, where he hoped to proselytize for a Jewish return to Palestine. The English novelist William Makepeace Thackeray, who met him there, said he had "no knowledge of Syria [then the name for the region] but what he derives from prophecy. I doubt whether any government has received or appointed so queer an ambassador."[1]

In 1891 a Chicago businessman, William E. Blackstone, a follower of John Nelson Darby's end-time theology who called himself "Reverend," circulated a petition that he delivered to President Benjamin Harrison calling for the United States to set up "an international conference to consider the condition of the Israelites and their claims to Palestine as their ancient home."[2] Blackstone got over four hundred signatures, including the devout John D. Rockefeller and J. P. Morgan, but failed to glean much support from American Jews, who feared that he wanted to send the Jews to the Holy Land in order to speed the second coming of Christ and the conversion of the Jews to Christianity. In the 1970s, after Israel's triumph in the Six-Day War, conservative Evangelicals would become similarly enchanted with Israel as the fulfillment of biblical prophecy.

The first stirrings of an American Zionist movement came in the 1880s when refugees from Eastern Europe established chapters of the Lovers of Zion along the Eastern Seaboard. That's where Henrietta Szold, growing up in Baltimore, learned about Zionism. But the movement took off after the appearance of Herzl's *The Jewish State* and the formation in 1898 of the Federation of American Zionists, a collection of local organizations including the Lovers of Zion. After an initial burst, the group's membership stalled, but it was then revived, as was the Zionist movement, during World War I, when Louis Brandeis took command of it. Under Brandeis, the federation gave way to the Zionist Organization of America and the American Jewish Congress.

American Zionists, like those in Europe and Palestine, favored the creation of a Jewish state. If anything, they were more outspoken in their advocacy than their counterparts across the Atlantic because they didn't have to fear repercussions from Arabs or Turks. But there were also very important differences between the American movement and the movement abroad. In Europe, being a Zionist meant wanting to *settle* sooner or later in Palestine to build a Jewish state there. But few American Zionists contemplated moving to Palestine. They had emigrated to the United States from Europe in order to escape anti-Semitism. "America is our Zion," the Union of American Hebrew Congregations declared in 1898.[3]

Americans became Zionists because they wanted to help. An American Zionist, the joke went, was someone who gave someone else five dollars to send a European Jew to Palestine.[4] Some Eastern European émigrés still had relatives who wanted to escape anti-Semitism, but for many American Jews their motives were moral and philanthropic. They wanted to aid the unfortunate, and they saw doing so as an extension of their liberal commitment at home. And for many Jews, particularly Reform Jews, being a Zionist came to define and enliven Judaism for them. It displaced traditional observances as the focus of being Jewish.

American Zionists also had less contact with Palestine and with those who had been to Palestine than their European brethren. An ocean and a sea separated them from the Holy Land. They formed their opinions of Palestine from books by travelers, articles in the Zionist press, and speeches by visiting Zionist leaders, many of whom had come to the United States to raise money. They knew next to nothing about Arab Palestine and assumed it was a desolate land waiting for Jews to inhabit it. That was an important factor, but not the only factor, in explaining how Jews who were noted liberals in America—champions of workers trying to unionize and of African Americans—seemed oblivious to the darker side of Zionism, to the attempt to impose a Jewish state on a people who had lived in Palestine for 1,300 years.

Judaism as a Denomination

The first Jews entered North America in the seventeenth century from Holland by way of what had become Portuguese Brazil. Almost two centuries later, there were only about 15,000 of these Sephardic Jews. As many as one in three of them had married gentiles. From 1840 to 1880, about 200,000 Jews came to the United States from Germany and Austria-Hungary. Then, between 1880 and 1920, more than 2.5 million Jews came from Eastern Europe. The severe restriction on immigration passed in 1924 halted the rapid growth of the Jewish population. In 1927 there were about 4.2 million Jews in the United States, amounting to 3.6 percent of the total population.[5] After that, the percentage of Jews in America steadily declined.

The first American Jews were "Orthodox"—a term that only began to be used in the nineteenth century to contrast traditional religious practices with those of Reform and later Conservative congregations—but most of the early leaders of the Zionist movement in the United States came from the Reform movement.

The first glimmers of Reform Judaism, inspired by Unitarianism, appeared in Charleston in the 1820s, but the real inspiration came from Central European émigrés Isaac Mayer Wise and David Einhorn, who introduced the German brand of Enlightenment Judaism to the United States in the decades immediately preceding and following the Civil War. By 1900 most Central European Jews who practiced Judaism attended Reform "temples" rather than Orthodox synagogues, and the number of Reform temples vastly outnumbered the Orthodox synagogues. The most important Jewish organization was the Reform rabbis' Central Conference of American Rabbis.

Reform rabbis tried to rid Judaism of any ritual that was not based on reason—from ancient dietary laws to the Saturday Sabbath. They applied the same daunting rule of reason to Old Testament prophecy, including the promise of a Messiah and of the resurrection of the dead. Well before there was a Zionist movement, Reform Judaism had rejected the religious premise of Zionism. Rabbi Gustav Poznanski, who was born in Poland but educated in Berlin, said at the dedication of the first Reform temple in Charleston in 1841, "This country is our Palestine, this city our Jerusalem, this house of God our Temple."[6]

American Reform Jews, like those in Germany, insisted that Judaism was a religion, not a nation. American Reform Jews argued that if they did define Jews as a national group rather than a religion, they would be inviting the same kind of anti-Semitism based on nationality that Eastern European Jews suffered. Jews who had emigrated from Central Europe and who had become prosperous were eager to counter any charges of "dual loyalty" to an American and Jewish nation in order to smooth their path into the highest reaches of American society.

They had American religious pluralism to back them up. During the Civil War, Jewish chaplains had initially been barred from the field during the Civil War, but the Congress, at Abraham Lincoln's urging, changed the chaplaincy law to define eligible chaplains as belonging to "some religious denomination" rather than to "some Christian denomination."[7] According to this definition, Judaism was a religious denomination like Methodism or Roman Catholicism.

By insisting that being Jewish was a religious denomination and not a nationality, Reform Judaism allowed these émigrés to proclaim their Americanism. "I am an American and cannot possibly belong to two nations," banker Jacob Schiff, the most prominent Jew of his day, declared.[8] Louis Marshall, a corporate attorney who worked closely with Schiff, made a similar declaration at a 1905 celebration in Albany of the 250th anniversary of the Jewish immigration to America. "The Jew," he declared, "is not a parasite, an exploiter of the country, or a newcomer within its gates. He is an American of the Americans—a Jew by faith and religion, an American in all that term can betoken."[9]

The Reform rabbis codified this understanding of nation and religion and of America as Zion in the Pittsburgh Platform, which was adopted in 1885 before the rise of a Zionist movement. "We consider ourselves no longer a nation, but a religious community, and therefore expect neither a return to Palestine, nor a sacrificial worship under the sons of Aaron, nor the restoration of any of the laws concerning the Jewish state," the platform read.[10]

The Reform rabbis reinterpreted the "realization of Israel's great Messianic hope" to mean "the establishing of the kingdom of truth, justice, and peace among all men." Their objective was not simply to aid Jews, or advance the Jewish religion, but to create the "reign of truth and righteousness among men." Their objective was *universal*, not particular to Jews.

The rabbis rejected the idea that Jews had been punished by being exiled from their homeland. Instead, they believed that through the gift of the Diaspora Jews had been "chosen" to take the lead in establishing the kingdom. But they didn't conceive of Jews as acting alone or primarily in order to advance the Jewish religion. The rabbis hailed Christianity and Islam's "providential mission to aid in the spreading of monotheistic and moral truth."

In rejecting Orthodox messianism and biblical-based ritual, the Pittsburgh Platform followed the lead of German Reform Judaism, but in embracing the objective of the new kingdom, it echoed American progressivism and the Protestant Social Gospel's attempt to establish the Kingdom of God on earth. The final, eighth provision of the Pittsburgh Platform made it very explicit, declaring that "in full accordance with the spirit of the Mosaic legislation, which strives to regulate the relations between rich and poor, we deem it our duty to participate in the great task of modern times, to solve, on the basis of justice and righteousness, the problems presented by the contrasts and evils of the present organization of society."[11]

Reform Jews could find the basis for many of these beliefs in the Old Testament, but they could just as easily find views that ran completely contrary.* During the Civil War, some Jews, including the

---

*In a lecture to the Harmonie Club in New York on May 15, 2001, Michael Walzer said of the Jews who espoused universalism: "Indeed, they could find what they needed in the Bible and Talmud to support a universalist politics and morality, but the discovery was too easy: they simply picked the nicest passages and ignored everything else."

Confederate secretary of state Judah P. Benjamin and the prominent New York rabbi Morris Raphall, claimed to reconcile Judaism with support for slavery. The Reform movement had the same relationship to Judaism and the Old Testament that the proponents of the Protestant Social Gospel like Walter Rauschenbusch had to Protestantism and the New Testament. Reform Jews were attempting to accommodate a religious belief to a political and social movement. By doing this, the Reform rabbis helped to win several generations of American Jews over to political progressivism.

Reform Judaism and Zionism

Out of Reform Judaism came three different responses to the rise of Zionism in Europe. The dominant response in the 1890s was clearly negative. In 1897 the Central Conference of American Rabbis declared that "we totally disapprove of any attempt for the establishment of a Jewish state."[12] Rabbi David Philipson, a graduate of the first class at the Hebrew Union, a Reform seminary in Cincinnati, dismissed the Zionist idea of an "ingathering of exiles." Wrote Philipson:

> Reform Judaism is spiritual, Zionism is political; Reform Judaism is universal, Zionism is particularistic; Reform Judaism looks to the future, Zionism to the past; the outlook of Reform Judaism is the world, the outlook of Zionism is a corner of Western Asia.[13]

Isaac Mayer Wise spoke disparagingly of the first Zionist Congress:

> The so-called Jewish Congress in Basel was, properly speaking, neither a Congress nor Jewish. It was really a convention of some voluntary advocates for a plan for the relief of the Jews in the Orient. It was not Jewish because it represented neither the sentiments nor the religious propensities of the Jews as a body.[14]

Some Reform Jews would continue to oppose Zionism. In 1942, Reform Jews founded the American Council for Judaism, which led the fight against American support for a Jewish state.

The second most visible response in the late nineteenth and early twentieth centuries was described as "non-Zionist" rather than "anti-Zionist." The key non-Zionist group was the American Jewish Committee, which was formed in 1906 in the wake of the Kishinev massacre by Marshall, Schiff, and the diplomat and Roosevelt cabinet member Oscar Straus. It was a select group—membership by invitation—of upper-class Central European émigrés. They tried to influence government policy through clout (and later campaign contributions) rather than through visible protest. As their critics noted, they were following in the footsteps of the *shtadlanim*, the rich Jews in Central Europe who interceded with, and often bribed, the gentile authorities on behalf of their ghetto coreligionists.

The committee's leaders raised money for the Jews of Russia and Palestine, but they opposed establishing a Jewish state. Zionism, Schiff warned, would "place a lien upon citizenship" and create "a separateness which is fatal."[15] But unlike the anti-Zionists who would end up in the American Council for Judaism, the Reform Jews of the American Jewish Committee worked closely with Zionist organizations after World War I—all the while insisting they were not advocating a Jewish state. After reports of the Holocaust surfaced, many of them embraced Zionism as the only alternative for Europe's displaced Jews.

The third group was the Zionists. They were a small minority of Reform Jews, but played a very large role in creating an American Zionist movement. The first president of the Federation of American Zionists was Richard Gottheil, a Columbia University professor of Semitic languages. The organization's youthful secretary was Rabbi Stephen Wise, who had studied under Gottheil. Wise, a large man with a broad forehead and square jaw, was a stirring orator who would eventually become America's best-known rabbi.

Gottheil, Wise, and other Reform Zionists were leading progressives. Wise became noted as much for his domestic politics as for Zionism. He described himself as an "ultra-liberal."[16] In Oregon, where he served as a rabbi from 1900 to 1906, he crusaded against child labor and became the state's first commissioner of child labor. He was a founder of the National Association for the Advancement of Colored People and the American Civil Liberties Union and a champion of women's suffrage. He walked the picket line with Passaic's striking textile workers. He devoted his sermons to social reform. He and Brandeis were the most prominent Jewish backers of Woodrow Wilson in 1912, and Wise later served as the unofficial Jewish liaison to Franklin D. Roosevelt.

Wise bridged the gap between Reform Judaism and the Social Gospel. When he was eighteen in 1892, he attended Glenmore in the Adirondacks, a "summer school for the social sciences" founded by Thomas Davidson, a Scottish immigrant and philosopher and leading proponent of the Social Gospel.[17] Wise became close to Davidson, and later to Walter Rauschenbusch, whom he described as "one of the real prophets of the religious social awakening of our times."[18]

Gottheil and Wise embraced Zionism largely through their émigré fathers, who were rabbis and ardent Zionists. Both men thought of themselves as disciples of Herzl, whom Wise met at the second World Zionist Congress in Basel. In 1899, Wise wrote fellow Reform rabbi Maximilian Heller, "As for the need of Zionism, there can be no question, and you know that well. Anti-Semitism is becoming worse and worse every day, more daring and unprincipled with every hour . . . We Zionists are pessimists, respecting the hope of securing justice from without. We are optimists in that we have the deepest faith in ourselves and our God-given powers to build up a country of our own."[19]

But other considerations probably moved these and other Reform Jews to become Zionists. As Nathan Glazer remarked, Reform Jews could not altogether abandon the national ethos of Judaism. They still opposed intermarriage and insisted on circumcision even though its health benefits (like those of kosher meat) had become suspect. Wrote Glazer, "Underneath the rational ideology of the leaders of Reform Judaism, there still remained a simple unreflecting attachment to the Jewish people, a subconscious insistence that the Jews be maintained as a people."[20]

For Schiff and the non-Zionists, that subconscious insistence was kept at bay by fears that their support for a Jewish state would cast doubt upon their loyalty as Americans and undermine their attempt to assimilate. But Gottheil and Wise—perhaps because one was a scholar and the other a rabbi—were less worried about assimilation. Wise would often repeat the story of his response to a woman who belonged to the Daughters of the American Revolution and who claimed that her ancestors wrote the Declaration of Independence. "Mine wrote the Ten Commandments," he replied.[21]

There was, finally, another consideration that was largely unspoken.

The rationalism of Reform Judaism—the repudiation of ritual, the purging of ancient belief—diluted Judaism's appeal as a religion. It removed the ties that bound together congregations; it robbed belief of its emotional component. "The thoroughgoing rationalism of the Reform leaders," Nathan Glazer wrote, "put them in opposition to the complex structure of Jewish ritual practice which had maintained Jews as a people apart."[22]

Reform Judaism, like its Protestant counterparts, Congregationalism and Unitarianism, lost members not only to secular politics but also to more orthodox religion; and after World War I, Reform Judaism tried to meet the challenge of the new Orthodox-influenced Conservative Judaism by restoring some elements of ritual. But for the Reform Jews of the early twentieth century like Wise, Zionism served as a bridge between the impassioned politics of progressivism, which they embraced, and the passionless principles of Reform Judaism. It was a way of being progressive—standing up for the oppressed Jews of Europe—and of being Jewish. In a more attenuated form, the same considerations would lead purely secular Jews like Louis D. Brandeis to Zionism.

The Eastern European Immigrants

If secular or Reform Central European Jews made up much of the early leadership of the American Zionist movement, Eastern European Jews began by the 1900s to provide many of the foot soldiers, and would later assume leadership, of the movement. They brought a different sensibility to American Zionism, one that was subordinate to that of Wise, Gottheil, or Brandeis in the beginning, but that later became the dominant strain of American Zionism.

The Eastern European émigrés arrived in earnest after the 1881–82 pogroms in Russia and the Pale of Settlement, although they were driven to emigrate as much by poverty as by anti-Semitic violence. If they were religious, they tended to be Orthodox, and most of those who were or became Zionists in the first decades tended to be Orthodox. Other Eastern European émigrés stayed out of politics or gravitated to the working-class politics of the labor or socialist movements.

One of the key figures in promoting Zionism among the Eastern European émigrés was an itinerant rabbi (a *maggid*), Zvi Hirsch

Masliansky from Belarus, who knew Ahad Ha'am, Pinsker, and Lilien-blum and taught Chaim Weizmann. Forced to flee Belarus, he emigrated to New York in 1895 and began touring the eastern United States giving sermons in Yiddish that blended Orthodox religiosity with Zionism. Masliansky inspired two future leaders of American Zionism, Louis Lipsky, the child of Polish Orthodox Jews, and Abba Hillel Silver, who emigrated with his parents from Lithuania in 1902.

There were obvious cultural as well as religious differences between the Eastern and Central European Zionists. The Eastern Europeans spoke and wrote Yiddish rather than English. Many of them started at the bottom of the economic ladder. They wanted to become Americans but, unlike the German Jews, they weren't worried about being accused of dual loyalty. They backed Zionism out of direct identification with the Eastern European Jews who continued to suffer from anti-Semitism. Many had friends and families who still lived in the Pale of Settlement. They had been raised with the idea that Judaism was a nationality as well as a religion and were comfortable with being American citizens and supporting a Jewish nation in Palestine.

The Eastern European Jews also had a different relationship to American politics. The Central Europeans like Wise, Brandeis, and, later, the Supreme Court justice Felix Frankfurter were known as much, if not more, for their contributions to American liberalism and progressivism. The Eastern European Zionists did not play large roles in American politics other than as Zionists. After Franklin Roosevelt's election, most became Democrats. But their primary focus was on establishing a Jewish state.

Visions of Palestine

The initial leadership of American Zionism was largely composed of German émigré and Reform Jews like Gottheil and Wise. The only Eastern European in the leadership was Lipsky, who was appointed editor of *The Maccabean*, the federation's monthly magazine; but in 1902, Lipsky was temporarily displaced by Jacob de Haas, an aide to Herzl whom he sent to guide the American organization, and who settled in the United States. Some of the Orthodox Eastern Europeans, who found Gottheil, Wise, and the Federation of American Zionists "Torahless," joined the Mizrachi. Working-class Zionists who were Socialists joined the American branch of Poale Zion, to which a young David Ben-Gurion belonged.

Most of these first-generation Zionists—and particularly those who belonged to the clubs in the Federation of American Zionists—looked upon Herzl's *The Jewish State* as their manifesto. They were political Zionists. Under de Haas and Lipsky, *The Maccabean* was highly critical of Ahad Ha'am's theories of cultural Zionism. The theories, de Haas wrote, "belong to an unreal world and an unreal age."[23] German émigré Horace Kallen, who would have a significant influence on Brandeis, dismissed Ahad Ha'am's Zionism as "an intensification of the status quo."[24] Wise scorned Ahad Ha'am's works as "an opiate for the Jewish masses, which would keep them in the bondage of a culture that could never lead them to a political rebirth."[25] That view of Ahad Ha'am was consistent with a Reform Judaism that scorned the accoutrements of Jewish culture but also reflected a lack of awareness of what establishing a Jewish state in an Arab majority region would mean.

The first generation of Zionist leaders had little knowledge of who actually lived in Palestine and what it would mean for Jews to establish a state there.

Much of their understanding of Palestine came from popular travel books about Palestine. These books portrayed Palestine as underpopulated and backward. One of the best known was Mark Twain's *Innocents Abroad*. Twain described arriving at a village where "not a soul was visible, but where the ring of the horses' hoofs roused the stupid population, and they all came trooping out—old men and old women, boys and girls, the blind, the crazy, and the crippled, all in ragged, soiled, and scanty raiment."[26]

This view of Palestine was articulated by early Restorationists in their talks and petitions. Writes the political scientist Kathleen Christison, "The notion that there were no Arab inhabitants in the Holy Land or that they were alien interlopers became a part of the popular imagination in the West, at least among the informed public and the religiously aware, well before the first Zionist settlers ever conceived of migrating to Palestine in the 1880's."[27]

The first Zionist leaders echoed these preconceptions about Palestine. By portraying Palestine as desolate, they could justify Zionist colonization without inviting questions about whether Zionists were subjugating the natives. Gottheil did not even mention Palestine's Arabs in his federation pamphlet *The Aims of Zionism*. Another pamphlet from 1899 described Palestine as a "neglected and deserted country."[28] An editorial in *The Maccabean* described it as "desolate."[29] The few mentions of Palestine's Arab population were plagued by wishful error. In 1901, *The Maccabean* estimated that there were "not as many as 150,000" Arabs in Palestine.[30] (It was probably between 550,000 and 600,000.) *The Maccabean* also asserted that that "one-third of the population of Palestine today is Jewish."[31] (It was probably 5 percent.)[32]

The Zionists voiced arguments that anticipated Jabotinsky's view that Palestine's Arabs were a fungible people that could as well live elsewhere. *The Maccabean* gave little credence to the skirmishes between Zionist settlers and the Palestinian Arabs. In 1913, *The Maccabean* asked incredulously, "Does anyone believe that the Arabs, in a contest for mastery in the land, are designed to overcome the Jews?" The Arabs would leave the area, the magazine editorialized, because there is "nothing that holds the Arab to Palestine." The "historic center of Arabs is Mecca and Medina." "As their land comes under cultivation," the Arabs are "bound to withdraw with the pressure of the population driving [them] Southerward."[33]

In the first decade of the federation, the authors also approvingly compared Zionist colonization to that of the British—a product, perhaps, of America's short-lived romance with imperialism under Theodore Roosevelt. In the January 1903 issue highlighting the federation's convention, de Haas and Lipsky featured an address, "What Has Zionism Accomplished?" by Leah Asher, a leader of the Worcester, Massachusetts, Zionists. Declaring that "colonization on a large scale is the greatest work of national life," Asher asserted that the Jews were following the example of the British in Southern and Central Africa and in Australia and New England who had turned "barren deserts . . . into places of habitation . . . The attempts of other nations in other parts of the world give us courage."[34]

In its first year, the federation expanded from 25 to 125 clubs or societies. It acquired 10,000 members from these clubs who agreed to pay 50-cent dues to the federation. But in the years up to World War I, it failed to grow further. On the eve of World War I, the American Zionist movement had only about 20,000 members out of 1.5 million Jews.[35] The number of Zionist societies had dropped from 304 in 1904, the year of the Kishinev Massacre, to 198.[36] Many of these had few members. In New York, three-fourths of the societies founded between 1898 and 1914 dissolved in less than two years.[37]

The federation was hampered by its decentralized structure and weak leadership. In 1904 both Gottheil and Wise resigned—Gottheil because he wanted to devote more time to his studies, and Wise because he felt the movement's European leaders did not take Americans seriously. Gottheil was replaced by a Baltimore physician who had little time to devote to the movement. After the 1914 convention of the Federation of American Zionists, Shmarya Levin, who had represented the Zionist Organization, reported back to Berlin that "if even now we do not interfere here *radically*, then everything will remain as it has been, and Zionism there will continue in the same miserable condition also in the future."[38]

But within five years, without radical intervention from abroad, American Zionists would boast 600 societies and 149,000 adherents. They would become the largest and most important group in the Zionist Organization.[39] That was partly the result of the world war, which dramatized the plight of Palestine's Jews, and the issuing of the Balfour Declaration in November 1917, but the most important reason for the movement's growth was Louis Brandeis. After the outbreak of World War I, the headquarters of world Zionism was moved temporarily to New York, and Brandeis agreed to become the head of the provisional executive committee. From then until his death in 1941 on the eve of World War II, he was the most visible—and, during the World War I years, the most active—figure in American Zionism.

8

ZIONISM AND AMERICAN LIBERALISM: BRANDEIS AND HIS CIRCLE

Many leaders of American Zionism were closely identified with progressive and liberal political movements. They backed unions and collective bargaining, government old-age and health insurance, workers' compensation, and civil rights and women's suffrage. In the early twentieth century, some of them were Republicans, the party of Lincoln and Theodore Roosevelt, but during Woodrow Wilson's and Franklin Roosevelt's presidencies most of them became Democrats. None of these individuals were as important as Louis D. Brandeis.

Brandeis, a key advisor to Wilson in the 1912 election, almost single-handedly revived the Zionist movement in 1914. He obtained Wilson's support for the Balfour Declaration. He was a founder of both the Zionist Organization of America and the American Jewish Congress. In speeches and pamphlets, he attempted to reconcile Zionism and Americanism. After he joined the Supreme Court in 1916, he took a less visible role in the Zionist movement. But acting through a circle of friends, protégés, and disciples, which included Stephen Wise and Felix Frankfurter, he retained his leadership of the Zionist movement over the next two decades.

From their liberal reputations, Brandeis and his circle might have been expected to espouse a very liberal version of Zionism—similar, perhaps, to that of the émigrés Judah L. Magnes and Henrietta Szold. As American liberals, they were, after all, outspoken defenders of the poor, the oppressed, and the disenfranchised and of democracy and self-determination. But their Zionism focused almost entirely on Jewish Palestine. They saw Palestine's Arabs largely through the prism of Western colonialism and Jewish nationalism. They either ignored them or assigned them to a lower rung of humanity than Palestine's Jews or America's multifold nationalities.

Becoming a Zionist

Brandeis, who was born in 1856, came from a well-to-do Jewish family that emigrated from Prague to Louisville, Kentucky, in 1851 after the failure of the 1848 revolution and the resurgence of anti-Semitism. His parents did not practice Judaism and he did not receive a religious upbringing. "My people were not so narrow as to allow their religious belief to overshadow their interests in the broader aspects of humanity," he wrote in 1910 before he had become a Zionist.[1] His parents' "religion" resembled Ethical Culture, which was founded by Felix Adler, a family friend who presided at Louis and Alice Brandeis's wedding and married a sister of Brandeis's wife.

Like Herzl or Ben-Gurion, Brandeis was not a believer and never belonged to a synagogue or temple. Initially, his link to the practice of Judaism was through his uncle Lewis Dembitz, who was an early adherent to Conservative Judaism and a Zionist, as well as a renowned lawyer and a Lincoln delegate to the Republican convention in 1860. Louis Brandeis admired his uncle. He didn't embrace his religious practices, but he took his uncle's last name for his middle name (his original middle name was David) and adopted his profession. And learning later that his uncle was a Zionist may have influenced his decision to become one himself.

Brandeis graduated from Harvard in 1876 and became a successful corporate lawyer in Boston. He hobnobbed with that city's Brahmin class. Like other upper-class Bostonians, he was a member of a boat club and a polo club, although as a Jew he was excluded from many upper-class homes, including that of his longtime law partner. Once he became wealthy, however, he devoted more of his time to defending labor unions and fighting monopolies. Known as the "people's lawyer," he helped formulate Wilson's "new freedom" in 1912.

Brandeis was striking in appearance. A Harvard classmate wrote of him that he "has a rather foreign look and is currently believed to have some Jew blood in him, though you would not suppose it from his appearance—tall, well-made, dark, beardless, and with the brightest eyes I ever saw."[2] He was aloof but had a commanding presence. Recalled a younger Zionist leader, Emanuel Neumann, "He appeared set on a higher level than virtually all the men I had known."[3]

Before 1912, Brandeis displayed virtually no interest in Zionism. In 1905 and again in 1910, he stated his support for the idea of a melting pot and his opposition to "hyphenated Americanism."[4] To protest Russian anti-Semitism, he put his name on appeals to end the Russo-American trade treaty, but he refused an invitation to speak at a fund-raising event in 1905 for the victims of Kishinev. Brandeis's transition to Zionism was incremental and started in a New York City labor dispute.

Brandeis certainly acknowledged he was Jewish, but he didn't think of himself as part of the same ethnic group as Eastern European Jews who migrated to the United States or to Palestine. That changed in 1910 when Brandeis mediated a garment workers' strike in New York where both owners and workers were Russian Jews. Brandeis, who had not ventured outside of upscale and reserved Central European Jewish circles, gained a newfound appreciation of raucous Eastern European Jewry. It was "the first time," he wrote four years later, that he "had come into contact with Jews en masse."[5]

In 1912, Brandeis had a long discussion with Jacob de Haas, who had become the editor of the *Boston Advocate*. De Haas informed him that his uncle (whom he called a "noble Jew") had been among Herzl's first followers in the United States.[6] That same year Brandeis attended a dinner where the Zionist Aaron Aaronsohn, who would later win over the British official Mark Sykes, spoke about his discovery of wild wheat in Palestine. Brandeis wrote his brother that Aaronsohn's talk was "the most thrillingly interesting I have ever heard."[7] What impressed Brandeis in Aaronsohn's talk was not only the Palestinian Jews' application of scientific agriculture but the cooperative community that the Jews had built. What Brandeis heard about Palestine conformed to his own vision of cooperative, small-scale democracy.

In May 1913, Brandeis invited Aaronsohn to his home, and soon afterward he gave his first speech in support of Zionism at the Young Men's Hebrew Association in Chelsea. "We cannot go as far as the pioneers in Palestine," he declared, "but we must make their example to radiate in our lives . . . In order that the world may gain from what is best in us, we should aid in the effort of the Jews in Palestine."[8]

At the time he heard Aaronsohn, Brandeis was also becoming estranged from Brahmin Boston and the myth of Pilgrim and Yankee New England. Brandeis had imagined the New England of the late nineteenth century as the heir to the Pilgrim and Puritan values of community that he esteemed, but the Brahmin opposition to his pro-labor and antimonopoly activities shattered these illusions and contributed to his identification with American Jews and the Jews in Palestine.

What Aaronsohn did for Brandeis, the historian Allon Gal suggested, was to supplant the myth of Puritan England with that of Jewish Palestine. The Zionist pioneer became the true heir of Pilgrim and Puritan values—and an older Christian Zionism that envisaged a Jewish return to Palestine as the counterpart of the Puritan emigration to the new world. "Zionism is the Pilgrim inspiration all over again," Brandeis declared in 1915.[9] In his speeches, he referred to Zionists in Palestine as "our Jewish Pilgrim fathers."[10] And he continued to do so. In 1923 he declared that "the same spirit which brought the Pilgrim west is the spirit which has sent many a Jew to the east, and should send many, many more."[11]

In speeches he gave during World War I, he did warn of the permanence of European anti-Semitism, but what most informed his conversion was the positive notion that Jews in Palestine were building the cooperative democracy that he wanted to create in the United States. He embraced the Jewish colonists of Palestine not only as the new Pilgrims but as an extension of the progressive movement in the United States. That became the basis for his attempt to reconcile Zionism with liberalism.

Men, Money, and Discipline

Brandeis brought to American Zionism immense prestige and influence—he was the most famous and honored Jew in America—along with a passion for organization and discipline. In August 1914, after the outbreak of war and the closure of the Zionist Organization's Berlin office, de Haas implored Brandeis to become the chairman of the provisional executive committee, which was established to take over from Berlin and London. De Haas expected him to be a useful figurehead, but to his surprise, Brandeis took the new committee in hand. His motto was "Men, money, discipline," and he enjoined his followers to "Organize, organize, organize."[12] Under Brandeis's leadership, the Zionist movement exploded; its fund-raising capabilities grew exponentially—in Brandeis's first nine months, the provisional committee raised more than the Federation of American Zionists and other bodies had raised in the prior fifteen years. The movement also gained new organizing arms.[13]

Soon after he assumed the chairmanship, Brandeis developed the idea for an organization that, unlike the Federation of American Zionists, would draw together members as individuals. At a convention in Pittsburgh in 1918, the new group, the Zionist Organization of America (ZOA), came into being. Some groups, like Hadassah, the women's organization, remained as affiliates, but the ZOA was primarily a membership group that could act with one voice.

Brandeis also teamed with Wise to found the American Jewish Congress as a counterweight to the American Jewish Committee. The American Jewish Committee claimed to speak for all American Jewry, even though it was a select group of wealthy American Jews of Central European origin. Brandeis and Wise wanted a congress of all Jewish organizations, which, given the preponderance of Zionist groups, would have a Zionist tilt. The congress would also represent Eastern European Jews, who were excluded from membership in the committee.

After Brandeis and his allies clashed with American Jewish Committee representatives at a planning meeting for the new organization, an article and editorial appeared in *The New York Times* (whose publisher, Adolph Ochs, had been a founder of the committee) criticizing Brandeis, who had recently been confirmed as a Supreme Court justice, for compromising his public position by getting involved in factional political controversies. In response, and partly, perhaps, out of pique, Brandeis resigned from all his public positions with the Zionist organizations, but behind the scenes he stayed extremely active in the movement. He was the most important connection Zionists had to the American presidency during the Wilson administration.

In April 1917, just after the United States entered the war, Brandeis received a cable from Weizmann, asking him, on behalf of himself, Ahad Ha'am, James Rothschild, and Herbert Samuel, to back a British protectorate for a Jewish national home in Palestine. When Balfour came to Washington the next month to solicit Wilson's backing for a British protectorate, he saw Brandeis. In response, Brandeis met with Wilson and persuaded him to back the British proposal, but because the United States still hoped to win Turkey over to the Allied side in the war, Wilson was unwilling to support a British protectorate publicly.

In September, the British sent Wilson through his advisor Colonel House the text of the Balfour Declaration and asked for his approval, but Wilson, on the advice of House and his secretary of state, Robert Lansing, held off. The British again called on Brandeis for help, and he met with House on September 23 and convinced him that the administration should endorse the declaration. When the British sent an official request to Wilson, the president responded positively, although he continued to insist that his statement not be made public for fear of alienating Turkey. Wrote Nahum Goldmann, onetime president of the World Zionist Organization, "If it had not been for [Brandeis's] influence on Wilson, who in turn influenced the British government, the Balfour Declaration would probably never have been issued."[14]

After he resigned his positions with the movement, Brandeis exercised leadership over American Zionists primarily through a group of protégés, friends, and disciples that was dubbed the "Parushim," after the Hebrew for "Pharisees," and that included Wise, de Haas, the Harvard law professor and later Supreme Court justice Felix Frankfurter, the philosopher Horace Kallen, the lawyer Robert Szold (who was Henrietta Szold's cousin), and the New York circuit court judge Julian Mack. Mack, who was a noted progressive and longtime ally of Hull House founder Jane Addams, became head of the ZOA in Brandeis's stead. Wise chaired the American Jewish Congress.

In 1921, Brandeis's allies lost a battle in the ZOA over what the funds raised in the United States should go for. The Parushim resigned from the organization and devoted their energies to the Palestine Development League and the Palestine Endowment Fund, which were run by de Haas and Szold, but by 1930, Louis Lipsky and Brandeis's other opponents in the ZOA had driven the organization into the ground, and at Weizmann's urging they invited the Parushim back into the leadership. When Szold and Wise returned to take control of the ZOA, they discovered that its membership had dropped from 180,000 at the end of World War I to 8,800 and its treasury contained only $8.[15] Under their leadership the ZOA recovered, and by the end of the decade its membership was back to 46,000.

Zionism and Americanism

During his tenure at the provisional executive committee, Brandeis developed his own version of Zionism, at the center of which were two propositions: first, that an American could be a Zionist *and* a good American at the same time; second, that an American could be a Zionist without having any intention of moving to Palestine. Wrote Irving Howe, "Brandeis kept quietly assuring American Jews that support for Zionism did not mean they would have to go to Palestine themselves— being a Zionist, to recall a phrase from a Hoveve Zion [Lovers of Zion] faction, was a *mitzvah*, a good deed, and few Jews could resist the claims of a good deed."[16]

Brandeis's views on Zionism were by no means original. His views were most influenced by the philosopher Horace Kallen. Kallen was born in Silesia (then part of Prussia) in 1882 and came to the United States in 1887. His father was an Orthodox rabbi, but his son eschewed the formal practice of Judaism. As for Brandeis and Frankfurter, Zionism became Kallen's religion. Brandeis had met Kallen when Kallen was an undergraduate at Harvard, but they first discussed Zionism in 1913 when Kallen became a professor of philosophy at the University of Wisconsin. The next year the two men traveled together on a boat from Boston to New York to attend the founding meeting of the provisional executive committee at the Hotel Marseilles. Kallen quickly became part of Brandeis's inner circle, responsible, among other things, for Brandeis's draft of the ZOA's founding platform.

By the time the two men traveled together, Kallen had already worked out a theory of cultural pluralism, which was intended as an answer to the notion of the melting pot and to the rejection of "hyphenated Americanism." In early 1915, Kallen published an essay entitled "Democracy Versus the Melting-Pot." Brandeis employed a version of Kallen's theory in his most famous speech, "The Jewish Problem: How to Solve It," which he delivered later that year before a conference of Reform rabbis in New York.

In this speech, Brandeis distinguished between a "nation" and a "nationality."[17] According to Brandeis, nations like the United States, Great Britain, Belgium, and Switzerland could be composed of several or even many nationalities. A nationality was a "fact of nature." A nation, by contrast, is "largely the work of man." The attempt to impose a single nationality on a nation—leading to the domination of one nationality by another—had led, Brandeis argued, to "some of our greatest tragedies," including World War I.[18]

Within a nation, Brandeis argued, a nationality should enjoy the same kind of equal rights as an individual. Letting nationalities flower within a nation led to great advances in culture and civilization. Brandeis was channeling Kallen. In his essay "Democracy Versus the Melting Pot," Kallen had compared a nation and its nationalities to a symphony played by an orchestra. "As in an orchestra, every type of instrument has its specific timbre and tonality [and] its appropriate theme and melody in the whole symphony, so in society each ethnic group is the natural instrument, its spirit and culture are its theme and melody, and the harmony and dissonances and discords of them all make the symphony of civilization."[19]

Brandeis made a case for Jews in America in these terms. As a nationality, Jews deserved equal rights to the Irish, the Italians, and other nationalities. And by acting in accordance with what was unique to their nationality, Jews could make a special contribution to America. "America's fundamental law seeks to make real the brotherhood of man," Brandeis said. "That brotherhood became the Jewish fundamental law more than 2500 years ago."[20] In expressing their nationality, Jews were expressing America's highest aims.

But what about Zionism? Like other nationalities in America, Brandeis explained, Jews looked toward a home overseas—in their case, Palestine. In Palestine, Jews were trying to create a society based on democratic brotherhood. So, argued Brandeis, in being a Zionist and building a home for European Jews suffering from anti-Semitism, an American Jew was upholding the brotherhood of man. The American Zionist was fulfilling his responsibility as a Jew *and* as an American.

"Indeed, loyalty to America demands rather that each American Jew become a Zionist," Brandeis said. "For only through the ennobling effect of its striving can we develop the best that is in us and give to this country the full benefit of our great inheritance."[21]

Brandeis implicitly drew a distinction between the European Jew who migrated to Palestine to escape virulent anti-Semitism and the American Jew who benefited from "America's detachment from the old world." The American Jew doesn't necessarily feel any need to migrate to Palestine; but instead he feels, or should feel, a moral obligation to support his fellow Jews in seeking their freedom there. It was important, Brandeis suggested in his speech, to "develop in each new generation of Jews in America the sense of *noblesse oblige*." Zionism for Americans was a moral obligation to help European Jews escape oppression. Brandeis concluded:

> Every Irish American who contributed towards advancing home rule was a better man and a better American for the sacrifice he made. Every American Jew who aids in advancing the Jewish settlement in Palestine, though he feels that neither he nor his descendants will ever live there, will likewise be a better man and a better American for doing so.[22]

Brandeis countered the view, put forth by Gordon and Ben-Gurion, among others, that the only way to be a Zionist was to settle in Palestine. And he also attempted to free American Jews from charges of dual loyalty by undermining the charge itself. Being loyal to Palestine, he argued, was being loyal to America, because America depends on the special contribution of its nationalities, including their support for their homes overseas, and because, in expressing support for Palestine, American Jews were expressing support for American values. In this sense, dual loyalty *was good*.

Brandeis's argument was ingenious, but it also suffered from a glaring contradiction. Like Gottheil, Wise, and other early American Zionists, Brandeis extolled a Jewish Palestine, but failed to address what it meant to establish a Jewish homeland or nation where another nationality already lived. In his speeches, Brandeis pictured Palestine as an empty room that Jews were entering. In his New York speech, he described Palestine as "treeless and apparently sterile" and "hopelessly arid" before the colonists arrived.[23] Brandeis gave no hint that anyone besides Jews actually lived in this desert land.

If he had acknowledged that another people—indeed, another nationality—lived in Palestine, then a moral contradiction would have loomed: he and American Zionists would be attempting to impose a single nationality on a nation that already contained other nationalities, and where the other nationalities vastly outnumbered the Jews who were establishing colonies there. He would be proposing to do to Palestine exactly what he objected to Russians doing in Finland or Germans in Alsace-Lorraine. And the results would be similarly tragic.

Brandeis Supports Transfer

After he became a Supreme Court justice and resigned his positions in the Zionist movement, Brandeis stopped giving speeches regularly or publishing articles on Zionism, but he spoke occasionally to organizations meeting in Washington and continued to opine in private meetings and to correspond with his circle and with leaders in Palestine, Great Britain, and the United States. What Brandeis said about Palestine and Palestinian democracy continued to conflict with his liberal opinions on American politics and economics.

In 1919, when Brandeis took his only trip to Palestine, he stopped in Paris on the way to visit the American delegates to the Versailles peace conference and see Balfour. In his discussion with Balfour, Brandeis revealed that he held the most expansive interpretation of the Balfour Declaration—one that promised not merely a Jewish homeland *in* Palestine but the equivalent of a Jewish state of Palestine. Palestine's Arabs were not mentioned. According to the minutes of the conversation, Brandeis asked:

> First, that Palestine should be the Jewish homeland and not merely that there be a Jewish homeland in Palestine. That, he assumed, is the commitment of the Balfour Declaration . . . Secondly, there must be economic elbow room for a Jewish Palestine . . . Thirdly, the Justice urged that the future Jewish Palestine must have control of the land and the natural resources which are at the heart of a sound economic life.[24]

In a letter to Wilson, Brandeis warned him that France might insist on the Sykes-Picot agreement, which would "defeat full realization of the promise of the Jewish homeland." And he urged Wilson to hold out for a Palestine that "on the North . . . must include the Litani River and the water sheds of the Mermon. On the East, it must include the plains of the Jaulon [Golan] and the Hauron [Hauran]."[25] One State Department official commented, "The frontiers proposed by Justice Brandeis would double the size of the Palestine agreed to under the Sykes-Picot treaty and bring the northern frontier right up to Beirut and Damascus."[26] But Brandeis cabled Balfour that the absence of these lands would "cripple [the] Jewish homeland project."[27]

The British, of course, rejected Brandeis's map of Jewish Palestine, which was similar to what British Zionists had proposed in 1919, but Brandeis never relinquished the idea of a greater Palestine. While Brandeis disagreed with the tactics of the Revisionists and with their opposition to Labor Zionism and the Histadrut, he agreed with them on the borders of a future Jewish state. In a letter to Julian Mack in 1930, he wrote that "the Revisionists are right in the essence of much of what they ask . . . Transjordan must become a part of Palestine."[28] In October 1936, when discussions began with the British in the wake of the Arab rebellion, Wise wrote Weizmann that after the discussion that he, Mack, and Szold had had with Brandeis, they had come to feel as strongly as Brandeis that "there can be no solution of any Palestine problem without ending the divorce between Palestine and Transjordan."[29]

Even after Brandeis became aware that many Arabs lived in Palestine, he refused to believe that they would object to a Jewish state. In a presentation to the ZOA after he returned from Palestine in 1919, he said, "So far as the Arabs in Palestine are concerned, they do not present a serious obstacle. The conditions under which immigration must proceed are such that the Arab question, if properly handled by us, will in my opinion settle itself."[30] After the 1929 riots, Brandeis once again downplayed the "Arab question." At a Palestine economic conference in Washington in November, he declared, "I have no fear of the Arab or any other question . . . I learned in Palestine, and I believe it is still true, recent occurrences to the contrary notwithstanding, that the danger of the Arabs is grossly exaggerated."[31]

Brandeis accepted the specious view—promoted by Zionists in Palestine—that the riots were instigated by wealthy Arab absentee landlords and implemented by Bedouins under "the cover of religious fanaticism." "The recent difficulties are in my opinion due largely to persons who own land in Palestine but live elsewhere and who object to the emancipation of the previously subservient fellahin and the improvement in their condition resulting from Jewish settlement," Brandeis said. "It is important not to mistake stimulated excitement for something deep-seated in the Arab nature; and it is also important not to forget that there is a very large number of Bedouins constantly coming into Palestine who are not Palestinians and who, in these troublous times, were led to serve as the militant force."[32]

In speeches, Brandeis, echoing Herzl in *Altneuland*, argued that the answer to the "Arab question" was economic development that would benefit Arabs and Jews. To his credit, Brandeis advocated opening labor unions and enterprises to Arabs and combating malaria among Arabs and Jews. Brandeis gave considerable money to Hadassah's medical clinics in Palestine, which served Arabs and Jews, and suggested that Hadassah put up signs saying that the services are "provided by Jews for the benefit of Arabs as well as of Jews."[33] In August 1930, Brandeis wrote Robert Szold that there is

> ample evidence in support of the argument that with a proper British attitude Jews can live in harmony with the Arabs; that friendly relations are being developing in many places; and that raising of the level of Arab existence has been, and is, not only a necessary incident of the Jewish upbuilding of P[alestine], but the Jewish desire.[34]

But while Brandeis urged that Palestine's Jews improve the social and economic situation of the Arabs, he did not urge political accommodation with the Arabs. And as the rebellion continued, and reached fever pitch in 1936, Brandeis began to advocate privately a much different kind of answer to the Arab question: the transfer of the Arab population to Iraq or Transjordan or to other unpopulated Arab lands. As pieced together by the historian Rafael Medoff in his book *Zionism and the Arabs*, Brandeis became interested in the midthirties in a scheme developed by Edward Norman, a financier and philanthropist and member of the Jewish Agency's executive council.[35] Norman wanted to "induce a large portion of the peasants of Palestine over a period to move to Iraq."[36] De Haas had also convinced Brandeis that there had been a huge influx of Arabs, including Bedouins, into Palestine who could safely be sent back to where they came from. In October 1938, Brandeis tried to interest Roosevelt in the idea of transfer. Brandeis wrote Frankfurter about the meeting. The president, he wrote,

> went very far in our talk in his appreciation of the significance of Palestine—the need of keeping it whole and of making it Jewish. He was tremendously interested—and on the whole surprised—on learning of the great increase in Arab population since the War; and on learning of the plenitude of land for Arabs in Arab countries, about which he made specific inquiries.[37]

Roosevelt took this idea to the British, but he wrote Brandeis afterward that they did not accept that "there is a difference between the Arab population which was in Palestine prior to 1920 and the new Arab population."[38]

Brandeis's population figures were certainly bogus, but that is beside the point. What he was proposing to do to the Arabs was very similar to what the mufti and Awni Abd al-Hadi had proposed doing to the Jews in their testimony in December 1936 before the Peel Commission: deport any of those who immigrated after World War I. Like the Palestinian Arab leaders, Brandeis opposed partition; while they wanted an Arab Palestine, he wanted a Jewish Palestine—and one that could include Transjordan. While Brandeis was much friendlier to Ben-Gurion and the Labor Party, and opposed the Revisionist tactics, his answer to the Arab question mimicked those of the Revisionists, who welcomed Norman's schemes.

Liberalism and Zionism

The tenuous relationship between Brandeis's liberalism and Zionism was not unique, but characteristic of almost all the early-twentieth-century American liberals who were Zionists. Horace Kallen was a social democrat, even to the left of most liberals and progressives, and a founder of the New School for Social Research. In 1918 he published a pamphlet, *Constitutional Foundations of the New Zion*, in which he outlined his vision of a social democratic Palestine.

Kallen's Zion is a "fundamental democracy," but it is a Jewish state in which the land is the "inalienable possession of the whole Jewish people." The term "Arabs" appears once in a comprehensive list of possible identities that a people might assume in any state (not in Palestine in particular) in addition to being citizens. There is no discussion of Palestinian Arabs or the role they would have in Kallen's Zion. They are simply absent from Kallen's account of the new state. As Pinsker wrote of Europe's Jews, the Arabs are ghosts in Kallen's Palestine.

Faced with Arab rebellions in Palestine, Kallen, like Brandeis, attributed them to outside forces. The 1920–21 riots, Kallen wrote, were fomented by "Egyptian and Syrian agitators."[39] He blamed the 1929 riots on the British, who had "manufactured" Arab nationalism.[40] Like Brandeis, Kallen refused to acknowledge the conflict between Zionism and Palestinian Arab nationalism. He blamed the "disturbances" on outside agitators or on the British.

Felix Frankfurter was a close friend of Kallen's and a protégé of Brandeis's. He was born in Vienna in 1882 and had come to the United States in 1894 when his family emigrated. His parents were observant, but he became what he called a "reverent agnostic."[41] After graduating from Harvard Law School, he served under Henry Stimson in the Taft administration's State Department, but in 1912 he became a fervent supporter of Theodore Roosevelt's "new nationalism." Brandeis helped to recruit Frankfurter to Harvard Law School in 1919, where he championed labor legislation and defended Nicola Sacco and Bartolomeo Vanzetti, Italian immigrants and anarchists who were, in his view, wrongly convicted of murder. Frankfurter became a friend and advisor to Franklin Roosevelt, who appointed him to the Supreme Court in 1939.

Frankfurter, who had been a member of the American Jewish Committee, was recruited to Zionism by Brandeis. He shared Brandeis's view of Palestine. Appointed as a Zionist representative to the Versailles peace conference, he urged a greater Palestine that included Transjordan and southern Syria and Lebanon.[42] And in 1930 he wrote an essay in *Foreign Affairs* attacking the British white paper for calling for compromise between Palestine's Jews and Arabs.

Frankfurter began by quoting Mark Twain's image of Palestine as "withered fields" and "weeds" and "bitter waters where no living thing exists," which he contrasted with the Palestine of 1930. It was a trope that went back to the Russian Zionists of the 1880s, as well as to the travel books of the nineteenth century. Frankfurter claimed that the Zionist effort in Palestine had benefited Arabs and that the resistance to Zionism came from "economically powerful Arabs . . . exploiting the religious feeling of Arab masses whom they themselves oppress." He insisted that the riots in 1929 belied the fact that "Jew and Arab are collaborating in the thousand intimacies of their common life as builders of a new country." Frankfurter denied any nationalist sentiment among Palestine's Arabs, whom he portrayed as "simple folk" misled by "extremists."[43]

In criticizing the report by Sir John Hope Simpson on Jewish land purchases and the exclusion of Arab labor from Jewish enterprises, Frankfurter suggested settling Arabs within Transjordan rather than Palestine:

> Moreover, the availability for settlement in Transjordania, with its large areas of fertile lands so sparsely populated and the thin stream of the Jordan only formally separating it from Palestine, was deemed by Sir John outside his terms of reference. And yet Transjordania is probably the key to the problem of land congestion in Palestine. Certainly, hill Arabs can as readily be settled there as on the plains.[44]

Frankfurter would later join Brandeis and the members of his circle in opposing any concessions to the Arabs after the 1936 rebellion. He opposed the Peel Commission's proposal for partition and insisted that Transjordan be returned to Palestine.

After Brandeis joined the court, Stephen S. Wise became the public face of American Zionism. In 1925, he took charge of the Keren Hayesod, the main Zionist fund-raising group. In 1936 he became chairman of the Zionist Organization of America. He had described himself as an "ultra-liberal" and was one on civil rights, labor rights, and women's suffrage.[45] But in his statements on Palestine, he displayed an uncanny ignorance of the country's Arab population.

In 1926 a noted scientist, Henry S. Pritchett, visited Palestine on behalf of the Carnegie Endowment for International Peace. The report that Pritchett submitted after his return was remarkably prescient. Pritchett found Palestine's Arabs desiring to be "free of foreign control and to have their own government" but held in check by the English and by a "Zionist movement [that sought] to make Palestine the 'National Home of the Jews.'" Pritchett warned that the "aggressive movement for Jewish colonization" could stoke "bitterness" among Arabs and lead to conflict between Arabs and Jews. He pointed to the growing tension over the Wailing Wall as a sign that even a "small incident" could arouse "sharpness of feeling between Jew and Mohammedan."[46]

Wise dismissed Pritchett's findings. "Surely, Dr. Pritchett must have seen with what scrupulous care the Jewish settlers have regard for the interests of the Arab population," Wise said. "Does not Dr. Pritchett know that a referendum today of the Arab population of Palestine would result in a great majority in favor of Jewish settlements in Palestine, because of what Jews have brought to and done for Palestine within a generation, transforming waste places and denuded hillsides into richly flourishing settlements which have brought new standards of life to Arab, Christian and Jew in Palestine?" Wise insisted that "as a people who love peace, we have made every sacrifice in the interest of peace and understanding in Palestine, and we have achieved it."[47]

Three years later, when the riots over the Wailing Wall broke out, Wise blamed them on the British administration. It had "so bedeviled a situation as to deepen Jewish-Arab differences, which at the outset were superficial." He denied that Zionist policies had excluded Arab workers, and blamed Arab unemployment on "incurable Arab nomadism." He described the 1936 riots and rebellion as "nothing more than passing disorders that take place between neighboring populations during a period of mutual adjustment." At the same time, he rejected Arab demands for political representation. They were, he wrote after the 1929 riots, "the forging of a weapon by which to expel the Mandatory."[48] In 1935, Wise branded the proposal for a legislative council a "grievous threat" and the "gnawing pains which herald carcinoma."[49]

Like Brandeis, Wise embraced the territorial ambitions of the Revisionists, but not their rejection of domestic Labor Zionism. In 1930 he urged Viking to publish a book by Jabotinsky, and he assured Jabotinsky that, with the return of the Mack-Brandeis group, "we shall now have a militant organization prepared to stand against the . . . [Jewish] Agency over whose minds Magnes and Brit Shalom have a tragic domination."[50] Lipsky accused Wise of being an "abettor of the Revisionists."[51] In the Zionist Organization in 1937, Wise led the battle against partition and insisted upon the inclusion of Transjordan in a Jewish state.[52] He called the proposal for partition "the gravest betrayal of a most sacred trust."[53] Of Brandeis's circle, he was probably the most active in American liberal politics, but the least liberal in his view of Palestine.

Imperial Mind-set

Brandeis and his circle were not, of course, the only American Zionists to express illiberal views about Palestinian Arabs. The ZOA's official organ, *The New Palestine*, was filled with them. In September 1928, when the British had won Arab agreement to a legislative council, one author wrote that Arabs "are illiterate and live under indescribably primitive conditions. The march of these illiterates to the polls can easily be pictured. As they cannot read the ballot which is handed them, falsification of election results is the easiest thing in the world."[54]

The New Palestine repeatedly published articles urging the transfer of Arab Palestinians to Jordan. In 1930, Abraham Goldberg, a member of the ZOA administrative committee, declared that moving Arabs to Transjordan "would have been a statesmanlike solution of the so-called Arab problems in Palestine."[55] In June 1937 the magazine editorialized that "the courageous and just policy would be to give the Jewish government of the Jewish area the power to expropriate Arab landowners on the basis of an equitable price for their land, coupled with an arrangement for land to be placed at the disposal of the owners or cultivators in the Arab area or Transjordan."[56]

These pronouncements reflected a narrow Jewish nationalism that did not recognize the claims of other national groups. Why did liberals like Brandeis or Wise take these kind of stances? One obvious explanation is their sheer ignorance of Palestine and Arabs. It's telling that the two American liberals who applied the principles of liberalism to Palestine, Judah Magnes and Henrietta Szold, emigrated to Palestine and made the acquaintance of Palestinian Arabs. They advocated compromise between Zionism and Palestinian Arab nationalism—to the disgust of American liberals like Wise, who thought Magnes was "mad" and even "treasonable."[57]

American Zionists also heard reports from those whom Emanuel Neumann described as "visiting stars," like Weizmann, who raised money by downplaying the difficulties that Palestine's Jews faced from the Arabs.[58] But it was more than that. After American Zionists became aware after the 1921 riots that Palestine was not an unpopulated desert, and after Wise and Brandeis and other American Zionist leaders had visited Palestine, they still discounted and belittled the Arab resistance to Zionism. That may be partly because they wanted to deceive the public but knew better privately. Their private correspondence, however, does not suggest that.

One factor that may have encouraged this was the imperial mindset with which many Americans and Europeans viewed Palestine's Arabs. Herzl had displayed this mind-set in saying that Palestinian Arabs could be won over to Jewish rule by the prosperity that Jews would bring to Palestinians. More advanced peoples might covet self-rule, but primitives would be satisfied with bread on the table. Brandeis and his circle shared this view. Palestine's Arabs, Wise wrote, "do not desire anything particularly except food. They are . . . in the depths of primitive life."[59] Frankfurter described Palestine's Arabs as "simple folk." Brandeis was certain that Arabs would appreciate "the work which has been done by the Jews for Arabs" in order to live "among them in perfect amity."[60]

Americans, of course, didn't have to look to Europe to acquire a hierarchical view of humanity that justified conquest. Americans had invoked the need to civilize savage races to justify Indian removal and Manifest Destiny. Brandeis and his circle viewed the Zionist settlers as "pioneers," "pilgrims," and "puritans" and the Arabs as "Indians." The comparison was partly an apt one. America was the original settler colony where the immigrants displaced the native inhabitants and eventually established a state of their own. Brandeis saw it as *justifying* Jews displacing Arabs in Palestine.

Until well after World War II, the rout of the Indians was seen as a triumph of civilization over savagery. In his *Winning of the West*, Theodore Roosevelt wrote of the Indian Wars that "the struggle could not possibly have been avoided. Unless we were willing that the whole continent west of the Alleghenies should remain an unpeopled waste, the hunting ground of savages, *war was inevitable* . . . It is wholly impossible to avoid conflicts with the weaker race."[61] Brandeis and other progressives saw the conflict between the Jews and Arabs in Palestine similarly.

When the Arab rebellion began, Brandeis drew an analogy between the Arabs and the Indians. In September 1929 he wrote Felix Frankfurter, "As against the Bedouins, our pioneers are in a position not unlike the American settlers against the Indians."[62] He repeated the comparison in a speech at a Zionist conference in Washington in November 1929. Of the riots that had occurred, he said:

> The situation reminds me of that in America, when the settlers who founded the Massachusetts Bay Colony had to protect themselves against the Indians. Only a few weeks ago I was reading an address on Petersham, where I once had a summer home. The orator described Colonial life there. Every man, as he went to church, stacked his gun at the church door, prepared for an incursion of the Redskin. There was danger in that settlement. But it is a great thing for the world, for business and industry, that the danger was incurred.[63]

At the urging of his close friend Stephen Wise and with funding from Macy's Department Store owner Nathan Straus, the Reverend John Haynes Holmes, a noted New York liberal, visited Palestine in 1929 and wrote a book about it, *Palestine Today and Tomorrow: A Gentile's Survey of Zionism*. Holmes was more sympathetic to Arab demands for self-rule than Wise was, but he, like Brandeis, saw Palestine through the prism of Pilgrims and Indians. "As I met and talked with these toilers on the land, I could think of nothing but the early English settlers who came to the bleak shores of Massachusetts, and there amid winter's cold in an untilled soil, among an unfriendly native population, laid firm and sure the foundations of our American Republic," he wrote. "It is obvious that the native Arabs, while no less stubborn and savage than the American Indians, cannot be removed from the scene."[64]

By World War II a decade later, Americans were beginning to have doubts about the justification for Indian removal. When the ZOA later reprinted Brandeis's 1929 address in a collection of his speeches and writings, they excised his comparison of Arabs and Indians. But its presence in that speech shows the extent to which American liberals in the early part of the century viewed the conflict through a mind-set developed over the prior two centuries to justify the conquest of one people by another.

Could the very commitment to Zionism have blinded Brandeis and his circle to the way their attitude toward Palestine contradicted their commitment to liberalism and democracy? Could it have blinded them to injustices committed in Palestine and led them to espouse patently contradictory theories of nations and nationalities? Saying that it was because of their commitment to Zionism seems too broad, but it is fair to draw a contrast between the kind of Zionism that they backed and that which Magnes and Szold supported.

Brandeis and his circle traced their own Zionism back to Theodor Herzl rather than to Ahad Ha'am. They were committed to establishing a Jewish state as soon as possible. There is not a necessary link between this commitment and the blindness to injustice, but there seems to be a psychological process that drove those who espoused *political* Zionism to rationalize away injustices to Palestine's Arabs and subordinate other liberal concerns to the single goal of achieving a Jewish state. It encouraged the willful ignorance that Wise displaced in critiquing Pritchett's report and the dismissal by Brandeis and his circle of the Arab rebellions.

Jabotinsky and the Revisionists reveled in this single-mindedness. They believed that the singular end of a Jewish state justified the means by which it was achieved. But Brandeis and his circle were liberals and progressives, just as Katznelson and Ben-Gurion were Socialists; they could not adopt a Thrasymachean might-is-right theory of justice or dismiss moral considerations altogether, as Wilansky suggested in 1919; they had to find moral justifications for their positions. But the justifications they adopted were rationalizations. A similar kind of psychological process would drive Abba Hillel Silver, who would lead the Zionist movement after Brandeis and Wise, and who in the 1930s would move from cultural to political Zionism.

9

ABBA HILLEL SILVER AND THE ZIONIST LOBBY

In April 1944, Rabbi Abba Hillel Silver, cochairman of the American Zionist Emergency Council (AZEC), met with Ohio Republican senator Robert Taft, who headed the platform committee at his party's upcoming convention. Silver convinced the dour Taft to back a provision to make Palestine a Jewish state. But opponents on the committee threatened to scuttle the proposal. It was only due to Silver's continuing pressure that Republicans voted at their July convention for a platform that called for Palestine to "be constituted as a free and democratic commonwealth."

The Republicans omitted the word "Jewish" before "commonwealth," but the provision was widely construed as endorsing a Jewish Palestine. The platform included, however, something Silver had not urged: condemnation of President Roosevelt for failing to get the British to "carry out . . . the Balfour Declaration." That spelled trouble for Silver within his own organization.

Silver lobbied Taft over the objection of his AZEC cochair Stephen Wise, an enthusiastic Roosevelt backer. Wise planned to campaign on his own for Roosevelt and wanted to keep the Zionist organization out of presidential politics. And Wise's enthusiasm about Roosevelt was shared by the Jewish electorate—in 1944, over 90 percent of Jews backed the president. When Silver recounted his success among Republicans at a meeting of AZEC's executive committee, Wise and other committee members rebuked him for urging a resolution that ended up attacking Roosevelt.

Silver was angered. "Many of the members of the committee," he complained to his friend and ally Emanuel Neumann, "are far more involved and committed in one way or another to the Democratic Party than they are to Zionism, and . . . in the case of a conflict of loyalties, they will sacrifice Zionist interests."[1] That wasn't strictly true. Wise, for one, insisted that his commitment to Democratic liberalism and wholehearted support for Roosevelt did not conflict with his Zionism, but Silver had a point.

Silver put the Zionist cause above party politics—and, in effect, above any domestic agenda. Silver was accused later of being a Republican, but his voting record—he voted three times for Roosevelt—showed no sign of a lasting partisan identification. If anything, Silver was a liberal like Wise who had championed unemployment compensation in the 1920s—he even helped draft the proposals in Ohio—and had resigned from the local chamber of commerce because it opposed labor unions. In a 1932 sermon he had insisted that only Norman Thomas, the socialist presidential candidate, understood the country's economic problems.

But his action as an individual was different from his actions as a Zionist leader. If a Democrat didn't fully endorse Zionism, Silver tried to use the Jewish vote and Jewish contributions against him. And he was willing to praise a Republican for his support of Zionism even if that helped him against a Democrat. That reflected a different view of American Zionist politics from that of Wise and members of the Brandeis circle.

Wise, Brandeis, and Mack encouraged public demonstrations or letter-writing campaigns over particular issues. Unlike the leaders of the American Jewish Committee, who operated behind the scenes, they openly rallied Jewish support for an issue. But they still had not broken decisively with the older tradition of the *shtadlanim*. Brandeis and Wise, with their connections to Wilson and Roosevelt, and Frankfurter, with his link to Hoover's secretary of state, Henry Stimson, and to Roosevelt, represented a continuation of that tradition. But Silver, who succeeded them as the leader of the Zionist movement, represented a sharp break. With Silver, the modern Zionist lobby began to emerge in American politics—and with it a less defensive but also more narrowly pressure-group-oriented Zionism even less inclined to consider the Arab side of the growing conflict in Palestine.

Intellectualized Thunder

Abraham Hillel Silver, who became known as "Abba," was born in Lithuania in 1893. His father, a rabbi, emigrated to America in 1898, where he taught at a Hebrew school on the Lower East Side of New York. Silver came to the United States with his mother and three siblings in 1902. At home, the Silvers observed Orthodox Jewish customs and even conversed in Hebrew, but Silver's father insisted that his children adapt to American ways. Upon his arrival, Moses Silver took the eleven-year-old Abba to a barber to shear off his long sideburns (called *peyes*) and sent him to public schools. Whereas many first-generation Eastern Europeans clung to the *Yiddishkeit* culture, Silver's principal link to his heritage was through the practice of Judaism, the use of Hebrew, and support for Zionism.

Silver's father was a Zionist, and in honor of Herzl's death in 1904 he persuaded his two sons to establish the Dr. Herzl Zion Club, which met initially at the Silver home and conducted much of its meetings in Hebrew. Its members included Emanuel Neumann, who was born in neighboring Latvia and was the same age as Silver, and who became Silver's lifelong friend—one of the few who addressed him as "Abba" in correspondence—and his closest ally in the Zionist movement. By 1907 the precocious Abba had become the club's leader, and he spoke that year on its behalf at the convention of the Federation of American Zionists.

Silver followed his father, grandfather, and great-grandfather into the rabbinate, but instead of enrolling in an Orthodox yeshiva he matriculated at the Hebrew Union College in Cincinnati, the citadel of Reform Judaism. The Hebrew Union was also a bastion of anti-Zionism, but something of a thaw had set in by Silver's arrival. After having purged three Zionist professors in 1907, the school hired David Neumark, a disciple of Ahad Ha'am, who would become the chair of its philosophy department and would also become Silver's mentor.

Silver was drawn to Reform Judaism by its commitment to the prophetic ethical mission that Jews would be a light unto nations. Silver was also attracted by Reform's attempt to blend into American society. "I and my young friends were reaching out, quite unconsciously," Silver wrote later, "for a more liberal type of Judaism."[2] In addition, Silver took comfort at the time from the fact that Wise and Judah Magnes were prominent Reform rabbis *and* Zionists.

Silver was the valedictorian of his class and rose swiftly in rabbinical circles. After two years at a Wheeling, West Virginia, temple, he was invited to become the rabbi at Cleveland's Temple-Tifereth Israel (dubbed "the Temple"), one of America's wealthiest and most prestigious synagogues. Silver's rise was due to his intellect and oratory—what one admirer called his "intellectualized thunder."[3] Leon Feuer, who served as Silver's assistant in Cleveland, described him in the pulpit as a "tall, gaunt figure in a cutaway coat . . . the dark eyes on fire with passionate conviction, occasionally tightly closed as though peering intently inward, the arms outstretched, the long talon-like but beautifully molded fingers seeming to encompass the entire audience which sat tense and utterly silent for fear of breaking the hypnotic mood, the incomparably beautiful voice gliding over the tonal range."[4]

As a Reform rabbi, Silver differed from Wise and the first generation of Reform rabbis who were Zionists. Wise was a rebel within the Reform denomination. He ignored the Central Conference of American Rabbis, the main Reform body. By contrast, Silver served on the leadership bodies of Reform Judaism and raised funds for and sent his protégés to Hebrew Union. Silver placed more importance on his profession and the promotion of Judaism than Wise did. At the Free Synagogue in New York, Wise emphasized social action and community service. At the Temple, Silver reinstituted Hebrew and stripped away activities that weren't relevant to religious education. While Wise boasted that he was more familiar with the Transcendentalists than the Talmud, one of Silver's early admirers said that he "knew Talmud like the Yeshiva prodigies in the old country."[5]

Silver kept many of the outward trappings of Reform Judaism. He held services on Sunday rather than Saturday. He offered confirmation rather than bar mitzvah to Temple teenagers. He dressed elegantly in the dark suit, white shirt, and tie of the Protestant minister. (When Silver returned to New York after graduating from Hebrew Union, Emanuel Neumann complained that "he seemed goyish. It all smacked of 'assimilation.'")[6] And Silver upheld the idea of America as a promised land in its own right. In 1926, Silver published a poem titled "America" that ended with these purple lines:

> God fashioned a nation in love,
> blessed it with Purpose sublime
> and called it America!

But Silver sought to change Reform Judaism by reintroducing some elements of Orthodoxy—most notably, the use of Hebrew—and by attempting to reconcile Reform Judaism with Zionism. Silver anticipated, and helped to bring about, many of the changes that overtook Reform Judaism in the late 1930s and that brought it closer to the growing Conservative denomination.

Silver and Ahad Ha'am

Under Neumark's influence, Silver became an adherent of Ahad Ha'am's cultural Zionism. He saw Zionism not as a defense against anti-Semitism but as a means of reviving the religious culture of Judaism. He envisaged Jewish Palestine as a cultural center of world Judaism that would include the American Diaspora. He rejected Herzl and Brandeis's objective of a Jewish state, and David Ben-Gurion's narrow definition of a Zionist as someone who had settled or planned to settle in Palestine.

Silver's cultural Zionism led to his first of many clashes with Wise. In 1916, when the Temple's longtime rabbi Moses Gries announced his retirement, Silver applied for the job. But there was one problem. Gries adamantly opposed Zionism. To sway Gries, Silver wrote him a letter trying to explain his Zionism. "The hope," Silver wrote:

> which prompts thousands of faithful Jews today to safe-guard their precious heritage, to intensify their Jewish life and to enrich its content by establishing a spiritual and cultural center in Palestine cannot but meet with my sympathy and approval. Not that I see in the establishment of such a center a solution of all Jewish problems the world over, but that such a center may be contributory towards a galvanization of Jewish life the world over . . . For me the political phase of

> Zionism has at all times been secondary and incidental and with the emancipation of Russian Jewry, it has become negligible.[7]

Silver's explanation satisfied Gries and the Temple's board of directors, but after he had assumed his post, Silver received a sharp rebuke from Wise. In a letter, Wise wrote that he had "learned not alone to my regret but to my dismay, that it was understood when you were elected to the pulpit that you were not a Zionist; that as someone put it, you had 'passed muster' after consultation with Dr. Gries with respect to Zionism; that, as it was put, your Zionism was so qualified as to be altogether unobjectionable."[8]

Silver was indignant. Describing himself as a "disciple of Ahad Ha'am," he wrote that "any suggestion which would intimate that I have revised or modified my views in order to 'pass muster' . . . is downright calumny and slander."[9] He enclosed the letter he had sent to Gries.[10] Silver was probably right to be annoyed. In speeches and sermons over the next fifteen years—well after he faced any need to ingratiate himself with the Temple's directors—Silver expressed similar views about cultural and political Zionism.

Silver's concern was to reconcile Reform Judaism's idea of mission with Zionism. Reform leaders of the late nineteenth century had contended that the exile and Diaspora were not a great misfortune but an opportunity for Jews to spread their ethical message. Attempts to reconstitute a Jewish state in Palestine would appear to run counter to that mission. Silver argued—consistent with Ahad Ha'am—that the creation of a Jewish national home would enhance that mission by establishing a center from which the international revival of Judaism could radiate. "I would not wish my people to become another little statelet, another little Montenegro somewhere, merely for the sake of existing as a separate entity there," Silver declared in a sermon in February 1926. "I wish my people to continue its historic mission as a light-bringer unto mankind."[11]

Like Ahad Ha'am, Silver rejected Herzl and political Zionism's argument that the main reason for a Jewish homeland was as a refuge from anti-Semitism. "A people that constructs a philosophy of life on suffering is a neurotic people, and I would be humiliated if the only claim which Israel had upon us was the fact of its age-old suffering and martyrdom," he wrote. "It isn't the misery of our people which makes

Palestine a burning issue today, nor is it anti-Semitism . . . It is not the persecuted bodies of my people that need Palestine so much as the persecuted and harassed spirit of the race that needs a refuge and a sanctuary."[12]

His prescription for American Jews was to "remain loyal to their faith," "preserve their racial and historical identity," and be a "contributing force to civilization."[13] He denied that American Jews had to worry about anti-Semitism. "What bothers me," he said, "what hurts me to the quick, is to see the moral debacle of our people, the breakup of moral idealism, the encroaching of materialism and the saturation of the whole body of Israel in this land with all the vileness and the corruption which comes from prosperity too quickly gotten and not readily assimilated."[14]

Silver did not, however, share Ahad Ha'am's awareness of the moral contradiction that lurked at the base of political Zionism: that by attempting to establish a Jewish state in Palestine, Zionists would be "encroaching upon the native population." That awareness also underlay Magnes's rejection of political Zionism. In much of Silver's writings and sermons, he either ignored Arabs or repeated the neo-imperial bromides about the Jews in Palestine clearing "the jungles" and bringing the benefits of Western civilization and economics to "a small, backward Oriental province."[15] But in the fall of 1929, Silver showed some appreciation for the moral difficulties of Zionism. In the wake of the riots in Palestine, Silver proposed dividing Palestine into Jewish and Arab cantons.[16] He also initially took seriously the proposal for a legislative council that would include Arabs and Jews.

The Nazi Threat

In the 1920s, Silver participated in the Zionist movement primarily as a fund-raiser for the World Zionist Organization's Keren Hayesod (Palestine Foundation Fund), which financed cultural efforts in the Diaspora as well as Palestinian and economic and social development. He spoke for Zionist causes and attended World Zionist Organization meetings and was widely esteemed for his oratory, but kept clear of any official leadership post in Zionist politics. He told one Zionist Organization of America official that he wished "to be a freelancer in the movement."[17] In the mid-1930s, however, Silver's attitude toward the Zionist movement and political Zionism began to change. The key event was the Nazi conquest of power, which Silver witnessed when he visited Germany in March 1933.

Silver quickly grasped the Nazi threat. The Nazi government, he wrote that year, "is deadlier than those of the Czars."[18] Silver worked with Wise and the American Jewish Congress on a boycott of German goods, and he became a vice president of the anti-Nazi American League for the Defense of Jewish Rights. With the United States and Western Europe virtually closed to German Jewish émigrés, he began to accord Palestine's role as a refuge against European anti-Semitism greater importance.

In May 1936, Silver warned at the graduation ceremonies of Hebrew Union College that Nazism "is a plague of lethal ideas, sweeping over the world today, victimizing the Jew wherever it reaches."[19] He advised the newly ordained rabbis to reaffirm the classic Jewish tradition against the "new paganism," but he also urged them to support "the Jewish National Homeland in Palestine." While he promised that this homeland "may become in the days to come a vast dynamo of creative Jewish cultural and spiritual elements," he no longer belittled its role as a refuge from anti-Semitism. A Jewish homeland, he said, "will remove the element of desperation—of fighting with our backs to the wall," and it will "serve as a haven for hosts of our people who must now seek new homes in a world where doors are everywhere closing."[20]

The Nazis turned Silver into a cultural *and* political Zionist. Silver accepted the new logic of political Zionism: if the Jews of Central Europe had to flee, and if the West was closed off to them, their only recourse was to go to Palestine; and the only way to guarantee that Palestine remained open to them in the face of Arab hostility and British resistance was to turn Palestine into a Jewish state. As Silver put it, "Our right to immigration is predicated upon the right to build the Jewish Commonwealth in Palestine. They are interlinked and inseparable."[21] Silver's acceptance of this logic led him to more full-fledged participation in the Zionist movement.

Silver didn't just abandon his equivocation about a Jewish state; he moved toward the Revisionist position on Palestine. Upon his return from Germany in 1933, he urged American Zionists to "think rapidly in terms of a 'great' Palestine capable of maintaining a large Jewish population . . . What is indicated is . . . a union of the two mandates of Palestine and Transjordania and the opening up of the empty and potentially rich ground of Transjordania for Jewish settlement." Silver also adopted the prevailing rationalization for Zionist colonization. Arab leaders, he argued, would be amenable because "they have seen . . . the improved conditions of the Palestine Arab brought about by Jewish immigration and enterprise."[22] In a newspaper column in 1934, he wrote that "Palestine must have more land . . . The separation of Trans-Jordania from Palestine is a political fiction."[23] The Nazi threat accelerated Silver's turn away from any accommodation with Palestine's Arabs. In 1935, when the Arabs, with British backing, reintroduced the idea for a legislative council, Silver denounced it as "legislative sabotage."[24]

In July 1937, Silver attended the fortieth annual conference of the Zionist Organization of America, at which he joined the Brandeis group in opposing a proposal for partitioning Palestine that the Peel Commission was rumored to be recommending. "We have no right to sign away the historic claims of the Jewish people nor the future of our children," Silver told the ZOA delegates.[25] The next month, at the Zionist Congress in Zurich, Silver opposed the Peel Commission's proposal.

Silver had ample justification in taking up the cause of political Zionism in response to the Nazi threat and the refusal of countries in the West to accept Jewish immigrants. But in moving toward political Zionism, Silver went down the same path as other political Zionists from Herzl to Brandeis and Wise: he dismissed the idea that Palestine's Arabs could have any claim to political rights within Palestine. He adopted a selective morality in viewing the future of Palestine: what was good for Palestine's Jews became good. That would become the mantra of the Zionist movement in America.

Silver's embrace of political Zionism led him, as it had the members of Brandeis's circle, to ignore or rationalize away the "Arab question." In 1939, when Hadassah, under the influence of Henrietta Szold, proposed that the ZOA establish an Arab-Jewish committee to ponder Arab-Jewish relations in a future Palestine, Silver fretted that it was "a potential source of trouble to the Zionist movement."[26]

Silver also kept his distance from any attempts to rescue Europe's Jews by arranging for them to emigrate somewhere other than Palestine. In 1938, James McDonald, whom Roosevelt designated as chairman of his advisory commission on refugees, and as a representative to an international conference at Évian to gather support for Jews who wanted to flee, tried to raise money for the refugees from Silver, who was then heading the United Jewish Appeal. Silver turned him down flat.

"Though I had known Rabbi Silver rather well," McDonald wrote in his diary, "I was shocked by his attitude toward not only the earmarking of this fund, but also toward the Évian effort and everything which has followed it. In substance, Mr. Silver not only said that he was personally opposed to earmarking the fund, but that he had been opposed to the Évian effort . . . that he thought the work of the President's Committee was useless . . ."[27] Silver was probably right to be skeptical about the Évian Conference, but he remained resistant to any efforts at rescue that didn't involve Palestine.

Silver Joins the Leadership

At the 1939 World Zionist Congress, the delegates created the American-based Emergency Committee for Zionist Affairs. The committee, chaired by Wise, was intended to play a coordinating role in the United States similar to that which Brandeis's provisional committee played in World War II. Neumann urged Silver to take an active political role in the Zionist movement. Silver told him that the proper moment had not come but that he might reconsider if the United States went to war. "At that point, I may do what you suggest," he told Neumann.[28]

What began to galvanize Silver was the reaction to a speech he made in May 1942 at an Emergency Committee for Zionist Affairs meeting in New York. The committee organized a conference at the Biltmore Hotel to discuss the fate of Zionism. More than six hundred delegates attended, including Weizmann and Ben-Gurion, who was head of the Jewish Agency. Ben-Gurion, convinced that the fate of Jewish Palestine was in America's hands, had started coming to the United States in 1938 to urge American support for a "Jewish commonwealth," a term that left open the possibility that the Jewish state would be an autonomous member of the British Commonwealth.

At the Biltmore conference, Ben-Gurion renewed his call for an end to the mandate and the establishment of a Jewish state. "A Jewish Palestine will arise," he declared. "It will redeem forever our sufferings and do justice to our national genius."[29] Silver agreed. He chided the "Bourbon mentalities" of those Jews who opposed a Jewish state.[30] And he dismissed "the unreal, spurious and dangerous" distinctions between "political Zionism" and "philanthropic humanitarianism."[31] Inspired by Silver and Ben-Gurion, the conference adopted the Biltmore Declaration. It pledged to support establishment of "Palestine . . . as a Jewish commonwealth integrated into the structure of the new democratic world."[32]

At the time, the American Zionist movement lacked an acknowledged leader. Brandeis had died the previous year. Wise, who chaired the meeting, was sixty-eight years old and ill. Mack died the next year. Frankfurter had withdrawn from public Zionist activities after joining the Supreme Court. And Neumann and Lipsky were relative lightweights. "In the momentum of the conference," Melvin Urofsky wrote in his history of American Zionism, "leadership passed to a new and more vigorous group, led by the militant David Ben-Gurion . . . and by Rabbi Abba Hillel Silver."[33]

At the conference, Weizmann lobbied Silver to take over the Emergency Committee, which had had little impact under Wise's chairmanship. Neumann, who had quit the Emergency Committee, also pressured him to take over. And so did Lipsky and Jewish Agency representative Nahum Goldmann, with whom Silver had clashed. Even Wise told Weizmann that he wanted Silver "to take over the too onerous duties of the chairmanship of the Emergency Committee."[34] But Wise, it turned out, was reluctant to give up control of the organization.

Silver, for his part, said he would take the job only if he could have "a concentration of the political work in my hands." He was incapable of sharing leadership. Leon Feuer recalled, "Once having made up his mind, he had supreme confidence in his own judgment, particularly in the areas of Jewish life where he considered himself the expert and, therefore, the authority."[35] Goldmann put it less charitably: "He was a typical autocrat, possessing the authority and self confidence to command, but not the flexibility to understand his opponent."[36] Wise and Silver finally signed an agreement in August 1943 to share power as cochairmen, but the matter was not really settled, and soon after he settled in the job, Silver would begin to clash with Wise. And the issue wouldn't simply be two strong personalities vying for control, but two different approaches to Zionist politics.

American Jewish Conference

The clash came over the platform of a new Jewish organization. In January 1943, at the urging of Wise and Weizmann, Henry Monsky, the president of B'nai B'rith, a hundred-year-old Jewish community service organization, convened a meeting of Jewish organizations. The seventy-eight men and women agreed to found an "American Jewish Assembly" to plan, as Wise put it, for the "vital postwar problems of the Jewish people."[37]

The American Jewish Committee, fearful that Zionists would dominate the proceedings, refused to attend the planning session, but Wise and Monsky worked out an agreement with Judge Joseph Proskauer, the new president of the committee. In return for Monsky and Wise changing the new organization's name from "assembly" to the weaker "conference" and delaying any discussion of Zionism and Palestine until after the founding meeting, the American Jewish Committee agreed to attend.

Silver and Neumann were not part of these initial discussions, but along with more than five hundred delegates they attended the opening session of the conference at the Waldorf Astoria on August 29, 1943, just after Silver had agreed to cochair the Emergency Committee. Silver was surprised to learn that the issue of Palestine statehood was to be deferred, and when he heard Wise speak without mentioning the need for a Jewish Palestine, he exploded in rage. He confronted Wise, accusing him of betraying Zionism. "What happened at the Biltmore?" Silver exclaimed. "We finally have a slogan, a battle cry for a Jewish state, and you, who claim to be a Zionist leader, refuse to talk about it!"[38] Neumann, who was present, later wrote, "In my whole Zionist career I had never witnessed such an awesome tongue-lashing as Silver administered to Wise; it was embarrassing to witness."[39]

Neumann persuaded Silver, who had been left off the program, to introduce a resolution committing the conference to establishing a Jewish state, and Neumann got the American Jewish Congress to give the podium to Silver. Silver gave his greatest speech. (That speech and Brandeis's speech "The Jewish Problem and How to Solve It" were the two most important addresses by American Zionists from the movement's founding until the recognition of Israel.) In rich, textured prose filled with historical allusion and metaphor, Silver laid out the case for the conference endorsing a Jewish state and for proceeding boldly rather than cautiously to lobby for it. Silver marshaled all the arguments that Zionists had invoked over the prior sixty years.

In the wake of revelations at the end of 1942 of Nazi genocide, Silver's appeal was rooted emotionally in the horror of the Nazi final solution:

> From the infested, typhus-ridden ghetto of Warsaw, from the death-block of Nazi-occupied lands where myriads of our people are awaiting execution by the slow or the quick method, from a hundred concentration camps which befoul the map of Europe, from the pitiful ranks of our wandering hosts over the entire face of the earth, comes the cry: "Enough; there must be a final end to all this, a sure and certain end!"

Silver also insisted that Jews were owed Palestine because of "their historic connection" with the land and because of the "incalculable and unspeakable suffering of our people and the oceans of blood which we have shed." He asked, "Should all this not be compensated for finally and at long last with the re-establishment of a free Jewish Commonwealth?" And he warned that only through establishing a Jewish Commonwealth could Jews escape future attempts to eradicate them. Nazi genocide was "the frightful aggravation of a situation which has continuously darkened the pages of history since the beginning of our dispersion," he said. Jews could escape anti-Semitism only by ending "our national homelessness."[40]

Silver's speech won over the delegates, who, after thunderous applause, rose to their feet to sing "Hatikvah," the Zionist national anthem, which includes the lyrics "to be a free people in our own land." Lipsky admitted that "the electric excitement it created seemed to bind every syllable uttered by the speaker to the nervous system of every listener."[41] Afterward, the delegates overwhelmingly voted to approve a resolution calling for the reconstitution of Palestine "as the Jewish Commonwealth."[42]

Silver's speech set the tone, and laid out the arguments, for what would become the American Zionist position. Unlike Wise or the "moderates," he aimed not to co-opt or conciliate the non-Zionist opposition but to bludgeon them into accepting the majority position. (Three delegates from the American Jewish Committee walked out after the delegates approved the resolution for a Jewish commonwealth.) "I am for unity," Silver said, "but here I must point out in all humility that unity of action in democratic organization depends *not* upon unanimity but upon the willingness of the minority to submit to the decisions of the majority."[43]

Silver's speech showed the extent to which he had embraced political Zionism. He forthrightly argued for a Jewish state and not a homeland. He portrayed the state as a refuge from an endemic anti-Semitism rather than as a spiritual or cultural center. He portrayed anti-Semitism as inescapable and integral to all non-Jewish majority societies. He dismissed "new immigration opportunities in other countries for fleeing refugees." And he cited the Arabs only as adversaries and not as a people who had a moral claim to the same lands. Silver's Zionism was now based on the relentless pursuit of ethno-religious nationalism, which was justified by centuries of persecution culminating in the Holocaust.

Subsequently, at the Statler Hotel in New York in March 1944, Silver hinted at support for a Jewish and an Arab-free Palestine. "The prosperity of Palestine will stimulate the prosperity of all adjacent Arab countries," he said. "The Jews are truly pro-Arab—perhaps the only truly pro-Arab people in the world, for we realize that the future prosperity of the Jewish national home is bound up with the prosperity of the entire Arab world which enclaves it. But the progress and development of the Arabs need not be achieved at the sacrifice of the Jewish National Home which at best occupies a fraction of a fraction of the lands open to Arab growth and development."[44] Later, Silver would contemplate schemes for transferring Palestine's Arabs.

Token Gestures

The challenge facing Silver was not just to win a conference dominated by American Zionists but to influence American administrations since Wilson's that had been leery of giving the Zionists more than token support. In 1922, Zionist leaders in Europe asked their American counterparts to obtain an endorsement from Congress and the White House of the Balfour Declaration's call for a Jewish national home in Palestine.

They thought a resolution would speed the League of Nations' approval of the British mandate and boost fund-raising internationally. Congress passed a resolution, but only after a House report assured its members that the resolution "commits us to no foreign obligation or entanglement."[45] It had no effect on the negotiation over the mandate.

During and after the 1929 riots, the Zionist movement and its supporters in Congress pressured the Hoover administration to intercede—first in Palestine itself and then with the British. New York congressman Samuel Dickstein demanded that Secretary of State Stimson send warships to Palestine. William Z. Spiegelman, the editor of the Jewish Telegraphic Agency, advised Stimson that "it is the human duty of other world powers to take over the mandate for Palestine."[46] Zionists in the United States blamed American inaction on State Department treachery and even anti-Semitism, but the Hoover administration was acting on long-standing American principles of letting another imperial power—and Britain in particular—manage its own possessions and of intervening only when Americans were directly threatened.[47]

In 1936, when the British seemed ready to mollify the rebellious Arabs, American Zionists appealed to the Roosevelt administration to prevent Britain from reducing Jewish immigration to Palestine. Wise, who had become chairman of the ZOA that year, wrote Roosevelt in the spring. Then in the summer he and Frankfurter asked Samuel Rosenman, Roosevelt's speechwriter and aide, to convey a message to the president.[48] But Roosevelt forwarded their messages to the State Department, which dealt with them indirectly by having the ambassador to Britain inform the British foreign secretary that "influential Jewish circles in the United States are deeply concerned about the possible consequences of suspending Jewish immigration into Palestine."[49]

In 1937, in response to the Peel Commission's proposal to partition Palestine, Zionists got the Senate to pass a resolution calling on the secretary of state, Cordell Hull, to convey American "anxiety over the situation" and to insist that Britain consult the United States before "any modification of the mandate."[50] This time, perhaps because of the Senate resolution, Hull sent a more pointed communication to the British. The British responded by politely telling the State Department to mind its own business.

Roosevelt was sympathetic to the plight of European Jews, but, unlike Wilson, he did not embrace a biblical Zionism that inclined him to back a Jewish state of Palestine. He wanted to help the Jews escape persecution, but not necessarily by creating a Jewish state. They could flee, he thought, to Uganda or to Guyana. The president was also over-whelmed by isolationist and anti-immigrant sentiments at home and later by the exigencies of fighting a world war on two fronts with Brit-ain as the United States' closest ally. Roosevelt and the State Depart-ment were reluctant to press the British over an issue that was at best a low priority. Silver's goal on the Emergency Committee was to get the Roosevelt administration and Congress to do more than token gestures, and he was willing to depart from past practice to do so.

Passing Resolutions

By 1943, Silver and many of the Zionist leaders in the United States, Great Britain, and Palestine shared Ben-Gurion's view that the center of foreign support for making Palestine a Jewish state was passing from a beleaguered Britain to the United States. In a meeting that year of the Emergency Committee, Nahum Goldmann declared, "I don't think the British Empire will play the role after this war that it played twenty years ago. It will be a combination of three powers, at least, after this war—the United States, Great Britain, and Russia . . . To change the Zionist position today depends 80 percent to 90 percent on the United States."[51] No one disagreed, and at these meetings almost everything was a subject for disagreement.

Silver's strategy was to do for the Biltmore declaration what British Zionists had accomplished with the Balfour Declaration. He wanted the United States to commit itself officially to establishing a Jewish state. He did this in an election year through lobbying the political par-ties to include statements in their platforms, but he wanted above all a congressional resolution that Roosevelt would sign and would become the basis after World War II for demanding American intervention in Palestine. Emanuel Neumann, who became vice chairman, wrote, "This may be our last chance in Congress before the postwar settlement of the Palestine situation is made. Therefore extraordinary importance attaches to the contests of the resolutions. They will be quoted and ar-gued about for years to come. The more teeth we can put in now the stronger will be our position in the future."[52]

In January 1944, Silver got two House members and two top-ranking senators, Ohioan Robert Taft and New York senator Robert Wagner, to introduce identical resolutions backing "Palestine as a free and democratic Jewish commonwealth." To win support for the resolution, Silver and Neumann organized a massive grassroots campaign. This kind of campaign would become the hallmark of the political activism of Silver and the American Zionist Emergency Council, the new name of the emerging committee. From August 1943 to January 1944, they set up a nationwide network of over two hundred emergency committees to pressure local and federal officials and win over local organizations. Eventually there were more than four hundred committees.[53] In 1944 they got endorsements of the resolutions from more than 2,000 unions, churches, and civic groups. They generated 12,000 letters from one Connecticut town whose Jewish population was about 1,500 and 10,600 from an even smaller community in Portsmouth, New Hampshire.[54] Thirty-nine state legislatures passed pro-Zionist resolutions.

But after an initial burst of enthusiasm for the resolutions on Capitol Hill, Silver ran into trouble in the Senate Foreign Relations Committee. On Roosevelt's orders, the State and War Departments sent out word to kill the resolution. "Our war effort would be seriously prejudiced," Secretary of War Stimson wrote the committee.[55] The Foreign Relations Committee tabled the resolution. On March 9, Roosevelt met with Wise and Silver. He chided them for favoring a course of action that could result in a war between Jew and Arab. "To think of it," Roosevelt said, "two men, two holy men, coming here to ask *me* to let millions of people be killed in a jihad."[56]

To appease Jewish leaders in an election year, Roosevelt offered a public statement that the United States had never given its approval to the white paper of 1939 and that "when future decisions are reached, full justice will be done to those who seek a Jewish national home." But after Arab protests, he authorized Hull to say that he had never disapproved or approved of the white paper and that he had mentioned a Jewish national "home" rather than a state.[57] Silver and Wise had come up with very little.

Wise continued to believe the president would back a Jewish state, but Silver had a much more realistic view of Roosevelt's priorities, which he expressed later that year in a sermon at the Temple:

The President is not sold on Palestine. He does not understand our movement . . . He entertains toward our movement the same attitude of general good will and uninvolved benignancy which he entertains toward a dozen other worthy causes, but having no intention of pressing for them vigorously on the international scene. Engrossed as he is in a global war, he cannot be counted on to go out of his way for use unless he is goaded and prodded into by the pressure of public opinion and by a real and earnest insistence on the part of a determined and not easily appeased Jewish community.[58]

Wise's view of Roosevelt led him to rely on "personal diplomacy" to advance the Zionist cause. That led Silver to accuse him of being a "court Jew."[59] Silver, on the other hand, relied on public pressure to move the president and Congress.

Silver and Wise

After the failure to get the resolution, Wise and Goldmann advised the Emergency Council to go slow on pressing the case for a Jewish state. Goldmann, who privately referred to Silver as "Mr. Cleveland" and "the Almighty" in his correspondence, said that it was "not wise to use high pressure methods continuously."[60] Silver countered that the council would not have gotten anything out of Roosevelt were it not for high-pressure tactics. Silver still had a narrow majority backing him, and kept up the pressure. He continued letter writing and demonstrations and lobbied to get both parties to come out for a Jewish commonwealth in their platforms.

Wise and Silver clashed over Silver's attempt to woo Republicans. The conflict between the two men highlighted Silver's conception of AZEC as a pressure group that tried to sway both parties rather than allying with one over the other. Silver would end up voting for Roosevelt in 1944, but he harshly criticized Wise for "going on the stump for Roosevelt," which violated, he wrote Neumann, "the position of neutrality on American politics which our Emergency Council and our leaders are supposed to maintain."[61]

Silver's success with the Republicans forced Wise to importune the Democrats, who went further than the Republicans and endorsed a "free and democratic *Jewish* commonwealth." And both the Republican candidate Tom Dewey and Roosevelt openly endorsed their platform statements. For Wise, that was enough, but Silver agitated for Congress to reactivate the resolutions on the Jewish commonwealth. That set off a chain of events that resulted, finally, in Silver quitting the council in protest.

In early November, Silver, Wise, and Goldmann met with the new secretary of state, Edward Stettinius Jr. The silver-haired Stettinius said he would consult the president, and on November 15 he phoned Wise to tell him that "the President feels that putting the resolution through now would just stir things up."[62] Roosevelt wanted the group to wait until after his meeting at Yalta in early February with Churchill and Joseph Stalin. Wise argued at the AZEC executive committee meeting that the group should hold off, but Silver called for making a new push to pressure the president.

When Silver met again with Stettinius on December 4, the secretary of state told him the president would not budge. He also told Silver that they had gotten a telegram from Wise promising to defend the president if he continued to oppose bringing up the resolution. A furious Silver complained that Wise's telegram "exposed our nakedness, revealed our division and confusion of counsel . . . and sealed the fate of the Palestine resolution."[63] AZEC's executive committee instructed Silver to give up, but he continued to lobby senators; and when the Senate Foreign Relations Committee, following the president's request, voted the resolution down, a furious Wise and his allies attacked Silver at the next executive committee meeting. Silver's defense was simple. "Does anyone really think that if Zionist pressure were removed, we would gain by it?" Silver asked.[64] But when it became apparent that the committee was lined up against him, Silver walked out, and Wise became the sole chairman.

Wise's victory in the executive committee was short-lived. While he had a majority on the committee, Silver and Neumann, who resigned with him, enjoyed the support on many of the rank and file. Neumann, whose abilities as an organizer matched those of Silver as an orator, created the American Zionist Policy Committee, which siphoned off funds and workers from AZEC. Much of the local Zionist press also came out for Silver. An article in *The Day*, a New York paper, said, "The last thing we are disposed to do is to throw our greatest

spokesman and most effective leader to the wolves as an act of appeasement."[65]

As AZEC floundered under Wise, Weizmann and other Zionist
leaders from abroad called for AZEC to recall Silver. Even Wise's allies,
like ZOA president Israel Goldstein, deserted him in favor of Silver.
Goldstein said of Wise, "I felt he was taken in, that out of the goodness
of his heart he was taken in by Roosevelt.[66] A "peace committee" was
formed, and in July 1945, Silver was reinstated as cochair and head of
the executive committee, and this time the committee was stacked
with his allies, including Lipsky and Neumann. Silver had won control
of AZEC and remained in control for the next three years.

Silver stands out for his abrasiveness. He was a singularly less attractive figure than Wise, as the subsequent portrayals of the clash between the two men reveal. He was unwilling to brook opposition to his
leadership. He was a thoroughly intimidating presence. Although
they were both large, imposing men, Wise admitted to Goldmann that
he "began to tremble" when Silver entered a room.[67] But if one grants
that the Zionist movement's goal was to establish a Jewish state, Silver
was basically right about the more combative direction that the movement had to take. While he was an autocrat as leader, his strategy of
mass, public pressure also brought many new recruits—and particularly
those Jews of more modest Eastern Europe ancestry who could identify
more with the Lithuanian-born and more religiously inclined Silver.
Wise's Zionism was an extension of his progressivism and Judaism;
Silver's of his commitment to Judaism. The Emergency Committee had
suffered under Wise; it flourished under Silver.

Silver's nonpartisan pressure group strategy also worked. AZEC
wouldn't have gotten the Democrats' endorsement if Silver had not first
gotten the Republicans'. What made Wise as well as the non-Zionists
at the American Jewish Committee uneasy about this strategy was that
it implied a threat that Jews would vote as a bloc on an issue that was of
special interest to them. That raised the specter of dual loyalty if the special interest of American Jewish voters turned out to be in conflict with
America's national interest. But that possibility didn't deter Silver. "He
is not afraid of dual loyalty," Ben-Gurion, who would later clash with
Silver, wrote another Jewish Agency official.[68]

With Silver's ascendancy, the American Zionist movement became a powerful weapon for the creation of a Jewish state. But, like most weapons, it was designed to cripple rather than conciliate its adversaries. Silver would establish a pattern of blind, unyielding, and uncritical support for Palestine's Jews that would carry over to American Jewish support for Israel. Silver's ascent, and transformation, said much about Zionism and American Zionism. He began as a cultural Zionist, aware, it seems, of the moral contradictions that afflicted political Zionism; but once, in the wake of the Nazi takeover of Germany, he embraced the quest for a Jewish state in Arab Palestine, he lost sight of these contradictions. And that would be true, too, of the movement he led as it entered the contest after World War II for statehood in Palestine.

PART THREE

TRUMAN

AND

ISRAEL

One thing seems sure. This problem can't be solved on the basis of abstract justice, historical or otherwise. Reality is that both Arabs and Jews are here and intend to stay. Therefore, in any "solution" some group, or at least its claim, is bound to get hurt. [The] danger in any arrangement is that a caste system will develop with backward Arabs as the lower caste.

—Ralph Bunche, July 1947

■ 10 ■

HARRY TRUMAN AND THE $64 QUESTION

Europe was in ruins when the Nazis finally surrendered in May 1945. There were as many as 8 million deportees, prisoners of war, concentration camp survivors, and other refugees. Many would soon be housed in camps for "displaced persons." Malnutrition and disease were rampant. And Europe's Jews were the worst off of all. The Nazis had killed about 6 million Jews. Of those who had been liberated from concentration camps, four of ten died soon afterward. In all, about 50,000 concentration camp survivors ended up in displaced persons camps. Within a year and a half, their ranks were swelled by several hundred thousand Jews fleeing anti-Semitic violence in former Nazi-occupied countries.

The Nazi final solution transformed the situation of Zionism. It reinforced the Zionist moral argument for a Jewish state—as did the resurgence, even after the Nazi defeat, of a virulent anti-Semitism in Eastern Europe and the refusal of Western Europe and the United States to let in the remaining survivors and refugees. But the Holocaust also undermined the argument for a state in all of British Palestine, let alone on both sides of the Jordan River. Zionists had assumed that millions of European Jews would migrate to Palestine after the war, but now there were only several hundred thousand, hardly enough to constitute a Jewish majority in a land where Arabs outnumbered Jews by two to one. "The extermination of European Jewry is a catastrophe for Zionism,"

David Ben-Gurion exclaimed in December 1942. "There won't be any-one to build the country with!"[1]

Britain emerged from the war still in control of Palestine, but weak and bruised. Its economy was a shambles. With exports at 40 percent of prewar levels and 30 percent of its lucrative merchant fleet destroyed, it could not finance the huge war debt it had accumulated. There was also a shortage of coal to heat houses. Rationing of food and clothing was stricter than it had been during the war.[2] And Britain still had to pay for a large occupation force in Europe and an imperial army and administration that included 50,000 troops in Palestine—with many more needed if a Jewish or Arab rebellion ensued.

The United States, by contrast, was vastly strengthened. Its econ-omy now produced more than half the total of the world's goods and services. The dollar had replaced sterling as the world's currency. The American military, having defeated the Germans and Japanese, now spanned the globe, with the Soviet Union its only rival. It had clearly replaced Britain at the apex of world capitalism. But it didn't want to replace Britain everywhere.

Harry Truman, who succeeded Franklin Roosevelt, initially as-sumed that Britain would remain in control of Palestine, allowing his administration, like its predecessor, to ignore promises of Jewish state-hood that had been issued in party platforms. But that assumption failed to survive Truman's first months in office. Truman, handicapped by his initial ignorance and confusion, and inclined to take a jaun-diced view of the creation of a Jewish state, had to make the decisions on Palestine and Zionism his predecessors had avoided—in the face of sharp disagreements within his own administration and unrelenting pressure from Silver and American Zionists.

Britain and Palestine

Palestine was quiet during World War II, leading British officials to believe that Britain could retain its mandate. Palestine prospered from British investment in bases and fortifications and the British military's demand for its goods and services. From 1940 to 1945, the Jewish economy grew 13 percent annually and the Arab economy 9 percent.[3] Arabs who had retreated to villages during the rebellion returned to the seacoast cities. An Arab working class took shape. The Arab violence of the late 1930s against the British or between Jews and Arabs abated.

While a breakaway faction of Revisionists—the "Stern Gang"—staged terrorist attacks against the British, the Zionist leadership in Jerusalem, London, and New York backed the British against the Nazis. About 30,000 Palestinian Jews joined the British army during the war.[4] The Palestinian Arabs were certainly not as supportive of the British, but they didn't make trouble, either. The mufti, housed in Berlin, enjoyed the adulation of the Arab working class and peasantry, but there was only passing enthusiasm for the Nazis. Almost 25,000 Palestinian Arabs joined either the British or the British-led Transjordanian army. Palestine's Arabs attempted to regroup during the war, but they were hamstrung by an absence of leadership—many of its leaders had been killed or exiled during the rebellion—and by continuing factional battles between the Husseinis and Nashashibis, which included assassinations.

After the Nazis surrendered, however, the conflict over who would control Palestine revived in earnest. Palestine's Zionists renewed their call to abrogate the white paper of 1939 and to establish a Jewish state. Weizmann and the Jewish Agency asked Britain to admit a million Jewish refugees. When that demand elicited unyielding opposition, the Jewish Agency proposed that the British immediately allow 100,000 refugees to enter Palestine. There were then only about 50,000 Jews in camps, but the demand was meant partly to highlight British intransigence. The Zionist parties also resumed ferrying refugees to Palestine in defiance of the white paper. At the same time the newly formed Arab League, composed of surrounding states and representatives of the Palestinian Arabs, declared that they regarded the white paper as "a solemn guarantee . . . and any attempt to go back on it now would be viewed as another breach of faith by England—and would cause the utmost prejudice to Anglo-Arab relations."[5]

During the war, Winston Churchill had adhered to the white paper. In July 1945, Britain's Labour Party, led by Clement Attlee and Ernest Bevin, defeated Churchill's Conservative Party at the polls. British as well as American Zionists cheered Labour's victory. Labour, which had worked with Ben-Gurion's Mapai Party in the Socialist International, had been supportive of Zionist goals in its official statements. In the

1945 election, Labour's platform called for unlimited Jewish immigration into Palestine with the aim of a creating a majority Jewish state. The platform even encouraged Arab population transfers out of Palestine. "Let the Arabs be encouraged to move out as the Jews move in," it declared.[6]

But, like many statements in political platforms, this one was the result of intense advocacy from a few party members, and of lobbying from an interest group—in this case Britain's Zionists—rather than of widespread enthusiasm within the party or public. Thomas Reid, a Labour Party MP, told a visiting American Zionist, "I think the average member who attended these [party platform] conferences had about as much knowledge of the Palestine problem as I have of the moon. These resolutions were put forward and accepted because nobody objected, as far as I can remember."[7]

Attlee and Bevin ignored their party's platform. Attlee left the policy on Palestine largely to Bevin, a big, beefy, pugnacious man who, with little formal education, had risen from dockworker to the head of Britain's largest union. In 1940, Churchill had tapped him to be the labor minister in the wartime coalition government, where he had performed brilliantly; and in 1945, Attlee, an austere, tight-lipped Oxford graduate, made Bevin his foreign minister. At Potsdam, Truman admired Bevin as a "tough guy" while putting Attlee down as a "sourpuss."[8]

Bevin had backed the minimal version of the Balfour Declaration promising a national home and in 1930 had cautioned Ramsay MacDonald on political grounds against supporting the Passfield white paper's restrictions on Jewish immigration and land purchases. But Bevin, who had been raised as a Baptist—a minority faith in Britain—regarded Jews as simply another religious denomination. He opposed suggestions that they were a nation or race.[9] And he didn't like the idea of establishing a Jewish state in Palestine. He told a Labour conference after the election that he did "not believe in absolutely exclusive racial states."[10] He initially proposed a federal union in Palestine with an Arab and Jewish part that would be ruled by Jordan's pro-British King Abdullah—a plan that other Arab states, jealous of Abdullah's power, quickly shot down.

Bevin was equally leery of Zionist pleas that Jewish refugees go to Palestine. He believed that if Jews were a religious group, they should go back to their countries of origin. "I am not absolutely sure we should be in too great a hurry to give up the idea that European Jews may live in the countries where they belong," he declared.[11] But like Bevin's proposal that Palestine become an Arab monarchy, his hopes for the integration of Jewish refugees into a tolerant new Europe were soon confounded by events. With the war's end, there was a renewed outbreak of anti-Semitism in Eastern Europe directed at the Jewish survivors—not as a religious denomination, but as an alien nationality. From the war's end through mid-1946, at least 350 and perhaps many more Jews were murdered in Poland.

Bevin and Attlee were particularly worried about how Arabs would react to the British allowing Zionists to pursue their aims. A cabinet committee on Palestine that they convened stressed that because of Middle East's oil and its location as a gateway to other parts of the empire, it was "a region of vital consequence for Britain and the British Empire." To maintain its regional presence, Britain could not afford to alienate the region's Arab leaders. "The future of Palestine bulks large in all Arab eyes and is a subject of deep moment to the Arab League," the committee warned. If the British repudiated the white paper, it would "undermine our position and may well lead not only to widespread disturbances in the Arab countries, but to the withdrawal of the co-operation on which our imperial interests so depend."[12]

Attlee and Bevin took these warnings about alienating the Arabs seriously, and they also remembered the costs of putting down the Arab rebellion in Palestine from 1936 to 1939. Faced with Zionist demands to admit 100,000 refugees and Arab insistence that Jewish immigration cease altogether, and with rival demands for a Jewish and an Arab state, the British opted for the status quo. They proposed no change in Palestine's sovereignty and the temporary admission after the white paper expired that year of only 1,500 Jews a month. That infuriated the Zionists, failed to appease the Arabs—who opposed even a single Jewish immigrant—and brought the United States actively into the conflict.

The American Democrat

Franklin Roosevelt had pursued a contradictory policy toward Palestine, which reflected his belief that nothing was going to get resolved during World War II and that it was therefore best to mollify both the Jews and Arabs. Publicly, Roosevelt promised Senator Robert Wagner in October 1944 that if he was reelected that November, he would "help bring about [the] realization . . . of the establishment of Palestine as a free and democratic Jewish commonwealth," but he stopped on his way back from Yalta in February 1945 to privately assure the Saudi monarch Ibn Saud that he "would do nothing to assist the Jews against the Arabs and would make no hostile move to the Arab people."[13]

When Truman became president on April 12 after Roosevelt died suddenly of a stroke, he knew nothing of the president's maneuverings. He learned of Roosevelt's promise to Ibn Saud only *after* he had assured Stephen Wise and a delegation from the Emergency Council in a White House meeting on April 20 that he would faithfully follow the late president's policies. And Truman himself had given little thought to Zionism or Palestine.

Truman was born in 1884 and grew up in semirural southwestern Missouri, the site of vicious guerrilla struggles during the Civil War, the memory of which was still fresh for his pro-Confederate grandmother and mother. He was extremely nearsighted and had to wear thick glasses, which ruled out boyhood athletics. He was an avid reader. He liked stories about great Americans, but also the Bible—partly because the family Bible had big print that was easy on his eyes.

Truman's interest in the Bible has given rise to speculation that he was a Christian Zionist like Wilson, Balfour, and Lloyd George, but he appeared to treasure the Bible for its stories of heroes and for its moral lessons.[14] The good book also had to compete with the works of impious Missourian Mark Twain, who was Truman's favorite author. Even as a teenager, Truman was distrustful of the pious. "I am not a religious man," he explained later. "Mrs. Truman takes care of that."[15]

Truman's parents sent him to a Presbyterian church, but when he turned eighteen he joined a local Baptist church and remained a Baptist for the rest of his life, even as his wife and daughter became Episcopalians. He ignored the Southern Baptist strictures on drinking and dancing, but he liked the lack of pomp and hierarchy and the simplicity of the liturgy. He liked the Baptist faith, he wrote in an unpublished autobiographical note, because it gave "the common man the shortest and most direct approach to God."[16]

What Truman drew from his infrequent churchgoing and Bible

reading was a Christian universalism that was similar to nineteenth-century Reform Judaism and clashed with the particularism of Zionism. Truman believed in a universal moral code drawn from the Ten Commandments and the Sermon on the Mount. From 1939 to 1944, when he ran for vice president and had to resign for fear of controversy, he was an avid follower of Moral Rearmament, a nondenominational movement that held out Christian teachings as an alternative to war and class conflict.

Truman disdained religious sectarianism. He believed in the separation of church and state. "In my opinion, people's religious beliefs are their own affair, and when I don't agree with them, I just don't discuss religion. It has caused more wars and feuds than money," he wrote his wife in 1939.[17] Given this view of religion, he was as put off by the idea of a Jewish state as he was by that of a Protestant or Catholic state.

Truman did not idolize the Jews. He wrote in his diary in 1945, "The Jews claim God Almighty picked 'em out for special privilege. Well I'm sure he had better judgment. Fact is, I never thought God picked any favorites."[18] Like many of his background, he was not free from anti-Semitism. When he visited New York in 1918, he wrote his cousin, "This town has 8,000,000 people, 7,500,000 of 'em are of Israelish extraction. (400,000 wops and the rest are white people.)"[19] In July 1947, after a visit from former secretary of the treasury Henry Morgenthau, whom he heartily disliked, he complained in his diary that Jews "have no sense of proportion," and are "very, very selfish."[20]

But Truman's casual anti-Semitism was entirely different from the toxic blend of nationalism and racism that infected Central Europe in the late nineteenth century. It was ethnic, not racial or even religious. It applied equally to non-whites and non-Protestants. And it coexisted with a democratic tolerance of individual Jews and Jews as a group. Truman had Jewish friends and a Jewish business partner—Eddie Jacobson—and was outraged by Nazi anti-Semitism. His biographer Alonzo Hamby writes, "His letters contain numerous nasty references to other races and ethnic groups. Yet he was equally capable of depicting America as a country whose greatness stemmed from mixing the best of many ethnic strains . . . he exemplified the American democrat, insistent on social equality but suspicious of those who were unlike him."[21]

A. J. Granoff, a Jewish friend from Kansas City who, along with Eddie Jacobson, visited Truman several times in the White House, said that before 1947, Truman "knew next to nothing about Zionism, a Jewish state, a Jewish homeland, [or the] Balfour Declaration."[22] That's overstated, but it is not far-fetched to say that Truman did not have the kind of deep sentimental attachment to the idea of a Jewish state that Balfour, Lloyd George, and Wilson had, nor anything like an extensive acquaintance with the issue. And his outlook on religious sectarianism, religion, and ethics—and his Jeffersonian view of America—inclined him, if anything, away from sympathy with political Zionism.

Truman and the Nazis

Before he became president, Truman had to respond to Zionist appeals from his constituents in Kansas City and St. Louis and from Zionist national organizations. He had two different kinds of reactions. He reacted politically as he might to any other pressure group. Truman was, above all, a politician. He had gotten his start as part of Kansas City's Pendergast machine and was the machine candidate for Senate. He had courted and raised money from prominent Jews in Kansas City and later St. Louis and was eager to win their favor as long as doing so wouldn't alienate another group or get him in trouble with another senator.

In 1941, Truman agreed to be one of scores of politicians to lend their name to the American Palestine Committee, a group that Emanuel Neumann and the Emergency Committee had set up and funded to "crystallize the sympathy of Christian America for our cause."[23] In November 1942, he was one of sixty-eight senators to sign a full-page ad put out by the American branch of the Revisionists commemorating the Balfour Declaration. Truman probably didn't know whose statement he was signing and later broke off his connection with the group when it ran an ad that was critical of a fellow senator. These were pro forma acts for a politician, but they also foreshadowed Truman's susceptibility to political pressure.

On one issue on which he was lobbied, Truman didn't respond politically, but out of heartfelt sympathy. Truman was ready to lend his name or speak on behalf of European Jews who were the target of Nazi genocide. Truman's compassion was rooted in his political outlook—

his dogged identification with the "little man" and his deep distrust of the wealthy and powerful and well connected. His political heroes were Thomas Jefferson and Andrew Jackson.

Truman was a pint-size man, as was his father, and quick to take offense and privately stew over slights. He grew up as part of the struggling rural middle class. His father was briefly successful as a grain trader, but failed as a farmer and ended up as a night watchman. Truman, too, was a flop as a haberdasher and banker. He acquired from his father a loyalty to the Democratic Party of the populist William Jennings Bryan. When he came to the Senate, he regularly attacked the banks, oil companies, and railroads for the damage they inflicted on ordinary Americans.

Truman approached foreign policy in the same spirit. He was, basically, a moralist. He saw international relations as a struggle of the common man and little guy against thugs and bullies. Of course, one didn't have to be a moralist and a populist to hate the Nazis and empathize with their victims, but Truman's outlook made him particularly inclined to do so. He was shaken by what the Nazis did to the Jews. Dean Acheson, who served as undersecretary of state during Truman's first term and secretary of state during his second, wrote of him that "the fate of the Jewish victims of Hitlerism was a matter of deep personal concern to him."[24]

That came out clearly in a rousing address Truman gave in 1943 at a rally in Chicago organized by a coalition of Jewish groups aimed at helping the victims of the Nazis. Truman attacked the "fiendish Huns and Fascists" who were planning "the systematic slaughter throughout Europe not only of the Jews but of vast numbers of other innocent people." And Truman concluded, "This is not a Jewish problem. It is an American problem—and we must and will face it squarely and honorably."[25]

But Truman's susceptibility to political pressure and his moralism and populism didn't guide him toward an answer when he was asked to endorse a Jewish Palestine. In early 1944, Taft and Wagner, at the behest of Silver and the Emergency Council, introduced a resolution calling for the creation of a "free and democratic Jewish commonwealth." Truman was one of only seventeen senators to oppose it. He may have dissented because he was deferring to the Roosevelt administration's fear that the resolution would anger the British and the Arabs. He wrote that "with Great Britain and Russia absolutely necessary to us in financing war, I don't want to throw any bricks to upset the applecart."

But he may have already been uneasy about a Jewish state. He tried to exempt himself from the Zionist movement's wrath by saying that "when the right time comes I am willing to help make the fight for a Jewish homeland in Palestine."[26] But Truman pointedly promised to help fight for a Jewish "homeland" rather than a "commonwealth." If he had been comfortable with the idea of a Jewish state, he probably would have echoed the language of the resolution rather than that of the Balfour Declaration.

White House Zionists

After Truman became president in the spring of 1945, he had to maneuver between an increasingly militant and growing Zionist lobby, which had allies within Truman's White House, and a State Department that, on most issues related to Palestine, took the opposite position from the Zionists. Truman was resentful of these conflicting pressures and insisted that he ignored them, but he did not. They framed the choices that he had to make.

The ranks of American Zionist groups had swelled with each new revelation of Nazi genocide. The total membership for the two largest groups, the Zionist Organization of America and Hadassah, rose from 50,000 in 1935 to 110,000 in 1939 to 280,000 in 1945.[27] A Roper poll taken in December 1945 showed that 80.1 percent of American Jews thought the creation of a Jewish state would be a "good thing for the Jews" and only 10.5 percent a "bad thing."[28] Prominent converts also joined the movement. The New York congressman Emanuel Celler recalled, "The Nazi terrors had brought many Johnny-come-latelies into the Zionist fold. I supposed I could be counted among those."[29]

In the first half of 1945, Silver and Wise were still vying for control of the movement, but that summer Silver, along with his friend and ally Emanuel Neumann, assumed control of the Emergency Committee. Silver turned the Emergency Committee into a militant pressure group that threatened to pull Jewish political support from the Democrats and Truman if they failed to back the committee's demand for a

Jewish state. Silver's slogan, on which he ran successfully for the presidency of the ZOA that fall, was "Put not your trust in princes."[30]

Silver continued to back the Biltmore program and a maximal objective for Zionism even after it became clear that Jews could not imminently create a majority in all of Palestine. Silver led the fight at the World Zionist Conference in London that year for a greater Jewish state "undivided and undiminished."[31] Silver also moved AZEC closer to the Revisionist position. He hired two Revisionists, Eliahu Ben-Horin and Benjamin Akzin, and commissioned Ben-Horin to work with former president Herbert Hoover on a four-hundred-word statement that the former president published in November 1945 recommending the transfer of Arabs out of Palestine.[32] AZEC praised the statement as "an expression of constructive statesmanship."[33]

Although hobbled by illness, Wise was still active in the movement through the American Jewish Conference. And Nahum Goldmann remained the Jewish Agency's representative in Washington and ostensibly Silver's equal in Zionist relations with the federal government. Both Wise and Goldmann regarded Silver as an "extremist." And they had important allies within the Truman White House who were fervent Zionists but wanted nothing to do with Silver's pressure tactics against Democrats. The most important ally was David K. Niles, who was an administrative assistant to Roosevelt and stayed on with Truman.

Niles was born of poor Russian Jewish immigrants in North Boston and never attended college, but during World War I, when he worked at the Department of Labor's information office, he caught the eye of a prominent Bostonian who hired him afterward to run a speakers' forum in Boston. Niles became acquainted with the northeastern liberal intelligentsia, including Frankfurter and Wise, whose daughter he unsuccessfully courted.

In 1933, Niles went to work in the New Deal, where Roosevelt's top aide Harry Hopkins took him under his wing. In 1940 he and Hopkins ran the campaign to draft Roosevelt for a third term. In 1942, Roosevelt made him his administrative assistant in charge of relations with labor and minority groups, including Jewish organizations. When Roosevelt died, Truman insisted that Niles stay on in the same position. As a liaison with Jewish groups, Niles became the prime link to the Zionist movement.

Described by one writer as "small, dapper, gray-haired, moonfaced, wearing horn-rimmed glasses," Niles worked entirely behind the scenes.[34] Niles collaborated with Goldmann and Goldmann's second-in-command, Eliahu Epstein, at the Jewish Agency in a way that would have drawn suspicion had it happened even a decade later. He enlisted Epstein to write speeches and draft statements for the president. In the White House, he worked on Zionist matters with Samuel Rosenman, who had been Roosevelt's chief counsel and speechwriter and stayed on in the same capacity with Truman for a year, and with Max Lowenthal, who had worked closely with Truman when Lowenthal served as chief counsel to the Interstate Commerce Commission, and continued to advise the president. Lowenthal was in the White House so often that Truman thought of him as being on his staff, even though he was not.

Niles, Rosenman, and Lowenthal were moderate Zionists who had initially been close to the American Jewish Committee, not the ZOA. They also were in the outer rung of Brandeis's circles. They had come to the conclusion during World War II that Jews needed a state and not just a homeland, but they were open to a variety of arrangements. They were leery of any tactics that smacked of dual loyalty or threatened Truman and the Democrats. Niles was an extraordinary political operator, adept at marshaling opinion and building coalitions; Rosenman was a first-rate speechwriter; and Lowenthal was able to draft persuasive memos on British policy toward Palestine and the Arab resistance to Zionism.

Truman became fond of Niles and had already come to rely on Rosenman and Lowenthal. After Rosenman had gone back to private practice in New York, Truman confided to a Democratic party official, "I have two Jewish assistants on my staff, David Niles and Max Lowenthal. Whenever I try to talk to them about Palestine, they soon burst into tears because they are so emotionally involved in the subject."[35] While Truman was typically exaggerating, his recollection gets at the intensity of Niles and Lowenthal's commitment to the Zionist cause, as well as Truman's fondness for them. Their importance lay in softening and making palatable to Truman the harsh message of Silver and the ZOA.

State Department Skeptics

Since the end of World War I, the State Department had been hostile to Zionist objectives in Palestine. In 1922, Allen Dulles, then heading the

department's Office of Near Eastern and African Affairs (NEA), had objected to a congressional resolution backing a Jewish homeland in Palestine and had withdrawn his objection only after a House committee report
declared that the resolution "commits us to no foreign obligation or entanglement."[36] The State Department worried about alienating the region's
Arabs, but also in deference to the British didn't want to assert any American interest in the region other than protecting American nationals.

After World War II, the department's first priority in the Middle
East was ensuring American access to the region's oil, which was essential to the American business and to American security in case of
war. The Arabian American Oil Company (ARAMCO) had a concession to produce Saudi oil, and American investors owned a quarter of
Iraq's oil fields.[37] State Department officials worried that by supporting
Zionism, the United States would alienate Arab leaders and risk losing
access to the region's oil.

These fears were exacerbated by the onset of the Cold War. In March
1945, after Roosevelt had reassured Wise that he still stood by his letter
to Wagner in support of a Jewish commonwealth, NEA director Wallace Murray warned that "the continued endorsement by the President
of Zionist objectives may well result in throwing the entire Arab world
into the hands of the Soviet Union."[38] Murray and his successor Loy
Henderson, who assumed office five days after Truman was sworn in,
viewed the region through the prism of the Soviet threat, as did a succession of secretaries and undersecretaries of state as well as top officials
at the Pentagon and the newly established Central Intelligence Agency.

Some Zionist leaders suspected that anti-Semitism was lurking behind the State Department's opposition to Zionism. They most often
singled out Henderson.[39] The straitlaced son of a Methodist minister,
Henderson joined the diplomatic corps after serving in the Red Cross
during World War I. He spent eighteen years as an envoy in the Soviet
Union, where he became obsessed with the danger of Soviet commu-
nism, and was finally transferred out in 1943 at the request of the Soviet foreign minister. Henderson didn't support either a Jewish or an
Arab state—an Arab state, he thought, would be unfair to Jews, and a
Jewish state unfair to Arabs.* What concerned him, above all, was that

*Henderson and other NEA officials have often been described as "Arabists," and
their opposition to a Jewish state attributed to their fondness for the Arab peoples of

American support for a Jewish state would open the Middle East to the Soviets.

Henderson aroused suspicion, too, because of the lack of compassion he sometimes displayed for Europe's Jews. With Henderson and perhaps also Murray clearly in mind, Truman wrote later of the "striped-pants boys" in the State Department who "didn't care enough about what happened to the thousands of displaced persons."[40] But Henderson's attitude was rooted in what he thought was a cold-blooded realism about American interests that State Department officials of his generation cultivated. For these officials, foreign policy decisions were to be free of sentiment and politics.

Truman at Potsdam

The first clash between the Zionist lobby and the State Department came within months of Truman taking office. At the end of July, Truman was scheduled to meet British and Soviet leaders at Potsdam, outside of Berlin. The Zionists wanted Truman to demand that the British allow Jewish immigration to Palestine and the establishment of a Jewish state. The Emergency Council and the American Jewish Conference staged a national campaign to get Truman to tell the British at the meeting to "open Palestine to mass immigration" and to "reconstitute" Palestine as a "Jewish commonwealth."[41] The groups got 54 senators

---

the Middle East. Certainly, that fit some British officials in the interwar period, but it doesn't seem to characterize Henderson's attitude or that of top consular officials. In *Imagining the Middle East* (University of North Carolina Press, 2011), the historian Matthew Jacobs writes, "It was not fondness for Arabs that led Loy Henderson to oppose a Jewish state in Palestine; he never held Arabs in especially high regard. Rather, Henderson considered Arabs to be 'childlike' and 'fanatical extremists' who would gain energy from U.S. support for a Jewish state in Palestine" (p. 203). In the State Department archives, one can find, for instance American consular officials in Jerusalem who are critical of Zionism regularly describing Arabs as "primitive peoples" (Set 1037, Reel 3, Report of Vice Counsel Robert G. McGregor Jr.). In *Great Power Discord in Palestine* (London, 1987), Amikam Nachmani says British foreign office officials saw American counterparts in 1945 as being "not necessarily always sympathetic to the Arabs." American officials would make "contemptuous comments about native Arabs, similar to the feelings Americans had had about the native American Indians" (p. 37).

and 250 House members, and the legislatures of 33 states, to endorse its demands.[42] New York senator Robert Wagner presented the demands to Truman.

The Zionist leadership's main objective was a Jewish state, which they saw not only as haven for the displaced persons, widely dubbed "DPs," but as a bulwark against any future outbreak of genocidal anti-Semitism—a fear that in 1945 did not seem entirely unwarranted. "Beware of refugeeism as a substitute for Zionism!" Silver proclaimed. "We must save the Jewish remnants, but the two things are complementary and do not cancel out each other."[43]

State Department officials were worried that the president would fall under the Zionists' influence. Edward Stettinius, who had replaced Cordell Hull as secretary of state, sent the president a condescending memo warning him that Zionist leaders would try to obtain his support for "unlimited Jewish immigration into Palestine and the establishment of a Jewish state," but that he should recognize that "the question of Palestine is . . . a highly complex one and involves questions which go far beyond the plight of the Jews."[44]

The State Department urged Truman not to raise the subject of Palestine at all at Potsdam. Henderson was worried that Churchill might propose concessions to the Jews on immigration. In a briefing paper, he warned Truman that if he gave his assent to any British concessions on Jewish immigration, the British would try to pass the blame for proposals "unpopular with the Arabs" onto the United States.[45] Henderson didn't conceive that the president might urge concessions. Henderson and the department were cheered when the presidential initialed "OK" next to their recommendations.[46]

But at Potsdam, Truman surprised the State Department by handing Churchill a letter expressing "the hope that the British Government may find it possible without delay to take steps to lift the restrictions of the White Paper on Jewish immigration into Palestine."[47] Churchill gave Truman's letter to Attlee and Bevin when the newly elected prime minister and his foreign minister arrived at Potsdam to replace him.

Truman's letter to Churchill represented a victory for the Zionists and a defeat for the State Department. And it reflected, above all, Truman's sympathy for the Jewish DPs. But after Truman returned to the United States, he made a statement that suggested that he had reservations about a Jewish state and unlimited Jewish immigration. At an

August 16 press conference, Truman was asked what "the American position on Palestine" had been during the talks. His reply was painfully ambiguous:

> The American view of Palestine is, we want to let as many of the Jews into Palestine as it is possible to let into that country. Then the matter will have to be worked out diplomatically with the British and the Arabs, so that if a state can be set up there, they may be able to set it up on a peaceful basis. I have no desire to send 500,000 American soldiers there to make peace in Palestine.[48]

The ambiguity lay in the term "the matter." One reading would suggest that Truman was referring to establishing a Jewish state and to the likelihood, suggested by the British at Potsdam, that establishing a state would require American troops. Silver certainly believed that and fretted that Truman was not committed to a Jewish state. But the subsequent reaction among his aides and in the State Department and in Arab capitals would suggest that he was also referring to unlimited Jewish immigration.

Niles and Rosenman assured him afterward that letting in Jewish immigrants would not provoke Arab violence, and Henderson, who wanted to reinforce the president's doubts, ordered a War Department study of how many American troops would be needed if immigration sparked "disturbances."[49] And Truman himself told an Illinois congressman that he wanted Jews to be able to emigrate, but was worried about Arab opposition. "The president is working at it both ways," Representative Adolph Sabath told the Jewish Telegraphic Agency.[50]

The Harrison Report

Over the next months, Truman would begin to clarify what he wanted to happen in Palestine—alternatively angering the British, the State Department, and Zionists. His first step was prompted by a report on the DPs that he had commissioned and that he received after his murky statement at the press conference.

In July, Chaim Weizmann sent his American representative Meyer Weisgal to persuade Treasury Secretary Henry Morgenthau Jr., who had been a member of the American Jewish Committee, to back a mission to Europe to examine the situation of Jews housed in the camps. Weisgal succeeded, and Morgenthau got the White House to agree. The treasury secretary suggested that Earl Harrison, the dean of the University of Pennsylvania and a former commissioner of immigration and naturalization, head the mission. Weisgal arranged for Dr. Joseph Schwartz, the head of a Jewish relief organization, to accompany Harrison. Weisgal wrote Felix Frankfurter that he and Weizmann had "absolute faith" in Schwartz's "Zionist convictions."[51]

Truman received Harrison's report a week after he gave his press conference, and he told his staff at a breakfast meeting the next day that it sickened him.[52] Harrison reported that "three months after V-E day . . . many Jewish displaced persons . . . are living under guard behind barbed-wire fences, in camps of various descriptions . . . including some of the most notorious concentration camps, amidst crowded, frequently unsanitary and generally grim conditions, in complete idleness, with no opportunity, except surreptitiously, to communicate with the outside world, waiting, hoping for some word of encouragement and action on their behalf." "As matters now stand," Harrison concluded, "we appear to be treating the Jews as the Nazis treated them except that we do not exterminate them."

Harrison reported that most survivors did not wish to return to their original countries; most wanted to go to Palestine. "The only real solution," Harrison concluded, "lies in the quick evacuation of all the non-repatriatable Jews in Germany and Austria, who wish it, to Palestine."[53] He endorsed the Jewish Agency's demand that 100,000 be allowed to emigrate immediately. That probably reflected the influence of Schwartz and the Jewish Agency on Harrison's views, since there were still considerably fewer than 100,000 Jews in DP camps.

Truman sent letters a week later, along with Harrison's report, to Dwight Eisenhower, who was in charge of the American forces in Europe, and to Attlee. In his letter to Attlee, Truman endorsed Harrison's (and the Jewish Agency's) recommendation for 100,000 immigrants. "No other single matter is so important for those who have known the horrors of concentration camps for over a decade as is the future of immigration possibilities into Palestine," Truman wrote.[54]

Truman bypassed his own State Department, which became aware of the letter two weeks later only when a former senator who had met with Truman mentioned it in a statement. After Gordon Merriam, the chief of the Near East division of the NEA, learned of the letter, he sent a memo to Henderson suggesting that the administration backtrack and issue a statement deferring to the British insistence that "it would be impossible to admit any large number [of Jews] to go to Palestine."[55] But Truman wasn't listening to the State Department on the matter.

Attlee replied to Truman briefly on September 14 warning if the president were to release publicly the Harrison report, along with a statement endorsing it, that would "do grievous harm to relations between our two countries."[56] Two days later Attlee wrote again, rejecting the idea, central to Harrison's report, that Europe's Jews should receive priority over other groups of DPs. Attlee expressed fear that granting admission to 100,000 Jews would poison British relations with the Arabs, and he offered to transfer 35,000 Jews from Germany and Austria to camps in Algeria and Morocco.[57] Truman responded curtly that he would take no public action on the matter until after James Byrnes, who had succeeded Stettinius as secretary of state, returned to the United States in early October from a Council of Foreign Ministers meeting in London.

Truman had also not consulted Zionist leaders about his correspondence with Attlee. But Weizmann had excellent sources in the British government, and on the same day that Attlee cabled Truman, Weizmann phoned Silver to inform him of the contents of the cable, including the offer to send concentration camp survivors to North Africa. Silver and Wise issued a statement calling on Truman to prevent "this shameful injustice."[58] And Silver and the AZEC staff began organizing demonstrations and publishing newspaper ads and sending telegrams— some 200,000 to the White House—to pressure the president.

The AZEC protests were specially centered on New York City, not only because of the large number of Jewish residents, but also because it was to hold a mayoral election in November. (Even more than today, New York's mayor was a major player in American politics, and the national parties wanted to win the post for their nominee.) A huge demonstration was planned for Madison Square Garden on September 30. And the demonstration carried with it the threat that the city's

Jewish voters might punish the administration for its stance on Palestine by opposing the Democratic mayoral candidate.

Truman understood the political stakes, and on the day before the Sunday rally he held his first extended meeting with Silver and Wise. Silver found him to be "under strain because of the failure of the London Conference" of foreign ministers. "War is far from over," Truman told them.[59] He said he hoped to convince the British to allow the 100,000 immigrants into Palestine, but he asked them to be patient and said he did not want to make a public statement on the issue. They warned him that he would lose Jewish votes if he did not side openly with the Zionists.[60]

The two leaders, and especially Silver, annoyed Truman, and when they urged him to endorse a Jewish state, he spoke his mind. He told them, as he had Sabath, that he wanted "good conditions for Jews everywhere," but he added that he objected to a religious state, whether Catholic or Jewish.[61] This was the first time Truman had voiced his ethical discomfort with the idea of a Jewish state. Silver and Wise argued with Truman and thought they had convinced him that a Jewish state was not a religious state, but they had not.

After seeing them, Truman met Joseph Proskauer and Jacob Blaustein from the American Jewish Committee, which had urged the president to back Jewish immigration to Palestine, but not a Jewish state. Truman complained to them of Silver and Wise "insisting as they do constantly for a Jewish state." Truman assured Proskauer and Blaustein that a Jewish state was not in the offing, and he expressed his concern that the attempt to impose one could cause World War III.[62] Truman had now combined his ethical objections to a Jewish state with his geopolitical concerns that trying to bring one about could enmesh the United States in war.

Silver and Wise had angered Truman and had provoked a candid response to their advocacy of a Jewish state, but their visit, coming on the eve of a major demonstration in New York, had its effect on Truman the politician. After seeing the rabbis, Truman broke his word to Attlee and did make a statement. At a press conference, his staff handed out copies of Earl Harrison's report, Truman's letter to Eisenhower, and a summary of the correspondence between Truman and Attlee. Truman made clear that he was fully behind the demand for 100,000 immigrants.

Byrnes explained to the British officials that Truman had released the materials because he was worried about the upcoming New York mayoral election. That infuriated Attlee and Bevin, leading them to believe that Truman had ceded his Palestine policy to Silver and the ZOA. But the two men also saw an opportunity in Truman's intervention to draw the United States into the looming conflict over Palestine.

Involving the Americans

The British had always been reluctant to seek the assistance of the United States in Palestine. They feared that the United States would try to undermine their political domination of the Middle East in order to win new export markets and concessions for American oil firms.[63] But their situation was growing dire. In response to Britain's refusal to abrogate the white paper, Ben-Gurion had united the Haganah and the Revisionist armed groups and had begun military operations against the British. With its economy tanking, and the Soviet Union threatening Britain's presence in Greece, Turkey, and Iran, the British could ill afford to put down another rebellion in Palestine, and Attlee and Bevin concluded that they needed to enlist the Americans to their side.

Bevin won cabinet support to propose the formation of a fact-finding committee to develop with the Americans a policy to deal with Europe's Jewish DPs. Bevin, Labour MP Richard Crossman observed, was "determined to drag the Americans off the side-line on which they have been 'rooting' for twenty years."[64] Bevin assumed—even after Truman's straightforward repudiation of an American military role—that he could win American aid in suppressing the growing Zionist revolt in Palestine.

Bevin thought the Americans would accept his invitation, but most other British officials believed that the Truman administration would demur out of fear of the American Zionists, who would brand acceptance of the proposal as capitulation to the British. And the proposal did spark a debate. While the State Department welcomed the British initiative, Samuel Rosenman, who was being advised by Wise and Silver, wrote to the president that he "shouldn't have anything to do with it." The proposal, he wrote, consists of "temporizing, appeasing and seeking to delay the settlement of the issue."[65] Rosenman wasn't wrong about the British plan. Bevin's strategy was to prolong the controversy over the DPs, hoping that it would eventually die out as Jewish refugees settled in Europe. But Truman sided with the State Department and agreed in principle to the committee.

Bevin had left any mention of Palestine out of his proposal. At Rosenman's urging, Truman called on the British to cite Palestine as a possible destination and to limit the investigation to thirty days. Truman the politician also asked that the announcement of the committee be delayed until after the New York mayoral election. After getting the 30-day limit raised to 120 days, Bevin accepted the American conditions. And on November 13, a week after the Democratic candidate had won the mayoral election , the United States and Britain announced the creation of the Anglo-American Committee of Inquiry.

Zionists in the United States and Great Britain denounced the committee. Silver and Wise called on Truman to base American policy "on the internationally recognized right of the Jewish people to reconstitute their national home in Palestine."[66] At the ZOA convention on November 18, Silver, the organization's newly elected president, expressed his disillusionment with Truman. "We had over-estimated the determination of the President. He was persuaded to accept the shabby substitute of an investigating committee—that very transparent device for delay and circumvention—against his own better judgment," Silver said.[67] Silver called for Zionists to boycott the committee hearings.

At a December meeting of the Inner Zionist Council, the highest decision-making body between World Zionist Congresses, Silver made his case that the committee's aim was "to put an end to Zionism." But Zionists in Great Britain and Palestine resisted Silver's hard line. Moshe Shertok, the political director of the Jewish Agency, argued that a boycott would isolate the Zionists and that nothing would be lost by participation. He prevailed over Silver.[68]

Truman's Strategy

Truman had decided to accept the British invitation because he had become more confident of what he could accomplish, and how to accomplish it. He got his chance to explain his approach in a discussion after the election with American diplomats from Egypt, Saudi Arabia,

Palestine, and Lebanon-Syria. The State Department had summoned the envoys home in early October to be briefed on the administration's Palestine policy, which had aroused anger and suspicion in Arab capitals. Niles, worried that news of the meeting could alienate Jewish voters, had convinced Truman to postpone it until after the New York election.

Truman met the envoys on the morning of November 10. George Wadsworth, the minister to Lebanon and Syria and senior member of the group, opened the meeting by asking the president four questions. The fourth was: What is American policy toward political Zionism? Truman answered each question in turn, and when he got to the fourth question, he smiled ruefully as if to acknowledge its difficulty. "That is the $64 question," he said. He explained that this question had been giving him and Byrnes "more trouble than almost any other question which is facing the United States."

He couldn't base his policy, he told them, on the pledges for a "Jewish commonwealth" that the parties had made in their platforms. These pledges "did not give consideration to the international political situation in that area"—in other words, they didn't take account of the opposition of the Arab majority in Palestine or of surrounding Arab governments to a Jewish state. Truman promised that in making policy he would heed the "international political situation."

Truman admitted to the diplomats, however, that he was under great political pressure at home to back the Zionist objective. He told the ministers that he hoped that when they returned to their posts, they would explain that "the question was a burning issue in American domestic politics and that the American Government would try to work out the whole matter on an international plane."

Then he unveiled his strategy. Truman, the minutes of the discussion said, "pointed out that if Palestine could take some refugees from Europe to relieve the pressure, it would alleviate for the time being the situation in Europe, and it might satisfy some of the demands of the 'humanitarian' Zionists and give us an opportunity to turn our attention to a permanent solution of the political problem." In other words, shipping the refugees to Palestine would pacify those Zionists who cared more about the welfare of the Jewish people than about establishing a state.

"There would be no immediate solution," Truman said. "Palestine

Theodor Herzl leans over a balcony at a
hotel in Basel, Switzerland, where the World
Zionist Organization held its conferences.

Ahad Ha'am poses with his daughter
and son in London in 1910.

Lord Arthur Balfour and Field Marshal Allenby
visit Jerusalem, where Sir Herbert Samuel is high
commissioner, for the opening of the Hebrew
University of Jerusalem in 1925.

(Courtesy of Passia Photography Archive)

Vera Weizmann, Chaim Weizmann, Sir Herbert Samuel, former prime
minister David Lloyd George, Ethel Snowden, and the Labour Party
politician Philip Snowden get together in the early 1930s.

Haj Amin al-Husseini, the grand mufti of Jerusalem, poses in 1929, the year of the Wailing Wall riots.
(Wikimedia)

George Antonius was the leading Palestinian Arab intellectual and the author of *The Arab Awakening*.
(Courtesy of Passia Photography Archive)

Sheikh Izz ad-Din al-Qassam organized guerrilla bands in the early 1930s to fight the Zionists and the British.
(Courtesy of Passia Photography Archive)

David Ben-Gurion was a private in 1918
in the Jewish Legion, which fought on the
side of the British in World War I.

Nahum Goldmann represented the
Jewish Agency in the United States
from 1940 to 1946.

Macy's Department Store owner Nathan Straus and Rabbi Stephen Wise
were both part of the circle of Louis D. Brandeis (center).
(Courtesy of the Library of Congress)

Rabbi Abba Hillel Silver and U.S. Ambassador to the
United Nations Warren Austin confer at the UN in May 1947.
(Courtesy of the United Nations)

Martin Buber and Judah L. Magnes testify before the Anglo-American
Committee of Inquiry in Jerusalem in 1946.

David Niles, who later became an aide to
Harry Truman, is seen as a young man in 1915.

(U.S. Navy, courtesy of the Harry S. Truman Library)

Max Lowenthal, the counsel to the Senate Interstate Commerce
Committee, confers with Senator Harry Truman in October 1938.
(Courtesy of the Library of Congress)

Clark Clifford, the White House counsel, sits alongside Truman in
Key West in December 1949. (Courtesy of the Harry S. Truman Library)

Count Folke Bernadotte was chosen by the United Nations in 1948 to mediate the Arab-Israel conflict. Ralph Bunche assisted him and later succeeded him. (Wikimedia)

Mark Ethridge, the vice president of the Louisville *Courier-Journal* and *Times*, was Truman's representative to the UN Conciliation Committee for Palestine. (Courtesy of the Library of Congress)

would probably be an issue during the election campaign of 1946 and 1948 and in future campaigns." And he concluded by returning to the political pressure that he faced. "I'm sorry, gentlemen," he said, "but I have to answer to hundreds of thousands who are anxious for the success of Zionism; I do not have hundreds of thousands of Arabs among my constituents."[69]

Truman's strategy was to put off "a permanent solution to the political problem" by satisfying the demands of the "humanitarian Zionists" for the emigration of European Jews to Palestine. He expected that the political issue (involving political Zionism) would recur not just in 1946 and 1948 but in "future campaigns." The $64 question would probably not be answered in his presidency. Truman saw the Anglo-American committee, he told the envoys, as a way "to work something out with Attlee" about the refugees, not about a Jewish or Arab state.

Truman's strategic assumptions were completely different from Bevin's. While Bevin believed that admitting the 100,000 would set Palestine on a slippery slope to Jewish statehood, Truman believed that admitting the 100,000 would *reduce* the pressure for a Jewish state. Bevin envisaged the Anglo-American committee as a way of postponing the question of immigration and enlisting American military and financial support. Truman saw it as a way of postponing the issue of statehood by settling the issue of immigration.

Truman now openly opposed the creation of a Jewish state. During the last week of November, Truman had to take a stance on a new version of the Taft-Wagner resolution, which the two senators had introduced at Silver's behest. This time, to make the resolution more widely acceptable, the senators had called on the United States to help "reconstitute Palestine as a free and democratic commonwealth" rather than a "free and democratic *Jewish* commonwealth," but the use of the verb "reconstitute" was a clear indication of what the resolution really meant, and how it would be used politically. Truman balked. At his press conference on November 29, the president replied brusquely when he was asked whether he supported it. "If that resolution is passed there isn't any use trying to have a fact finding commission finding facts and making recommendations," he said.[70]

On December 4, Truman received a delegation from the American Council for Judaism, an organization that was founded in 1943 by Reform rabbis unhappy with their denomination's growing rapprochement with Zionism. It advocated a Palestine that was neither Jewish, Christian, nor Muslim. Because of the prominence of its members, who included Lessing Rosenwald, the chairman of the board of Sears, and Arthur Sulzberger, the publisher of *The New York Times*, it gained entrée into the highest circles of government.

The council members voiced their rejection of Zionism. Afterward, one of the participants, J. David Stern, the publisher of *The Philadelphia Record*, who was not a member of the council, held a press conference. He said that he had Truman's permission to clarify the president's position on Palestine. According to Stern, Truman "was still in favor of a free Palestine and of making Palestine a haven for Jews as well as opening the country to immigration, but he did not favor making Palestine a Jewish state. As a true American, the President said that he did not feel any government should be established on religious or racial lines." The president, Stern said, "felt that the government of Palestine should be a government of the people of Palestine irrespective of race, creed or color."[71]

At a meeting later that day with Weizmann, which Niles had arranged, Truman voiced exactly the same objections. While he welcomed what Weizmann had to say about immigration to Palestine, he rejected the idea of a Jewish state, calling it a "theocracy." Weizmann tried to dispel Truman's fears by conjuring up the illusion of a pacified Arab population. According to Weizmann's report of the conversation, he told the president that all religions would enjoy equal status and that reports of Arab hostility were "highly exaggerated" and were "being used as an excuse to prevent a pro-Jewish solution." Weizmann was dissatisfied with the results of the conversation. He thought the earlier group had "confused the President, who was confused anyway and was angry with the Jews who were adding to his problems."[72]

At this point, though, Truman was no longer confused. He had a strategy that was based on his support for Jewish immigration and his opposition to a Jewish state. The question was whether this answer to the $64 question would work. Would the British give way on immigration? And if they did, would the Zionists table their demands for statehood and lay down their arms, and would the Arabs put aside their threats and acquiesce in several hundred thousand more Jews in Palestine? This was Truman's clearest attempt to reconcile his support for the refugees and his opposition, born out of his Jeffersonian politics, to a Jewish state. But his strategy would founder because of opposition from the British, the Zionists, and the Arabs, leaving the president no alternative that he could unequivocally support.

11

THE SEARCH FOR AN ANGLO-AMERICAN CONSENSUS

There was probably never a time after December 1917 that the Jews and Arabs in Palestine could have agreed on their own to share or divide the country. When the Arabs indicated some willingness to deal in the late 1920s, the Jews backed off; and when the Jews might have agreed to partition in the late 1930s, the Arabs weren't interested. So if any agreement were possible, it would have had to be imposed by outside powers, and then enforced by them until the Jews and Arabs agreed to abide by it. In the fall of 1945, Attlee and Bevin invited the United States to join them in developing a plan for the refugees in Europe and the Jews and Arabs in Palestine. That was the agenda for the Anglo-American Committee of Inquiry.

Committee deliberations can be tiresome to witness, and even more so to read about, but those of the Anglo-American Committee revealed publicly for the first time just how far apart the Zionists and the Palestinians were, as well as the differences in approach between Truman and the British. The committee proposals for implementing the final recommendations also came very close to what both Truman and the British wanted to do. They laid the basis for a solution that the Americans and British might have imposed. But in the end Truman backed out of the committee's final proposals, even though he had overseen and approved them. Why he did so says much about the obstacles America faced then and now in formulating a policy toward the Jews and Arabs.

Overstating Their Case

In November 1945, Truman sent the State Department a list of ten candidates to fill the six American slots on the committee. They included an old Truman friend, Texas judge Joseph Henderson, who shared Truman's ambivalent view of a Jewish state, and two of Niles's choices, San Francisco lawyer Bartley C. Crum and James G. McDonald. Crum was sometimes known as "Comrade Crum" for his defense of Negroes and Communists. McDonald had been the League of Nations high commissioner on refugees and an advisor to Roosevelt on the fate of Europe's Jews. Both men backed a Jewish state.

The State Department tried to knock Crum and McDonald off the list, but Niles succeeded in getting them included in the final six.[1] Hutcheson was named committee chairman. Bevin chose representatives who he thought shared his objective of continuing British control of Palestine, which meant restricting Jewish immigration. Thinking he had six votes in his pocket, Bevin felt comfortable promising the committee members, when they visited London, that if they issued a unanimous recommendation, he would abide by it.

The committee held hearings in Washington, D.C., London, Cairo, and Jerusalem and toured the DP camps in Europe and Palestine. In the hearings in Washington, Wise, Neumann, Hadassah head Judith Epstein, and Reinhold Niebuhr of the American Palestine Committee testified for the Zionist cause (Silver was still boycotting the hearings). The Zionists made a powerful case for removing the white paper's restrictions on immigration. Epstein brought tears to the eyes of the commissioners when she described how in one camp in Palestine that Hadassah had established for refugee children, the children fled and hid when they first heard the dinner bell. "When we investigated we learned that a bell meant only one thing to these children," Epstein said. "We found out that in the extermination camps a bell had rung daily as a signal for the children to line up. Each day new ones were picked for extermination. One child had been in that dreadful line 30 times and survived."[2]

The Zionists also made a case for a Jewish Palestine, but it proved to be far less compelling. Neumann contended that the Balfour Declaration had assumed an eventual Jewish majority in Palestine and assured the committee members that, in a Jewish state, Arabs and Jews could coexist amicably. Niebuhr, perhaps the most famous liberal of his day, put forth Jabotinsky's old argument that "while Palestine was the logical place for homeland for the Jews . . . the Arabs have a vast hinterland in the Middle East." Niebuhr also endorsed the Revisionist case for population transfer. "Perhaps, ex-President Hoover's idea that there should be a large scheme of resettlement in Iraq for the Arabs might be a way out," he told the committee.[3] It was another example of how American liberals, in the wake of the Holocaust and the urgency it lent to the Zionist case, simply abandoned their principles when it came to Palestine's Arabs.

Crossman was "surprised and irritated . . . by the almost complete disregard of the Arab case."[4] But Crossman was equally unimpressed by the Arab witnesses. The Princeton professor Philip Hitti, a Christian Arab originally from Ottoman Syria, insisted that Palestine was really a part of Syria. Hutcheson asked Hitti whether, if the goal of a Jewish state were eliminated, the Arabs would agree to any Jewish immigration. "Frankly, no," Hitti replied, "Jewish immigration seems to us an attenuated form of conquest."[5] Both the Zionists and Arabs, Crossman concluded, were "overstating their case."[6]

In Jerusalem, the hearings took place at the lecture hall of Jerusalem's imposing YMCA building. Chaim Weizmann, always the diplomat, acknowledged that there would be "some slight injustice if Palestine is made a Jewish state" but, following Jabotinsky's old argument, insisted that "Arab national sentiments can find full expression in Damascus and in Cairo and in Baghdad." The Arabs, he told the committee, "have so many kingdoms," while the Jews have none.[7] Ben-Gurion added a point that Zionists would repeatedly make over the next years and can be heard today, claiming that Palestine had never existed as an Arab land. "Arab history was made in Arabia, Syria, Persia, and in Spain and North Africa. You will not find Palestine in that history."[8]

Ben-Gurion unflinchingly defended the Biltmore platform. He demanded statehood immediately. "Our aim," Ben-Gurion said, "is not a majority. Our aim is a Jewish state. As 'Jewish state' we mean Jewish soil, Jewish labor, a Jewish economy, Jewish schools, language and culture. We also mean Jewish security. We mean complete independence."[9] Hutcheson, mirroring Truman's views, objected strenuously to these arguments. He didn't think it was right to "import people into a country for the deliberate purpose of creating there a majority in order to dominate the country and take control from its inhabitants."[10] And he also didn't accept the idea that a Palestinian Arab could easily move or be moved to Baghdad to accommodate Zionism, which he compared to forcing a Texan like himself to "go to Virginia."[11]

Ben-Gurion had threatened any Jews who repudiated the Biltmore platform with expulsion from the Zionist movement, but two men defied Ben-Gurion. Magnes, who had become the president of the Hebrew University in 1935, and faculty member Martin Buber, who had migrated to Palestine in 1938, spoke in opposition to political Zionism. In 1942, Magnes, Buber, and other intellectuals associated with the Hebrew University had founded the Ihud (Union) Association to promote a binational Palestine, leading Lipsky and other American Zionists to issue a statement demanding that Magnes resign as president of the university.[12] Magnes deplored political Zionism. In 1943 he had charged that the Biltmore declaration was "equivalent, in effect, to a declaration of war by Jews on the Arabs."[13] Ihud's plan was to establish a state in which Jews and Arabs enjoyed equal and autonomous political rights. "We regard the Arab natural rights and the Jewish historical rights, as under all the circumstances, of equal validity," he told the committee.[14] He favored unrestricted Jewish immigration until Jews and Arabs had reached a parity, which he estimated would occur in 1957.

Magnes and Buber were the only Zionists to testify who acknowledged that Palestinian Arabs had an equal, if not greater, claim to Palestine. Magnes's timetable for unrestricted immigration was probably realistic. His testimony was warmly received by the entire committee. McDonald admitted afterward that Magnes "reached the hearts of more than perhaps any other speaker."[15] There was only one point that the committee couldn't accept, and it wasn't unimportant. That was Magnes's contention that "the vast majority of plain, inarticulate Jews and Arabs . . . want understanding and cooperation, and to achieve this they would make many concessions and sacrifices."[16]

Magnes was questioned repeatedly on this point and had to acknowledge that, if anything, relations between Jew and Arab "have deteriorated."[17] And the deterioration was reflected in the political fortunes of the Ihud Association itself, which, like its predecessor Brit Shalom, enjoyed scant support except among a few prestigious Jewish intellectuals like Buber and Hannah Arendt. It had no Arab support. State Department official Evan Wilson, who traveled with the American

delegation, reported that the Arabs viewed Magnes as "more dangerous than the official Zionist spokesman. They know that in any scheme
of bi-nationalism on a parity basis they will tend to be out-maneuvered
by the more aggressive, more efficient Jews and so they oppose all such
proposals quite as vigorously as they do the Jewish state."[18] In a conversation with the Jewish Agency official Elias Sasson, the Palestinian leader
Awni Abd al-Hadi said he did not have "any respect toward Dr. Magnes's
attitudes and proposals."[19] In short, the one person in Jerusalem who
took seriously the moral claims of both sides was spurned by the leaders of both sides.

The Arab Case

As the hearings opened, the Arabs were far less prepared to make their
case than the Zionists were. To win over the newly sovereign Arab states,
the British had help set up the Arab League at the war's end, but the
league's states were bitterly divided between the Hashemite kingdoms
in Iraq and Transjordan on one hand, and populous Egypt and wealthy
Saudi Arabia on the other hand, with Syria and Lebanon usually siding
with the latter. The Palestinians were not just "caught in between," as
the historian Walid Khalidi has written, but had their own internal
conflicts that were reinforced by the conflicts between the Arab states.[20]

The Palestinian camp was crippled by the murderous family feud
between the Husseinis and Nashashibis. Many of the leaders who had
survived the rebellion of the 1930s, including the mufti and his cousin
Jamal al-Husseini, were still in exile. The mufti suffered from a toxic
reputation outside the Arab world due to his collaboration with the
Nazis and was distrusted by Arab and Palestinian leaders, including
his cousin, but he still enjoyed enormous popularity among the Palestinian Arab rank and file. "Among the Palestine fellahin," British officials reported in September 1945, "there is an almost religious veneration
of Haj Amin and any attack of him would be regarded as an attack on a
good Moslem."[21]

In 1945, acting on behalf of the Arab League, Syrian prime minister Jamil Mardam Bey revived the Palestinian Arab Higher Committee. He created a leadership composed of five representatives from the
Husseini faction, five from rival parties, and two independents, but no

chairman—a tribute to the absent mufti. In early March, however, the British allowed Jamal Husseini to return from Rhodesia, where he had been exiled. Upon his return, he claimed the chairmanship of the higher committee and kicked out the representatives of the rival parties, who set up another rival group, the Arab Higher Front. On the eve of the hearings, the Palestinian Arab movement was, in Evan Wilson's words, "badly organized and lacking in leadership."[22]

The Zionists had welcomed the Anglo-American Committee to Palestine, and lobbied them energetically outside the hearings and during their tour of Palestine. By contrast, the Palestinian Arabs, outside of a few sumptuous meals at the homes of notables, made little effort to win over the committee. Testifying in Jerusalem, Palestine's Arabs employed a strident, abusive, and inflated rhetoric. Labor leader Sami Taha charged that Zionism was "an imperialist trick" that Zionists were using the Holocaust to justify. "Zionism," he said, "is an auxiliary instrument of imperialism, racism and Nazism."[23] Jamal Husseini described Zionists as "pampered . . . spoilt children of the British government."[24] He threatened war if Jews were allowed to immigrate. "Why should not we have this war?" he explained. "It is quite natural. This is God's way."[25] Ahmad al-Shukeiri, who staffed the Arab League's Jerusalem office, warned that "if it is a question of degree of violence, the Arabs are prepared to break the record."[26]

What also hurt the Arab case was the specter of the mufti, ensconced in Paris but soon to arrive in Cairo. Both Jamal Husseini and Awni Abd al-Hadi had clashed with the mufti in 1939 over his rejection of the British white paper, but both were forced by the tortuous circumstances of Palestinian Arab politics to describe him to the committee as their leader. They did nothing to counter the committee's impression that an Arab Palestine would be led by the mufti, which neither the American nor the British members were prepared to accept. (After World War II, Ben-Gurion would regularly advise his colleagues to "rely on the Mufti" to discredit the case for an Arab Palestine.[27]) For that reason alone, the Arabs failed to convince the committee that an Arab Palestine was viable or desirable. They made their greatest and perhaps only impact in arguing against a Jewish state. By the time the hearings closed, the committee members had heard a compelling case for Jewish immigration and against either a Jewish or an Arab state.

The Committee Proposals

After Jerusalem, the twelve committee members—dubbed the "twelve apostles"—repaired to the quiet beauty of Lausanne, Switzerland, to formulate their findings at the Beau-Rivage Palace Hotel on Lac Léman. They quickly agreed that the 100,000 Jewish DPs should be admitted, but could not agree on Palestine's future.

Three Americans—Crum, McDonald, and the *Boston Herald* editor Frank Buxton—and one Englishman, Crossman, favored some form of Jewish state; Buxton and Crossman had been won over to the Zionist cause during the trip. Buxton's reasoning was revealing. "He argued," McDonald wrote in his diaries, "that the principle of eminent domain, used to justify the American conquest of Mexico and the movement of American Indians into a modern society, applied to the situation in Palestine."[28] Buxton, like Brandeis and Jabotinsky, thought of the Palestinians as the Indians or Mexicans whom the United States had, to his mind, justifiably displaced.

Five of the British committee members balked at any idea of a Jewish state, and they were joined by Hutcheson, who, as Truman's representative on the committee and as a powerful voice in his own right, carried the day. The committee dismissed partition, which Crum, McDonald, and Crossman favored, because of the "tendency of the dam to burst"—that is, for one side to overrun the other. They saw a binational state as a form of partition. It would have to be based on creating political parity between Arabs and Jews even though Arabs were in the majority. Otherwise, it would become an Arab state and, like the other alternatives, would require outside force in order to maintain. They rejected creating an Arab state out of a merger with Transjordan because "Palestine is maritime, part of the Mediterranean region, having ties with the West and with Egypt. Transjordan is Arabian, with a traditional orientation towards Damascus and a dynastic bias toward Iraq."[29]

To the committee, that left only one option: the continuation of the status quo—"No Arab, no Jewish state," in Magnes's words, but under overall British control. The committee spelled out its reasoning in its report:

> We have reached the conclusion that the hostility between Jews and
> Arabs and, in particular, the determination of each to achieve domi-

nation, if necessary by violence, make it almost certain that, now and for some time to come, any attempt to establish either an independent Palestinian State or independent Palestinian States would result in civil strife such as might threaten the peace of the world. We therefore recommend that, until this hostility disappears, the Government of Palestine be continued as at present under mandate pending the execution of a trusteeship agreement under the United Nations.[30]

The committee assumed that by prolonging the mandate as a UN "trusteeship," the United States and Britain would forestall rather than perpetuate the violence. That was, certainly, wishful thinking.

In its recommendations, the committee tried to include something for each of the interested parties. The Americans got their 100,000 DPs but the committee also recommended that destinations other than Palestine be explored for the remaining Jewish DPs. The British got an affirmation of their mandate; Palestine's Jews didn't get a state, but they got the 100,000 immigrants and, besides that, the elimination of the white-paper restrictions on immigration and land sales. The Arabs didn't get an Arab state (but got no Jewish state, either) and did get a promise of economic aid to bring Arab standards of living and education up to Jewish levels.

Arab leaders denounced the report. Jamal Husseini called for Arabs to fight to prevent the immigration of the 100,000 Jews. The U.S. Information Center in Beirut was burned down. There were strikes in Palestine; money was raised for arms. There was a violent demonstration in Baghdad. Ben-Gurion acknowledged in his diary that the Arabs had gotten the worst of the deal:

> The Arabs will most probably protest because the White Paper is to be abolished, immigration on a large scale is to be permitted, independence for Palestine is rejected and the country will be put under foreign trusteeship. The "sweeteners" offered the Arabs are expressed mostly in the negative; no Jewish state; protection of tenant farmers and small landowners . . . in essence the Arabs will be able to raise a cry that they have been defrauded and dispossessed.[31]

But in his public statements, Ben-Gurion contended that the report created a "crisis of unprecedented gravity" for the Zionist movement.

That was because "there was no mention of a Jewish state." Palestine, Ben-Gurion foresaw, was to become "neither Arab nor Jewish but . . . a national home for the British army in the Middle East."[32] Weizmann, however, and other moderates saw the report as more positive because of its concessions on immigration. "We cannot have both things [and] it would be better to discuss [immigration] than the imaginary Jewish state," Weizmann declared.[33]

At an April 29 meeting of the Jewish Agency Executive in London, Ben-Gurion acceded to the fears of Weizmann and British Zionists that rejection of the report would alienate the British government and public opinion. The Zionist leaders decided to make a test case of the 100,000 while continuing the "fight for the Jewish state."[34] In the United States Silver and Neumann recoiled sharply at the committee's report. When McDonald met with Silver in New York over breakfast on Sunday, April 28, and showed him the report, Silver said that it was "both bad and sad, and represented a complete repudiation of the Zionist program."[35] Silver threatened to denounce the report when it was officially released on the thirtieth.

In Washington, Niles, Frankfurter, and other "moderates" were annoyed by Silver's reaction. Silver, Frankfurter told Niles, "prefers a Jewish state on paper rather than doing something real for human beings."[36] Crum and McDonald convinced Silver that if he denounced the report, he would permanently alienate the White House and probably lose any chance of getting the 100,000 to emigrate to Palestine. They proposed recommending to Truman that he praise the report's decision to allow 100,000 to emigrate, while taking no position on the report's recommendations for Palestine's future.

Silver finally agreed, and he and Neumann drafted a statement that they wanted Truman to make; and Crum and Niles convinced Truman to issue the statement himself rather than waiting, as Byrnes had promised Bevin, to make a joint statement with the British. Truman added sentences praising the report for "guaranteeing" Arabs' "religious and civil rights" and for seeking to protect the Jewish, Muslim, and Christian "holy places."[37] Truman issued the statement on April 30.

For the British, the timing and content of Truman's announcement was another betrayal. The announcement, the government's press secretary wrote later, "threw Bevin into one of the blackest rages I ever saw him in."[38] The next day, in a speech before the House of Commons,

Attlee insisted that the report "must be considered as a whole in all its implications." And Attlee went on to break Bevin's promise that the British would carry out whatever unanimous decision the committee reached. Attlee now set out two conditions before Britain would allow the 100,000 into Palestine. First, the Zionists in Palestine had to dissolve their "private armies." That applied not just to the Revisionist terror groups, which a week before had ambushed seven British soldiers, but the Haganah. That was not going to happen. Secondly, Attlee demanded that the United States share the "military and financial responsibilities" that would result from carrying out the report. That was also not going to happen. Truman was prepared to make a financial contribution, but he and his cabinet, with the Cold War looming and with the army still demobilizing, remained dead set against any American military involvement in Palestine.[39]

Both Ben-Gurion and Silver felt vindicated when Attlee and Bevin reneged on their promise to respect the committee's decision, but Truman was unhappy with the exchange. He supported the short- *and* long-range recommendations that the committee had made, and he sympathized with the British demand that the recommendations be considered as a whole. Truman, after all, backed both the admission of the 100,000 and some alternative to a Jewish or Arab state.

Niles wanted him to wage a public campaign to get the British to agree to the 100,000, but Truman sided with a State Department proposal to continue the talks with the British. Bevin proposed that the two sides appoint a group of experts to decide how the total plan could be implemented. In June, Truman appointed a cabinet committee to survey the situation and, in July, sent former assistant secretary of state Henry Grady on behalf of the committee to meet with a British group headed by Deputy Prime Minister Herbert Morrison.

An All-out Struggle

When Attlee reneged on Bevin's promise, Silver and AZEC immediately initiated a campaign against the British. Members of AZEC's different organizations began bombarding the White House with letters and telegrams demanding that Truman pressure Britain. AZEC members picketed the British embassy and consulates. After it became clear that Truman was going to allow the British to delay a decision, the American Zionists turned their fire on Truman's State Department. On May 18, Silver announced an "all-out struggle" against "the delaying tactics designed to keep the doors of Palestine shut to Jewish immigration, currently being pursued by the British Government and, it would seem, also by our own State Department."[40] On June 12, AZEC held a large rally in Madison Square Garden.

Silver, Wise, and Crum were the leading speakers. Crum showed that he had become a foot soldier in the Zionist cause and was willing to propagandize for it. He insisted that Jew and Arab were actually getting along quite well. "We found no anti-Semitism in Palestine," Crum declared. "The opposition of the Arab 'leaders' is opposition to western democratic civilization. But these leaders do not speak for the masses . . . They have vested interests; they wish to maintain their power position . . . You will not find this objection among the people."[41]

The featured speaker was Silver, and he unveiled a weapon meant to force the British to take the Zionist demands seriously—but one that divided the American Zionist leadership. The administration had proposed a $6 billion loan to Britain to help the British economy, which was on the brink of insolvency. The Senate had approved the loan, but the House had yet to do so. Silver railed against the loan: "In view of this shocking record of broken pledges and the repeated violation of solemn obligations," he declared, "American citizens have the right to turn to their representatives in the Congress of the United States, who are now discussing the granting of a loan to Great Britain, and inquire whether the Government of the United States can afford to make a loan to a government whose pledged word seems to be worthless."[42] In an AZEC meeting on June 21, Neumann called for a coordinated public campaign against the loan. Council members were divided on the issue, but they agreed to a private campaign to influence members of Congress to hold up the loan pending resolution of the situation in Palestine.

Wise, Niles, and Frankfurter—the older Brandeis circle of Zionists—thought Silver and Neumann's opposition to the loan raised a genuine issue of dual loyalty: Silver and Neumann seemed to be putting the interest of Palestine's Jews above that of Americans, who had a legitimate interest in rescuing America's staunchest wartime ally from insolvency. Wise published an essay backing the loan. "A great wrong will not condone another wrong," he wrote. "Wrong is wrong, and if the general denial of the loan to Britain is wrong to the British people and to our own country, we as loyal American Jews have no right to insist upon that."[43]

Niles organized Zionists who opposed Silver and Neumann to come out publicly for the loan. On July 8, Wise issued a public letter endorsing the loan. Two days later Silver counterattacked. "It should be clear that Dr. Wise in urging approval of the British loan spoke for himself only and for no Zionist body in the United States," Silver said.[44] But on July 15 the House passed the loan. The *Boston Herald* wrote that "the most clear-cut factor in the shift of attitude was Stephen S. Wise's statement."[45] All in all, the debate over the loan bore out how the Zionist movement under Silver had increasingly become a single-minded pressure group for Palestine's Jews. Unlike Wise and Brandeis, Silver and Neumann did not see the Zionist movement as an extension of American progressivism, or Zionism as an expression of Americanism. What mattered, above all, was establishing a Jewish state in Palestine.

At the same time that Silver and AZEC were trying to pressure the British in the United States, the Zionist movement in Palestine was taking the offensive. In a May 12 broadcast, the Haganah warned against the British plan to concentrate their military bases in Palestine and promised that if Britain didn't "fulfill its responsibilities under the mandate . . . the Jewish Resistance Movement will make every effort to hinder" the creation of these bases.[46] On the nights of June 17 and 18, the Haganah knocked out ten of the eleven bridges connecting Palestine with its neighbors.

On Saturday, June 29, the British struck back with a nationwide sweep involving 17,000 troops that arrested 2,700 Jews, including Shertok and other prominent Jewish Agency leaders. The British called the plan Operation Agatha, but the Zionists dubbed it the "Black Sabbath." In response, the Haganah decided to focus on illegal immigration rather than military operations, but the Revisionist Irgun, led by the future Israeli prime minister Menachem Begin, refused to abide by the cease-fire. On July 22 it blew up the King David Hotel, killing ninety-one British officials, Arabs, and Jews. Ben-Gurion repudiated the Irgun act and even called on the Haganah to turn Irgun members in to the British, but the British reacted by imposing a curfew across the country and sending in more troops.

Civil War Along the Potomac

In July, Truman's representative Henry Grady arrived in Britain to conduct talks with Morrison. Grady discovered that the British cabinet had junked the Anglo-American Committee's plan for a unified Palestine. Instead, they endorsed a federated Palestine with autonomous Jewish and Arab provinces. The coast would be Jewish; the inland Arab; Jerusalem, Bethlehem, and the Negev would be under direct British control. The British would exert control over Palestine's finances, foreign relations, and immigration. All other policies would be handled by the autonomous provinces and by a national legislation in which Jews and Arabs enjoyed equal seats in the upper house. The "ultimate objective"—after a period of transition—would be "self-government for the inhabitants."[47]

Truman did not favor a particular proposal for Palestine's future. He was insistent only that it not be a Jewish or Arab state. The new British proposal for a federation sat well with him. With his approval—the president had been conferring with Grady daily—the Americans agreed to the new British proposal to admit the 100,000 Jewish immigrants as part of a long-range plan for a federated Palestine.

In a telephone call afterward, Truman assured Secretary of Commerce Henry Wallace that the Jews were getting the "best part" of Palestine.[48] And that was probably true. The Jews were getting the coastline ports and the richest agricultural land, including the citrus fields, while the Arabs were getting the less cultivatable lands. Only 15,000 Jews compared to 815,000 Arabs were actually living in the area designated for Arabs, while 301,000 Arabs would fall in the area to be governed by 451,000 Jews. This division of Palestine reflected damage already inflicted on Arab aspirations and Arab economic development by Zionist immigration, labor, and land policies and by the abortive rebellion of the 1930s, which led more Palestinian Arabs to leave the coast for native villages in the hills.

But measured in sheer acreage, it was as good a deal as the Palestinian Arabs, who still outnumbered the Jews almost two to one, had gotten. James Byrnes was happy with the plan, and he told his British counterparts that he expected the United States would endorse it and help implement it. Neither Byrnes nor Truman anticipated the furor the plan would cause. "The center of battle interest," Acheson wrote, moved "from Israeli-British fighting in Palestine to civil war along the Potomac."[49]

The Morrison-Grady proposal was leaked to *The New York Times* on July 25, before the White House had expected to unveil it, and it immediately caused a firestorm of protest among Zionists and their supporters in Congress. Speaking for AZEC, Silver denounced it as a "conscienceless act of treachery, dooming the helpless Jewish survivors in Europe to further death and humiliation and driving the Jews of Palestine to further desperation." Silver objected to making the admission of the 100,000 contingent upon "the ghettoization of the Jews in their own homeland."[50] Silver summed up the issue: "For the Jews of Europe, it is now Palestine or death; for the Jews of Palestine it is now liberty or death."[51]

AZEC began a massive letter-writing campaign. Probably at Silver's instigation, senators and House members began visiting the White House to urge Truman to reject the plan. McDonald brought Senators Mead and Wagner to see the president. New York representative Emanuel Celler led a delegation of New York House Democrats to the White House. Wagner and Taft denounced the plan on the Senate floor. The New York Democrats were particularly worried about the Jewish vote in the upcoming congressional elections in November 1946. Paul Fitzpatrick, the chair of the New York State Democratic Committee, wrote Truman, "If this plan goes into effect it would be useless for the Democrats to nominate a state ticket for the election this fall."[52] Niles and Rosenman also spoke against the Morrison-Grady plan.

Truman reacted angrily to the intense lobbying. When McDonald warned Truman that if he accepted the Morrison-Grady plan in order to get the 100,000 immigrants, he would "go down in history as anathema," Truman shot back, "The Jews aren't going to write the history of the U.S. or my history."[53] When Celler, who had warned Truman of the effect his actions could have on the forthcoming election, and had read him a three-page statement denouncing the plan for ghettoizing the Jews, Truman responded, "This is all political. You are all running for re-election."[54] And he said he was sick of hearing from Jews, Irishmen, Poles, and Italians about *their* interests and wanted to hear from "Americans."[55]

Afterward, in a letter to Crum, McDonald wrote that Truman "showed what in a person of lesser office could be regarded as annoyance."[56] In a memo to the AZEC, McDonald attributed the president's support for Morrison-Grady to a "mind set which incapacitates him from understanding Jewish psychology."[57] Like other supporters of a Jewish state, McDonald simply dismissed Truman's qualms about a Jewish state. With a Democratic loss of Congress looming in November, he saw putting political pressure on the president as a way to get around his insensitivity to Zionist concerns, while for Celler, domestic politics was at the heart of his concern.

Truman never liked to admit it, but he was highly susceptible to political pressure. Byrnes had urged Truman to endorse the Morrison-Grady plan on July 31, the same day that Attlee was to unveil it in a House of Commons speech. But on July 30, Truman held a cabinet meeting at lunch to discuss whether he should go along with the plan. Truman brought into the meeting a stack of telegrams protesting the Morrison-Grady plan that, according to Henry Wallace's recounting, was "four inches thick."[58] Truman said how "put out" he was about the pressure he was getting from Jews. "Jesus Christ couldn't please them when he was here on earth, so how could anyone expect that I would have any luck?"

Truman might have been put out, but as he had done before, he acceded to the pressure while complaining loudly about it. Although Acheson and Secretary of War James Forrestal continued to advocate for the Morrison-Grady plan, Truman finally told Acheson that he was not going to endorse the plan the next day. Both Acheson and Byrnes blamed political influence for Truman going back on his support for the recommendation. Acheson told the British ambassador that "in view of the extreme intensity of feeling in centers of Jewish population in this country neither political party would support this program at the present time."[59] Byrnes, who came from one-party South Carolina, blamed the influence of Niles and Rosenman.[60]

Truman said he was still considering the Morrison-Grady plan, but it was, to all intents and purposes, dead. Just to make sure, Niles arranged on August 7 that the members of the Anglo-American Committee, who were annoyed that the British had gone back on their committee's recommendations, meet with Grady and his group in Truman's presence. Crum said, "Hello, sucker," upon greeting Grady, and even Hutcheson, who might have been expected to back Grady, criticized him for failing to take their report as his "Bible."[61] On that day, Truman wired Attlee that he was rejecting the plan. That spelled the end of Truman's attempt to get the 100,000 Jewish refugees passage to Palestine without committing himself or the United States to the creation of a Jewish state.

Truman continued to see the Morrison-Grady plan for a federated Palestine as an ideal solution to the conflict between Zionists and Arabs, but he would abandon any attempt to implement it. From then on, Truman had no solution of his own, but was buffered between competing plans from the Zionist movement and his own State Department. In the end Truman would accede to the Zionists' pressure—not because he believed in their cause, but because he was worried about Democratic losses in 1946 and again in 1948. A pattern had been established that would prevail for the rest of the century.

12

NAHUM GOLDMANN AND THE ROAD TO PARTITION

On August 2, 1946, the Jewish Agency Executive opened a critical meeting in Paris to decide what to do about the Morrison-Grady proposal. Nahum Goldmann, the Jewish Agency's chief representative in Washington, had come to Paris for the meeting, and he was worried. Goldmann called his second-in-command, Eliahu Epstein, who had remained in Washington, to ask him to contact David Niles in the White House. Goldmann wanted to know what the president was thinking.

Epstein called back with bad news. According to Niles, the president had become exasperated with the Zionists. He had kept asking Niles, "What is it that the Jews want?" Truman, Niles said, "had become convinced that the Jews objected to what was offered them without having a proposal of their own which would have chances to fulfill at least part of the demands and requirements of all the interested parties, which would make it possible to advance the Palestine problem toward a peaceful solution."[1]

Silver and the American Zionists did have a proposal of their own: they wanted to establish all of Palestine as a Jewish state. But for Truman, that was precisely the problem. As the president wrestled with the $64 question, the Zionists had become even more insistent that there was only one answer—a Palestine "undivided and undiminished." The British rejected this proposal; the Arabs threatened to go to war over it;

and some leading Zionists privately admitted it was not feasible given the absence, in the wake of the Holocaust, of a Jewish majority that could fill all of Palestine. As the experience of the Anglo-American Committee had shown, something had to give—and for Goldmann it became Silver and other American Zionists' insistence on a greater Jewish Palestine. Goldmann became the first mainstream Zionist leader since 1937 to propose compromise with the Arabs.

Goldmann's Zionism

Nahum Goldmann—who was second only to Weizmann as an international negotiator—was born in 1895 in Lithuania. He lived in a small Jewish town with his grandparents for his first six years until he joined his parents, who had moved to Frankfurt, where his father taught Hebrew and belonged to one of the first Zionist groups, the Jewish Colonization Society. In his youth in Russia, Goldmann's father had been part of a study circle with Ahad Ha'am. Goldmann wrote that "even as a child I was a Zionist without knowing it, inasmuch as I took over my father's concepts and his positive attitude to everything Jewish as axioms of my heritage."[2]

Goldmann studied law and philosophy at the University of Heidelberg, where Karl Jaspers and Max Weber taught. In 1913 he took his first trip to Palestine as part of a student group and stayed over for an extra five months. He wrote articles for a Zionist newspaper in Germany, and after he got his degree from Heidelberg, he became a journalist. In 1925 he founded a publishing house in Berlin, which brought out, among other things, the first volumes of the German *Encyclopedia Judaica*; but Goldmann's career as a publisher—and his work on the encyclopedia—was cut short after the Nazis took power in 1933.

Goldmann first made his reputation in Zionist circles as a writer and lecturer, but in the late 1920s he became active in Zionist politics in Europe and began attending regularly the World Zionist Congresses. In 1935 he became the Jewish Agency's representative to the League of Nations in Geneva, and in 1943, after he had moved to the United States, he became the chief representative of the Jewish Agency there. For years in Germany, he had been a man without citizenship and passport—in Wilhelmine Germany, Russian Jewish émigrés had not been allowed to become citizens. He would remain virtually stateless for the rest of his life, even while acquiring various passports and becoming a citizen, successively, of the United States, Israel, and Switzerland.[3]

Goldmann's Zionism was much closer to that of Ahad Ha'am and Weizmann than to the political Zionism of Herzl and Jabotinsky. Goldmann supported a Jewish state, but he was an evolutionary Zionist who favored the emergence of a state out of a full-blown polity and economy. Goldmann didn't see a Jewish state in opposition to the Diaspora, but, like Ahad Ha'am, as the center of a thriving world Jewry. He saw Jews as a "global people"—a description that fit his own life and experience.[4] Goldmann also insisted that Zionists come to terms with Arab nationalism. In 1921, after the Jaffa riots had broken out, Goldmann wrote, "It was as if, only now, the Yishuv [the Jewish Community in Palestine] had suddenly discovered that there was such a thing as an Arab problem. We have overlooked the most obvious, the most important and the most elementary of all our political and social problems— the Arab question."[5]

In the Zionist political battles of the 1930s and early 1940s, he was generally allied with Weizmann and with Stephen Wise, who became his closest friend and collaborator in the movement and with whom he founded the World Jewish Congress in 1935. At the Jewish Agency in Washington, Goldmann continually clashed with Silver. The differences were partly personal and partly institutional. Silver wanted the AZEC to have authority over all Zionist dealings in the United States, particularly those with the U.S. government; Goldmann thought the Jewish Agency was the primary representative of the world movement to the U.S. government. Silver wanted the movement to speak to the administration with one voice, and he was determined that the voice be *his*. Where Wise had quaked at Silver's rage, Goldmann either ignored "Mr. Cleveland" or tried to humor or deceive him without giving ground, which only enraged Silver further.

The two men differed sharply in their choice of tactics and in their ideas about Zionism. While Silver relished a public fight with Roosevelt or Truman, Goldmann was much more cautious than Silver about pressuring the president. When Silver pressed the Taft-Wagner resolution in the face of Roosevelt's opposition, Goldmann sided with Wise. Goldmann's methods were closer to the *shtadlanim* of the American

Jewish Committee. In this respect, Silver had a better grasp of what made American presidents and political parties pay attention. But Goldmann had a more realistic and equitable view of what could be achieved in Palestine.

Silver was close to Revisionists like Ben-Horin and to Begin's Irgun; he privately approved of the Irgun's terrorist tactics. Goldmann, even before the bombing of the King David Hotel, wanted the Yishuv and Jewish Agency to dissociate themselves from Begin and the Irgun. In his advocacy of a Jewish Palestine, Silver tended to ignore the existence of an Arab majority except to promote the idea that they could be transferred to Iraq, while Goldmann recognized that, to live peacefully, the Jews would have to reach some kind of compromise with the Arabs. That led to his advocacy of a partitioned Palestine.

The Case for Partition

In 1937, before the Peel Commission had completed its findings, Weizmann, based on his access to British officials, warned Goldmann that the commission would recommend partitioning Palestine. Goldmann told Weizmann that he favored partition as long as the Jewish area was large enough to allow the several million immigrants Goldmann expected. At the World Zionist Congress that year, which debated the Peel recommendations, Goldmann was the most fervent proponent of partition.

After World War II, Goldmann renewed his call for accepting "territorial compromises." In a letter in February 1946 to Moshe Shertok, the head of the Jewish Agency's political department, Goldmann laid out the case for partition. He dismissed the Biltmore program of a Jewish Palestine as "practically out of the question" because it would mean "no concessions to the Arabs" and would make "the independence of Palestine dependent on the attainment of a Jewish majority" at a time when it was unattainable because of the Holocaust.

Goldmann ruled out a federal Palestine with an autonomous Jewish canton because he feared that the "Arab majority" would find some way to "sabotage" Jewish immigration. That left partition as the only proposal that made possible a Jewish majority state that would be able to open its gates freely to immigrants. To quiet Arab fears that the Jewish state would be a vanguard of European imperialism, Goldmann proposed that it become part of a "Middle East Federation."[6] Goldmann's was the first proposal by a Zionist official that took account of the Holocaust *and* that sought to come to terms with the Palestinian Arabs.

By the spring, Ben-Gurion, Shertok, and Weizmann were telling members of the Anglo-American Committee privately that they could accept the partition of Palestine, but officially the Zionist movement was still committed to a Jewish Palestine, and in the United States, Silver and the Emergency Council were publicly *and* privately in favor of the Biltmore program. As usual, American Zionists were the last to recognize that circumstances had changed. That set up a confrontation between Goldmann and the American movement's leadership.

When Goldmann broached the subject at an AZEC meeting in May 1946, the party leaders backed Silver's argument for an "undivided Palestine."[7] Then, in early July, Goldmann gave an interview to *The New York Times* about partition. The *Times* reported that "Zionist spokesmen, who asked that their names not be made public, revealed that they had reluctantly concluded that the only practical method of ending the Palestinian conflict would be partition—'a fair partition, not one giving the Jews Tel Aviv and two villages.' "[8] Silver and Neumann recognized who the "spokesmen" were and fired off a response to the *Times*, which reported the next day that AZEC "took exception" to the "misleading impression" created by a "Zionist leader."[9]

On July 17, Goldmann made his case before the national board of Hadassah, the group most sensitive to Palestine's Arab majority. As before, he ruled out the Biltmore program because of the lack of a Jewish majority. He also dismissed binationalism: "You force Jews and Arabs today to live together in Palestine, and there will then be civil war," he observed. But he suggested that partition could lead over the long run to reconciliation between Jews and Arabs. "It often happens in friendships and marriages, you separate in order to unite. Let them outlive their national intention for a while."[10]

Two weeks later Neumann, speaking to the same group, denounced Goldmann's proposals as "spurious." Referring to Goldmann's statement to *The New York Times*, Neumann said, "For any responsible member of the Zionist movement to take it upon himself, no matter how highly placed he may be, to launch these compromise proposals is not merely a disservice, in my opinion such persons forfeit their right to continue to act as responsible men for the movement."[11]

But Goldmann was not deterred by opposition from the American Zionists. He urged that the members of the Jewish Agency Executive meet to frame a response to the Morrison-Grady plan for a federalized Palestine. Goldmann wanted to use the meeting to broach the question of partition. The group convened in Paris on August second. It included Wise; Golda Meyerson (Meir), a future prime minister of Israel; Louis Lipsky, who worked at the Jewish Agency's New York office; Israel Goldstein, the head of the ZOA; and Rose Luria Halprin of Hadassah. Shertok and Bernard Joseph, whom the British had detained, were absent.

Also missing was Silver. Ben-Gurion, who was the chairman of the Jewish Agency Executive and had been abroad when the British sweep occurred, tried twice to convince Silver to attend. Silver said he was too busy with political work in the United States, but the real reason was his rivalry with Goldmann. He would only go if it would be made clear at the meeting that there was a single authority representing Zionists in the United States. Ben-Gurion did not consent, so Silver stayed home. As the meeting was to begin, Silver fired off a telegram "requesting that no contacts be made with Government officials [in Washington] . . . without prior consultation" with him.[12]

At the meeting, there was considerable support for accepting a Jewish state in part of Palestine, but the members of the Jewish Agency Executive disagreed over how to broach the plan to the American and British governments. Goldmann argued that partition should be presented as an ultimate goal that would be realized after a transition period of several years. During that period, Jews and Arabs would inhabit the kind of autonomous zones that the Morrison-Grady plan recommended, but the Jewish zone would have control over immigration into it.

Goldmann's plan was meant to draw in Truman and officials of the State Department, who, he knew, had been favorably disposed to the Morrison-Grady plan. Goldmann was "very much afraid," he wrote Felix Frankfurter, that the British would throw the whole issue into the lap of the new United Nations, where the Arab countries were represented but the Jewish Agency was not, and where the Soviet Union had a Security Council veto.[13]

By contrast, Ben-Gurion proposed rejecting the Morrison-Grady plan and insisting on statehood, whether in a part or in the whole of Palestine. Unlike Goldmann, he had already given up hope of winning British support for any Zionist initiative, while Goldmann thought that by winning over the Americans, the Zionists would win over the British. Goldmann warned that if upon returning to Washington he were simply to demand statehood, the president would reject it outright. The members of the executive backed Goldmann by 6 to 0, with three members, including Ben-Gurion, abstaining. "The Executive," the resolution read, "is prepared to discuss a proposal for the establishment of a viable Jewish State in an adequate area of Palestine."[14]

But who would convey this new program to Washington and London? Ben-Gurion asked Goldmann whether they should ask Silver to query the Truman administration about partition. Goldmann warned that the White House and the relevant cabinet officials were already hostile to Silver, whom they saw as a Republican who was willing to embarrass them and damage their party's prospects in order to get his way. (Indeed, Truman had been so offended by what he saw as Silver's rudeness during a July 2 visit to the Oval Office that he would never agree to see him again.) The meeting decided to delegate Goldmann to negotiate by himself on behalf of the Jewish Agency Executive.

Ben-Gurion cabled Silver that Goldmann was going to arrive in Washington to carry out the Jewish Agency Executive's decision. "I hope that the two of you will work in full cooperation and harmony," Ben-Gurion wrote.[15] The details of what subsequently happened between the two men remain murky, but one thing is clear: they did not work together harmoniously.

Goldmann and Silver

Goldmann arrived in Washington on Tuesday, August 6, and that evening attended a meeting at the Statler Hotel with Silver, Neumann, Epstein, and other staff people from AZEC and the Jewish Agency. At the meeting, Silver, who remained opposed to partition, insisted that Goldmann not bring it up on his own with administration officials but focus instead on the demand for the admission of 100,000 immigrants. If administration officials introduced the subject in the course of discussing the Morrison-Grady plan, then Goldmann could say that the Jewish Agency "would be prepared to consider partition as a possible compromise." Goldmann must not "whittle down the full Zionist program" on his own.[16]

In his minutes of the meeting, Silver protégé Leon Feuer, AZEC's representative in Washington, reported that Goldmann agreed to Silver's recommendation. Goldmann claimed he did not—and Epstein backed him up. What likely happened was that Goldmann gave Silver and Neumann the *impression* that he agreed but never explicitly said so, leaving himself the option of acting otherwise, which is what he did. The next day, when Goldmann met with Acheson, he introduced the proposal for partitioning Palestine.

Acheson wanted to know why the Jewish Agency couldn't accept the Morrison-Grady plan as the basis for negotiations. Goldmann replied that the Zionists were prepared to give up part of Palestine only if they could be assured that what they kept was a Jewish state with control over its immigration. "If a ghetto is a state, it is no longer a ghetto," Goldmann told Acheson.[17] Acheson was also worried that establishing a Jewish state, even on a part of Palestine, would provoke a war between Jews and Arabs. Goldmann assured Acheson that Jewish Agency representatives had learned that partition would be received "enthusiastically by Trans-Jordan and would be acceptable to Syria and Lebanon."[18] And he laid out the plan for the new Jewish state joining an Arab-dominated Near East Federation.

Acheson was impressed with Goldmann's presentation—it was "the first sign of reasonableness in an incredibly difficult position," he later told two AZEC representatives.[19] The acting secretary promised to back the plan for partition if Goldmann could secure the endorsement of Niles, the secretaries of war and the treasury (both of whom sat on Truman's Palestine policy-making committee), and the American Jewish Committee.

For Goldmann, Niles presented no problem, nor did Secretary of the Treasury John Snyder, but AJC president Joseph Proskauer and Secretary of War John Patterson did. Goldmann's strategy was to first win over Proskauer, who was a friend of Patterson's and who, he learned from Wise, had already come to Washington to see the secretary of war. Goldmann made a date to see Proskauer that evening in his hotel room.

Proskauer had become the president of the American Jewish Committee in 1943 on a platform that called for the international trusteeship for Palestine rather than a Jewish state and for the right of Jews to immigrate subject only to the absorptive capacity of Palestine's economy.[20] When Silver got the American Jewish Conference to endorse the Biltmore program that year, Proskauer pulled the committee out of the organization. Proskauer had been born in Mobile, Alabama, in 1877. His parents were German and Austrian Jewish émigrés. He got a law degree from Columbia and became a leading corporate attorney in New York City. In 1923, he was appointed to the New York State Supreme Court by Democrat Al Smith, whose campaign for governor he had backed. Proskauer left the bench in 1930 to return to private practice, but was still known as "Judge."

Goldmann and Proskauer had been at odds over Zionism, but Proskauer put Goldmann immediately at ease. "Call me Joe," he insisted.[21] To win Proskauer over, Goldmann invoked the Holocaust. He asked him if he wanted "to fight the Jews in Palestine after Auschwitz because they want to have a Jewish state? You will be torn to pieces between your loyalty to America and your loyalty to the Jewish people."[22] Goldmann tried to allay Proskauer and the committee's fears that a Jewish state would put American Jews in an ambiguous position. The word "Jewish" would not be included in the name of the new state. It would be Jewish only in the sense that Jews would be a majority. The creation of a Jewish state, Goldmann promised Proskauer, would remove Zionism from American politics.[23]

What appears to have most impressed Proskauer was Acheson's tentative endorsement of the plan. That meant it had a serious chance of success. What worried him was the possibility that support for *any* Jewish state could provoke a war with the Arabs. The non-Zionist American Jewish Committee had a much more lively and liberal concern with the fate of Palestine's Arabs than the Zionist Organization of America did—again bearing out the idea that the embrace of Herzl's Zionism encouraged willful ignorance about Palestine's Arabs. Proskauer told Goldmann he would accompany him the next morning to visit Patterson. The secretary of war, upon hearing the judge speak favorably of the plan, agreed to back it.

Goldmann wanted to meet personally with Truman, but Niles warned him that the president was fed up with being pressured by Zionists. Instead, Niles and Acheson met with Truman about the plan while Goldmann and Epstein waited anxiously in Goldmann's hotel room to hear the result. According to Goldmann, Niles came in and threw himself upon the bed. He was in tears and began to shout in Yiddish, "If my mother could hear that we are going to have a Jewish state."[24] Truman had approved the plan and instructed Acheson to inform the British. But Niles's celebration turned out to be premature.

The next day Goldmann met with Acheson and Henderson to work out a statement that would be given to the British. They asked him about the summary of his proposal and also about a $300 million loan they planned to offer the Arabs to agree to the plan. Would the Jewish Agency approve? Goldmann's reply was revealing. He suggested that the loan be "used to encourage the Arabs to leave Palestine and settle elsewhere."[25] Like Wise, who also expressed support privately for transferring Arabs out of Palestine, Goldmann would not publicly advocate achieving a majority or a greater majority by transferring Arabs to Jordan or Iraq, but he wanted it to happen and privately urged steps that would make it more likely.[26]

Acheson and Henderson read Goldmann what they planned to have American ambassador Averell Harriman tell the British about the administration's position. Acheson wrote Harriman a description of the plan and an account of his conversation with Goldmann, and told him to convey to the British that "in our view, this recent development offers hope that Jewish Agency will realistically join in search for practicable solution. As first step we suggest possibility that Brit Govt might let it be known that coming consultations will not be rigidly bound to consideration [of] one plan and the possibility of early creation of viable state of Jewish portion not precluded." Acheson endorsed partition as a *possible outcome* of "consultations with Arabs and Jews."[27] He didn't say the United States now favored the plan.

A Wasted Opportunity

Over the summer of 1946, stretching out, perhaps, through the early winter, the Jews and Arabs of Palestine stood the best chance since the period from 1928 to 1930 of achieving a compromise in their conflict, but for it to have happened, each of the players in the conflict would have had to play their part perfectly. First was the British. Unbeknownst to American officials, British foreign minister Ernest Bevin, whom Silver and other Zionists reviled, had quietly become a proponent of partitioning Palestine. On July 11, while Grady and Morrison were still deliberating, the British cabinet first took up Bevin's proposal for partition. But Bevin himself was not there. He had to be in Paris for the postwar peace conference.

Bevin's position was backed by the British high commissioner in Palestine, Alan Cunningham, but it was opposed by the British military, who feared alienating the Arabs, and by everyone in the Foreign Office except Bevin. Attlee was also unsympathetic. Instead of proposing partition, the cabinet opted instead for what became the Morrison-Grady plan. That was the first flubbed line in the drama.

Bevin was enraged by the King David Hotel bombing, but when Goldmann met with him in mid-August, he found him still receptive to the plan for partition. Bevin, Goldmann wrote Crum in September, "has a certain amount of goodwill and ambition to reach a settled agreement—which can only mean partition."[28] But there was another snag. In late July, Bevin had suffered a heart attack and for the rest of the year rarely attended cabinet meetings, including those where decisions about Palestine were made. With Bevin sidelined, much of the initiative went to George Hall, the colonial secretary, who was determined to bring the Jews and Arabs to the table to reach an agreement on the basis of the Morrison-Grady proposal. When Goldmann urged Bevin to come out forthrightly for partition, Bevin told him there were "departmental difficulties."[29]

Then there were the Arabs. During August, Elias Sasson, the director of the Arab section of the Jewish Agency, made trips to Egypt and Transjordan to sound out Arab leaders about partitioning Palestine. Sasson found considerable interest in the plan among the Egyptians, who believed that the British "would not withdraw from Egypt as long as the Palestine problem is unsolved."[30] In a trip to Transjordan, Sasson also found King Abdullah as amenable as ever to partitioning Palestine if he could annex the Arab part. But the Arab League leaders warned the British to work out matters privately with the contending parties before calling a conference. If they had to air their opinions initially at a public conference, these Arab leaders would have to harden their stands to accommodate a public and a Palestinian Arab leadership that would not brook any compromise.

At a conference in Bludan, Syria, in June 1946, the leaders of the Arab League had tried again to unify the Palestinian leadership around a new Arab higher executive that would be amenable to compromise. The group, which subsequently retook the name of the Arab Higher Committee, contained only four members: Jamal Husseini, who was vice chair; Dr. Hussein Fakhri al-Khalidi, representing a rival party to the Husseinis; Hilmi Pasha, an independent; and Emile Ghouri, a Christian Arab aligned with the Husseinis. The chairman's seat was left vacant for the mufti. But in mid-June the mufti, who had escaped confinement in Paris, landed in Cairo and began reassuming control of the Palestinian Arab movement. While Jamal Husseini would have been willing to compromise, the mufti was not—at least, not without the public stroking that the British refused to give the former Nazi collaborator.

In the United States, the Zionist leadership was in a typical state of upheaval. Silver was furious with Goldmann for going behind his back to the administration and for not obeying what he thought were AZEC's orders. And Silver had reason to be mad. Goldmann had attended an AZEC meeting later in the same afternoon that he had had his first meeting with Acheson, but had failed to mention that he had met with the acting secretary of state. Then, on August 14, *The New York Times* published an account of Goldmann's negotiations that included details that Silver was unaware of. Silver fired off a telegram to Ben-Gurion resigning from the Jewish Agency Executive, but Ben-Gurion refused to accept his resignation. In his meetings with government officials, Silver played the good soldier and expressed support for partition, but he continued to oppose it in Zionist meetings.

Within the Jewish Agency, a disagreement broke out over whether to attend the London conference that the British government had called. Goldmann, Weizmann, and the British Zionists wanted to attend and advocate the plan for partition—and Acheson urged them to attend. But Ben-Gurion, Silver, Golda Meyerson, and a majority on the executive thought that the Zionists had already compromised significantly and feared being put in a situation where they would be asked to compromise between partition and the Morrison-Grady plan. As a result, the Jewish Agency Executive set as a condition of their attendance that partition and not the Morrison-Grady plan be the basis of the discussion and that the Jewish leaders taken prisoner during the Black Sabbath roundup be released and allowed to attend.

That led to a stalemate. Hall was unwilling either to abandon the Morrison-Grady plan or to release the prisoners. And American officials, while willing to make an elliptical endorsement of the partition plan, were unwilling to pressure the British. So, with Morrison-Grady the chief item on the agenda, the Jewish leaders failed to show up on September 9 in London when the conference opened. The Arab League representatives did show up, but not the Palestinian Arab representatives, who were protesting the British refusal to invite the mufti. As the Egyptians had warned Sasson, the Arabs, forced to air their views publicly, took a hard line, calling for a unitary Arab-majority state, a cessation of Jewish immigration, and Arabic as the only official language. The talks broke down.

The Yom Kippur Statement

American Zionists, publicly committed to partition as a strategy, sought to get the Truman administration to break up the stalemate in London and Jerusalem. They wanted the president to take a more definite stand in favor of partition *and* to persuade the British to agree. Silver and Neumann planned to use the 1946 elections to pressure the administration. In a talk with Hadassah, Neumann warned that "unless the administration is made to realize that its disregard of its pledges to the Jews would have harmful consequences to them and their party, they will continue to act as they have acted, or worse."[31]

In 1946, the Zionist lobby had a chance to threaten Democratic control of the country's direction. A little over a third of the Senate and the entire House of Representatives was up for reelection. The Democrats had controlled both bodies since 1932. If the Republicans could take back one or both houses in that November, they would be able to block the president's agenda or even enact their own. That would mean, among other things, crippling or reversing the New Deal reforms passed during the Roosevelt years.

Jews made up only about 4 percent of the electorate nationally, but they had considerable clout in New York—the nation's largest and most important state—and some influence over results in Ohio, Pennsylvania, Illinois, and Maryland. In New York that year, a Senate seat, the governorship, and forty-five House seats were being contested. Ohio had a closely watched Senate race. And with Truman unpopular—a dismal 40 percent approval rating in that fall's opinion polls—these races were expected to be so close that a shift of a few percentage points toward the GOP in the Jewish vote could make a large difference.[32]

Silver and Neumann advocated that Zionist leaders remain neutral in the elections and focus instead on winning government support for Zionist proposals. They got the AZEC to pass a resolution, aimed at Wise, forbidding its board members from endorsing candidates. But by focusing their ire of the failure of the Truman administration to make good on its support for Zionism, Silver and Neumann were, in fact, calling on Jews to cast a protest vote against Democratic candidates. If that meant electing Republicans who would gut the nation's labor laws, so be it. It was a bold strategy, but also one, as Wise had warned, that raised the question of dual loyalty.

At a Hadassah board meeting, Etta Lasker Rosensohn, who later became president of the organization, described Silver and Neumann's strategy as "suicidal." "It seems to me when you come straight out and say that you are going to make that . . . the one criterion as to whether we should elect a man or not, you are saying something, if you permit, that is morally wrong, utterly indefensible and puts us in the same class as the Communists, whom all of us despise . . . because voting in American life they make the good of Russia the criterion of what is going to happen in America."[33]

When the AZEC debated the election strategy at its September 10 meeting, Wise and Rose Halprin of Hadassah opposed it, but to no avail. Silver and Neumann had a majority in favor. Afterward, Harry Shapiro, the AZEC's executive director and a Silver ally, sent out a memo to the local emergency committees advising them to hold public meetings and to run ads in local newspapers. For ad copy, he enclosed an "open letter to the Democratic party" that could be "signed by your leading rabbis, officers of groups within the Zionist ranks, etc." The ad, which appeared in New York City papers on October first, evoked the Biltmore platform rather than the proposal for partition. It accused the

Democratic Party of betraying its pledge to support "unrestricted im-migration and colonization" and a "Jewish commonwealth."[34]

While Silver, Neumann, and Shapiro were building public pressure on Truman and the Democrats to back the Zionist demands, Wise, Goldmann, Niles, and Democratic officials lobbied Truman and Acheson privately to come out strongly for partition. On August 30, Goldmann wrote Acheson asking him or the president to indicate support "for such a scheme."[35] On September 19, Niles and Democratic Party chairman Robert Hannegan, a close friend of Truman's from St. Louis, arranged for the president to meet with Wise, former New York governor Herbert Lehman, who was running for Senate, and prominent New York Democrat Monroe Goldwater. They urged him to take a public stand on the 100,000 immigrants and partition.

Goldmann's purpose was to use the United States to nudge the British, but Niles, Hannegan, Lehman, Wise, and Goldwater were equally if not more worried about the Jewish vote in the upcoming election. On October first, at Niles's suggestion, Hannegan forwarded to Truman a letter from Bartley Crum urging Truman to "put heart into the more than 5,000,000 citizens of Jewish blood in the United States who are now most disheartened."[36] Niles warned Truman that Thomas Dewey, who was running for governor of New York and who, if he won, was the likely Republican presidential nominee in 1948, planned an appeal on Palestine to New York's Jews on October 6. Abraham Feinberg, a wealthy New York businessman, Zionist, and Democratic fund-raiser, urged Truman to issue a statement on October 4, the eve of the Jewish holiday Yom Kippur, because in their sermons "every single Rabbi in every single synagogue will broadcast what you say."[37]

Truman had been reluctant to make a statement. After the uproar over Morrison-Grady, he didn't want to get involved in another public row over Palestine. Earlier in September, he had turned down a plea from Niles to issue a statement on immigration and partition that had been drafted by Eliahu Epstein and another Jewish Agency staffer, Leo Kohn. More important, Truman remained cool to the idea of a Jewish state in Palestine. On September 26, Truman told George Wadsworth that he was deeply concerned about the European Jewish refugees but, according to Wadsworth's memo, rejected the idea of a Jewish state and would only support "some local autonomy arrangement under the control of a power."[38]

But Truman was also a politician and was worried about his party's and his own election chances. After meeting Wise and three New Yorkers, he told Niles that he would make a statement. Niles enlisted Epstein to write a draft. Niles went over Epstein's draft and sent it to Acheson to make his own changes. In the final version, which he issued, as Feinberg advised, on the eve of Yom Kippur, Truman reiterated his "deep interest . . . that steps be taken at the earliest possible moment to admit 100,000 Jewish refugees to Palestine." Truman also promised to try to liberalize "the immigration laws of other countries, including the United States . . . with a view to the admission of displaced persons."

What attracted the most attention was what Truman said about partitioning Palestine. Acheson had weakened Epstein's formulation. He had the president cite the Jewish Agency proposal for "the creation of a viable Jewish state in control of its own immigration and economic policies in an adequate area," but then, instead of endorsing it outright, say that "it is my belief that a solution along these lines would command the support of public opinion in the United States." Acheson also had Truman add, "I cannot believe that the gap between the proposals [from Morrison-Grady and the Jewish Agency] is too great to be bridged by men of reason and goodwill. To such a solution, our Government could give its support."[39] This wording had the effect, if read carefully, of distancing the president from saying that he actually supported partition.

Silver was disappointed in the president's statement. While he was quick to take credit for the statement's existence—which, he wrote Ben-Gurion, had been precipitated by "mounting pressure inaugurated a few weeks ago by the Emergency Council"—he also noted that "our government is not backing the partition proposal of the Agency." "The danger now," Silver wrote, "is that having cashed in on whatever good will this statement may have produced among the Jews of America, the White House will be content to let the matter drop—as it has done time and again in the past after similar maneuvers on the eve of elections."[40]

Silver was partly right about the statement. It wasn't a clear endorsement of partition. But what mattered was not how Silver carefully parsed it but how the public and press *interpreted* it. Epstein, who complained to Goldmann about Acheson's changes in his statement, also acknowledged that "not a single newspaper has pointed up this part of the statement and all the headlines carried by the papers read 'Truman's Support of a Jewish State.'"[41] And that was how Truman's statement was read in Britain and the Middle East as well. The Jewish Telegraphic Agency, which was owned by the Jewish Agency and which aspired to be the Associated Press of the Zionist movement, headlined its own story, "Truman Urges Establishment of 'Viable Jewish State' Within Palestine."[42] Just as had happened with the Balfour Declaration in December 1917, the media and the public ignored whatever subtleties and ambiguities policy makers had intended.

The president, who still privately favored a federal Palestine, was content afterward to let the matter of a Jewish state drop. That fall, an exasperated Truman wrote Ed Pauley, a wealthy oilman and the Democratic National Committee treasurer, that the "situation is insoluble in my opinion. I have spent a year and a month trying to get some concrete action on it. Not only are the British highly successful in muddling the situation . . . but the Jews themselves are making it almost impossible to do anything for them."[43] Burned-out by the controversy—feeling he could do no more to accomplish what he thought was right—Truman decided to let the State Department handle any further negotiations.

Truman also dropped the idea of liberalizing American immigration laws, which had been urged sarcastically by Bevin and recommended by the Anglo-American Committee.* When Representative William Stratton introduced a bill the next year to allow entry of 400,000 refugees to the United States, Truman wrote Niles that "the idea of getting

---

*In April 1947, Representative William Stratton introduced a bill that would have allowed entry of 400,000 refugees to the United States. The bill won the support of the AFL and American Legion, but hostile House members amended it to penalize Jewish immigrants. Total immigrants were limited to 202,000. Those admitted from particular countries were to be counted against the future quotas for those countries. Jewish DPs were limited to those who arrived in camps before December 22, 1945, disqualifying many Jewish DPs, including all those who had fled from Poland, and preference was given to occupational groups such as farm laborers and construction workers that did not generally include Jews. Truman threatened a veto, but "with very great reluctance" signed the bill in June 1948. See *Truman Public Papers*, Aristide R. Zolberg, *A Nation by Design* (New York: Harvard University Press, 2006), pp. 307–308.

400,000 immigrants into this country is, of course, beyond our wildest dreams."[44]

But the Yom Kippur statement nevertheless represented a milestone in the struggle for a Jewish state. By making the statement, Truman unwittingly passed a threshold. He gave up trying to reconcile his own moral convictions about a Palestine that was neither Arab nor Jewish with the political imperatives created by Silver and the American Zionist movement. He put partition on the political agenda—not just that of the Zionist movement but of the United States and later the United Nations. It now became a question of whether partition could be implemented peacefully and, relatedly, whether it could be done in a way that acknowledged Jewish and Palestinian Arab national aspirations.

Silver did not acknowledge it, but Truman's endorsement of Jewish statehood would not have occurred without Goldmann having persuaded the Jewish Agency to abandon the Biltmore program for the more viable and less morally objectionable goal of partition. Nor would it have happened without insider lobbying by Niles and Wise. But it also would not have occurred without the unrelenting and obnoxious political pressure that Silver, Neumann, and the AZEC brought on the White House.

In Britain, Truman's Yom Kippur statement sparked still another angry response from Attlee and Bevin. The British had asked Truman to delay his statement of support for partition while they were attempting to reach a compromise between the Arabs and Jews, but Acheson explained to the British ambassador that Truman needed to make his statement before Dewey made his. That particularly infuriated Bevin. "In international affairs, I cannot settle things if my problem is made the subject of local elections," Bevin declared.[45]

Bevin charged that Truman's statement had derailed negotiations with the Jewish Agency that were about to bear fruit. That is not clear. What it did was undermine Bevin's own strategy, which depended on the United States joining Britain to enforce an agreement in Palestine that might not be entirely acceptable to one or both of the parties. To Bevin, Truman's Yom Kippur statement suggested that even if he were to make a commitment to enforce a genuine compromise between Jew and Arab, he could not be trusted to keep it if the American Zionist lobby put sufficient pressure on him. Bevin wrote in a memo to his colonial secretary "that the United States government will to the end remain an uncertain and unreliable factor in the problem."[46]

Could negotiations have borne fruit? It seems possible that if the Truman administration had defied the AZEC and withheld its support for partition and if Truman had been more supportive of British efforts, then Bevin could have won the Jewish Agency's agreement either to postpone their quest for statehood or to partition Palestine on somewhat equitable terms. With the threat of British and American intervention, the Arab states might have been able to persuade their Palestinian colleagues to go along. That may sound implausible, but at the end of negotiations, when it was too late, David Ben-Gurion showed that part of this strategy might have worked.

Silver's Victory

With the talks in recess and any agreement unlikely, Silver and his allies in the AZEC reaffirmed their hard-line stances. At the October 14 AZEC meeting, when Wise complained that local committees were running ads against Truman and the Democrats even after Truman had issued his Yom Kippur statement, Silver dismissed the significance of the statement. "The issuance of the statement was harmful not advantageous," he said. Silver declared that "the proposals for partition are pretty well dead."[47] When Wise defied the AZEC's ban against endorsements by endorsing the Democratic candidates for Senate and governor in New York, he was roundly denounced. A New York AZEC committee put out a press release declaring that "Dr. Wise spoke for no one but himself."[48]

At the annual ZOA convention in Atlantic City on October 27, Silver, backed by a majority of delegates, took aim at Goldmann and Wise and their positions. Silver criticized Goldmann for his "irresponsible announcements" and "harmful" political activities and Wise for supporting the loan to Britain.[49] The convention debated Goldmann's proposal for partition, but when Robert Szold proposed that Goldmann be invited to speak on its behalf, the ZOA's Committee on Political Resolution, which Silver controlled, rejected Szold's proposal. The delegates, Meyer Weisgal later commented, "were whooped up to the point of being ready to burn Nahum at the stake."[50] The convention rejected partition in favor of "the historic claims of the Jewish people to the whole of mandated Palestine."[51]

Silver's vendetta against Goldmann and Wise seems to have been at least partly driven by pique at having his authority undercut. (Ben-Gurion, who was tacitly allied with Silver during this period, nonetheless referred to him privately as "the Führer.")[52] But his and the AZEC's rejection of Goldmann's initiative also reflected their utter indifference to the Arab side of the dispute over Palestine. American Zionists conducted themselves as if it were still 1943. Silver would finally become a champion of partition, but only when it had become patently obvious that the attempt to secure the whole of Palestine was not politically viable. Goldmann had figured this out a decade before.

At the World Zionist Congress in Basel, which began on December 9, Silver and Neumann, armed with a majority of American delegates, continued their crusade to drive Goldmann, Wise, and their allies, including Weizmann, out of power. They attacked Goldmann's partition plan and won support for a resolution backing the Biltmore program. A resolution favored by Wise, Goldmann, and Weizmann to join the London talks was also defeated. And Goldmann's notion of a new Jewish state being part of a Middle Eastern federation was also shelved for a Eurocentric resolution that "Palestine should become a Jewish Commonwealth integrated into the structure of the democratic world."[53]

Silver and Neumann's hardline position enjoyed support not only from their American followers—of 385 delegates, 121 were Americans—but also from the Revisionists, who had decided to dissolve their New Zionist Organization and rejoin the Zionist Organization, and from two small labor parties on the left who favored a binational Palestine. Ben-Gurion, who couldn't stand Silver but was eager to oust his old rival Weizmann, also backed the Americans' position.

Silver and Neumann scored a political and a personal victory over their adversaries. Goldmann was transferred from Washington to London—to be replaced by Shertok, who was more agreeable to the two Americans, though no pushover. Wise was removed from the Jewish Agency Executive. And Weizmann—whose speech to the congress Neumann interrupted, loudly denouncing the aging statesman as engaging in "demagoguery"—was denied reelection as president of the Zionist Organization. Ben-Gurion remained as chairman of the Jewish

Agency Executive, and Silver became the sole chairman of the Jewish Agency's American section.[54] Silver told *The New York Times* that "the old leadership was repudiated" and the congress had come out with "a clear purpose and a clear line."[55]

Wise resigned from the AZEC. When Eliahu Epstein, who remained in Washington, wrote Wise regretting his decision, Wise replied, "I assure you that I will not be silent in this critical hour, but I cannot have [a] part in any work with Silver and . . . Neumann . . . I am liable to attacks of nausea, and I do not wish unduly to facilitate these."[56] A sickly Wise, who had loomed so large in American Zionism's first four decades, ceased to play a leading role in the American movement. Goldmann, too, was relegated over the next two years to a secondary role in the world movement.

Bevin's Last Stand

At the same time as Silver and Neumann were trying to inoculate the Zionist movement against compromise, the Arabs were hardening their stance against any accommodation with the British or the Jews. In December, the main Egyptian advocate of accommodation with Zionism, Premier Sidky Pasha, was forced out of office. And Saudi king Ibn Saud vigorously protested Truman's Yom Kippur statement. But the greatest obstacle to any compromise came from a new Palestinian Arab leadership.

In November, the British released twelve Palestinian Arabs who had been close to the mufti and allowed them to return to Palestine. That move, along with the release of imprisoned Jewish leaders, was supposed to create goodwill, but it had the opposite effect on negotiations among the parties. Three of the exiles and two others close to the mufti were put on the Arab Higher Committee, which meant that eight of ten places belonged to the Husseini faction. This faction took their cue from the mufti, who was now installed in Cairo, and who rejected even a hint of compromise with the British or the Jews.

Just prior to the January meetings, the mufti-controlled Arab Higher Committee publicized a memorandum that it had sent to the Arab League laying down its conditions for an agreement with the British. These included immediate independence, cessation of immigration, recognition of Jews only as a religious minority, and citizenship only for those Jews who had arrived in Palestine before 1917 and their direct descendants.[57]

In Palestine, the Higher Committee consolidated control over the militarized youth movements that had sprung up after World War II partly in response to Zionist terrorism. These groups, the Najjadah and Futuwwah, which numbered between 10,000 and 30,000, staged parades and drills and became known as the Higher Committee's "army."[58] When the Palestinian Arabs sent representatives to the London talks that reopened in January, the presence of this army emboldened the Husseinis to threaten war if the British tried to enforce partition or unrestricted immigration on Palestine.

The January 1947 talks took the same form they had in September. The Arabs conducted formal discussions, the Jewish Agency informal ones, and the results were exactly the same: stalemate. The Jewish Agency was less forthcoming than before. Earlier, it had argued for partition. Now it introduced partition only as a last resort and refused to specify how it would work or where the boundaries would be.[59] At a Jewish Agency Executive meeting on February 7, Goldmann strenuously objected to the "method of negotiations" being employed. He urged the agency to "put forward its own plan for partition."[60] But Neumann, Shertok, and Ben-Gurion, who were conducting the negotiations, did not heed Goldmann's advice.

The Arab negotiators were even less forthcoming. They insisted that in accepting prior Jewish immigration, they had made a sufficient compromise, and were unwilling to allow any further immigration. According to the British minutes, the "Palestinian Arabs recommended strongly that British should pack up and get out leaving Palestinian Arabs to handle the situation." They ominously declared that with the aid of the Arab League countries, they could "handle" any "prospect of bloodshed" from the Jews. Husseini gave a "fighting speech" warning that he didn't think it was possible for "the Arab governments . . . to restrain their populations . . . for much longer."[61]

To salvage the negotiations, Bevin and the British made a proposal modeled on the Morrison-Grady plan but that incorporated elements of the white paper. Palestine would be divided into Jewish and Arab majority cantons with some degree of self-rule—similar to Switzerland— but the British would oversee the country with the help of a Jewish and

Arab advisory council. The Jewish Agency would be dissolved so that the British no longer had to deal with America's Jews but only with those in Palestine. After five years, Palestine would become an independent unitary state under joint Arab-Jewish rule, but in fact under Arab majority rule.

The proposal tilted markedly to the Arabs. The Jews immediately and unconditionally rejected it; for them, it was a step down from Morrison-Grady. But the Arabs, who were unwilling to compromise even on 100,000 immigrants, also rejected it unconditionally. As they had done in 1939, the Arabs turned down a plan that under the circumstances was very favorable to them. The Palestinian Arabs suffered from a profound lack of national leadership. Their resentments—their continuing fury at the Balfour Declaration and at the Zionist attempt to deny them self-determination—were understandable, but these sentiments clouded their view of reality and made it impossible for them to recognize and accept genuine concessions.

Bevin, faced with rejection from both the Jews and Arabs, and with an economy that would no longer support Britain's overseas commitments, told the two sides on February 13 that he was giving up. Indeed, Bevin may have decided to give up months earlier and in the last month was merely making an offer he knew the parties would refuse. But Bevin's decision took the Zionist representatives by surprise.

The next day a chastened Ben-Gurion, who had always shown flexibility when the occasion required it, and was clearly worried about what would happen if the UN had to decide Palestine's fate, offered a dramatic compromise. In a meeting with Lord Jowitt, a member of the British cabinet, Ben-Gurion proposed that in exchange for the British allowing 100,000 Jews into Palestine over two years and the abrogation of the white paper, he would abandon the Zionist demand for a Jewish state for the time being. The mandate could continue "for five or ten years more," Ben-Gurion said. Jowitt replied, "I can tell you we met just in time."[62]

But it was actually too late. Bevin was no longer interested—with the treasury drained, Britain could no longer afford its overseas empire. The only way Britain could have continued the mandate was with a promise of American help, which was not forthcoming. Truman had become reluctant to get involved, and the State Department didn't want to put the United States in the midst of a civil war. The British cabinet never even considered Ben-Gurion's proposal. The window closed at the same time Ben-Gurion revealed that it had been open all along—if the United States and Britain had been willing to apply pressure. But in the end, both countries balked, and the stage was set for civil war.

On February 14, Bevin announced that Britain was ceding responsibility for the future of Palestine to the United Nations. Over the next week Britain also announced that it was granting independence to India and terminating military and financial aid to Greece and Turkey. Britain's new colonial secretary, Arthur Creech Jones, intimated in a speech to Parliament that the government hoped that the UN would reaffirm Britain's mandate, but Bevin seems to have given up trying to reconcile the parties. In a meeting on February 27, Goldmann tried to re-raise the proposals that Ben-Gurion had made, and Bevin stopped him. Britain would agree to continue the mandate only if there was "Jewish-Arab cooperation," he said.[63]

In a speech to Parliament, Bevin laid much of the blame for the failure to reach an agreement in Palestine on the American government and American Zionists, but he also blamed the mandate itself and, by extension, the Balfour Declaration:

> The problem of Palestine is a very vexed and complex one. There is no denying the fact that the Mandate contained contradictory promises. In the first place it promised the Jews a National Home, and, in the second place it declared that the rights and position of the Arabs must be protected. Therefore, it provided for what was virtually an invasion of the country by thousands of immigrants, and at the same time said that this was not to disturb the people in possession. The question therefore arose whether this could be accomplished without a conflict, and events in the last 25 years have proved that it could not.

Bevin had reached the same conclusion as the Peel Commission had reached a decade earlier. The Balfour Declaration was itself to blame. That was correct. The British and Zionists had conspired to screw the Arabs out of a country that by the prevailing standards of self-determination would have been theirs. But saying that did not lead to an answer of what to do now in Palestine. Here Bevin had no answer and fell back on blaming the Americans.

Truman's thinking at this point had become muddled. He didn't support the idea of establishing a Jewish state in a place where another people had lived for centuries. He believed that the Zionists were treating the Arabs unfairly. The Zionists, he had written Pauley, "seem to have the same attitude toward the 'underdog' when they are on top as they have been treated as 'underdogs' themselves."[64] But Truman refused to recognize that any attempt to resolve the conflict in Palestine along the lines of the Morrison-Grady plan would have required at least the threat and probably the use of force. And the British, with the treasury exhausted, were in no position to do that without American help.

Truman had, of course, good reasons for ruling out the use of American troops: the army was demobilizing while facing what appeared to be a growing threat in Europe from the Soviet Union. But by ruling out American intervention, Truman made it difficult to achieve what he continued to believe was the fairest outcome in Palestine. Relentless Zionist pressure made what was difficult impossible. After he had given in to the Zionists and issued his Yom Kippur statement, Truman put his own vision of Palestine in the back drawer of his mind. It no longer defined for him what the choices were. Instead, he allowed the nationalism of the Zionist movement and the realpolitik of the State Department to define what was possible. Truman would refer back to his own vision, but in the form of nostalgia about what could have happened if various parties had not dismissed the findings of the Anglo-American Committee and Morrison and Grady's plan to implement these findings. It was Truman's enduring lament about Palestine.

Silver, for his part, had now achieved in the American Zionist movement the absolute control that he had sought since 1943. But at his moment of triumph, he was forced to recognize that he didn't know what to do with his power. Like other Zionists, Silver feared that throwing Palestine's future into the lap of the UN would mean delay and obstruction. On the day that Bevin announced he was giving up, Silver went to see Acheson. Acheson found him "subdued and rather frightened by the impasse that has been produced."[65] Silver had ousted Goldmann, but—faced with the prospect of a debate over Palestine's future at the UN—he was going to be forced to accept the leadership of Ben-Gurion and Zionist leadership in Palestine and to plead, cajole, and thunder for a partitioned Palestine.

13

PASSING THE BUCK

Sitting on Truman's desk in the Oval Office was a small, rectangular glass sign in a walnut base that read *The Buck Stops Here!* Truman's conduct as president has often been summed up in those words. He is remembered for being decisive, for taking responsibility for his decisions, and for not second-guessing himself or his advisors. But while Truman may have acted decisively toward the Soviet Union or toward the Republican Congress, he was, after the failure of the Morrison-Grady proposal, anything but decisive in dealing with the future of Palestine.

The pattern, established in the fall of 1946, looked like this: Convinced that no just outcome was possible in Palestine, Truman would try to withdraw from the issue altogether, leaving it to the State Department. But as the threat of civil war loomed larger in Palestine, and after the conflict over policy between the American Zionist movement and State Department had grown louder, Truman would reluctantly reenter the fray. At first, he would side with the State Department, whose positions were actually closer to his own, but under relentless political pressure from the Zionists, he would give in and do what they asked. Afterward, he would insist that he hadn't bowed to pressure, but—probably because he knew that he had and was disgusted with himself—would withdraw again from the issue and leave it to the State Department. That happened with the Yom Kippur statement and would happen the next year after the British had thrown the issue of Palestine into the lap of the UN. Truman hoped the UN, with some guidance from the State Department but with the United States clearly taking a backseat, could resolve the conflict in Palestine. That proved to be wishful thinking.

By ceding the issue of Palestine to the UN, the British were, in effect, throwing it into the lap of the United States. The UN had only existed a year. Its offices were housed temporarily on Lake Success— about a fifty-minute drive from New York City—in a converted gyroscope factory, and the General Assembly met at an old World's Fair auditorium in Flushing Meadows. The United States supplied the bulk of the funds and controlled more votes than any other country. It couldn't necessarily get its way on contentious issues—in the Security Council, each one of the five permanent members of the council, including the Soviet Union, enjoyed a veto—but no significant proposal could get through the General Assembly or the Security Council without American support. The UN would be unable to reach a meaningful decision on Palestine without clear American support and direction.

An exhausted Dean Acheson, who would go back to his private law practice in June, understood what the British action portended. "It is hard to see how we can escape the responsibility for leadership," Acheson wrote Loy Henderson the day after Bevin had announced his decision.[1] But Truman didn't see it that way, and his illusions were reinforced by Secretary of State George Marshall, who, facing a Soviet challenge in Western Europe, hoped that the department itself could evade final responsibility for the outcome in Palestine.

A Low Priority

Truman tossed the folder for Palestine onto the State Department's desk at the worst possible moment—just as Foggy Bottom was becoming preoccupied with the Cold War. Communists were taking power in Poland and Hungary; Greece was embattled; the Soviets were waging a struggle for Iranian oil concessions; and Communists in Western Europe were gaining support because of continuing economic hardship. In March, Truman announced that the United States would take over Britain's role in guarding Greece and Turkey from communist insurgents.

In June, Marshall announced his huge economic recovery plan for Europe.

Marshall, Acheson, and the former investment banker Robert Lovett, who succeeded Acheson as undersecretary in June, accorded a relatively low priority to the events in Palestine.[2] Their objective was to resolve the conflict between the Jews and Arabs without having to send in troops that they thought were needed in Europe and in Turkey and Iran. (The number of soldiers in uniform had dropped from 3.5 million in 1945 to 400,000.) They also didn't want to become identified with an "American plan" that would either infuriate the Jews and bring political pressure upon the president or offend the Arabs and drive oil-rich countries into the waiting arms of the Soviet Union. Peace and quiet rather than justice were their goals.

Marshall, Acheson, and Lovett were relatively unversed in the politics of Palestine, so they relied on Henderson and the office of Near Eastern and African Affairs to guide them. After the British threw the issue to the UN, Acheson wrote to Henderson asking his advice about what to do. Acheson wondered whether the United States should favor partition or "conclude that despite its domestic advantages for us that policy carries too great a weight of international difficulty to put across."[3] Henderson replied that "we should move slowly in committing ourselves in any direction."

Henderson was particularly concerned that if the United States committed itself to partition, pressures from "highly organized groups in the United States" would make it impossible for the administration to compromise in the face of widespread opposition to partition in the UN. Henderson didn't say whether he still favored partition, which he seems to have supported during the fall of 1946 only out of loyalty to Acheson. He said that the NEA was "reviewing all plans for Palestine."[4]

With Marshall attending to the Cold War and Truman disgusted with anything related to Palestine, Henderson's advice of inaction easily carried the day. As deliberations began at the United Nations, the State Department refused to take any substantive position. The United States insisted that it not be a member of a special committee that UN secretary-general Trygve Lie appointed to make recommendations on Palestine. The United States and Britain backed putting the issue in the hands of what Acheson called "a small committee of neutral nations."[5] Lie appointed representatives of Australia, Canada, Sweden, Peru,

Guatemala, Uruguay, India, Iran, Yugoslavia, Czechoslovakia, and the Netherlands to a UN special committee that was supposed to present a proposal to the General Assembly by September first. This was a hallmark of British and American irresponsibility.

As the committee began deliberating, Marshall wrote the chief UN representative, former senator Warren Austin, that "we are inclined to believe that it might be preferable not to make any public statement of our views with regard to the future government of Palestine." Marshall added, "We are convinced that there is no solution of the Palestine problem which will not meet with strong opposition from one or several quarters."[6]

American Zionists attacked the administration for failing to take a clear position on Palestine's future. The Emergency Council staged an Action for Palestine Week in May calling on the president and Austin to "speak out for the American policy on Palestine."[7] At a UN press conference, Silver accused Truman of appealing to Arabs by slighting the Jews.[8] Truman was infuriated by Silver's charge. When Niles sent Truman a report on the mufti that *The Nation* had produced in order to discredit Arab testimony at the United Nations, Truman scrawled a note to Niles on the first page: "We could have settled this Palestine thing if U.S. politics had been kept out of it. Terror and Silver are the contributing causes of some if not all of our troubles . . . I surely wish God Almighty would give the Children of Israel an Isaiah, the Christians a St. Paul and the Sons of Ishmael a peep at the Golden Rule."[9] Silver, of course, was being unfair in accusing Truman of favoring the Arabs, but not in sensing that something was amiss.

The Soviet Turnaround

While Truman looked to the UN for a solution, Zionist leaders, who assumed joint opposition from the Arab states and the Soviet Union, feared that the organization would decide against them. The AZEC staff member Frank Akzin wrote that "the chances of a favorable action by the UN is extremely remote."[10] At a meeting in April, the Jewish Agency Executive decided to demand from the UN merely that the British continue its mandate under the conditions of relatively unrestricted immigration and land sales that prevailed before the white paper of 1939. But as the Zionists would soon discover, they had misjudged their own prospects.

During the early debate at the UN's special session, the Soviet Union had sided with the Arab states' demand that the special committee focus on establishing independence from the British, which would lead to an Arab-majority state. As late as May 10, the Soviet representative to the UN, Andrei Gromyko, seconded the Arab stance; but four days later, Gromyko gave a speech that shocked American, Arab, and Zionist diplomats and created "jubilation" among Jews in Palestine.[11] Gromyko reiterated his support for "an independent, dual, democratic, homogeneous Arab-Jewish state," but he then went on to say that "if this plan proved impossible to implement because of the deterioration in the relations between the Jews and the Arabs . . . then it would be necessary to consider . . . the partition of Palestine into two independent autonomous states, one Jewish and one Arab."[12]

The American ambassador to the Soviet Union, Walter Bedell Smith, attributed the Soviet turnabout to the special importance the Soviet Union attached to ousting Great Britain from the Middle East.[13] With the British out of the way, the Soviets believed they would stand a much better chance of gaining influence in the region. Both options that Gromyko presented would have knocked out the British. And it was probably significant that the first two-thirds of Gromyko's speech consisted of a denunciation of the British mandate, charging Britain with having turned Palestine into a "semi-military and police state."[14]

But there was probably an added factor. In the United States, the Soviet Union hoped to build opposition to the Truman administration's Cold War policies among the remnants of the New Deal Popular Front, led by former vice president and cabinet official Henry Wallace, whom Truman had dismissed in September 1946 over Wallace's disagreement with Truman's aggressive anti-Soviet policies. Jewish liberals and leftists were an important part of this New Deal coalition; and like the older generation of Wise and Brandeis, many of these Jews, including the writer I. F. Stone and the labor leader David Dubinsky, were Zionists. By favoring partition, the Soviet Union hoped to curry favor among them, leading them to question the administration's Cold War policies as well as its policies in Palestine.

In a conversation in March 1948 with the Jewish Agency representative Eliahu Epstein, the Soviet UN representative Semen K. Tsarapkin hinted at this strategy. The Soviet diplomat drew a sharp contrast between Soviet and Truman administration support for Palestine. According to Epstein, Tsarapkin "expressed satisfaction with the fact that the Jewish public in the United States is beginning to understand who the 'real friends' of an independent Palestine are, and who is giving 'lip service' only to such support."[15] That suggests that one Soviet motive was to outflank the Truman administration in support for Palestine.

The State Department in Washington, preoccupied with the Soviet challenge in Europe, failed to grasp the significance of Gromyko's speech. A State Department memo suggested that he was paving the way "to come out forthrightly on the side of the Arabs . . . later at a moment when the Soviets could reap the greatest benefits in the Moslem world."[16] By contrast, the Jewish Agency fully appreciated the significance of Gromyko's statement. "There should be no differences of opinion among the major powers now, when even Russia has expressed itself in favor of partition," a Jewish Agency spokesman told the Jewish Telegraphic Agency.[17]

Gromyko's statement put an end to the Jewish Agency proposal for continuing the mandate and put partitioning Palestine back at the top of the Zionist agenda. Most members of the Jewish Executive began to close ranks around obtaining "a viable Jewish state in an adequate area of Palestine." And Ben-Gurion, who, of all the interested parties, could see most clearly down the road, secretly began readying the Jewish community to take power when the British left and to defend itself against Arab attack. "It is essential to continue to build up the strength of the Yishuv," Ben-Gurion wrote his wife.[18]

Silver also grasped the significance of the Soviet reversal, but he drew different conclusions from Ben-Gurion. Silver took the Soviet support for partition as a reason to reassert the Basel program of an undivided Palestine. When Ben-Gurion proposed partitioning Palestine, Silver sternly rebuked him, reminding him of the "full Zionist program" adopted in Basel. Ben-Gurion, whose alliance of convenience with Silver had expired, fired back an angry letter of his own. "When myself or other executive member expresses views not on your behalf, it does not call for your public explanation," he wrote.[19]

The UNSCOP Proposals

At the United Nations, the Truman administration had ceded the initiative to the United Nations Special Committee on Palestine (UNSCOP), which arrived in Jerusalem on June 16. It had not held hearings in New York out of deference to the Arabs, who feared the hearings would provide a platform for American Zionists. The committee members were chosen from nations that hadn't taken a stand on the conflict, and as the committee sailed from New York, at most three of the eleven members were favorably inclined to Zionism; but by the time they completed their stay in Palestine, a majority were backing some form of a Jewish state. That was largely because of the way in which the Jewish Agency, the British, and the Arab Higher Committee (AHC) and Arab League dealt with the committee members during their visit. As had happened in 1937 and in 1946 when the Anglo-American Committee visited, the Jews tried to win over the unconverted, while the Arabs squandered what support and sympathy they had.

The Jewish Agency appointed two rising stars, David Horowitz, an economist, and Abba Eban, a young Cambridge graduate, to accompany the group. Their instructions, reflecting Silver's eclipse, were to work for a "Jewish state in a suitable area of Palestine."[20] They inundated the group with information, especially about economic development. The American consul general in Jerusalem reported back to the State Department that when the committee visited Tel Aviv on June 25, "crowds clapped and sang for the delegates and pressed around their cars to shake their hands. Hebrew newspapers extolled the individual members and at the Great Synagogue, the committee heard Chief Rabbi Unterman call upon the Almighty to 'instill in the hears of the United Nations Committee knowledge, wisdom, and intelligence, to judge honestly and to gather the people of Israel in their Holy Land to revive and rebuild it.'"[21]

In the hearings held at the YMCA auditorium in Jerusalem, the Jewish Agency representatives stressed their goodwill toward the Arabs. On July 4, Ben-Gurion, who was preparing for war with the Arabs, made the case for a Jewish state that would enjoy excellent relations with the Arabs inside and outside it: "Only by establishing Palestine as a Jewish state can the true objectives be accomplished: immigration and settlement for the Jews, economic development and social progress for the Arabs . . . Nothing will further the Jewish Arab alliance more than the establishment of the Jewish state."[22]

What best made the Jewish Agency's case was the British response that summer to the arrival of the immigrant ship *Exodus 1947.* The Jewish Agency designed the *Exodus*'s journey to embarrass the British, and it succeeded beyond their wildest expectations. The dilapidated ship left for Palestine from France on July 11 with 4,554 Jewish refugees on board. Before it arrived in Haifa, it was intercepted by British destroyers. British soldiers boarded the *Exodus* and killed two immigrants and a crew member and wounded about one hundred other immigrants. The ship was then escorted to Haifa, where in plain view of three committee members the immigrants were forced to board three ships for deportation back to France. When the ships arrived back in France, the immigrants refused to disembark and were sent to displaced persons camps in Germany. The incident profoundly affected the committee and also boosted public support in Europe and the United States for a Jewish state. It reinforced the argument that establishing a Jewish state was a necessary and appropriate response to Nazi genocide.

UNSCOP invited the Arab League and the Arab Higher Committee to send representatives to testify before it in Jerusalem, but the Arabs were bitterly divided. Privately, Jordan favored partition as long as it could annex the West Bank. The Egyptians, Saudis, and Syrians distrusted the Jordanians as much as they distrusted the Zionists. None of the Arab leaders trusted the mufti, but because Jordan's King Abdullah wanted to displace him entirely so that he could take over Arab Palestine, the other Arab states continued to defer to the mufti publicly. Competing Palestinian Arab leaders like Musa al-Alami and Jamal Husseini were afraid to buck the prelate because of his popularity in Palestine. As a result, the mufti's unyielding stance against the Jews and the British carried the day.

The AHC boycotted the committee hearings and, on the committee's arrival in Jerusalem, staged a general strike in protest. The committee members were offended. The head of UNSCOP, Chief Justice Emil Sandström of Sweden, went on the radio to plead with the AHC to cooperate. One of the Yugoslav delegates, who were thought to be sympathetic to the Arab cause, read a statement at the first public meeting of

UNSCOP condemning the boycott. The AHC also refused to cooperate with the committee during UNSCOP's travels in Palestine. When the committee visited Arab-owned factories in Jaffa and Haifa, the owners spurned the group because Jewish journalists were traveling with them. When UNSCOP visited an Arab village, the villagers evacuated it in anticipation of their arrival.

During the summer, several representatives from the Arab League and the AHC, outside the earshot of the mufti and their fellow Arab officials, told Jewish Agency representatives and British officials that they opposed the mufti and would have considered some plan for a federal or cantonized Palestine. King Abdullah reiterated to the British his support for partition. Publicly, however, they retained a united front in favor of the mufti and his hard-line position. When several representatives from the Arab League met with the committee in Beirut, they called for a unitary Arab Palestine. Hamid Frangié, the foreign minister of Lebanon, told the committee that all the Jews who had arrived since 1917 were in Palestine illegally.[23] Paul Mohn, the deputy chairman of the delegation, later wrote, "There is nothing more extreme than meeting all the representatives of the Arab world in one group . . . when each one tries to show that he is more extreme than the other."[24]

By August, when the committee arrived in Geneva at the old League of Nations Headquarters to formulate its proposals, there was no support for the Arab position. And the British, too, through their lack of cooperation with the committee and their handling of the immigrants aboard *Exodus 1947*, had eliminated any support for reaffirming the mandate. The committee members' choice came down to partition or some version of the Morrison-Grady plan.

In Geneva, the delegates studied the Peel Commission recommendations on partition and invited Richard Crossman, the Labor representative on the Anglo-American Committee and the author of *Palestine Mission*, to speak to them. Crossman favored partition but thought it had to be done fairly and quickly. "British evacuation without any solution being provided will lead to the Jews capturing the larger part of the country, and thereby obtaining very much more territory than under organized partition," Crossman warned.[25] That was a warning that would have been worth heeding.

Seven of the committee members backed partition, three backed a federal plan similar to Morrison-Grady, and one, the delegate from Australia, abstained, but none of the members could agree on the details. They relied on Ralph Bunche, whom the United Nations secretary-general had appointed as a special assistant to UNSCOP, to draft the majority and minority report. Bunche, an African American, was raised by his grandmother in Los Angeles. An outstanding student, he graduated summa cum laude from UCLA and received a doctorate in political science from Harvard. He taught at Howard University but also worked for the United Nations as a troubleshooter. He received the Nobel Peace Prize in 1950 for his work in Palestine.

Bunche had little prior acquaintance with Palestine. From Jerusalem he wrote a friend, "I am now a Near East expert, completely befuddled."[26] But Bunche was a quick study, and as a genuine outsider who also had a personal acquaintance with racial and ethnic discrimination, he acquired a keen understanding of the conflict between the Jews and Arabs. He wrote in his diary on July 4, the day of Ben-Gurion's testimony, "One thing seems sure. This problem can't be solved on the basis of abstract justice, historical or otherwise. Reality is that both Arabs and Jews are here and intend to stay. Therefore, in any 'solution' some group, or at least its claim, is bound to get hurt. [The] danger in any arrangement is that a caste system will develop with backward Arabs as the lower caste."[27] The future of Palestine was encapsulated in that observation.

Bunche had a low opinion of the committee members, whom he described as "just about the worst group I have ever had to work with ... they are all so petty, so vain, so striving and not infrequently either vicious or stupid."[28] That was borne out in the frenetic last week at Geneva when Bunche had to cobble together the proposals. The majority plan for partition was roughly modeled on the Peel Commission's proposal, but added the Negev to the Jewish state, which the Jewish Agency representatives had pushed hard for. The Zionists' public rationale was that the Jews alone were equipped to develop the desert into an inhabitable region, but privately they hoped the desert contained valuable minerals and were even more interested in developing a port on its southward tip that opened onto the Gulf of Aqaba and the Red Sea. A port there would provide a Jewish state with a passage to the east in case the Egyptians blocked off the Suez Canal. That, again, was another indication that the Jews were thinking ahead.

Under the plan that Bunche negotiated by shuttling between delegates with map in hand, the Jews got the coast, the Negev, and the fertile Western Galilee. The Arabs got the West Bank of the Jordan and a slice down the south and along the border with Egypt. Jerusalem and its holy places would remain under UN control. The Jewish and Arab states would be united in an economic union with a common currency and means of transportation.

All in all, the Jews who made up about a third of the population would get about 55 percent of the land; the Arabs would get about 40 percent, and the UN would administer the rest. The Jewish state would include 498,000 Jews, 407,000 Arabs, and some 90,000 transient Bedouins. The Jewish population would soon be augmented by 150,000 immigrants from Europe, but in the long run the higher Arab birthrate would probably lead the Arab population to exceed the Jewish in the Jewish state. The Arab state, by contrast, would contain 725,000 Arabs and only 10,000 Jews.

The plan was unfair to the Arabs. Their state lacked a viable seaport and a capital, and Jaffa, an Arab city of 70,000, would be included in the Jewish state. It was also unworkable. Former State Department official Evan Wilson wrote that "the scheme depended for its success on some form of economic union: without it, the two proposed states would not be economically viable. In fact the entire plan, with its checkerboard-like division of the country into six different zones (not counting Jerusalem) converging at only two meeting points, and with its four separate entities—Jewish state, Arab state, internationalized Jerusalem, and the economic union, was far too complex to be workable without a maximum of good will on all sides."[29] And needless to say, there was not even a minimum of goodwill.

The AHC and the Arab League rejected not only the majority but the minority report, which would have set up a federated Palestine governed by a popularly elected constituent assembly. The AHC warned that "any attempt to impose a solution contrary to the Arabs' birthright will lead to trouble, bloodshed, and probably a third world war."[30] The mufti—determined to kill any chance for a deal—described the minority proposal as "partition in disguise,"[31] which it was to some extent, but the borders of the Arab and Jewish quasi-states were to be decided by an Arab-majority national assembly. While Jordan's Abdullah told a Greek diplomat that he was counting on partition so that he could annex the Arab portion, he joined other Arab League leaders in denouncing the plans publicly.

In Geneva, the two Jewish Agency representatives, Nathan Epstein and Arthur Lourie, wired Ben-Gurion and Shertok, warning them not to reject the majority proposal or even dwell on its failings. "Must earnestly emphasize danger any public statement that would make possible for British to say that Jews like Arabs have rejected majority report," they wrote. Epstein and Lourie advised the Jewish Agency to gear its response to the "high authority [of] the United States."[32]

Ben-Gurion agreed with Epstein and Lourie. While he lamented the exclusion of Jerusalem and the Western Galilee from the Jewish state, he advised the Jewish Agency general council—the agency's second-highest decision-making body, which was to meet in Zurich on September 3—to "respond favorably" to the majority report. And he warned that the support of Marshall and the United States was "most important" to the proposal's passage in the UN.[33]

The Revisionist movement rejected the proposals, and so, initially, did Silver. Speaking for the Emergency Council, Silver told a New York Yiddish daily that the majority report "represents a great step forward in comparison with former proposals and should be viewed as the expression of the conscience of mankind . . . [But] the territorial boundaries set for the Jewish state are a great blow and we must fight against this. I still maintain my previous position that we must demand all of Palestine and wait for such an offer on the part of the UN Assembly as will prove acceptable to us."[34]

Silver still harbored dreams of a Palestine "undivided and undiminished," but his view was not shared at the Jewish Agency general council. At the Zurich meeting, the agency representatives voted 61 to 6 to back the majority report. The Jewish Agency planned to propose amendments in the fall, but to take a generally positive outlook toward the plan. And they intended to focus on gaining the Truman administration's support for the proposal. To the surprise of the other delegates, Silver and Neumann went along with the decision. Wrote David Horowitz, "Dr. A. H. Silver and Emanuel Neumann astonished us by displaying a positive attitude, wishing us every success in achieving the creation of a Jewish state in a suitable area of Palestine."[35]

Silver and Neumann lost another key vote at the meeting. Ben-Gurion proposed vigorous opposition to Irgun terrorism against the British, which had continued unabated during the UNSCOP visit when Irgun terrorists in Jerusalem had even tried to kidnap a government liaison officer with UNSCOP. (The official, who was struck on the head with a hammer, escaped because his wife's screams attracted attention.) Silver and Neumann opposed the resolution, but backed off when they saw the Zionists in Palestine united against them.[36]

That meeting marked a milestone in the relationship that the Emergency Council, and more broadly the American Zionist movement, had to the Zionist leadership in Palestine. In the past, Silver and the Emergency Council had hewn to their own path—either taking leadership in the agency or noisily dissenting—but after the Zurich meeting, the American movement subordinated itself to Ben-Gurion and the leadership in Palestine. There would be disagreements, especially after the war in 1948, but in these disagreements Ben-Gurion and his successors would invariably prevail. The American Zionist movement was consigned to doing what Silver and Neumann did best: pressure the American administration to back what the Zionist leaders in Palestine wanted.

At the time, Silver and the AZEC's subordination to Zionist leaders in Palestine was a net plus. Silver and Neumann had become uncomfortably close to Begin and the Irgun. And Silver's strategy of pressing for an undivided Palestine was unrealistic and would have undermined support for Zionism in the UN. But in the long run the subordination of the American movement to the leaders in Palestine and later Israel would lead to the creation of a Zionist and pro-Israel lobby in the United States that lacked a mind of its own, except on such purely tactical matters as how to best lobby Congress or the White House.

Battle in Washington

In September, after UNSCOP produced its report, Lie convened an ad hoc committee on Palestine, made up of one representative from each member state, to consider the UNSCOP proposals and choose which one the General Assembly should vote on. The Truman administration finally had to take a position. That led to a renewed struggle over what American policy toward Palestine should be. It pitted American Zionists and their allies in the White House—Niles, Rosenman, Max Lowenthal, and Rosenman's replacement as special counsel, Clark Clifford—against the State Department and its allies in the Pentagon. Truman tried to stay above the fray, but he was invariably drawn in by political pressures.

The first battle was over personnel and not directly over policy. The United States had nine representatives to the United Nations, including such luminaries as Eleanor Roosevelt, future secretary of state John Foster Dulles, and future Democratic presidential candidate Adlai Stevenson. Austin was the chief representative and diplomat Herschel Johnson was his deputy. The State Department designated Johnson to be the U.S. representative on the ad hoc committee. And it appointed Henderson and Wadsworth to be advisors to the committee.

Niles sent a memorandum to Truman complaining about the choice of the two advisors. Niles expressed his misgivings by appealing to Truman's political fears, warning that their appointment would provoke lobbying against him and his party. "Because both are widely regarded as unsympathetic to the Jewish viewpoint, much resentment will be engendered when their appointment is announced and later," Niles wrote.[37] Niles also circulated an unsigned "Note on Ambassador George Wadsworth," which described the official as an "anti-Semite and an anti-Zionist."[38] In backing up this charge, the note equated Wadsworth's opposition to a Jewish state with anti-Semitism.

Niles acknowledged in his memo to Truman that "it may not be feasible to oppose Henderson and Wadsworth as advisors to the delegation." He proposed instead to counter them by adding as an advisor the former general John Hilldring, who had served as assistant secretary of state for the occupation, oversaw the DP camps, and was known to be sympathetic to Zionism. Truman let Niles have his way—partly, it seems, out of fondness for Niles, but also because Niles knew how to appeal to Truman's political fears. The president sent a memorandum to Robert Lovett recommending that Hilldring be appointed as an advisor. And when one of the nine UN representatives resigned because of ill health, Hilldring became part of the American delegation and a pipeline into the delegation for Niles and the Zionist movement.

Policy, however, was still in the State Department's hands, and on September 15, Marshall, with Henderson in tow, met with the UN delegates in New York. Marshall was, perhaps, the most respected figure in American public life; the country's military leader during World War II and now its secretary of state. Dour, humorless, impersonal—no one except his wife and oldest army friends called him by his first name—he exuded authority. Members of Congress, who had been willing to badger administration officials to back Zionist measures, spoke softly in Marshall's presence. In a letter to his superior Moshe Shertok, Eliahu Epstein, who had continued to be the Jewish Agency representative in Washington, rued the passing of the "good old times" when they could get Congress to gang up on a secretary of state.[39]

Marshall, Henderson later recounted, felt that Palestine was "more of an internal than an international problem and had to be faced in a way quite different from most foreign affairs problems."[40] Marshall's recognition that domestic pressures had to be taken into account made him more amenable to compromise on the issue than Henderson and the NEA were. That fall, he tried to reach an accommodation among the opposing perspectives on the subject. His refusal to take a firm stand frustrated the Zionists, but also disturbed Henderson, Wadsworth, and other NEA officials who had reverted to their strong opposition to a Jewish state, whether in all or part of Palestine.

In his presentation to the UN delegates, Marshall echoed Henderson's warnings, even after Gromyko's speech, that the "adoption of the [UNSCOP] majority report . . . would mean [a] very violent Arab reaction" that could push the Arabs into the arms of the Soviet Union. Unlike Henderson, however, he didn't take that as a reason to oppose partition but to temper the way the United States went about supporting it. He advised the delegates that the United States "should avoid actively arousing the Arabs and precipitating their rapprochement with the Soviet Union *in the first week or ten days of the General Assembly*" (my italics). In other words, Marshall accepted as a fait accompli that the United States would eventually heed "evident popular desire" and come out in favor of partition, but he wanted to postpone the reaction. His argument was tactical. He was concerned that arousing the Arabs early in the debate would "create difficulties . . . in subsequent General

Assembly maneuvering" and would also oblige the United States to take the lead in enforcing a resolution if it was resisted militarily.[41]

Marshall read the U.S. delegates the statement he planned to deliver before the General Assembly on September 21. It praised UNSCOP's effort without endorsing either the majority or minority proposal. Hilldring told Marshall that such a statement "would certainly be a disappointment to American Jews and Jews everywhere."[42] Eleanor Roosevelt took a different tack. While she had not been in favor of a Jewish state, she wanted the United States to support the UN's effort at peacemaking by endorsing the majority report. "Support of the United Nations report would strengthen the United Nations in the minds of the American people," she said.[43] Roosevelt and Hilldring downplayed any danger that the attempt to implement partition could lead to war.[44]

When Marshall spoke four days later to the General Assembly, he took account of Hilldring's and Roosevelt's objections. He added a telltale clause at the conclusion that left open the possibility of the United States backing the majority position. "The Government of the United States," he said, "gives great weight not only to the recommendations which have met with the unanimous approval of the Special Committee, but also to those which have been approved by the majority of that committee."[45] That wasn't exactly an endorsement—the Jewish Agency wasn't satisfied at all—but it was enough to infuriate the Arab representatives at the UN and to worry Henderson that he was losing the debate over U.S. policy.

Alarmed by Marshall's concessions to Zionism, Henderson produced a memo quaintly entitled "Certain Considerations against Advocacy by the U.S. of the Majority Plan." In it, he predictably warned that American support for partition would throw the Arabs into the arms of the Soviet Union. But he also argued that the plan for partition was "unworkable." The plan's economic union could not work without "Arab-Jewish friendship and cooperation," which did not exist. And if the UN tried to implement partition, it would lead to permanent hostilities that would pose a continuing challenge to the United States and would require "major contributions in force, material and money" from the U.S. government as well.[46] Henderson recommended that instead of backing either the majority or minority proposal, the United States should support an extended UN trusteeship over Palestine that would allow "long and protracted discussions during the course of which moderate Jews and moderate Arabs would find common ground."[47]

Henderson's warning that the partition plans would lead to American military involvement came directly on the heels of a decision by the British cabinet not to help implement a UN plan unless both the Jews and the Arabs agreed to it. For Bevin, who believed the majority plan was "manifestly unjust to the Arabs," that was tantamount to saying that the British were giving up any responsibility for Palestine's future.[48] While other countries at the UN continued to assume that the British would implement whatever plan they came up with, Henderson feared that any military responsibility for implementing partition would devolve upon the United States.

Henderson was certainly right that attempting to partition Palestine would lead to war and that American troops might be enlisted to keep the peace, but he overlooked the possibility that the attempt to impose a trusteeship could also lead to war. If judged by the criterion of whether force would be needed to make it work, Henderson's alternative was no more workable than UNSCOP's majority proposal. Nonetheless, Henderson and other foes of partition continued to insist over the next seven months that the United States should back a plan for trusteeship because it would not require force to implement it.

Henderson's memo was widely circulated, and several days later he was invited to the White House to defend it. In Truman's presence, Niles and Clifford, who had become a recent convert to Zionism, harshly cross-examined him. Finally, according to Henderson, Truman got up. "Oh hell, I'm leaving," he said. In recalling the incident decades later, Henderson astutely said of Truman:

> Although I was not in a position, of course, to know what his real feelings were, I had the impression that he realized that the Congress, the press, the Democratic Party, and aroused American public opinion in general, would turn against him if he should withdraw his support for the Zionist cause. On the other hand, it seemed to me, he was worried about what the long-term effect would be on the United States if he should continue to support the policies advocated by the Zionists. He was almost desperately hoping, I thought, that the Department of State would tell him that the setting up in Palestine of Arab and Jewish

States as proposed by the U.N. Commission would be in the interest of the United States. This, however, the State Department had not been able to do.[49]

Putting Pressure on Truman

By mid-October, the Truman administration could no longer equivocate. It had to announce whether it backed the majority proposal and, if so, under what conditions. The Zionist movement, aware of Truman's determination to avoid any decision on a Jewish state, and concerned about Henderson's influence on the American position, began a campaign to force the president to come out clearly for the majority proposal. Silver and the AZEC initiated scores of letters and telegrams to Truman and Marshall. Rhode Island's Democratic State Committee, for instance, wrote Truman a letter, signed by all the major Democratic officeholders in the state, calling for him to pursue a "pro-Jewish policy in Palestine."[50] The AZEC got twenty-three governors to wire Truman to demand that he "give full and vigorous support" to the majority proposal.[51]

The organized Zionist movement got a strong boost from the liberal and left-wing media, led by New York's two left-wing dailies, *PM* (for which I. F. Stone wrote) and the pre-Murdoch *New York Post*; *The Nation*; *The New Republic* (which Henry Wallace, another recent convert to Zionism, was editing); the *Washington Post* editorial page; and *Collier's*. Before television came to dominate the news in the 1960s, these publications were central to the political debate in the country. Washington officials read them carefully, and politicians feared incurring their displeasure.

In this campaign, Silver and the AZEC had powerful allies in the liberal and left-wing media, particularly *PM* (of which Crum had become the publisher) and *The Nation*. Wise's former assistant Lillie Shultz covered the UN debate for *The Nation* and conferred regularly with David Niles, and Niles had made sure that the *Nation*'s report on the mufti and the Arab Higher Committee landed on Truman's desk. Crum and the *Nation* editor Freda Kirchwey regularly exchanged information with Jewish Agency representatives in New York. These relationships were not those between journalists and sources, but between political allies.

Most of the writers and editors for these liberal publications saw Zionism as a fitting response to the horrors of Nazi genocide. Stone became a Zionist when covering the attempt of Holocaust survivors to reach Palestine. The Holocaust cast a long shadow over the moral debate about Palestine's future. "We desperately need . . . to recapture the moral prestige which the Western democracies have forfeited," Crum wrote in a review of Stone's *Underground to Palestine*.[52]

Most of these liberal Zionists also discounted the moral claims of Arab Palestinians, employing every rationalization that the Zionist movement had used since its founding. *The Nation*'s authors wrote that Palestine's Jews were bringing the blessings of "Westernization" to "primitive countries."[53] They insisted that Palestinian Arab nationalism was "not at all nationalism in the Western sense."[54] They identified the Arab cause entirely with the mufti and the Nazis and framed the conflict as one between Zionism and the mufti. They also shamelessly promoted the AZEC's current line. After Niles had warned the Jewish Agency that Truman's assent depended on his believing that the resolution would not lead to war, the AZEC had issued a memorandum declaring that "there is no danger of any large-scale Arab attacks upon public order in Palestine."[55] And the liberal media followed suit. "Seasoned observers," *The Nation* declared, "do not believe that the Arabs will revolt or have the strength to revolt."[56]

In the last week of September, in line with the AZEC's campaign, these publications ran articles and editorials questioning Truman's commitment to a Jewish state. the *New York Post* accused him of making "a deal with the Arabs on Palestine," warning that "any deal involving further concessions to the Arabs would be not only an unconscionable betrayal of the Jews but also open, calculated destruction of American honor."[57] *The Nation* organized a forum on Palestine, warning in the invitation that "there is a gigantic double-cross in the offing at the United Nations."[58]

At the same time, Niles and Clifford recruited Democratic officials to remind Truman of the effect that opposition to a Jewish state could have on Jewish voters in the 1948 presidential and congressional elections. Ed Flynn, a New York City party boss, relayed to Truman a warming from the state's top Democrats that he could lose the Jewish vote in the next year's election. Niles and Clifford got three cabinet members to lobby Truman.[59] At a cabinet luncheon in early October, Robert

Hannegan, whom Truman had made postmaster general and chairman of the Democratic National Committee, told him that Jewish contributors to the party wanted assurances that the administration would back the Zionist position.[60]

Truman also got a letter from an old Kansas City friend, Eddie Jacobson, pleading with him to support the majority plan. "The lives of one and one-half million souls depend on what happens at the United Nations meeting within the next few weeks," Jacobson wrote.[61] Jacobson had served under Captain Truman in France during World War I, and they had opened a clothing store in Kansas City after the war that failed during the 1921 recession. Jacobson hadn't paid any attention to Palestine and Zionism, but in the summer of 1947 two officials from B'nai B'rith, which had embraced Zionism in 1943, suggested that Jacobson and his friend A. J. Granoff, who also knew Truman, use their influence with the president. After that, both men, and Jacobson in particular, became frequent visitors to the White House and conferred regularly with Niles.

Truman was determined to stay out of the cross fire. He told Hannegan that if the Zionist movement would keep quiet, everything would be all right, but that if they persisted, they would destroy all chances of a settlement.[62] He wrote to Jacobson that he didn't think "it would be right or proper for me to interfere at this stage" and that "General Marshall is handling the thing."[63] But that wasn't inconsistent with acceding to pressure. Marshall, cognizant of the political pressure the president was under, had already had a statement drafted endorsing the majority plan, and at the beginning of October, Truman communicated to Marshall and Lovett that he wanted to support partition, as long as it was clear that the United States was unwilling to take the lead in enforcing it with troops.

The AZEC and the Jewish Agency claimed responsibility for Truman's decision to back the partition plan. Leo Sack, who was on the AZEC's Washington staff, told a meeting that they had won "a great victory . . . because of the sheer pressure of political logistics that was applied by the Jewish leadership in the United States."[64] Michael Comay, a South African who was with the Jewish Agency at the UN, and whose reports on the UN offer a vivid chronicle, reported back to a colleague in South Africa: "Our friends pulled every string they could and [so did] the leaders of the Democratic Party machine headed by their great anxiety as to the election consequences of a sellout."[65]

On October 11, Herschel Johnson unveiled the new American position before the Ad Hoc Committee on Palestine. Johnson reiterated American support for the Balfour Declaration and Palestine Mandate and backed the "basic principles of the majority plan which provides for partition and immigration." It was a clear endorsement of partition. But in line with Marshall's wishes, Johnson called for "certain amendments and modifications" to the plan and mentioned including Arab Jaffa in the Arab state as an enclave within the Jewish state.

Johnson also included Truman's rejection of an American-led armed intervention. He said the United States was willing to provide "economic and financial . . . assistance through the U.N.," but when he came to describing how the UN could deal with "the problem of law and order," Johnson, reflecting both the White House and State Department, proposed "a special constabulary or police force recruited on a volunteer basis." He concluded that "in the final analysis, the problem of making any solution work rests with the people of Palestine."[66]

The administration's concrete proposals were an unworkable hodgepodge that any members actually familiar with Palestine saw through. The British delegation said that the plan for a constabulary "could not have been thought out carefully by the United States."[67] The British ambassador told Lovett that "a voluntary constabulary would hardly be sufficient to handle any major Arab disturbance."[68] The ambassador recounted Britain's difficulties in the late 1930s when it had to station 100,000 troops (in addition to police) in Palestine.

Nonetheless, American support helped carry the day on the Ad Hoc Committee. According to Comay, it "had a decisive influence in the Committee. Most countries were holding back until then." But to the surprise of the State Department, the Soviet Union went along without American prodding. The Soviets agreed in principle with the majority plan, while asking for modifications in borders and stipulating that the UN and not Britain should oversee the transition to two states. Marshall, Henderson, and the Pentagon fretted that the Soviet Union would now volunteer to insert troops into Palestine, but the Jewish Agency cheered the Soviet stand; and so did American officials sympathetic to Zionism. Herschel Johnson acknowledged that the Soviet position was "very similar" to the American.[69]

After the vote in the Ad Hoc Committee, Truman reacted in the same telltale way he had reacted after the Yom Kippur statement. He railed against pressure from the Zionists and at the same time claimed it had had no effect on him whatsoever, and he also fretted about the failure of the Morrison-Grady plan. He told the Florida senator Claude Pepper, "Had it not been for the unwarranted interference of the Zionists, we would have had the matter settled a year and a half ago. I received about 35,000 pieces of mail and propaganda from the Jews in this country while this matter was pending. I put it all in a pile and struck a match to it."[70]

Amending the Proposal

A subcommittee of the Ad Hoc Committee was now charged with amending the majority proposal before it headed to the General Assembly for a final vote. The attempt to amend the proposal would provoke another confrontation between the State Department and the Zionist movement—with a reluctant Truman finally being forced to intercede.

In drafting Herschel Johnson's presentation, Marshall and the State Department had attempted to make partition more palatable to the Arabs by introducing amendments of a "pro-Arab nature."[71] These would include putting Jaffa and Safed, two majority Arab towns, in the Arab rather than Jewish state, and giving the Negev, which was populated almost entirely by Arabs and Bedouins, to the Arab state. "If partition is to be successful," Marshall wrote Austin, "it should be as equitable and just as possible."[72]

The most controversial of these amendments was giving most of the Negev to the Arabs. With the Negev included, an Arab state would be larger than the Jewish state, and it would have a direct link to the sea and a contiguous border with Egypt and Jordan. Such a plan, combined with the threat of UN intervention, might have at least brought the Arab League into negotiations. And it would have been a far fairer distribution of Palestine's assets. Truman approved the State Department's amendments, which fit his own sense of fairness. But the Jewish Agency was determined to defeat the proposal.*

The Jewish Agency launched what it called "an extensive campaign in Congress and the President against this scheme."[73] The AZEC called on its local emergency committees to send a "large number of telegrams" to Truman and Lovett protesting the "exclusion of the large and important area of [the] Negev from the Jewish state contrary to UNSCOP majority recommendations which our government has endorsed."[74] Johnson and Hilldring also urged Lovett to withdraw the proposal, which they described as being "vigorously opposed by the Jewish Agency and probably by all the friends of partition."[75] When Lovett held firm, the Jewish Agency called on Chaim Weizmann to meet with Truman.

Epstein, who was in charge of the Jewish Agency's Washington office, got Niles to arrange the meeting on November 19. In his talk with Truman, Weizmann, who was briefed beforehand by Frankfurter and Epstein, stressed the importance of the Gulf of Aqaba as a trade route and as a "parallel highway to the Suez Canal" in case "the Egyptians chose to be hostile to the Jewish state."[76] But he also talked of the promises of irrigated farming in the desert. Truman's daughter wrote afterward, "His vivid description ignited the enthusiasm of the ex-senator who had toiled for years to create regional development and flood controls in the Missouri Valley."[77]

Weizmann's words may have done the trick, but Truman also received that day a memorandum on the 1948 election from Clifford that was actually written by former Roosevelt aide James Rowe. Clifford's memo, which became a guidebook to Truman's campaign, was very explicit about the importance of winning the Jewish vote in New York in the coming election. And the way to do that was through the administration's taking a favorable stand on a Jewish state:

---

*The Jewish Agency also opposed making the whole of Jerusalem an international, UN-run city. It wanted at least the Jewish sections included in a Jewish state, but rather than fighting the UN directly on the issue, the Jewish Agency began quietly moving "public institutions" there even if it couldn't move formal government bodies there.

The Jewish vote, insofar as it can be thought of as a bloc, is important only in New York. But (except for Wilson in 1916) no candidate since 1876 has lost New York and won the Presidency, and its 47 votes are naturally the first prize in any election. Centered in New York City, that vote is normally Democratic and, if large enough, is sufficient to counteract the upstate vote and deliver the state to Truman. Today the Jewish bloc is interested primarily in Palestine and somewhat critical of the Truman Administration on the ground. The bungling of the British in the Exodus case is sure to intensify these already complicated and irrational resentments. Unless the Palestine matter is boldly and favorably handled there is bound to be some defection on their part to the alert Dewey.[78]

By midafternoon, Truman decided to reverse the State Department's position. He called John Hilldring just as the former general and Johnson were about to go into the subcommittee to present the U.S. position on the Negev. When Hilldring complained to the president about the problems that the State Department's instructions would cause, Truman told him nothing should be done "to upset the apple-cart."[79] Hilldring took that to mean that the delegation should withdraw their proposal on the Negev. Truman insisted later that evening to Lovett that he had not intended to change the State Department's instructions, but that denial of intention didn't ring true.[80] When it came to Palestine, the man known for the motto "The buck stops here" had had trouble making up his mind, and even when he did, he denied responsibility for his decisions.

The final proposal that the subcommittee submitted to the Ad Hoc Committee on Palestine was virtually the same as the UNSCOP proposal except it was even less feasible. To appease the Arabs, the subcommittee made Jaffa part of the Arab state and shifted part of the Galilee to the Jews, but that meant that Jaffa, an important part of any Arab state—indeed, a potential seaport—was entirely enclosed by the Jewish state. The overall proportions were about the same as the UNSCOP plan: 55 percent Jewish, 40 percent Arab, with the rest UN controlled. But the Jewish state continued to have an Arab near majority. And both states contained geographic anomalies like Jaffa that could only work if the two peoples were committed from the beginning to live in harmony. And that was even more true of the proposal for an economic union.

The Jewish Agency in Palestine recognized that the proposal was a monstrosity. While Jewish Agency speakers at the UN promised cooperation between Jew and Arab in the Jewish state, Jewish leaders in Palestine had their doubts. They understood that a Jewish state that was 40 percent or more Arab was a contradiction in terms, and that a Jewish state was only viable if Jews made up the overwhelming majority of citizens.

At a meeting in Tel Aviv in November, Ben-Gurion speculated that if war broke out, the Arabs in the Jewish state would constitute a dangerous "fifth column." Yitzhak Gruenbaum, a member of the Jewish Agency Executive, described them as a "permanent irredenta." The Zionist leaders preferred that Arabs in a Jewish state become citizens of the Arab state. In that case, Ben-Gurion said, "we would be able to expel them."[81] But the Jewish Agency backed the proposal as a first step toward Theodor Herzl's goal. That reflected a certain cynicism, but also an assessment of what lay in store for the Jews and Arabs.

Another Commission

There was, perhaps, a chance that a proposal for partition, if better framed and fairer to the Arabs, could have kept the Jews and Arabs at bay for years, and even laid the basis for an eventual agreement between them on one or two states. It would, however, have had to be backed by military force and the prestige of the UN. But when Austin, Johnson, and Hilldring attempted to draw up a plan for implementing the partition proposal, they did so with a view toward winning votes rather than meeting the threat of a rising conflict between Jews and Arabs.

The United States proposed that the plan be implemented by a small commission from nations that had backed partition but that were not on the Security Council. That was intended to keep the United States and the USSR out of any armed conflict. When the Soviet Union proposed that the Security Council be directly in charge, the United States got them to agree to a compromise by which the United Nations Palestine Commission reported regularly to the Security Council but was responsible to the General Assembly. Five nations—Bolivia, Czechoslovakia, Denmark, Panama, and the Philippines—were selected to send representatives to the five-person commission.

On November 24, Henderson made a last-ditch effort to warn Marshall, Lovett, and Truman that a war could break out after the resolution passed. "I wonder if the President realizes," Henderson wrote Lovett, "that the plan which we are supporting for Palestine leaves no force other than local law enforcement organizations for preserving order in Palestine. It is quite clear that there will be wide-scale violence in that country, both from Jewish and Arab sides, with which the local authorities will not be able to cope."[82] Lovett read Henderson's memo to Truman that day, but it does not seem to have had any impact on the president's thinking.

What *was* Truman thinking? Perhaps he believed the propaganda about a peaceful transition to two states that the AZEC and *The Nation* were peddling. But it seems more likely that he had stopped thinking seriously about Palestine and was responding reflexively to events. His underlying views of what should have happened remained the same as ever. He had suggested to Claude Pepper in October that he still favored something like the Morrison-Grady plan and that "had it not been for the unwarranted interference of the Jews, we would have had the matter settled a year and a half ago."

On November 19, ten days before the final UN vote, Truman responded to a letter from Utah Democratic senator Elbert Thomas urging him to back partition. Truman complained to Thomas of the role of "New York Jews" in knocking out the Morrison-Grady plan. He also expressed a fatalism about events. "I have about come to the conclusion that the Palestine program is insoluble, but I suppose we will have to keep working on it," he wrote Thomas.[83] That attitude allowed him to put the prospect of war along with other potential disasters that might have been avoided if "New York Jews" had not pressured him to repudiate the Morrison-Grady plan.

Vote on Partition

As the vote for the partition proposal neared, there were roughly five groups of nations with different opinions on what should happen in Palestine. Strong backers of partition, which included Guatemala,

Uruguay, and Poland, invoked the Nazi genocide to back up their position. They focused on Palestine as a safe haven for oppressed Jewry and gave little thought to how the proposal was to be implemented or how it would affect Arabs. Ben-Gurion later characterized the resolution, and the support for it, as "Western civilization's gesture of repentance for the Holocaust."[84] The Arab countries were on the exact opposite side of the debate. They insisted that Jews would have to give up their dreams of statehood and threatened that if they did not, they would face war. As they had done before, Arab representatives went to such violent extremes in making their case that they frightened away potential supporters.

Another group of small nations—in Africa, Latin America, and Asia—were susceptible to pressure and bribes. Still another, including France and the Netherlands, leaned toward backing partition but were worried about offending their Muslim populations. Finally, there was a group of countries, led by Sweden, Denmark, and New Zealand, that fully understood the grave weakness of the partition proposal but still ended up backing it. The plan lacked, in the words of the Swedish representative Gunnar Hagglof, "a practical and efficient means for enforcement." Hagglof said his country would vote for the resolution because "if no decision at all were taken, it would have still more serious consequences." [85]

Months later, Hagglof told Lionel Gelber from the Jewish Agency that a majority of nations felt that the United States and the chairman of the ad hoc committee, the Australian Herbert Evatt, had manipulated the issue so that the countries were forced to choose between "partition and some pro-Arab scheme." They would have preferred an "attempt at conciliation," but that was not among the choices they were given. [86]

On November 24, the Ad Hoc Committee on Palestine passed the partition plan and rejected the plan for a unitary Arab state. But the plan for partition fell one vote short of the two-thirds majority it would need to get adopted by the General Assembly. The Jewish Agency panicked and, with Thanksgiving two days away, got countries sympathetic to the majority proposal to filibuster on November 25 so the vote would be delayed until November 29. That set up four days of feverish lobbying, but the Jewish Agency could not have swayed enough votes on its own. They believed they needed Truman's support, and they ended up getting it.

Truman initially balked at pressuring other countries. After the ad hoc committee vote, Lovett telephoned Johnson and Hilldring. He told them that "the President did not wish the United States delegation to use threats of improper pressure of any kind on other Delegations to vote for the majority report." Lovett reminded Johnson and Hilldring of U.S. "commitments to the Arabs . . . that the United States was not to be an advocate and was not to use improper pressure on other Delegations."[87] Truman and Lovett's instructions reflected a desire on the part of the United States not to alienate the Arab nations; but also to retain the ability to mediate between the Jews and the Arabs.

After the vote on the ad hoc committee, however, officials in the administration and Congress—and Truman himself—came under intense pressure to use whatever power they had to sway countries that were sitting on the fence to vote yes on partition. The Jewish Agency and the AZEC mobilized every congressman, businessman, and former and current administration official. At a luncheon with the president and James Forrestal afterward, Lovett "said he had never in his life been subject to as much pressure as he had been from Jews in the three days beginning Thursday morning and ending Saturday night."[88] In a letter to Joseph Proskauer that Truman never sent, he wrote, "I don't think I've ever had as much pressure put on the White House."[89]

And the Zionist effort to sway the president worked. When Henderson asked Herschel Johnson about pressure being exerted on wavering nations, Johnson told him that Niles "called us up here a couple of days ago and said that the President had instructed him to tell us that, by God, he wanted us to get busy and get all the votes that we possibly could; that there would be hell if the voting went the wrong way."[90]

After the final vote, when the majority report eked past by one vote, Michael Comay, who was watching the process from the ground, gave Truman credit for the turnaround. Truman, he wrote, "became very upset and threw his personal weight behind the effort to get a decision. From then on Washington exerted itself to rally support and the situation improved."[91] And privately Truman himself acknowledged his role. Several days after the vote, Truman told Jacobson, who was visiting the White House, that he and "he alone was responsible for swinging the votes of several delegations."[92]

As he had done repeatedly after succumbing to pressure, Truman expressed resentment at the lobbying. "The pressure boys almost lost themselves. I did not like it," he wrote to Emanuel Celler on December 1.[93] And Truman insisted later that he did not give in to the pressure. "I have never approved of the practice of the strong imposing their will upon the weak," he wrote in his memoirs in a curious reference to the lobbying.[94] But Silver knew better. "We marshaled our forces, Jewish and non-Jewish opinion, leaders and masses alike, converged on the government and induced the president to assert the authority of his administration to overcome the negative attitude of the State Department," he said.[95]

There were wild celebrations in New York after the vote. Writing in *The Nation*, Lillie Shultz praised the vote "as the first constructive act of the United Nations."[96] But there were already storm clouds on the horizon. Arab delegates walked out of the hall in protest after the vote, and within days of its passage, the violence that Jamal Husseini and other Arab speakers at the UN had threatened broke out in Palestine and in surrounding countries. There were large demonstrations in Egypt, Syria, and Lebanon. The AHC called a general strike in Palestine. Arab rioters in Jerusalem attacked shops and passersby in Jerusalem. A Jewish bus was ambushed in Jaffa, and Arab snipers began firing in Tel Aviv. At first the violence was sporadic, but by the month's end Jews and Arabs were at war in Palestine.

The UN had rested its hope for a peaceful transition to two states on the work of the Palestine Commission. But they assumed that the Palestine Commission would enjoy the close cooperation of the British, who would tamp down violence and facilitate the emergence of provisional Jewish and Arab governments. That assumption proved to be entirely false. After the majority plan was adopted on November 29, the British once again said they would not cooperate with a plan that the Jews and Arabs had not agreed to. And they also declared that they would not cooperate with the commission and would not allow it to make preparations for Jewish and Arab states until two weeks before the British were due to leave—the final date for Britain's evacuation now being May 15.

Trygve Lie appointed Ralph Bunche to be the principal secretary to the commission and the Spaniard Pablo de Azcárate to be his deputy. When the commission tried to begin work in December, the Arabs boycotted it and the British ignored it. The State Department official Evan Wilson wrote of the commission: "The members were an undistinguished and timorous lot who feared, with some justification, for their safety if they were to set foot in Palestine. They were determined not to budge from New York, in spite of the terms of their mandate from the General Assembly. Aside from the Czechoslovak chairman, none of them had any knowledge of the Palestine problem."[97]

Azcárate, who was sent to Jerusalem in February as an advance guard for the commission, wrote that the British were preoccupied with "impeding by every possible method the presence in Palestine of anybody or anything remotely connected with the UN, and in particular with the Palestine Commission."[98] After the commission had disbanded, Azcárate concluded, "If the plan was defective, and if its adoption by the General Assembly took place in conditions which were far from ideal, what barred the last hope of seeing it executed was the Palestine Commission."[99] Yet the United States had seriously proposed the commission as a means to implement partition.

Truman himself was beaten down by the struggle at the UN and by the pressure he had been under. On December 2 he wrote Henry Morgenthau, asking him to "caution all our friends who are interested in the welfare of the Jews in Palestine that now is the time for restraint and caution and an approach to the situation in the future that will allow a peaceful settlement."[100]

All in all, the debate at the UN had been disastrous. The British had thrown the problem into the lap of the United Nations, but the United Nations couldn't help to resolve it without strong American participation. The United States initially wanted to have no role, but when the Truman administration did join the debate, it sought to forge a solution that, while acceptable to a majority of nations and to the Jewish Agency, was patently unworkable and set the stage for a civil war. Truman was ultimately to blame for the muddled American response, but few of the parties escaped responsibility for what happened.

■ 14 ■

UNMATCHED INEPTNESS

American Zionists who wrote for the top dailies and magazines had insisted the Arab threats of war were bravado, and at the United Nations, some delegates hoped that the sheer fact of the UN's endorsement of partition would discourage Arabs from making good on their threats of war. But as Henderson had warned, the UN decision led to war. Truman, still brimming with resentment against the "pressure boys," withdrew from the discussion about what to do next and let the State Department set American policy. He passed the buck again.

Over the next six months, the State Department and the Zionists would battle over whether to continue backing partition and, finally, whether to recognize the new state of Israel. Truman would intermittently intercede along the same lines as before—initially in favor of the State Department, but eventually siding with the Zionists. American recognition of Israel has often been heralded as a triumph of Truman's diplomacy and foresightedness, but it was, like the fiasco at the UN, a product of political pressure and strategic indecision.

Arab Discord

During the UN debate over partition, Jamal al-Husseini had warned that Palestine's Arabs "would fully defend with their life-blood every inch of the soil of their beloved country."[1] The war in Palestine had begun the day after the UN passed the partition resolution. But in those first six months, while the British still occupied Palestine, the Palestinian Arabs carried the burden of war against the Jews. The Arab states, deeply divided among themselves and distrustful of the mufti, backed the war but initially kept their own armies at home.

The leaders of Egypt, Saudi Arabia, Syria, and Lebanon might have accepted a deal along the lines of Morrison-Grady or the UN's minority plan, as Lebanon's representative Camille Chamoun, speaking on behalf of the Arab states at the UN, had belatedly revealed on November 29.[2] The Arab leaders might even have eventually accepted a small Jewish state.[3] Jordan's King Abdullah came closest to making a deal that would grant him Arab Palestine. In the fall of 1947 he conducted clandestine negotiations with Golda Meir. But the Arab leaders in Egypt and other states were afraid of incurring the wrath of their own populaces, which opposed any compromise. And Abdullah was still unwilling to break with the other Arab leaders. So they applauded the Palestinian Arab decision to go to war.

But while the Arab states vocally supported the Palestinian cause, they continued to distrust the mufti and the AHC. His presence, they believed, precluded future compromise and discredited their opposition to Zionism by identifying it with a former Nazi collaborator. Jordanians and Iraqis opposed the mufti's quest for an independent Palestine because it conflicted with their ambition to take over the whole or part of the country for themselves.

At an October meeting in Aley, east of Beirut, the Lebanese, Jordanians, and Iraqis had vetoed the mufti's plan for establishing a provisional Palestinian government. And in the wake of the UN majority resolution, they continued to block any attempt to establish a provisional Arab government to counter the Jewish government that was already administering Jewish Palestine. As a result, Palestine's Arabs failed to develop the means of administering the territories that the UN had granted them, let alone the whole of Palestine.

The Arab League countries were also unwilling to stage a formal invasion of Palestine as long as the British still ruled. They did form a military committee, based in Damascus, to recruit volunteers to conduct guerrilla operations. About 4,000 volunteers, organized into the

Arab Liberation Army (ALA), entered Palestine in January 1948. But the mufti and the AHC were excluded from the committee.

The mufti was opposed to other Arab countries sending armies into Palestine. He suspected, rightly, that their real motives were to carve up Arab Palestine for themselves. He refused to cooperate with the ALA and the Arab League's military committee. Instead, he organized his own military committees in Palestine. But the mufti himself was out of the country, as were other AHC leaders. As a result, the mufti's indigenous military committees largely operated on their own. They were armed bands similar to those that had roamed the Palestinian countryside during the last phases of the rebellion in the 1930s after the British had exiled or imprisoned the AHC members. They teamed up with impromptu and poorly armed village militias to stage sporadic ambushes and operated independently of the ALA guerrillas. While they constituted a disruptive force, they were incapable of taking power in Palestine. They were destined for defeat at the hands of the better-organized Jewish forces.

Palestine's Jews had been preparing for war with the Arabs since the end of World War II. They built their own fledgling arms industry with surplus machinery purchased in the United States and smuggled into Palestine. When war broke out in December 1947, the Haganah had 15,000 trained soldiers at its disposal and the Irgun and Stern Gang a total of several thousand. The Haganah immediately pressed into service and began training all seventeen- to twenty-five-year-old men and women.

In addition, Palestine's Jews had the benefit of its fully organized government and a military leadership, led by Ben-Gurion, that enjoyed centralized control over the Haganah.[4] Ben-Gurion, who had performed brilliantly as the head of the Jewish Agency, proved to be talented as a war commander. Former secretary of state Henry Kissinger once said of Ben-Gurion, "It's a pity his shoes are too small for him. He could have been given his real measure in a bigger state than Israel."[5]

Except for a few weeks when Jewish Jerusalem was seriously threatened, Ben-Gurion and his generals did not take very seriously the threat of the disorganized, ill-equipped bands or of the volunteer ALA. During the winter Ben-Gurion remained confident, as he wrote Shertok, that the Haganah could "secure the establishment of [the] Jewish state."[6]

But Ben-Gurion was worried about an invasion from trained Arab state forces, which he expected after the British departed on May 15.

Ben-Gurion and the Haganah spent the early months of the war preparing for this invasion by creating a professional army. Against the mufti's disorganized forces and the ALA, the Haganah and Revisionist groups practiced a strategy of "aggressive defense." They retaliated against Arab attacks and attempted to defend the territory that the UN allotted for a Jewish state, but because they were worried that they would provoke British intervention, they didn't attempt to inflict a final defeat on their adversaries. That created a misleading impression at the State Department, in the United Nations, and among American Zionists that Palestine's Jews were at best holding their own against Arab attacks and at worst—as the road from Tel Aviv to Jerusalem became closed to Jewish convoys—were facing defeat.

Kennan's Memo

With Truman's mind elsewhere, State Department officials had sole responsibility for responding to the war in Palestine. And as before, they harbored their own illusions about what was going on. This time, the illusions were not about Soviet intentions but about the strength of the Arab forces. State Department officials, along with officials from the Pentagon and the newly established CIA, believed that if war did break out, the Arabs, by virtue of their superior numbers, would win. A CIA report predicted that "the superior organization of the Jews" would initially lead to success, but that "as the situation develops into a war of attrition, the Jewish economy, disrupted by total mobilization, will break down . . . Unless able to obtain significant outside aid in terms of manpower and materiel, the Jews will be able to hold out no longer than two years."[7]

What the State Department and Pentagon feared most was that in the case of a looming Jewish defeat, the United States, because of political pressure and humanitarian concern, would have to send arms and even troops to aid the Jews. This was, Evan Wilson wrote, "a contingency that the State and Defense Departments wished to avoid at all costs."[8] That wasn't because of anti-Semitism, although there was a strong current of anti-Semitism that surfaced in some Pentagon analyses of the Palestinian conflict, but because defense planners feared that such an intervention would undermine the conduct of the Cold War against the Soviet Union.

The Cold War conflict was looming larger: in December, the Communist Party seized power in Romania and in February took control in Czechoslovakia. On March 5, General Lucius Clay, in charge of American forces in Germany, warned that war with the Soviet Union was imminent. Pentagon planners feared that if the United States intervened directly on behalf of the Jews against the Arabs, that would alienate Arab states and then the United States could lose access to their oil in case of war. A Pentagon report in October 1947 declared, "A great part of our military strength is based on oil. It now appears that loss of the Iraq and Saudi Arabia sources of oil would mean that in case of war the United States would fight an oil starved war."[9]

American Zionists charged that the State and Defense Departments' concern about access to oil was being hyped by industry lobbyists and by Forrestal because of his prior business connections with the oil industry, but American, German, Soviet, and British war planners had been concerned about access to Middle Eastern oil since World War I; and by the end of World War II, American planners were beginning to fear that domestic oil production was eventually going to outrun domestic demand. In addition, foreign policy officials were worried about sustaining the Marshall Plan in Western Europe, which depended upon oil imports from the Middle East.

To avoid entanglement, the State Department, at Henderson's urging, announced on December 5 an embargo on all arms sales to Palestine and the surrounding Arab countries. And as soon as the fighting erupted that month, the State Department, along with Forrestal and the Joint Chiefs of Staff, called for a reevaluation of the UN's partition decision. Marshall had shared their doubts about partition. In Britain in early December, the secretary of state told embassy staff that he thought the United States had made a mistake in supporting partition.[10] At a meeting on December 12 of the newly established National Security Council, George Kennan, the director of the State Department's policy planning staff, was asked to prepare a paper on the feasibility of partition.

Kennan was a diplomat who, while stationed in Moscow, had become famous for his long telegram, later published as an essay by "Mr. X" in *Foreign Affairs*, that laid out what became the American strategy of containment. Kennan had been recalled to Washington and elevated to the top job in the policy planning staff. He was not, however, an expert on the Middle East, and he sought out the advice of Henderson and Dean Rusk, the assistant secretary of state for international organization affairs. In line with their analysis, Kennan argued in his paper that because of Arab opposition, "the partition of Palestine cannot be implemented without the use of force, and . . . the U.S. would inevitably be called upon to supply a substantial portion of the money, troops, and arms for that purpose."

Kennan recited the familiar reasons for opposing any use of American or of volunteer troops, which could easily include Soviet forces. He concluded that the United States "should take no further initiative in implementing or aiding partition" and that when "the march of events has conclusively demonstrated" that it is impossible to carry out partition "without the use of outside forces," the United States should call for the issue of Palestine to "go back to the General Assembly," where the United States "should cooperate loyally" in encouraging a "pacific settlement between the Palestine Arabs and Palestine Jews" or "a federal state or trusteeship, which would not require outside armed force for implementation."[11]

Kennan's recommendations, which echoed those of Henderson, rested on the questionable assumption that the UN *could* achieve a "pacific settlement" between Arabs and Jews and that establishing and conducting a trusteeship would be possible without "outside armed force for implementation." But Kennan had nonetheless hit upon the weakness of the UN plan, which, as formulated, could not be implemented peacefully. As a result, Kennan's paper met with wide agreement in the State and Defense Departments.

That winter, high officials in the State and Defense Departments began hinting of a change in the American position on partition. On January 19, Forrestal appeared before the House Foreign Affairs Committee. He was asked by a congressman whether the UN decision on partition had "rendered our situation more insecure, considering the 350 million people of the Moslem world—are we in jeopardy of having those pipelines cut?" Forrestal replied without pausing, "The answer is yes."[12] A month later Marshall commented in a press conference that the "whole Palestine thing" was under "constant consideration."[13]

Then on February 24, in response to a report from the virtually defunct Palestine Commission calling for the UN to sponsor an international force to carry out the partition plan, Warren Austin gave a speech before the Security Council in which he rejected the very idea of the Security Council enforcing the partition plan. The November partition plan had said that the Security Council could act against "any attempt to alter by force the settlement envisaged by this resolution," but in a display of legal sophistry, Austin insisted that "the Charter of the United Nations does not empower the Security Council to enforce a political settlement . . . The Council's action . . . is directed to keeping the peace and not to enforcing partition."[14]

Privately, the State Department began drafting a speech for Austin to give the next month that would advocate, along the lines Henderson and Kennan had suggested, that the General Assembly junk partition and create instead a trusteeship. But they had to get the White House's approval for a change in strategy.

Getting Truman's Attention

To get Truman's approval, the State Department first had to get his attention. As visitors to the White House discovered during the two months after the UN vote on partition, Truman was preoccupied with the Cold War and with presidential politics. When asked about Palestine, he reverted to his opinions about Jewish obstructionism and the superiority of the Anglo-American Committee proposals.

On January 23, Truman received Theodore O. Thackrey, the editor and publisher of the *New York Post*. Thackrey had published an editorial attacking the administration for its "shameful failure to provide either the United Nations or the Jews of Palestine with the means for enforcing the U.N. partition decision."[15] He had requested a meeting with the president to talk about Palestine. According to Thackrey's account of the conversation, Truman was "very nervous, jumpy and cursing throughout the conversation. Time and again he jumped off his seat, walked the room and said repeatedly 'damn this, that and the other': 'Damn the Russians, damn the British, damn the Jews.'" Thackrey didn't think he had to remind Truman about the potential political fallout of the president's Palestine policy because the president "was fully aware of this implication," so he concentrated on the policy itself.

When he asked the president about ending the arms embargo, Truman said he was not going to lift the embargo but that he was for "the establishment of an international army" for the UN. In fact, his administration had opposed such an army for Palestine. When Thackrey remarked that there was "little evidence" of the United States pressing for such a force, Truman said Thackrey was being unfair. When Thackrey asked him whether he thought such a force could be assembled in time to intervene in Palestine, Truman said, "I hope so," but when Thackrey pressed him about whether it was actually going to happen, Truman finally said "To hell, no."

Thackrey tried to keep the conversation focused on Palestine, but Truman veered off onto "Russia and the possibility, even the probability, of a new world conflict." When Truman finally got back to the Middle East, the president pointed out "how adversely the American position in the Middle East was affected by partition."[16] Truman seemed to be thinking along the same lines as Marshall, Kennan, and Forrestal. All in all, however, Thackrey's report suggests a president not paying attention to Palestine.

On February 4, Truman talked about Palestine with Wadsworth, now the ambassador to Iraq. Wadsworth had given Truman a paper he had written describing the Arab opposition to partition and advocating a move away from partition toward trusteeship.[17] Wadsworth told him that he was hoping that the National Security Council would come up with "something positive which we in the field might say, something constructive which we could use to build better and mutually beneficial relations." According to Wadsworth, Truman expressed confidence in the State Department. He assured him that "the whole problem was being worked on actively and constructively."

But Truman then reverted to his experiences in 1946. "The basic problem," he told Wadsworth, "was and had been that bullheadedness and fanaticism constantly interfered. Two years ago, [I] had found a sound approach. The British had gone along with [my] proposals for an Anglo-American Commission . . . There had been a unanimous report. Grady had gone to London to get it implemented but had failed because of British bullheadedness and the fanaticism of our New York

Jews. [Truman thought of Silver as a "New York Jew."] The British were still being bullheaded and American Jews were still being fanatic about it."[18]

State and Defense Department officials were determined to turn Truman's attention to Palestine's future. In Marshall's regular meeting with Truman on February 19—the day before Truman was to sail to the Caribbean for a vacation—the secretary of state informed him that the State Department was developing a new position on Palestine that he and Lovett would like him to consider, but he did not tell him what the position was. Marshall asked for and got assurance from Truman they should "disregard all political factors."[19]

Three days later, the State Department sent Truman, who was already at sea, a "working draft" of their position on Palestine. The first eleven points of the working paper went over what Austin planned to say in his speech before the Security Council on February 24 about not enforcing partition. But the last three numbered points contained new and controversial ideas. The State Department proposed that if partition could not be implemented "without enforcement measures," and

> if the Security Council is unable to develop an alternative solution acceptable to the Jews and Arabs of Palestine, the matter should be referred back to a special session of the General Assembly. The Department of State considers that it would then be clear that Palestine is not ready for self-government and that some form of United Nations trusteeship for an additional period of time will be necessary.

The State Department proposed that to manage the trusteeship, the Security Council ask the British to "retain the mandate."[20] The State Department simply refused to heed Britain's pledge that it was leaving Palestine on May 15.

The working draft's plan was similar to Henderson's original proposal for trusteeship as updated by Kennan. Theoretically, it was not inconsistent with eventually achieving partition, but Henderson and the State Department were opposed to partition, and the draft didn't say that the "additional period" was intended to make it work. Truman wrote back, "I approve in principle your basic position. I want to make it clear, however, that nothing should be presented to the Security Council that could be interpreted as a recession on our part from the position we took in the General Assembly."[21]

Did Truman embrace partition? In talking to Thackrey, he shared the State Department's doubts about it, and a month later, while cruising in the Caribbean, Truman seemed more positive about it but still doubtful whether it could be implemented. He told William Hillman, the bureau chief of *Collier's* in Washington, who was with Truman on the cruise, that he thought it was a "just solution." According to Hillman (as recounted later to Gideon Ruffer of the Jewish Agency), Truman "said that he was the sponsor of partition and still believed that this was the solution . . . He does not know what should be done to implement partition in the face of strong Arab resistance. He knows that it is the only just solution."[22]

Two weeks later, after the Security Council had balked at an American resolution that would have affirmed its responsibility to implement the November resolution, Truman approved the working draft as the basis for a new American position. At a White House meeting, Lovett and Marshall got Truman's approval to present the "alternative and that was the trusteeship proposal."[23] There's conflicting evidence about whether Truman ever received the actual draft of what Austin was going to say, but he did know and approve of the message. That set the stage for a blowup within the administration and between the administration and American Zionists.

Jewish Support for Partition

As the State Department was urging that the United States back off on the November resolution, support for partition had become almost universal among American Jews. United Nations backing for partition had inoculated non-Zionist American Jews from fear that supporting a Jewish state could be seen as dual loyalty. They could now say they were supporting the UN and not simply the national aspirations of their coreligionists. As a result, most non-Zionist Jews and Jewish organizations now favored a Jewish state. The American Jewish Committee's Proskauer was as energetic as ZOA president Israel Goldstein in pressing for partition. And the formerly anti-Zionist Sulzberger and *The*

New York Times also came on board. During the UN debate over partition, *The New York Times* published thirty-one editorials in favor of partition and none opposing it.[24]

All the Jewish religious groupings came out in favor of Zionism and partition. That included the Reform Jews, among whom Silver and Wise had been outliers. Nelson Glueck, the newly installed president of the Hebrew Union College, the citadel of Reform Judaism, used his presidential address in March 1948 to affirm his support for "the United Nations plan of partition." "To abandon it because it is being attacked," Glueck declared, "is to give freedom to frightfulness and lend license to terror."[25]

Support for a Jewish state had become axiomatic for most American Jews. Hannah Arendt wrote in 1948, "With the exception of a few anti-Zionist die-hards, whom nobody can take very seriously, there is now no organization and almost no individual Jew that doesn't privately or publicly support partition and the establishment of a Jewish state."[26] Golda Meir raised $50 million for arms during a brief fundraising trip to the United States that winter. Support for Jewish statehood also resonated in elections.

On February 17 a special election was held in the Bronx to fill a congressional seat from which the incumbent had resigned. Jews made up the largest voting bloc in the district, which Democrats usually carried easily. But the handpicked Democrat was challenged by Leo Isacson, formerly the chair of ZOA's Bronx branch, who ran on the American Labor Party ticket. Isacson, who was endorsed by Henry Wallace, took aim at Truman's Cold War policies and his lack of enthusiasm for Zionism. His campaign slogan was "Peace, Prosperity and Palestine."[27] He charged that "it is part of the Truman Doctrine and the Marshall Plan to sacrifice Jewish blood for Arab oil."[28] Isacson was supposed to lose, but he won in a landslide, largely, it appeared, because the district's Jews wanted more straightforward support by the administration for a Jewish state.

As Jewish support for Zionism rose, one might have expected the power and authority of the AZEC and the leading American Zionist groups to rise as well. But the contrary occurred. The AZEC remained vital to affecting the political climate for Zionism. So did liberal media like

The Nation and the *New York Post*. But by early 1948, Ben-Gurion and the Jewish Agency in Palestine set the AZEC's strategy. At one meeting Silver had to inform his frustrated subordinates that the "AZEC could not determine fundamental Zionist policy, but merely action policy."[29]

If there was a center of Zionist influence in the United States, it lay in the close working relationship binding supporters of a Jewish state in the White House and former and existing Democratic officials with Shertok, Epstein, and the other Jewish Agency representatives from Palestine. Some of the former officials were actually employed by the Jewish Agency. David Ginsburg was a Frankfurter protégé who had served in the Securities and Exchange Administration and during the war in the Office of Price Administration. He had become a prominent Washington lawyer and liberal who helped to found the Americans for Democratic Action. In 1948 he was also on retainer to the Jewish Agency.

Other officials occupied a gray area between the Jewish Agency and the American government. Ben Cohen was another Frankfurter protégé who drafted New Deal legislation and served during the war as a foreign policy troubleshooter for the government. In 1948 he was advising the Jewish Agency and at the same time serving as an American representative to the UN. Robert Nathan served as an economist in the Roosevelt and Truman administrations but at the same time had done the bidding of Chaim Weizmann, who convinced him to go to Palestine in 1944 to do a study of the country's economy.[30]

Occupying the outer circles of this informal network were several people who would later became controversial. The former State Department official Alger Hiss, who was later revealed to have been a Soviet agent, had left government to become president of the Carnegie Endowment for International Peace, but he still retained close ties to the State Department. Hiss backed the Jewish state and regularly advised Max Lowenthal at the White House about State Department efforts to block Zionist initiatives.

David Wahl, another former Roosevelt administration official who was also identified as a Soviet agent, had become the head of the Washington-based Americans for Haganah.[31] Wahl talked regularly to Niles and Lowenthal in the White House and was an informal contact between them and Jewish leaders in Palestine, including Ben-Gurion and Weizmann, whom he shepherded on his visits to Washington.* Hiss seems to have left the Soviet service after he left the government, but according to recent revelations, when Wahl was conferring with the White House, he was still meeting regularly with a Soviet agent who hoped to learn from him about administration stands on Palestine.[32]

Support for the Jewish state wasn't a Soviet plot. But the participation of Hiss and Wahl may indicate that, on this issue, some leftists enthusiastically backed a Jewish state at least partly because the Soviets did. That may explain the enthusiastic support for Zionism in Henry Wallace's Progressive Party, which opposed the Cold War and which was increasingly run by Communist Party members.

At the urging of the Jewish Agency's Washington staff, a meeting of this informal network was held on February 3 at David Ginsburg's home to decide how to prevent the administration from turning against partition. Cohen and Nathan were at the meeting, along with Shertok, Epstein, and other Jewish Agency operatives. No one from the AZEC was there. That was a clear indication of who counted in Washington.

The participants adopted an elaborate two-part strategy to sway the Truman administration using "rational argument" to convince American officials that supporting partition was in line with "long term United States national interests" and using "political pressure" to convince those officials that "it would be most unwise, from a strictly electioneering point of view, to jettison the United Nations decision and to accept a new position on Palestine less considerate of Jewish needs and desires."[33] The key element of this strategy was getting an appointment with the president for Weizmann, who was about to return to the United States.

---

*In June 1948, Niles and Lowenthal became involved in trying to quash a congressional investigation of Wahl. They were in touch with Ralph Becker, who was chairman of the Young Republican National Committee. Told that a Republican committee had a letter tying Wahl to "some espionage agent," Lowenthal got ahold of Wahl through Eliahu Epstein. According to Lowenthal, Wahl "says he knows of no such letter and I so reported to Becker, who is trying to help because of his interest in Dave's Palestinian activities." Lowenthal Papers.

On this, the group got nowhere at all. Epstein asked Niles to arrange a meeting between Weizmann and the president, but Niles told him that Truman was unwilling to see any Zionist leaders. Frankfurter also failed to get Weizmann an interview with Marshall. Frank Goldman, the president of B'nai B'rith, got wind of the problem, probably from Epstein, and asked Eddie Jacobson to convince the president to see Weizmann. Truman was due to leave for the Caribbean the next day, and Goldman offered to charter a plane for Jacobson to make the trip, but Jacobson couldn't leave Kansas City at that time. So instead he wired the president urging him to see Weizmann. "He is very old and heartbroken and [the] finest leader that my people have," Jacobson wrote.[34]

Truman wrote back at some length. He said that he was sorry that he had not had time to see Weizmann, but "there wasn't anything he could say to me that I didn't already know." Truman added that he had made a point of not seeing anyone about Palestine until the "United Nations has had a chance to act on our suggestion for a police force to enforce partitioning"—a remark that indicated once again that the president wasn't paying attention. Truman then went into his lament: "The situation has been a headache to me for two and a half years. The Jews are so emotional, and the Arabs are so difficult to talk with that it is almost impossible to get anything done . . . The Zionists, of course, have expected a big stick approach on our part, and naturally have been disappointed when we can't do that." And his letter ended, characteristically, on an apparent contradiction. "I have come to the conclusion," he wrote, "that the situation is not solvable as presently set up; but I shall continue to try to get the solution outlined in the United Nations resolution."[35] Truman, in other words, no longer believed that partition would work, but he was still trying to get it to work.

The White House Zionists

Within the White House, the locus of support for Zionism was also shifting. In 1945 and 1946, the key White House officials had been Niles and Rosenman. Niles was still important in 1948 but was ill part of the winter and was superseded during the crucial part of 1948 by Clifford and Lowenthal. Clifford was the most important addition to the pro-

Zionist faction at the White House. An ambitious trial lawyer from St. Louis, he had first joined the White House in 1945 when the St. Louis businessman J. K. Vardaman, whom he knew socially and who had become Truman's naval aide, hired him as his assistant. Without much to do, Clifford gravitated to Rosenman, who was writing speeches and making policy recommendations for the president; and when Rosenman left after a year, Clifford succeeded him.

Clifford had evinced little interest in Palestine until the fall of 1947 when the issue's connection with Truman's electoral chances the next year became very apparent, but he was probably favorably inclined toward Zionism from his service under Rosenman. By the winter of 1948, the tall, suave, Hollywood-handsome Clifford ("Big fella, ain't he," the slight Truman had remarked upon first meeting him) had become a dogged defender of partition. He served as another White House link for Epstein and the Jewish Agency and he sent memoranda to Truman recommending a Jewish state.

Clifford did not, however, write or conceive most of these memoranda. They were based on drafts by Max Lowenthal. Lowenthal, whose given name was Mordechai, was the child of Orthodox Jewish immigrants from Lithuania who had settled in Minneapolis. He got a law degree at Harvard in 1912, where he became a close friend of Felix Frankfurter's. He clerked for Julian Mack, whose niece he later married, and became a law partner in New York of another key member of the Brandeis circle, Robert Szold.

Like other members of the Brandeis circle, he was a leading left liberal. In the early 1920s he won a landmark decision for Sidney Hillman's Amalgamated Clothing Workers of America. As counsel for the Commerce Committee, he defended the consumer and small investor against big corporations. He was a champion of civil liberties and critic of J. Edgar Hoover's FBI. He was close to left-wing New Dealers as well as to people like Wahl and Hiss who would later be accused of being Soviet agents.

Lowenthal was a diminutive man, which probably contributed to Truman's comfort with him. Like Niles, he also was wary of becoming a public figure. He wrote thousands of memoranda but would invariably not sign them. He was a proverbial backroom operator. During 1948, Lowenthal became a fixture at the White House, even though he held no formal position and did not have an office. Working out of the

Cosmos Club, which was then located near the White House, Lowenthal could come and go as he pleased at the White House. He remained a trusted advisor to Truman on commerce and labor issues, but Truman came to rely on him for advice on Palestine as well. So did Clifford, whom Lowenthal cleverly won over by shamelessly flattering him. "You are the key to this election," he told Clifford.[36]

Clifford's Zionism was probably driven more by politics; Marshall, Lovett, and Henderson certainly believed so. But as the White House aides became engaged in a tussle over Truman's support for the Jewish state with the State Department, Clifford and Lowenthal adopted a strategy of framing their recommendations entirely in terms of foreign policy and America's national interest. And Clifford himself later insisted that politics had been irrelevant, even though it was constantly lurking around the edges of their conversations.[37]

It was a clever strategy. In basing their arguments on something other than the president's electoral chances, Clifford and Lowenthal grasped what Henderson had sensed in that heated meeting the previous September with Truman and his aides—that Truman wanted a strategic justification for supporting a Jewish state that allowed him to respond positively to the political pressures he was under without confirming the British charge that he was simply bowing to political pressure. Henderson had not provided this justification, but Clifford and Lowenthal tried to do so.

Clifford was aware of the State Department initiatives on trusteeship and was determined to block them. He sent Lowenthal, who was not a foreign policy expert, to Epstein at the Jewish Agency offices to research a memorandum that would answer the State Department.[38] From Lowenthal's drafts, Clifford produced two memos in his own name that he sent to Truman. In the first, dated March 6 and entitled "Proposed Program on the Palestine Problem," Clifford listed a series of steps that the United States could take that matched those recommended by the Jewish Agency. In the second, longer memo, Clifford tried to address Truman's own anxieties. The memo was a lawyer's brief that didn't so much attempt to ascertain the truth as to meet Truman's objections with whatever arguments sounded plausible.

Clifford insisted that his memo had nothing to do with politics.

"One's judgment in advising as to what is best for America must in no sense be influenced by the election this fall," he wrote. Partition was, he wrote, "the only hope of avoiding military conflict for the United States in the Middle East" and "the only course of action with respect to Palestine that will strengthen our position vis-à-vis Russia." Clifford also argued that, by remaining committed to partition, the United States would strengthen the United Nations, which would strengthen the United States vis-à-vis Russia because "the United Nations is a God-given vehicle through which the United States can build up a community of powers in Western Europe and elsewhere to resist Soviet aggression." Needless to say, the UN was not set up or designed to do this.

Clifford assured Truman that the United States need not worry about a cutoff of Arab oil because "the Arab states have no customer for their oil supplies other than the United States." On this point Clifford turned out to be right—at least until 1973. However, he also assured Truman that he didn't have to worry about alienating Muslims. "While the British-Moslem alliance is undoubtedly extremely important to Britain, a similar alliance between the United States and the Moslem world is much less important to the United States," he wrote.

In Clifford's memo, which Lowenthal drafted, he warned Truman that by constantly framing policies designed to appease Muslims and Arabs, "the United States appears in the ridiculous role of trembling before the threats of a few nomadic desert tribes"—the implication being that most Arabs were Bedouins.[39] Like other Zionists who in their domestic politics were prime supporters of civil rights and civil liberties, Lowenthal displayed little sympathy for Arabs. And the same, of course, was true of Clifford.

Jacobson and Weizmann

In early March, the news from Palestine was filled with stories of Arab assaults on Jewish settlements and convoys. On March 3, Arab irregulars, led by Syrians and Iraqis, attacked a settlement ten miles west of Jerusalem. A battle lasted for three hours before British troops intervened. Two days later, three hundred Arabs ambushed a twenty-three-man Haganah detachment trying to clear a road from a settlement to Jerusalem, and killed seventeen of the Jews.[40]

The news from Palestine worried Eddie Jacobson, who feared that "the British were hoping for an Arab victory which would drive the Jews into the sea." On March 12, at the urging of B'nai B'rith's Goldman and the Jewish Agency, Jacobson finally flew to Washington to see the president. Truman always had time for old friends, and on Saturday, March 13, Jacobson was shown into the Oval Office. Truman's secretary, Matt Connelly, had warned Jacobson not to bring up Palestine, but after the usual pleasantries Jacobson did just that, pleading with the president to see Weizmann. According to Jacobson's account, Truman "immediately became tense in appearance, abrupt in speech and very bitter in the words he was throwing my way." Truman railed about "how disrespectful and how mean certain Jewish leaders had been to him"—most likely a reference to Silver.

Jacobson was about to give up, but he made one last try to convince Truman. Pointing to a small statue of Andrew Jackson on a horse that stood in Truman's office, he compared Truman's admiration for Jackson with his own for Weizmann, whom, in fact, he had never met. Weizmann, he said, "is a very sick man, almost broken in health, but he travelled thousands and thousands of miles just to see you and plead the cause of my people."[41] Truman gave in and agreed to see Weizmann.

Weizmann visited Truman on Thursday, March 18. He was shown in through the East Gate so that the press would not be aware of his visit, and no minutes were taken of their conversation. Weizmann talked to Truman of industrial achievements in Palestine and of the need for land and of the importance of the Negev—topics he had touched upon during their visit in October. Truman assured Weizmann that he wanted "justice done without bloodshed" in Palestine.[42] But Truman's version of the conversation differs on one important point from what Weizmann recalled in his own memoir, *Trial and Error*. Weizmann wrote that Truman "indicated a firm resolve to press forward with partition."[43] But in his memoirs, Truman made no mention of any discussion about partition.

Truman may be correct on this score. On April 5, Nathan Epstein, who would have made it his business to know what had transpired during Weizmann's visit, delivered a report to a meeting of Mapai, the Jewish Labor Party, about the conversation. Truman, Epstein said, "encouraged [Weizmann] to believe that there would be some favorable changes, especially on the matter of the arms embargo." According to Epstein, Truman had left some of Weizmann's questions "unanswered," but what he said about the embargo had made Weizmann "feel that at least no adverse changes had occurred or were likely to occur during the following days."[44]

Epstein's is the most contemporary account, and it strongly suggests that Truman did not make any specific promises about partition. But at this point, Truman, in contrast to the State Department, may not have distinguished clearly between supporting partition and favoring a trusteeship. So while he may not have specifically responded to a question about whether he backed partition, he most certainly did not tell Weizmann he opposed it in favor of trusteeship.

Truman did mislead Weizmann about ending the arms embargo. Truman may have wanted to end it, but he had to know that the State Department was adamantly opposed to doing so. With Thackrey, Jacobson, and now Weizmann—and even with Marshall and Lovett— Truman was telling them what he thought they wanted to hear. But Truman was under Weizmann's spell. Even the appearance that he had betrayed him would upset Truman.

Austin's Bombshell

Marshall and Lovett were waiting for a pretext that would allow Warren Austin to give the speech on trusteeship they had cleared with Truman earlier in the month. They got their chance on Friday, March 19, after the Palestine Commission had reported its "inescapable conclusion that when the Mandate is terminated Palestine is likely to suffer severely from administrative chaos and widespread strife and bloodshed."[45] Austin's proposal could then be framed as a way to avert strife and bloodshed.

In his speech, Austin said that, based on "clear evidence that the Jews and Arabs of Palestine and the Mandatory Power cannot agree to implement the General Assembly plan of partition through peaceful means," the UN should establish a "temporary trusteeship . . . to maintain the peace and afford the Jews and Arabs of Palestine, who must live together, further opportunity to reach an agreement regarding the future government of that country."⁴⁶ Austin's plan not only prolonged the settlement of the conflict in Palestine by introducing a temporary trusteeship, it left undetermined the "future government." Austin did not mention partition except to say that it could not be implemented peacefully. The message of the speech was clear: partition was out.

At the UN, Silver, representing the Jewish Agency, was slated to speak after Austin. Although caught entirely unawares by Austin's speech, he managed a stinging rebuttal. Calling Austin's speech a "shocking reversal" of the American support for partition, Silver got at its central contradiction. "It should be clear to everyone that the establishment of a trusteeship by the United Nations in Palestine will not automatically ensure peace in that country, and that force will have to be used to maintain that arrangement, just as it would have been necessary to carry out the partition decision of the United Nations."⁴⁷

At a special all-day meeting that the ZOA called in Washington three days later, Silver was even harsher, threatening reprisals against American troops if they were used to police the trusteeship. "It makes no difference whether the soldiers of the trustee power wear French or Chinese or American uniforms, the opposition will be there. The only question will be who is on the other side of barbed wire," he said.* Silver did not try to reconcile his American and Jewish identities. His "we" were Palestinian Jews who would shoot American soldiers if they tried to impose a new mandate on Palestine.

Silver blamed Austin's speech on Forrestal and the "oil interests." Forrestal had become an easy target for attacks from Silver, Crum, and other Zionists even though he was not nearly as important as Marshall or Lovett in determining administration policy toward Palestine. Neumann, who had been elected president of the ZOA, said it was "not too late for President Truman to shake himself loose from this conspiracy fostered by oil profiteers."⁴⁹ The liberal and left-wing press chimed in. The *New York Post* and *PM* editorialized against what *PM* called "Black

---

*On March 29, Ephraim Marks, the president of the Zionist Emergency Council of Omaha, wrote Silver, chastising him for exposing "Zionists to charges of disloyalty." "What do you suppose the effect on American Jewry [would be]," Marks asked, "if, after such statements are made by you as the chosen representative of our people, American soldiers were sent to Palestine and they were killed by Jewish forces?"⁴⁸ Silver Papers.

Friday."[50] *The New York Times* condemned the speech, which, it said, "comes as a climax to a series of moves which has seldom been matched, for ineptness, in the handling of any international issues by an American administration." And *The Times*, echoing Silver, noted the paradox that haunted the State Department's proposals—that trusteeship "may well require an even larger armed force than would be required for partition."[51]

Austin's speech got a hostile reception at the UN. Eleanor Roosevelt threatened to resign as UN representative; Trygve Lie protested that the speech was a rebuke to the United Nations itself and suggested to Austin, who he thought had spoken under duress, that the two of them resign in protest. (Austin demurred.) The Soviet representative denounced the speech. The French demanded to know who would be responsible for implementing trusteeship. Only the Arab delegates greeted the speech favorably, but their enthusiasm would be short-lived.

Truman claimed to have been blindsided by the speech. His immediate reaction was vintage Truman. He lashed out at those whom he suspected of betraying him, but not to their faces. "The State Department pulled the rug from under me today," he wrote in his diary. "This morning I find the State Department has reversed my Palestine policy. The first I know about it is what I see in the papers . . . I am now in the position of a liar and a double-crosser." Not yet ready to blame Marshall and Lovett, he pointed his finger at "people on the third and fourth levels of the State Department who always wanted to cut my throat."[52] Truman was upset on a personal level that Weizmann would think he had lied and double-crossed him. He lamented to Clifford that Weizmann must think him a "shitass." He asked Clifford to investigate "how this could have happened."[53]

Clifford lent credence to Truman's view that the State Department had blindsided him. But it was not really true. Clifford's assistant George Elsey wrote in his memoirs that Truman "had personally read and approved some days earlier the Austin speech."[54] And Marshall reported in a memorandum that when Truman talked to Marshall on March 22, he admitted that he had "agreed to the statement but said that if he had known when it was going to be made he could have taken certain measures to have avoided the political blast of the press."[55]

Truman did have some reason to be angry, but he couldn't really drive the point home. Austin's speech had not incorporated Truman's instruction that "nothing should be presented to [the] Security Council that could be interpreted as a recession on our part from the position we took in the General Assembly." Instead, it was rightfully taken as a repudiation of the November plan for partition. What probably happened was that Truman—who, in Elsey's words, was "beset by worries on all sides" and "trying to juggle too many problems without allowing his staff to help"—either did not read the speech carefully or did not remind Marshall and Lovett on March 8 that a commitment to partition had to be included in it.*

Truman's biographer Alonzo Hamby wrote that "Truman appears to have been overwhelmed by the Palestine issue."

> He was subjected to intolerable pressures of either alienating his Jewish constituency or sending American troops as part of a UN force to impose partition. He did not want to get into a fight with Marshall or Lovett . . . One senses that some sort of a mental withdrawal process occurred. . . . Confronting a situation he had described as "insoluble" . . . and wanting to avoid conflict—he agreed with Marshall and Lovett, reassured Weizmann, and convinced himself that he was following a consistent policy until reality hit him like a sledgehammer on March 19.[56]

Austin's speech, and the sharp reaction to it, also brought home the politics of the Palestine issue. Washington's Democrats were already panicking over Isacson's victory in the Bronx. Isacson was backing Wallace's challenge to Truman, and Wallace was accusing Truman of selling out the Jews. Truman, Wallace declared, "talks like a Jew, and acts like an Arab."[57] If Wallace could siphon away Jewish votes the way Isacson had, he could easily deny New York to Truman. Nationally, Truman's approval rating was 36 percent—even below what it had been

---

*Something very similar had happened in September 1946 when Henry Wallace, who was then secretary of commerce, submitted to Truman a speech he was going to give on American foreign policy. Truman approved the speech and only realized after Wallace gave it, and an uproar had ensued, that it contained a sharp criticism of the administration's policy toward the Soviet Union. Truman then asked for Wallace's resignation.

in the fall of 1946 when the Republicans took back the Congress. Some top party figures were calling for him to get off the ticket.

Critics of the Austin decision were warning of its political effects. Immediately after the Austin speech, former Democratic National Committee vice chairman Oscar Ewing, now the head of the Federal Security Agency (forerunner of the Department of Health and Human Services), told Truman about a meeting he had held of sympathetic administration officials at which Robert Nathan assessed the political repercussions of the speech. Ewing also forwarded to Clifford a memorandum on partition from the research director of the DNC.

The clearest indication that politics had come front and center was who attended a meeting that Truman called on March 24 to contain the damage from Austin's speech. On one side were State Department officials Marshall, Henderson, Rusk, and Charles Bohlen, but on the other were several political staff or associates, including Ewing, DNC chairman Howard McGrath, and press secretary Charles Ross, as well as Niles, Lowenthal, and Clifford. The political officials outnumbered the foreign policy experts. That would never have happened at, say, a discussion of how to respond to the Berlin crisis.

The meeting took place in the cabinet room and lasted all afternoon. Niles, who had returned to duty, got into a heated argument with Henderson over partition. Finally, Truman called a halt to the meeting, declaring, "This gets us nowhere. All I want is a statement I can read tomorrow at my press conference."[58] Truman asked Clifford to work with State Department officials on a statement that would reconcile prior American support for partition with Austin's proposal for trusteeship and that would call for a truce between the Jews and Arabs.

The statement Truman read was a masterpiece in equivocation that reflected both the State Department and White House perspective but did little to repair the political damage that Austin's speech caused. The statement declared that "trusteeship is not proposed as a substitute for the partition plan but as an effort to fill the vacuum soon to be created by the termination of the mandate on May 15." That suggested that partition was still the goal. But it went on to say that "trusteeship does not prejudice the character of the final political settlement."[59] That suggested that the political settlement could take some form other than partition.

Truman's statement failed to calm the fury of the Zionist movement.

The AZEC held a day of protest and prayer on April 8 "giving expression to the Jewish people's indignation over the U.S. government's reversal of policy on Palestine" and sent thousands of postcards (they claimed more than a million) to Truman "assailing the administration's betrayal."[60] But Arab leaders were also not pleased. In Truman's question-and-answer session, he had intimated that he was still in favor of Jewish immigration. Now they, too, rejected the proposal for trusteeship. The confusion generated by Austin's speech and the administration follow-up continued. When Austin actually submitted his proposal to the General Assembly on April 20, it was framed in exactly the same terms as his speech. Arabs and Jews were to agree on "the future government."[61] There was no mention of the UN partition plan. Truman's attempt to contain the damage had been fruitless.

Futile Efforts

For six weeks after Austin's speech, Henderson and the State Department tried to sell the United Nations, the British, and the Jews and the Arabs on the proposal for a temporary trusteeship. But their approach once again fell afoul of the reality on the ground. It showed that, for all their purported realism, they still hadn't come to terms with what was happening. They kept thinking that they could induce the British to remain in Palestine after May 15 either to be the trustee or to prepare the way for a UN trusteeship. The British kept saying that they were leaving. When the British wouldn't accede to the State Department request, the State Department proposed a tripartite force of American, French, and British troops, but the French and British rejected the plan outright.

The State Department thought that if they could get the Jews and Arabs to negotiate face-to-face, they would reach an agreement on a truce and trusteeship. The British had tried to do this repeatedly since 1923 and had failed, but the State Department believed it could succeed. An attempt at negotiations on April 9 at UN headquarters lasted a day before collapsing. Then the United States proposed a last-ditch plan that had a Jules Verne touch to it. At the State Department's urging, Truman offered the presidential plane, the *Sacred Cow*, to fly Arab, Jewish, American, and possibly French and Belgian representatives to

Palestine to conduct negotiations toward a truce. It was a stunt, and the Jewish Agency immediately rejected it.

The State Department even made a qualified offer to send American troops—if they were part of a UN force. But James Forrestal and the Defense Department shot that down. In a letter to Marshall on April 19, Forrestal warned that, according to the Joint Chiefs, even if the United States shared the responsibility with other countries, it would still have to supply "approximately 50,000 men," which "represents our entire present ground reserve, both Marine and Army. In other words, there would be no troops available to any other area."[62] In a discussion with the UN delegation that day, Rusk made clear that the American offer of troops was not without strings attached. "The United States," Rusk assured the delegates, "was not going to buy into any war between the Jews and Arabs of Palestine."[63] Other delegations concluded that the United States was not serious about sending troops and continued to oppose the trusteeship plan.

Henderson had one last idea. He thought that if he could bring together "moderate Jews and Arabs," he could undercut Silver and Ben-Gurion on one side, and the mufti on the other. He and Lovett both sent letters to Judah Magnes urging him to visit the United States. Magnes and his small organization, Ihud, remained committed to a binational Palestine, and Magnes had applauded the administration's plan for a truce and trusteeship as a way to lay the groundwork for a joint Arab-Jewish administration of the country. Henderson and Lovett hoped that he could help build support for the plan in the United States.

Magnes was old and sickly—he had only seven months to live—and needed to have a physician as well as his wife accompany him on the trip, which Lessing Rosenwald paid for. By the time Magnes arrived on April 26, the prospects for a truce and trusteeship had already dimmed. Magnes had once had a following in the American Jewish Committee, but he failed to win support for binationalism among the group's leadership. He got a better reception in Washington. After he saw Marshall on May 5, the secretary of state was so impressed with Magnes's views on Palestine that he urged Truman to see him.

Truman received Magnes in the Oval Office for a half hour on the morning of May 6. After Magnes had recounted what he had told Marshall about his hopes for a binational Palestine, Truman began to talk about the Anglo-American Committee's report. He said it was a great document and claimed to know it almost by heart. "It was a thousand pities that report had not been carried out," he told Magnes. He pulled the report out of his desk drawer. "Here it is. You see that it is a document that I could consult. I do consult it." Turning finally to the present, Truman lamented the failure of the negotiations between the Jews and Arabs. "The Jews refused my plane offer," he said.

He told Magnes of his hope that Jews, Christians, and Muslims—who lived according to the same moral code—would be able to live together. "But here it is," he told Magnes, "you Jews and your Arabs are spoiling things." In parting, Magnes told Truman not to give up. And Truman replied, "Dr. Magnes, we won't give up. We shall hang on to this until we find a way. That is our duty."[64] But Truman had not found a way—and his mind was still dwelling on the failure of the Anglo-American Committee's report.

Magnes's visit to the United States had no impact on the attempt to achieve a truce and trusteeship in Palestine. Indeed, the entire administration effort—from Austin's speech through Truman's offer of the presidential plane—turned out to be an irrelevant sideshow to what was actually going on in Palestine. In the absence of an effective American policy, Palestine's future was being determined by forces on the ground.

The Haganah Takes the Field

The State Department's decision to press for trusteeship and a truce had been based on the notion that the Jews were losing the war with the Arabs and that, as a result of Zionist pressure at home, the United States would be called upon to intervene militarily to save the Jews. The change in policy, Henderson wrote in a memorandum after Austin's speech, "is being inaugurated in the belief that American public sentiment would insist on American armed intervention if necessary in order to avoid the slaughter of the Jews in Palestine" and that "such slaughter would take place following British withdrawal unless either American or Soviet troops intervene."[65]

The continuing events in Palestine during March suggested that Henderson and other policy makers' fears of a Jewish defeat were well-founded. On March 27, Arabs inflicted heavy casualties on Haganah-led convoys in the Galilee and on the road to Jerusalem. Even top officials of the Jewish Agency in Jerusalem were beginning to fear defeat. One memo from the political department in late March declared that "there is little likelihood of Jews being able to overcome [the] Arab world by force of arms."[66] But in fact the State Department and the political department in Jerusalem were dead wrong about the Yishuv's prospects.

In early March, the Haganah's operations chief, Yigael Yadin, had circulated among his commanders a new strategy, Plan D (for the Hebrew letter *dalit*) that was to be put into effect in early May as the British departed. It called for securing the roads and the borders of the new Jewish state against the expected attack from Arab states. Villages that housed militias or that were on or near critical roads were to be "taken, cleansed or destroyed."[67] And Jewish settlements outside the UN borders of the Jewish state were also to be protected from attack.

Ben-Gurion, worried about Jerusalem's encirclement and also about the American reversal of its support for partition, decided, in effect, to move up the execution of Plan D to the beginning of April by launching a large-scale Haganah attack against Arabs and Arab villages that were threatening Jewish Jerusalem. By then the Haganah had a trained force of 40,000 or so men and women; in early April, arms shipments had begun arriving from Czechoslovakia; and the British evacuation was proceeding apace. Once the Haganah, aided by the smaller terrorist groups, took the offensive, the Palestinian Arab resistance crumbled.

In the initial engagement in Jerusalem, the Haganah cleared the roads by seizing control of the Arab villages that overlooked them, driving out the inhabitants, and routing the militias. Abd al-Qadir al-Husseini, the son of Musa Kazim Husseini, and the most effective of the Arab commanders, was killed. The Haganah and Irgun also took control of Jaffa, Tiberias, the Arab sections of Haifa, and Safed. After a brutal Irgun assault against Jaffa, only 4,000 to 5,000 of 80,000 Arab inhabitants remained. The rest fled in fear—some to Lebanon, some to Gaza, and some to the West Bank. The other Arab towns were also emptied out. In all, about 300,000 Arabs fled their homes during this first phase of the war between the Jews and the Arabs.

A key event was the attack by the Irgun and Stern Gang against the village of Deir Yassin on April 9. The Arab village was just north of Jerusalem. It had refused to host the Arab Liberation Army and had signed agreements with a neighboring Jewish settlement not to attack each other. It was also of little military value. But the terrorist groups attacked it, killed at least 110 of its inhabitants, including women and children. Women were raped. Houses were blown up with their residents in them. Women, children, and old men were carted through West Jerusalem in a victory parade reminiscent of the Romans. Prisoners were executed on the spot. The Jewish Agency and Haganah denounced the action, but the Irgun produced a letter from the Haganah regional commander urging the Irgun to capture Deir Yassin.[68]

The massacre at Deir Yassin struck fear in the hearts of Arab villagers. It was "a decisive accelerating factor" in their flight, according to the IDF intelligence service.[69] That was to the benefit of the Jewish Agency's war effort, and helped to lead to the Jewish majority that Weizmann and Ben-Gurion had dreamed about but never thought would be realized without a decade of strenuous immigration. But Deir Yassin also became—and has remained—a potent symbol of Jewish injustice toward Palestine's Arabs. On April 22, Jordan's King Abdullah announced that as a result of the events in Deir Yassin and the flight of Arabs from Haifa and Tiberias, he had lost hope of a peaceful solution to the Palestinian conflict and was ready to go to war against the Jews.[70]

The terrorist groups had used similar tactics before; to a great extent, they were modeled on the brutal British attempt to put down the Arab rebellion after the Peel Commission failed. But while the British aimed at pacifying villages, the terrorist groups and often the Haganah aimed at inducing flight—and wittingly or unwittingly (the historian Benny Morris seems right to reject a grand conspiracy at work) at achieving the transfer of Arabs out of Jewish Palestine. What was particularly shocking about Deir Yassin was that the villagers were, to all intents and purposes, neutral in the war. They were like the Orthodox Jews of Hebron and Safed, many of whom were opposed to Zionism, whom the Arab rioters slaughtered in 1929.

In the United States, *The New York Times* published reports of the massacre, but there was no discussion of it in the meetings of the AZEC's leadership, and except for a brief reference in *Palestine Affairs*, no mention of it in Zionist publications. That may have been because the threat of Jewish defeat still loomed large and because the Arabs themselves had committed their share of atrocities. But the absence of *any* discussion seems to indicate a willingness to overlook the morality of Zionism. As Jabotinsky had argued two decades before, the ends of Zionism justified the means.

On April 16, Ben-Gurion reported to Shertok that "the military situation has changed radically in favor of the Jews."[71] By early May, when the State Department was still pushing for a truce, the Yishuv was in control of the territories allotted to it by the United Nations (with the possible exception of the Negev, which was still under attack) and was on its way to incorporating into a Jewish state Safed and the Western Galilee, Jaffa, and part of Arab Jerusalem that had been assigned to the Arabs or to the UN's authority. And the issue had shifted in Washington from how to win support for a truce and trusteeship to whether to recognize the Jewish state when the British left on May 15.

Premature Recognition

On March 23, in the wake of Austin's speech, the Jewish Agency and the Va'ad Leumi announced that when the British left, a Jewish government would take charge in the territories allotted to a Jewish state by the UN. Over the next six weeks some Jewish Agency leaders wavered. In early May, Shertok and Goldmann thought that the Jewish Agency should consider accepting the American-sponsored UN proposal for a truce in the hope that a war with the Arab states could be averted, but Ben-Gurion held firm and carried the day.

In Palestine, the state within a state that the Jews had begun building in the 1920s fully emerged during the war and took over the administration of Jewish Palestine even before the British had left. On the other hand, in Arab Palestine, where the Arab League and King Abdullah had blocked the installation of a provisional government, anarchy reigned. On May 3, Wasson, the American consul in Jerusalem, reported back to the State Department:

> In Palestine, [the British] Palestine government has generally ceased to function and central public services no longer exist. In Jewish areas, Jews have taken effective control and are maintaining public services within those areas. Preparations for [the] establishment [of the] Jewish state . . . are well advanced. Confidence in future [is] at high peak and Jewish public support for leaders overwhelming. In Arab

areas, only municipal administration continues without any central authority. In Samaria food and gasoline are in very short supply. Morale following Jewish military successes [is] low with thousands of Arabs fleeing [the] country.[72]

In Washington, Truman's aides, prodded by the AZEC and the Jewish Agency, began in early May to agitate for the president to announce that he would recognize the new state before the state actually came into being. At lunch on May 5, Lowenthal gave Matt Connelly, Truman's appointment secretary, a bunch of clippings for the president. The White House staff in those days was quite small, and while Connelly's title was modest, he enjoyed considerable influence with the president. Lowenthal contended that the president should say "he would recognize the Jewish state." Connelly agreed to work with Lowenthal to convince the president, but he warned Lowenthal that when Clifford, who also favored a presidential announcement, said something about it to Lovett, the undersecretary "hit the ceiling."[73] Lowenthal also began deluging Clifford with position papers and arguments for a recognition announcement.

Lowenthal's argument, which Clifford and Niles adopted, was partly commonsense realism and partly disguised politicking. They argued on good grounds that the attempt to get UN approval for trusteeship and to get the Jews and Arabs to accept a truce had failed and that the Jewish state was going to come into being, like it or not, and would do so in accordance with the UN resolution of November 1947 that the United States had sponsored. Lowenthal provided Clifford with a statement that the president could read announcing that he would recognize the new state.

What was tendentious was their insistence that Truman should say he *would* recognize the new state before the new state even existed. Lowenthal and Clifford claimed that, by doing so, the United States would gain a step on the Soviet Union; but they could also do that, as they later acknowledged, by recognizing the new state minutes or even seconds after Ben-Gurion announced its existence. Their purpose in this case seems to have been to forestall any opposition to recognition and to ingratiate Truman and the administration with American Jewry during an election year.

The AZEC and other Zionist organizations, which had harshly criticized Truman, had planned hundreds of rallies across the country on the night of May 14, when the announcement was expected in Palestine. Lowenthal, Niles, and Clifford feared that if the president didn't do anything to win over the Zionists, he would be denounced at these rallies. And if the Soviet Union were to beat the United States to recognizing the new state, it would be a black mark on Truman among American Jews.

On May 5, Dean Alfange, who was the chairman of the American Christian Palestine Committee, sent a letter to Truman's friend and military aide Harry Vaughan to pass on to the president. Alfange warned that Truman "could not carry the state of New York in the present circumstances. Only a dramatic move on the President's part that would electrify the Jewish people would change the situation. Such a move might well be the recognition of the Jewish state."[74] Alfange's warning was echoed by Democratic Party bosses in New York and Chicago.

Having gotten wind of Clifford's plan, the State Department adamantly opposed it. But their response was far from straightforward. They had good grounds for opposing the initiative as framed. There was little precedent for recognizing a state before it came into existence, and doing so in this case would make the United States—which had been pressing at the UN for a truce and a delay in the formation of a new state—look foolish and hypocritical. But Marshall and Lovett seemed to go beyond rejecting the timing of the announcement. They insisted that the president should allow more time to win the UN and the warring parties in Palestine over to a truce—a truce that could lead to trusteeship and a negotiated agreement between the Jews and the Arabs.

By early May, most of those directly involved with negotiations at the UN had given up on trusteeship and were about to give up on getting a truce. "At the present stage, trusteeship as a concept for the solution of the Palestine problem seems virtually to have been abandoned by almost all delegations," the State Department official and UN advisor John Evarts Horner wrote on May 4.[75] Horner said there was some support for a truce, but only a minority conceived that a truce would lead to a "neutral regime."[76] And in a meeting with Marshall and Lovett, Shertok and Epstein had removed any doubt that the Jewish Agency would oppose the American truce plan.

What was likely driving Marshall and Lovett to reject Clifford's plan was their anger at the politicization of the issue. Both Marshall and Lovett saw Clifford's proposal for a premature announcement as being patently political. Marshall, who had tolerated political considerations when they figured in the deliberations in the previous September at the UN, may have also rejected Clifford's plan out of a particular dislike of him, perhaps because of Clifford's attempt to blame the State Department for the furor caused by Austin's speech.

At this point Truman seems to have been more worried about internal politics than about the Jews and Arabs of Palestine. He wanted to please Clifford, Niles and Lowenthal, Jacobson, and Weizmann; but he also wanted to placate Marshall, whom he revered. He had put aside his own vision of Palestine and was adjudicating between the people he had appointed and the alternatives they had given him.

When Eddie Jacobson saw Truman in Washington on April 12, he told Jacobson that he would recognize the Jewish state. On April 30, Truman told Dean Rusk that he supported the American plan for a truce. When Rusk asked Truman what he would do if the Arabs accepted the proposal and the Jews did not, Truman replied, "If the Jews refuse to accept a truce on reasonable grounds, they need not expect anything else from us."[77] A week later Truman told Magnes that his heart was still with the Anglo-American plan for a federated Palestine.

When Truman met with Clifford on May 7, he tacked back in the direction of recognizing the Jewish state. According to Clifford, Truman was "sympathetic to the proposal" to say he would recognize the new state, but he wanted to get Marshall's reaction.[78] He called Marshall, and when the secretary of state objected strenuously to the statement, Truman proposed that they have a meeting to discuss it. The meeting was set for May 12, a day before Clifford had wanted the president to issue the statement. Truman instructed Clifford to prepare an argument on behalf of his proposal that could counter Marshall's objections. "I want you to present it just as though you were making an argument before the Supreme Court of the United States," Truman told Clifford.[79]

The Oval Office Meeting

The meeting took place in the Oval Office at 4:00 p.m. on an unusually hot, sunny day in May. Truman sat behind his desk, with the sign reading *The Buck Stops Here!* prominently displayed. On his left were Marshall, Lovett, and two junior State Department officials. On his right were Clifford, Niles, and Connelly. The meeting has sometimes been portrayed as a turning point in American relations with Zionism. Clifford uses it as the prologue to his memoir, *Counsel to the President*, as if it epitomized his service to presidents. But it was really more about the conflict between people—particularly Clifford and Marshall—than it was about the policies under discussion.

Marshall and Lovett led off by complaining about the unwillingness of the Jewish Agency to agree to a truce, which Marshall attributed to overconfidence after recent military successes. Marshall was interrupted by a telephone call from the military telling him that Shertok had said he was flying to Tel Aviv with messages from Marshall to Ben-Gurion. Marshall expressed disbelief about the report, saying he had never heard of Ben-Gurion. That indicated, if anything, how little he knew about Palestine. Marshall concluded by recommending that the administration continue to pursue the truce and trusteeship and defer any decision on recognizing the new state.[80]

Truman then asked Clifford to speak. Clifford's key point, drawn from Lowenthal's memoranda, was that the effort to secure a truce and establish a trusteeship had failed; partition, at least as far as the Jewish state was concerned, was a fact; and it was in the nation's interest to acknowledge that fact, which accorded with the UN resolution of November, and recognize the new Jewish state. Clifford recommended that, in his press conference the next day, the president announce his intention to do so, and urge other countries to do likewise.

Marshall's face reddened as Clifford spoke, and when Clifford was finished, Marshall turned to Truman. "Mr. President, I thought this meeting was called to consider an important and complicated problem in foreign policy. I don't even know why Clifford is here. He is a domestic advisor, and this is a foreign policy matter." Truman responded, "Well, General, he is here because I asked him to be here."[81]

Lovett pounced on Clifford's proposal for "premature recognition," which he said would be "injurious to the prestige of the President."

Lovett charged that it was a "transparent attempt to win the Jewish vote." Marshall seconded Lovett's argument. "The counsel offered by Mr. Clifford," he charged, "was based on domestic political considerations, while the problem which confronted us was international." And Marshall ended by saying that "if the President were to follow Mr. Clifford's advice, and if in the elections I were to vote, I would vote against the President."[82] Truman, shocked by Marshall's implied threat, brought the meeting to a close. "I understand your position, General, and I'm inclined to side with you in this matter," Truman said.[83] And he initialed a State Department proposal to continue trying to negotiate a truce and trusteeship.

Truman consoled Clifford afterward. "Well, that was rough as a cob," he told Clifford. He agreed that Clifford could try again after letting "the dust settle a little bit" but that he would have to be careful. "I can't afford to lose General Marshall," he said.[84] At his news conference the next day, Truman was asked what he would do if the new state asked for U.S. recognition. "I will cross that bridge when I get to it," he replied. Truman had told Clifford that he was still in favor of recognition, but he seems to have been genuinely undecided. What swayed him, finally, was the "unbearable pressure" (as Clifford later put it) that he found himself under to recognize Israel.[85]

After his press conference, Niles pulled Truman aside to tell him of a call he had received from Jake Arvey, the Jewish head of the Democratic Party in Chicago. Arvey, who earlier had threatened to try to draft Dwight Eisenhower as the Democratic nominee, had reconciled himself to Truman running, and he wanted Truman to know that he could advance his chances by recognizing the Jewish state before the celebrations took place. Truman told Niles that he had heard the same thing from the New York party boss Ed Flynn, who said there were going to be three hundred mass meetings around the country. Niles assured Truman that he and Lowenthal were trying to prevent "adverse references to him at these meetings." Truman told Niles that he was going to show him and Lowenthal how much he appreciated what they had been doing.[86]

That same afternoon Clifford called Lovett to try to work out a deal. Connelly had pointed out to Clifford that while Marshall and Lovett had "carried the day" in rejecting Clifford's suggestion that the president announce that he *would* recognize the new state, they "did not take the position that recognition should be refused after application [was] made."[87] In other words, the real pro-and-con debate had focused on the less important and easily decidable question of whether Truman should recognize the new state before it asked for recognition. If the question were to shift back to recognizing the state after it had requested recognition, the onus would be on Marshall and Lovett to show that doing so was unreasonable or against the national interest.

Clifford told Lovett that he and Marshall had been right about premature recognition, but he thought they should still consider what to do if the new state asked for recognition. Lovett said that the State Department was considering that question. Clifford realized, he told Lowenthal later, that Lovett was "thinking of yielding."[88] The next day Clifford called Ben Cohen to work on a letter asking for recognition. Cohen suggested calling Epstein, and Epstein directed Clifford to Ginsburg, who, together with Clifford, drew up a letter asking for recognition. At lunch with Lovett that day, Clifford stressed that Truman needed to recognize the new state that weekend rather than the following week. "A week later would be too late to do the President any good," he told Lovett—a fairly clear reference to the political pressure that Truman was under.[89]

After much back-and-forth, Lovett gave in, while Clifford for his part agreed that the recognition should be "de facto" rather than "de jure": it should recognize the existence of the new state, but not its government or borders; and ambassadors should not yet be exchanged. At 4:30, Marshall sent word that while he did not support recognition, he would abide by the president's decision. In Tel Aviv, David Ben-Gurion, speaking at the museum of art, announced that the new state of Israel would come into existence at midnight, 6:00 Washington time. Ben-Gurion, who hoped to enlarge the territory that the UN had allotted, did not specify borders for the new state. At 6:11 p.m. in Washington, Truman issued a statement recognizing the existence of the new state of Israel.

The next morning Truman's aides gathered in Connelly's office to await their regular Saturday morning meeting with the president. Lowenthal was there. When Truman entered the room to welcome his aides, he saw Lowenthal and asked him what he was doing. Lowenthal, who had drafted Clifford's statements arguing that the president should recognize Israel because it was in the national interest rather than in Truman's political interest, replied, "I am smiling because you are going to win the election."[90]

"I Thought We Had the Problem Solved"

In his earlier meeting with Weizmann, Truman told him that he wanted to achieve "justice done without bloodshed" in Palestine. At a meeting on May 8 that Marshall and Lovett had with Shertok and Epstein, Shertok had asked Lovett what the State Department was trying to achieve in Palestine, and Lovett had answered, "Peace."[91] But the administration's policies did not produce either peace or justice without bloodshed. That went for the original UN partition plan and for the decision to recognize the state. These policies—like those of Balfour and Lloyd George in 1917—were characterized by wishful thinking and a disconnect between means and ends.

Zionists, of course, continued to tell the administration what it wanted to hear. During the final battle over recognition, Lowenthal was telling Clifford that, by recognizing the new state, "bloodshed will be prevented." Lowenthal was predicting that the "Arabs would not fight the Jews much, did not dare, did not have the strength."[92] But no sooner had Ben-Gurion completed his announcement of the new state than the first and by no means the last Arab-Israeli war began. An Egyptian force crossed into the Negev; Egyptian aircraft bombed Tel Aviv; Syrian and Lebanese troops entered from the north and Jordan's Arab Legion from the east. Palestinian Arabs, many of whom had fled what would become the new Jewish state during the winter and spring and were now a forgotten people, looked on fearfully from the sidelines.

Truman would later revel in the honors that the Jewish state bestowed upon him, but in the immediate aftermath of recognizing Israel he remained unconvinced of its necessity or its moral wisdom. On May 15 he wrote Bartley Crum, who a week before had importuned him to recognize the new state: "You, of course, are familiar with all the effort put forth by me to get a peaceable and satisfactory settlement of the Palestine question. I am still hoping for just that. I think the report of the British-American Commission on Palestine was the correct solution and, I think, eventually we are going to get it worked out just that way."[93]

On May 18, after the fighting had resumed, he replied to Dean Al-fange's earlier plea to recognize the new state. "My soul [sic] objective in the Palestine procedure has been to prevent bloodshed," Truman wrote. "The way things look today we apparently have not been very successful." And then the president went down a familiar road. "Nobody in this country has given the problem more time and thought than I have. In 1946 when the British-American Commission on Palestine was appointed and Mr. Bevin had made an agreement with me that he would accept the finding of that Commission, I thought we had the problem solved but the emotional Jews of the United States and the equally emotional Arabs in Egypt and Syria prevented that settlement from taking place . . . I sincerely hope that sanity will come to both sides so that a peaceful approach can be made to a settlement which should have been worked out by the British some twenty years ago."[94]

It's not clear what Truman was referring to when he complained that the Arabs in Egypt and Syria had prevented the Anglo-American Committee's recommendations from taking place. Truman's pattern was to evoke the promise of the committee report and then to put the blame on whichever groups had been most recently frustrating him. The one constant in his reproaches were the "emotional Jews" of the United States. But that may be because they were his most persistent critics and because he eventually gave them what they wanted.

TRIUMPH AND CATASTROPHE

Many a study of Truman and Israel ends with his recognition of Israel.[1] Even those that acknowledge his indecision over the years end on a note of decisiveness, as if that one moment—when Truman decided to issue a statement recognizing the new state—balanced out the prior three years of frustration, equivocation, second-guessing, and regret. But Truman's policies toward Palestine and then Israel—his encounter with Zionism and Arab nationalism—did not end in May 1948. They continued for at least another fifteen months, in which he and his administration tried to convince the new state of Israel to adjust its borders and to repatriate the war's refugees.

These months replicated the difficulties of the months that preceded them. With the Cold War heating up and an election in progress, Truman kept trying to shift responsibility for the Israeli-Arab conflict onto the State Department, but when State Department policies drew the ire of the Israelis and their allies in the United States, he was forced to take sides. His first impulse was to express concern about an outcome that clearly favored the Jews over the Arabs, but as had happened repeatedly over the last three years, he eventually gave up trying to achieve a just resolution to the conflict. Truman's policies toward Palestine and then Israel began and ended on a note of indecision.

Airlift and Elections

In the summer of 1948, Truman had to worry about a conflict with the Soviet Union over Berlin. After the United States had merged its zone in Germany with that of the British and French to form what would become West Germany, and began pouring money into West Germany to rebuild its economy, the Soviet Union, fearful of a revived Germany, imposed a blockade on Berlin, which was an international city inside what would become Soviet-controlled East Germany. The Russians prevented any cars, trucks, or trains from entering the city from the west. Berliners faced starvation, and the Truman administration a choice between abandoning the western part of Berlin, confronting the blockade directly, or attempting to run it through an airlift. Truman decided on an airlift.

In 1948, Truman was also running for president. With his approval ratings hovering around 40 percent, Truman was expected to lose to the Republican candidate Tom Dewey, but Truman, who had been an underdog before, was determined to make a race of it. Preoccupied with the Berlin crisis and his campaign, Truman had little time to think about Israel and about the war that had broken out between the new state and its Arab neighbors. As he had done earlier, he ceded responsibility for American policy to the State Department.

Marshall himself was equally caught up with the Berlin crisis, but after his clash with Clifford and Truman over recognition the secretary of state was determined not to lose control of Palestine policy again. In a meeting with Truman on May 24, Marshall warned Truman of "the tragic results which might well follow any action not carefully considered."[2] Truman agreed to clear any White House initiatives with Lovett. But that still didn't solve the problem of who would devise policies.

With Truman and Marshall paying little attention to the Arab-Israeli war, that put more responsibility for the policy on Lovett, but he also had to run the State Department during Marshall's frequent absences. The initiative for policy devolved to the lower ranks in the department, whose recommendations in the past had led to clashes with the supporters of the Jewish state. What happened then was entirely predictable: more pitched battles between the proponents of the Jewish state (including Truman's White House aides) and the State Department, which could only be settled, finally, by a distracted and disgruntled president.

The first of these battles resulted in victories for the Zionist network. Niles, Clifford, and Lowenthal lobbied Truman to fire Henderson. Truman, who saw the abrasive Henderson as the anti-Zionist counterpart of Silver, asked Marshall to dismiss him, but Marshall could not fire him because he was protected by civil service regulations. The best he could do was to move him out of Washington by making him ambassador to India. Henderson's replacement, his deputy Joseph C. Satterthwaite, had the same views of Palestine and Israel but was less insistent in pressing them upon the president.

Niles, Clifford, and Lowenthal also sought to influence the administration's choice of a special representative to the new state of Israel. The State Department sent over the name of the foreign service officer Charles Knox, who was already serving in Tel Aviv. Niles asked Hilldring's opinion about Knox, who had served briefly on Hilldring's staff at the UN, and Hilldring said he was pro-Arab and "no damn good."[3] Hilldring's judgment that Knox was "pro-Arab" was wildly unfair—another example of taking the slightest criticism of the Jewish state as an indication of "pro-Arab" sympathies. But Niles accepted Hilldring's judgment and got Truman to reject Knox.*

Niles, Clifford, and Lowenthal first set their sights on Hilldring, but Hilldring was worried his health would not permit him to take the job. They then turned to James McDonald, who had been on the Anglo-American Committee and had become a dependable part of the Zionist network, willing, when asked, to pressure the president. Niles was particularly confident about McDonald, he told Lowenthal, because

---

*Knox continued to serve in Tel Aviv in 1948 and early 1949 under Ambassador James McDonald, who praised him effusively. McDonald wrote in his memoirs that Knox would have been "a perfect choice as the United States representative." (*My Mission in Israel*, New York: Simon & Schuster, 1951, p. 7.) After Knox left Israel, he wrote his successor, William F. Penniman, a glowing letter about the Israelis. "The Jew in Israel," he wrote, "is less picturesque in his western work clothes, not humble, nor subservient, holding fast to a personal moral code which is the historical basis of Christian ethics, with a resilience that somehow has enabled him to survive despite recent disasters that would have eliminated a less strong people. I feel sorry for the Arabs. I am anxious to help them, I do not admire them, I pity them." Lowenthal Papers.

he had "been working closely with the ZOA and has lectured at their expense."[4]

McDonald, tall, austere, gray haired, had made his reputation as an early proponent of human rights. He had worked for the League of Nations in the 1930s getting Jews out of Germany and had been a delegate to the ill-fated Évian Conference. When Clifford approached him about the job, he said that he might not be able to afford it. According to Lowenthal, Niles then made the "necessary arrangements" with Henry Morgenthau to supplement McDonald's salary. Morgenthau, like other American Jewish Committee members, had become a strong supporter of Israel. With McDonald's consent, Truman appointed him.

In pushing for McDonald, Niles, Clifford, and Lowenthal were running roughshod over the tradition of an impartial foreign service by promoting someone who had been paid by the ZOA and appears to have been paid on the side by Israel's supporters. McDonald himself seems to have been a man of integrity, as witnessed later by his sympathy for the Palestinian Arab refugees; and, unlike Crum, he would not stoop to being a propagandist for the Zionist cause. But McDonald was a true believer—perhaps out of his experience with the refugees from Nazism in the 1930s—whom Israeli officials could easily spin and manipulate.

The First Arab-Israeli War

The war over Israel and Palestine began on May 16, but the Arabs probably lost it before it started. At the end of April, Arab leaders and military officials had met in Transjordan to devise a strategy. They settled on a plausible plan: the Iraqi, Syrian, Lebanese, and Jordanian armies would conduct a pincer movement in the north-central region that would cut the Galilee off from the rest of Israel, and the Egyptians would head northward up the coast toward Tel Aviv. But this plan—and the war effort as a whole—fell victim to the enduring quarrels among the Arab countries.

Transjordan's King Abdullah had agreed to the plan, but, in spite of his protestations after Deir Yassin, he had no intention of following it. The war plan was an attempt to destroy the Jewish state, but Abdullah wanted to divide Palestine up with the Israelis. "Their plan was to prevent partition; his plan was to effect partition," the historian Avi Shlaim has written.[5] Instead of adhering to the war plan, King Abdullah directed his British-financed, trained, and led Arab Legion, the only effective Arab fighting force, to advance across the West Bank in order to occupy what the UN had resolved to be Arab Palestine. That single move undermined the Arab strategy.

With Abdullah no longer committed to an assault on the north, Lebanon balked at invading Israel, and Syria and Iraq settled for more limited objectives. Egypt's leaders, who were more concerned about preventing Abdullah from capturing Arab Palestine than about destroying the Jewish state, split their forces, sending some armies up the coast and others toward the West Bank to prevent a Jordanian takeover. As the historian Benny Morris put it, the Arab war plan changed from a "united effort to conquer large parts of the nascent Jewish state . . . into an uncoordinated, multilateral land grab."[6] The Israelis might have had difficulty with a coordinated offensive, but they had little trouble defeating scattered forces fighting at cross-purposes with each other.

Even at the beginning of the war, the Israelis enjoyed a numerical advantage in total troop strength. And their commanders and forces—in contrast to those of the Egyptians, Syrians, or Iraqis—were battle tested. (Egypt's war minister had risen to his post from having been director of prisons.) But because the Israelis still lacked heavy equipment, their overall advantage didn't surface immediately. They blocked the invasion from the north and the south but could not drive out the opposing armies. Israel defended its borders, except in the Negev, where the Egyptians had set up camp, but its positions, Shertok complained to Nahum Goldmann, were "tenuously held."[7]

The UN came to the rescue of Israel's weary forces. On the same day that Truman had recognized Israel, the UN had earlier adopted a resolution affirming the "efforts of the Security Council to secure a truce in Palestine" and empowering the General Assembly to appoint a "mediator" who would "promote a peaceful adjustment of the future situation of Palestine."[8] A week later a UN committee appointed a Swede, Count Folke Bernadotte, as mediator, and Trygve Lie appointed Ralph Bunche to be his deputy. One of Bernadotte's first acts was to negotiate a one-month truce in the Arab-Israeli war. Both sides agreed to stop fighting on June 11. With the guns temporarily silenced, Bernadotte began to formulate a proposal to end the conflict altogether.

Bernadotte was working with Bunche and another UN official, the British-born South African economist John Reedman, to develop his plan. Bernadotte had been vice president of the Swedish Red Cross during World War II and had negotiated the release of about 15,000 people from Nazi concentration camps in 1945. Bunche described Bernadotte in his diary as "affable, speaks good English, fairly tall and slender, deep-lined face, but nice-looking."[9]

As a diplomat, Bernadotte was known for his persistence, whirlwind energy, courage, and commitment to human rights, but not necessarily for his grasp of what contending parties might be willing to accept. He was guided in part by a kind of abstract idealism. Bernadotte's first proposal, which he unveiled as "suggestions" on June 28, was an unwieldy compromise between the American and British approaches.[10] He adopted the idea of exchanging the western Galilee for the Negev; Transjordan would get the West Bank and most of the Negev. But Bernadotte also granted Transjordan control of Jerusalem, granted any refugees from the Jewish state the right of return, and allowed each country to appeal after two years each other's immigration policy to a joint council.

Bernadotte had reasons for his surprising proposals: he thought, for instance, that the Berlin crisis exposed the weakness of trying to internationalize or divide a city like Jerusalem. But the Jews peremptorily dismissed Bernadotte's plan for a Transjordanian Jerusalem and for their loss of sovereignty to a joint council. The one thing Ben-Gurion had vowed not to concede was control over immigration.

Israeli leaders were also opposed to granting any Arabs the right to return, and they did not plan to budge on that issue, either. They saw the flight of Palestinian Arabs as a godsend. On June 15, Shertok wrote Goldmann:

The most spectacular event in the contemporary history of Palestine— more spectacular in a sense than the creation of the Jewish state—is the wholesale evacuation of its Arab population which has swept with it also thousands of Arabs from areas threatened and/or occupied by us outside our boundaries. I doubt whether there are 100,000 Arabs in Israel today. The reversion to *status quo ante* is unthinkable. The opportunities which the present position opens up for a lasting and radical solution of the most vexing problem of the Jewish state, are so far reaching as to take one's breath away . . . we must make the most of the momentous chance with which history has presented us so swiftly and so unexpectedly.[11]

The day after Shertok wrote Goldmann, the Israeli cabinet decided to bar refugees—who already numbered over 300,000—from returning to their homes. An order went out to the IDF to fire upon any Arabs trying to return. That marked the beginning of the Palestinian refugee crisis. It also put the Israelis on the other side of the right to return, a principle of international law that would be codified by the United Nations in December 1948. If the Israelis had gained the moral high ground in the late 1930s when they sought a safe haven for Europe's endangered Jews and the Arabs talked of deporting even those Jews who were already in Palestine, they retreated into the marshes over their determination to drive Palestine's Arabs out of the country and not let them back in.

However, Bernadotte's plan was also dismissed by most of the Arab League nations. Egypt, Saudi Arabia, Syria, and Lebanon still rejected any plan based on partition. But they were especially dismissive of a plan that they thought unfairly favored Jordan. Even the British were embarrassed by the gifts that Bernadotte had bestowed on their ally. Bernadotte had to withdraw his proposal and plead to the Arabs and Israelis to continue to honor the one-month truce.

Israel on the Offensive

During the truce, the Israel Defense Forces (IDF) almost doubled its size and added armored vehicles and airplanes. The Israelis were ready and eager to fight, but they wanted to put the onus of breaking the truce onto the Arabs, so they agreed to extend the truce by thirty days, into August. The Arabs predictably played into the Israelis' hands. At a July 6 meeting of the Arab League in Cairo, all the countries except Jordan favored breaking the truce. Some of the Arab leaders were still under the illusion that they could defeat the Israelis, but the Arab leaders were driven primarily by domestic concerns. They were more fearful of their public opinion at home, which strongly favored renewing the war, than they were of defeat in battle. The Egyptians broke the truce on July 8, a day before it was to expire. "What madness!" Pasha Glubb, the British officer commanding the Arab Legion, exclaimed.[12]

The renewed war lasted only ten days, until the Security Council demanded a truce. In the north, the Israelis consolidated their control over the Eastern and Western Galilee region by taking Arab Nazareth. In the south, they fought off an Egyptian offensive. In the center, they cleared the road from Tel Aviv to Jerusalem, ending Jewish Jerusalem's isolation from the Jewish state. The Arabs weren't yet driven out, but they were beaten, as evident in their ready acceptance of the Security Council's demand for a truce. Bunche wrote that "if Arabs accept, this means virtual surrender on the question of the Jewish state."[13]

The ten-day war had also aggravated the refugee crisis. When the IDF had taken the Arab villages Ramle and Lydda on the way between Jerusalem and Tel Aviv, they expelled all the inhabitants, who numbered around 60,000, on specific orders from Ben-Gurion. Neighboring Arab villagers also fled, frightened, perhaps, by stories of IDF soldiers firing indiscriminately into houses in Lydda. The refugees were driven eastward. The IDF reported that "some 30,000 women and children from among the inhabitants of Lydda, Ramle and the area are dispersed among the hills, suffering from hunger and thirst to a degree that many of them have died."[14]

In the wake of the ten-day war, the plight of the refugees drew widespread international attention. On August 1, Bernadotte sent a message to the Security Council asking its members to demand that the Israelis permit those of the 300,000 or more refugees who were not of military age to return. The British urged action. Dean Rusk sent a memorandum that Lovett forwarded to the president, registering the department's concern about the refugees. "They are destitute of any belongings, are without adequate shelter, medical supplies, sanitation and food," he wrote. Truman approved the department's recommendation to "urge upon the Provisional Government of Israel and other governments concerned the need for repatriating Arab and Jewish refugees under conditions which will not imperil the internal security of the receiving states."[15]

But the Israelis doubled down. During the second truce, the IDF was ordered to prevent any Palestinian Arabs from returning to their villages. They blew up huts, burned down villages, destroyed crops, and killed livestock. They killed military-age men whom they found. Where they didn't destroy houses, they gave them to Jewish immigrants that were flocking into the country. Abandoned fields were leased to new immigrant settlements. Immigrants were moved into what had been Arab Jaffa and the Arab section of Haifa.[16]

In August, Shertok assured Weizmann that the Israeli government would not compromise. "With regard to the refugees, we are determined to be adamant while the war lasts. Once the return tide starts, it will be impossible to stem it, and it will prove our undoing. As for the future, we are equally determined . . . to explore all possibilities of getting rid, once and for all, of the huge Arab minority which originally threatened us," he wrote.[17] And he sent Comay instructions at the UN on how to respond to criticism. "Arab exodus direct result folly aggression organized by Arab States and sponsored by British," he wrote Comay. "Present distress masses refugees and their future settlement responsibility war-mongers. No question allowing Arabs return while state of war continuing."[18]

In the United States, Silver and the AZEC backed up Israel's refusal to readmit the refugees. Silver blamed the British for the refugees' flight. The Arabs "need never have left their home if the Government of Bevin had not so arranged things that upon its withdrawal from Palestine the country would be turned over to chaos and war," he declared. Silver insisted, incredibly, that the Jews of Israel "were entirely agreeable to live in harmony with their Arab neighbors within the state."[19] The AZEC's regular publication, *Palestine*, contended that "the overwhelming majority of the Arab refugees from Palestine were instigated by their own leaders and their leaders' British friends to flee from Jewish occupied territory, where, had they remained, they could have enjoyed as much safety as their Jewish compatriots."[20]

Silver and the AZEC magazine's statements bore out the extent to which the Zionist movement had become a propaganda arm of the Israeli government. In 1948, however, Silver and other American Zionist leaders were in a much better position to know what was really happening in Israel than their forebears, who had to get their news from visiting fund-raisers. But they weren't interested in conveying that to Americans. By spreading falsehoods and distortions about an important foreign policy issue, Silver and the AZEC did American democracy a disservice. Silver, too, showed how a narrow nationalist agenda had undermined his own moral integrity. The truth had become, in effect, whatever served Israel's cause at that moment.

Bernadotte's Assassination

In August, Marshall and Bevin decided to put a peace plan of their own on the table. By the end of the month, they had worked out a common stance that envisaged similar land swaps to Bernadotte's June plan but that recognized Israel's full sovereignty and put Jerusalem in UN hands. Their plan also included a provision on the refugees' right to return. But to avoid the inevitable conflict with both Jews and Arabs, the Americans and the British wanted Bernadotte to present the plan as his own. Bernadotte wasn't willing to simply adopt their plan—he and Bunche wrote their own—but his thinking was close to theirs, and he knew that his plan would have more chance of being accepted if the Americans and British enthusiastically backed it.

Marshall had kept Truman apprised of the negotiations with the British over Bernadotte's proposal. On August 31 he sent Truman a memorandum that included a proposed letter to James McDonald outlining the British-American approach to Bernadotte. Truman approved the response to McDonald and the overall strategy.

On September 13, Marshall sent Robert McClintock, a foreign service officer who was Rusk's assistant at the State Department office of the United Nations, and the British sent Sir John Troutbeck from the Foreign Office to confer with Bernadotte and Bunche on a final draft.

Bernadotte agreed with the Americans and British on Jerusalem and on Israeli sovereignty. The only difference among them, McClintock reported two days later to Marshall, was over the Negev. McClintock thought that "from [the] point of view of impartial equity that Bernadotte [was] right" to swap the whole Negev for Western Galilee, but he thought it would be "political good judgment to give Israel a token holding in that area." However, McClintock told Bernadotte that, whatever they finally decided, he would recommend that the State Department support the proposals "in their entirety." [21]

The United States and Britain wanted Bernadotte to negotiate with the Arabs and Israelis before bringing the proposal back to the UN, but

Bernadotte, displaying an indifference to diplomacy, insisted on sending it to the secretary-general for presentation to the General Assembly. On September 16, Bernadotte and Bunche finished the 130-page proposal and sent it to Lie for publication. Bernadotte gave all of the Negev to the Arabs, and he also sharply criticized the Israelis for driving out Palestinian refugees and for refusing to take them back:

> The exodus of Palestinian Arabs resulted from panic created by fighting in their communities, by rumors concerning real or alleged acts of terrorism, or expulsion. It would be an offense against the principles of elemental justice if these innocent victims of the conflict were denied the right to return to their homes while Jewish immigrants flow into Palestine, and, indeed, at least offer the threat of permanent replacement of the Arab refugees who have been rooted in the land for centuries.[22]

Having handed in his proposal, Bernadotte arrived the next day in Jerusalem to inspect a new headquarters for his operation. Bunche was supposed to join him but was held up at an Israeli checkpoint after leaving the airport. Grown tired of waiting for Bunche, Bernadotte set off instead with Colonel André Sérot, a French observer who credited Bernadotte with rescuing his wife from a concentration camp. Their car was stopped by a jeep and three armed men got out and fired point-blank at Bernadotte and Sérot, killing them both.

Bernadotte had been reviled in Israeli newspapers, but there was no sign that the Israeli government had a hand in his murder. The killers were members of the Stern Gang, the breakaway Revisionist faction led by Yitzhak Shamir, who later became prime minister of Israel. In 1944 the Stern Gang had assassinated Lord Moyne, Britain's pro-Zionist minister in Cairo. It was a particularly senseless act of terror that alienated Moyne's close friend Winston Churchill, and probably contributed to Britain's rejection of Jewish statehood after World War II. This time, by murdering Bernadotte, the terrorists breathed life into his proposal.

On September 21, Marshall released a statement, which he had earlier sent Truman for approval, eulogizing the mediator and praising his report. "My government is of the opinion that the conclusions are sound and strongly urges the parties and the General Assembly to accept them in their entirety as the best possible basis for bringing peace to a distracted land."[23] Marshall's endorsement of the recommendations "in their entirety" set off a firestorm in Washington and Tel Aviv that was reminiscent of the uproar after Austin's trusteeship speech the previous March. And, as before, Truman found himself thrust into the middle.

Battle over the Plan

Truman continued to rue the defeat of the Anglo-American Committee plan, telling Julius Klein and a visiting delegation of Jewish War Veterans that he and Bevin "had agreed on the best possible solution for Palestine, and it was the Zionists who killed that plan by their opposition." Forced to take a position on the British-American initiative—and, by extension, the Bernadotte plan, which closely resembled it—he had given his approval. Truman believed that if the Israelis gained additional territories at the expense of Palestine's Arabs, they should have to compensate them by ceding territories that had been allotted to Israel by the UN.

But Truman's and the State Department's approach angered the Israelis and their American supporters. The Israelis insisted upon the lands allotted to them by the United Nations *plus* those lands they had conquered in repelling the Arab invasion. In his talks with Bernadotte in June, Shertok insisted that "the facts created by the war had also to be taken into account, as they contributed to the broad outline of a political settlement, as it existed." This idea of creating facts and *only then* negotiating dated back at least to Ben-Gurion in 1936, if not to Jabotinsky's "Iron Wall," and was central to Israel's strategy during the 1948 war.

Israel enlisted its network in the United States. Epstein and Eban had a Rolodex of what they called "friends" whom they summoned. Truman, who was on a nationwide whistle-stop tour, was subjected to an intense lobbying campaign that was coordinated by Eban in Paris, where the General Assembly was meeting that fall, and by Epstein in Washington. The AZEC and Silver struck first. Speaking on behalf of "all official Zionist bodies in the United States," Silver appealed to Truman "to prevent the imposition of such iniquitous terms on Israel as the

Bernadotte plan recommended." Silver threw in Truman's face the "platform pledges of the Democratic party" that "modifications" to the November 29 resolution could be made "only if fully acceptable to the state
of Israel."[24] The AZEC also ran full-page ads headlined: "Mr. Truman,
Where Do You Stand on This Issue?" denouncing the Bernadotte plan.[25]

The *New York Post* asserted that the report demanded that Israel
"surrender territory to the Arabs which Israel paid for with the lives of
her citizens."[26] *The Washington Star* quoted the New York State Democratic Party chair warning that Marshall's statement would cost the
Democrats every large city in the country.[27] When Truman still did
not stir, Eban wrote Weizmann suggesting that he ask Eddie Jacobson
to talk to Truman. Jacobson would do it, Eban wrote, "if he had a signal
from you."[28]

Weizmann sent Truman's old business partner a long telegram
urging him to go see the president. Jacobson also heard from Epstein,
who was "very much alarmed that the Bernadotte plan would be put
through the UN." Jacobson traveled to Oklahoma City, where he joined
the presidential train on September 28. That evening Jacobson sat in
on a meeting of Truman with Clifford and other advisors. According
to Jacobson, Truman said he "would not budge from the U.N. decision
of November 29th, regardless of what Marshall, Lovett, or anyone else
said." He also said that the United States "would not endorse the Bernadotte proposal as written."

According to Jacobson, Clifford then read Truman the plank in the
Democratic Party platform, which, he said, the State Department had
approved at the time. "Now they want to do just the opposite," he said.
Clifford warned Truman that he could be accused of hypocrisy for supporting the platform but then repudiating it through his State Department. According to Jacobson, Truman then interjected that he "had
nothing to do with the American delegates at the UN affirming the Bernadotte plan." Marshall had acted, he claimed, without consulting him.[29]

Truman decided to send a telegram to Marshall that would amount
to a repudiation of Marshall's stand. In the telegram Truman would
state that "my position as to boundaries has not changed." But Clifford
decided to consult Lovett before sending it to Marshall, who was in
Paris, where the General Assembly, in the absence of a permanent home,
was meeting. Clifford phoned Lovett from the presidential train on the
afternoon of September 29. Clifford read him the telegram and ar-

ranged for the two men to talk at 4:30 that afternoon when the train stopped at freight yards in Tulsa. Lovett could hear train whistles in the background as they talked.

Lovett sought the opinion of Kennan, McClintock, and other State Department officials about the statement, and they agreed that disavowing Marshall in this manner would put him in an "intolerable position." Back on the phone with the White House aide, Lovett read Clifford the memorandum that the president had approved on September 1 laying out American agreement with Bernadotte's approach, and he also recounted how he had sent Marshall's statement to the president on September 18 but had not heard back.[30] Clifford got off the phone, and when he came back, he said that the president would send an innocuous statement instead to Rabbi Wise saying that the Bernadotte plan "offers a basis for continuing efforts to secure a just settlement."[31] That put a little distance between the president and the Bernadotte plan without repudiating Marshall's stand.

But while Truman agreed not to disavow the plan he had endorsed, he did throw up a roadblock. Marshall and Bevin had originally planned to use the shock of Bernadotte's assassination to win General Assembly support for the plan. But Truman instructed Marshall through Lovett to delay consideration of the Bernadotte plan until after the election on November 3. He advised Lovett that the American delegation should employ "any parliamentary procedures available" and "use every effort to avoid having U.S. delegation drawn into the debate."[32] The American effort was aided by the Arab delegates, who, oblivious to the Israeli strategy of creating facts, foolishly believed that they would do better in the General Assembly after the American election.

The Silly Season

Truman was worried about losing New York to Dewey because of his administration's association with the Bernadotte plan, but he was reluctant to anger Marshall, who was steering the United States through the Berlin crisis. (Truman's decisive handling of the Berlin crisis was a major source of his rising popularity, which would surface on Election Day.) The only thing that could force Truman's hand would be an attack by Dewey on Truman's support for the plan. On October 22,

Dewey, prodded by Silver, circulated a letter he had written to Dean Alfange.

Dewey's letter didn't specifically criticize Truman for supporting the Bernadotte plan but it reaffirmed his "wholehearted support" for the Republican platform pledge of "full recognition [of Israel] with its boundaries as sanctioned by the United Nations."[33] Clifford told Truman that Dewey was attacking his integrity by implying that he had "reneged on [the] Democratic platform."[34] Interestingly, Lovett agreed. Two days later Truman issued a statement reaffirming his own support for the Democratic platform's pledge to make modifications in Israel's borders "only if fully acceptable to the State of Israel" and pledging de jure recognition of Israel, the revision of the arms embargo, and "aid to the state of Israel in developing its economy and resources."

Still, Truman's stand was muddled. He also said that he continued to support the principle behind the Bernadotte plan, even if he didn't support its exact details. "A plan has been submitted which provides a basis for a renewed effort to bring about a peaceful adjustment of differences," he said. "It is hoped that by using this plan as a basis of negotiations, the conflicting claims of the parties can be settled."[35] As the Republican majority leader Robert Taft noted, Truman's statement was contradictory. He was pledging to support whatever Israel wanted while also endorsing a plan whose principle—not merely its details—ran afoul of what Israel was willing to accept.[36] Truman's statement on the Bernadotte plan, like his statement on March 25 affirming and yet denying the Austin plan for trusteeship, was a model of equivocation.

Truman's response to Dewey brought a brief respite from his critics. Eban wired Epstein, "Presidential statement despite all reservations regarded here as considerable weakening American support Bernadotte plan, especially as Republican support that plan never been given."[37] Epstein wrote Wise, "I think that it would be just to President Truman and useful to us, to give a favorable interpretation to his statement, emphasizing the most important part of it, namely, that portion which makes it clear that no territorial changes should be made without our consent. That gives us the first official US backing in our defense of the Negev."[38]

But a new imbroglio loomed ahead. Since July 19 a truce had prevailed between the warring parties in Palestine, but by late September the Israelis were determined to break it. Having acquired decisive superiority in numbers and hardware—the Israelis now possessed even a small air force—they wanted to create new "facts" on the ground that would undermine the Bernadotte plan, which had been based on the existing military geography, with the Israelis holding their allotted areas in the north and center plus the Western Galilee, the Jordanians holding the West Bank, and the Egyptians holding much of the Negev.

At a cabinet meeting on September 26, Ben-Gurion proposed conquering the West Bank, but he was narrowly outvoted. Instead of trying to seize the West Bank, which they now implicitly ceded to King Abdullah, the cabinet voted to oust the Egyptians from the Negev. Ben-Gurion didn't want the Israelis blamed for breaking the truce, so the IDF tried to create a pretext for their offensive by driving a convoy through an Egyptian-controlled area to one of their settlements. When the Egyptians didn't respond adequately, the Israelis blew up one of their own fuel trucks.[39] The next day the Israelis attacked. McDonald was predictably taken in—on October 14 he reported back to Washington, "The activities of Egyptian army in south are causing major concern Israeli army"—but few UN delegates were fooled.[40]

At the UN on October 19, the British and Chinese supported a resolution calling on the parties to resume their truce and to leave any positions "not occupied at the time of the outbreak."[41] With Truman's approval, the United States backed the resolution. But while the UN debated, the Israelis pushed ahead. With the Egyptian army on the run, the Israelis began a new offensive in the north-central Galilee to oust Syrian and Iraqi forces from all of the Galilee. They defeated the Arab armies and drove Palestinian Arab villagers out of lands that the UN had allotted to the Palestinian Arab state.

The Israeli offensive in the north was particularly brutal. In one village, Israeli troops put the local males and prisoners in a building, killed them, and then blew up the building. Word of atrocities like this impelled Arabs to flee. In both the south and north, the Israeli army expelled Arabs. According to Benny Morris, the two operations added another 200,000 to 230,000 refugees, who now numbered about 700,000.[42] At the UN the British and Chinese introduced a new resolution on October 28 that would lead to sanctions if the parties didn't return to their pre–October 15 positions. That set up a new battle between the Zionist network and the State Department over what position the United States would take.

Truman arrived by train in New York on October 28 for a Madison Square Garden speech that was to close out his cross-country whistle-stop tour. He invited Eddie Jacobson to the event, and when Jacobson arrived, he was struck by the "screaming headlines" in the city's newspapers announcing that "England and China [were] asking the US to join them in asking for sanctions against Israel."[43] Israeli representatives in New York and Washington had organized a lobbying campaign. Arthur Lourie, an Israeli representative at the UN, wrote Eban, who was in Paris, that in response to the Anglo-Chinese resolution, he had been

> in touch with Eliahu [Epstein], [journalist Herbert Bayard] Swope, Silver, the *Nation* people, the Emergency Council and others. At a short notice an energetic offensive has been mobilized. The President . . . is on his way to New York today and immediate contact with him has been difficult, but a number of the Democratic leaders, including [the New York mayor William] O'Dwyer, Flynn, and others are on the trail.[44]

O'Dwyer, the former New York governor Herbert Lehman (who was active in Wahl's Americans for Haganah), and the labor leader Jacob Potofsky (whose clothing workers filled what would have been empty seats at Truman's Madison Square Garden rally) got to see Truman to urge him to oppose the British-Chinese resolution. Once more Truman buckled under pressure.

While Truman was speaking at the rally, he had Clifford draft a message to Marshall. Clifford dictated the message to Lovett to forward to Marshall. In the message Truman said he was "deeply concerned over reports here of action taken in [the] Security Council."[45] Lovett, incredulous, reminded Clifford that Truman had approved of the delegation's support for the Anglo-Chinese initiative, but Clifford insisted that the president wanted the telegram sent. When Marshall got the message, he didn't know what to make of it, and asked Lovett to get the president to clarify it. When Lovett finally got ahold of Truman, the president backtracked. While not wanting to oppose the resolution, Truman told Lovett that he wanted "every effort [to] be made to avoid taking position on Palestine prior to Wednesday [the day after the election]."[46]

Nonetheless, Israeli's lobbying community had scored another victory. Epstein wired Shertok on October 29 that "under strong pressure friends, Truman yesterday evening sent instruction delegation Paris oppose Anglo-Chinese resolution. Furious Lovett attitude . . . very helpful in moving Truman yesterday were Lehman, O'Dwyer and Potofsky."[47] The State Department had suffered another defeat, but Truman seems to have assured Lovett in their phone conversation that, after the election, the State Department could resume control of American policy. Lovett wrote Marshall, "Am told removal of restrictions on normal procedures may be expected next week when silly season terminates."[48] But these hopes would soon be dashed.

The Power of Money

By early November, when another cease-fire went into place, Israel controlled all of the Galilee (the western and central Galilee had been allocated to Palestinian Arabs in the UN partition plan), some of southern Lebanon, and most of the Negev. A large force of Egyptians—numbering 3,000 or 4,000, and including Egypt's future ruler Gamal Abdel Nasser—were trapped and surrounded in the northern Negev. The Jordanians controlled East Jerusalem and the West Bank.

The Israeli strategy was still to create facts on the ground that negotiation couldn't alter. The Egyptians and Jordanians had sent out peace feelers to the Israelis, but Ben-Gurion wasn't interested until he had consolidated Israeli military gains. One Israeli official summed up the situation: "The IDF is occupying more and more of the Arab parts of Palestine, setting up faits accomplis and making the political plans obsolete before they have crystallized," he wrote on November 2. "In addition, Ben-Gurion himself is highly skeptical—almost scornful—of all these political schemes and the impression is that he prefers to solve all these problems by force of arms."[49]

Bernadotte's proposal for borders, swapping the western Galilee for the Negev, had been based on the divisions of the country on September 16 between the Israelis and the Arabs. The Israeli offensive wiped out these divisions, and in order to restore them, the UN would have had to force the IDF back to positions it had occupied beforehand. That could conceivably be done by economic sanctions or even by armed intervention, but the United States, which would have had to lead the effort, was unwilling to coerce the Israelis. That didn't change after the "silly season" was over.

During a post-election meeting with Lovett and the ambassador to Great Britain, Lewis Douglas, with Clifford present, Truman affirmed his support for the principle of the Bernadotte recommendations—any new territories acquired by the Jews would have to be balanced by new territories given to the Arabs—but he was equally insistent that nothing could be done "without Israel's consent."[50] Instead of coercion, Truman wanted to rely on persuasion. He wanted the American effort "directed toward having the two parties settle the matter or stick to the Nov. 29 boundaries."[51] But Israel had never been amenable to simple persuasion, and the Arabs had been defeated on the battlefield. If the United States wasn't willing to coerce Israel, that meant the gains achieved in October would remain Israel's.

After the election, the informal Zionist network, centered in Washington, remained intact, but with a new addition. Dewey had won New York, but Truman still won the election. That suggested that Jewish votes were no longer that important. But Truman's whistle-stop tour in the Midwest, which had turned the election, had been financed by two Zionists, the businessmen Abe Feinberg and Ed Kaufmann. Feinberg had bankrolled Wahl's Americans for Haganah, and Kaufmann had been the president of ZOA. With Truman's campaign treasury empty, the two men had raised $100,000 in two days—a huge sum in 1948—to finance Truman's campaign trip. That gave them both, and particularly Feinberg, unmatched access to the White House. Lowenthal termed Feinberg "the man through whom the White House can best be approached."[52]

Feinberg's clout became apparent midway through November. The Canadian delegate on the Security Council introduced a resolution prepared by Bunche, who had succeeded Bernadotte as the mediator, to negotiate a permanent truce between the two sides. The resolution included a proposal for creating "broad demilitarized zones."[53] On November 8, Shertok called Feinberg to complain about this provision. Feinberg contacted Clifford, and Clifford got the American delegation to introduce an amendment to remove the provision. The provision was gone from the resolution that was adopted on November 16, along with other language that the Israelis had deemed offensive.[54]

A day after this UN vote, Douglas met with Attlee in London. The British prime minister complained to Douglas that the president's actions, beginning with his October 24 promise of an Israeli veto on any border changes, had "undermined the common ground" that the United States and Britain had developed over the Bernadotte proposals. In his dispatch to Washington, Douglas warned that Truman's new plan of relying on the Israelis and Arabs to reach agreement was "a delusion."[55] Douglas was right, but Truman preferred to suffer delusions rather than acknowledge the power that Israel and its supporters had over his decision making.

The Refugees

To resolve the conflict, and to repatriate the refugees, the United Nations delegated Bunche in the November 16 resolution to organize a "permanent armistice." On December 11, the UN, in Resolution 194, established a three-member Palestine Conciliation Commission (PCC) to negotiate a peace between Israel and the Arab states that would include agreements about borders and refugees.[56] The PCC, with a representative from the United States, France, and Turkey, was to operate in tandem with Bunche.

The December resolution said that "the refugees wishing to return to their homes and live at peace with their neighbors should be permitted to do so at the earliest practicable date, and that compensation should be paid for the property of those choosing not to return and for loss of or damage to property which, under principles of international law or in equity, should be made good by the Governments or authorities responsible."[57]

Israel responded to the resolution by creating new faits accomplis. On December 12 the Israeli ministry of finance issued new regulations, "Relative to the Property of Absentees," that allowed the government to confiscate the lands, homes, buildings, and offices that the refugees had abandoned. By the spring of 1950 the government had confiscated about 1 million dunams (or 250,000 acres) of land as well as 7,800 shops, offices, and stores.[58] The refugees' homes that were confiscated were given to Jewish immigrants, who, beginning in May, had been entering Israel at a rate of about 25,000 a month. The rate would soon exceed that as Jewish refugees from Iraq and other Arab countries, who became subject to persecution in retaliation for what had been done to the Palestinians, poured into Israel.

The resolution also called for setting up Jerusalem as an international city under UN control. Ben-Gurion and the Israeli cabinet responded by announcing on December 13 that Israel's government offices and the Knesset (Parliament) would be moved from Tel Aviv to Jerusalem. The Israelis also turned up their noses at the commission's mandate to negotiate borders. Ben-Gurion and the IDF launched a final offensive on December 22 that by January 7 had driven Egypt out of most of the Negev. Resolution 194 was dead even before the peace negotiations had begun, but the Truman administration still believed in it.

Refugee Negotiations

Truman appointed Mark Ethridge, the editor of the Louisville *Courier-Journal*, to represent the United States on the commission. Ethridge, fifty-three, was an outspoken Southern liberal who as editor of the Louisville newspaper had championed voting rights and economic development for Southern blacks. During World War II, Franklin Roosevelt, whom he had met decades earlier in Georgia, had appointed Ethridge chairman of the Fair Employment Practices Commission. After the war, Truman's secretary of state, James Byrnes, tapped him to go on a fact-finding mission to the Balkans.

Ethridge, like Truman, was a bellwether of liberalism. How he reacted to the negotiations would say a lot about the moral issues at stake. A large, silver-haired man with clear-rimmed round glasses, he arrived in Jerusalem in January. His instructions were to adhere to the UN resolution on refugees and Jerusalem and to insist that if Israel wanted to add to the boundaries that the UN had prescribed in November 1947, it would have to swap other territories in exchange. Ethridge and the commission had two talks with Shertok before they set out on February 12 for a tour of Arab capitals. The Israelis, to whom Truman had granted de jure recognition after their elections in January, were determined not to give ground on any of the issues. Ethridge found Shertok "unyielding" on Jerusalem, borders, and refugees. He found his refusal to even discuss the repatriation of the refugees "inhuman."[59]

Ethridge toured Arab capitals. Iraq refused to participate in the commission's deliberations. Saudi Arabia said it would abide by the decisions but would not send a representative to meetings. The Arabs made a condition of negotiation that Israel agree to the principle of repatriation and compensation stated in the December 11 resolution. Ethridge took that to mean that if Israel would accept the resolution on refugees, the Arabs would join in peace negotiations.

As Ethridge pursued the subject with the Arab leaders, he got what he thought were concessions. Jordan and Syria agreed that the Israelis would not have to take back all the refugees. They were willing to take some of them. And the Arab leaders agreed to participate in the commission's conferences in Beirut and Lausanne, Switzerland, even if Israel still hadn't accepted the principle of repatriation, but they wouldn't formally negotiate with the Israelis. Ethridge then sought to wring some concessions from the Israelis.

On February 24, Ethridge and the other two members of the commission met with Shertok in Tel Aviv. He asked the foreign minister whether Israel would accept "the principle [of the resolution on refugees] no matter how it is worked out in negotiations between the parties." Shertok simply refused to reply. "With regard to our attitude, our readiness to re-admit a certain number of Arabs, and the extent to which we would be ready to admit them at all directly depends on the general spirit and also fundamental provisions of the peace settlement," he said.[60] Ethridge got nothing out of other Israeli officials. He wrote Acheson on March 14 that "six weeks of effort to get the Israeli government to commit itself on the refugee problem have resulted in not one single statement of position. That is true also of Jerusalem and the other problems with which we have to deal."[61]

Two weeks later, after the commission had held meetings with the Arabs and Israelis in Beirut, Ethridge wired Acheson asking for the administration to put pressure on the Israelis to make concessions on refugees. "If Jews would only make conciliatory gesture on refugee problem, PCC could get on with its work of trying to get peace," he wrote.[62] But Ethridge continued to strike out. On April 7 the commission met with Ben-Gurion and the foreign ministry staff. Ben-Gurion insisted that Israel had nothing to do with the existence of the refugees. "Israel had not expelled the refugees; their flight had been organized as part of the Arab offensive worked out by Arab leaders and British agents," Ben-Gurion told the commission.[63]

On April 11, Ethridge appealed to Truman. "This is by far the toughest assignment you have ever given me," he wrote. "The Arabs are shocked and stupefied by their defeat and have great bitterness toward the UN and the United States. The Jews are too close to the blood of their war and their narrow escape, as they regard it, from extinction, too close to the bitterness of their fight against the British mandate to exercise any degree of statesmanship yet. They still feel too strongly that their security lies in military might instead of in good relations with their neighbors."[64]

But the last straw for Ethridge came when he visited Ben-Gurion in Tiberias on April 18. He had been told that the prime minister wanted to confer with him about Israel issuing a conciliatory statement about the refugees and backing some form of internationalization for Jerusalem, but Ben-Gurion, Ethridge wrote Acheson, "mentioned neither question and apparently had no intention of doing so. Instead, Ben-Gurion analyzed at length Britain's mistaken imperialistic policy in the Middle East" and the humanitarian role he wanted the United States to play.[65] After that meeting, Ethridge told Dean Acheson he was resigning from the commission, but Acheson talked him into staying on.

Truman had kept his distance from the negotiations going on between Israel and the Arabs, but Eliahu Epstein warned Shertok that the president was "sentimentally sympathetic" to the Arab refugees.[66] Truman couldn't understand how the Israelis could deny the Palestinian Arabs the "right to return" that the Jews had fought for. When Acheson described to him the State Department and Ethridge's difficulties in getting Israel to agree to the principle of repatriation, Truman, Acheson wrote, "was disturbed over the uncooperative attitude being taken and said that we must continue to maintain firm pressure."[67]

The Israelis worried that Truman was turning on them due to what Epstein called "instigating reports by Ethridge."[68] They began a campaign to convince Truman and the American public that the best solution was to transfer the Palestinian Arab refugees to other Arab countries. Shertok got Silver's approval to recruit the former Revisionist Eliahu Ben-Horin, who was still working for the AZEC, to revive the Hoover plan. Ben-Horin penned an op-ed in *The Christian Science Monitor* recommending Iraq as a good site for the Palestinian Arabs. Ben-Horin also got this scheme endorsed by the former State Department official Sumner Welles, Interior Secretary Oscar Chapman, Frankfurter, and Niles.[69] Epstein created an "advisory committee" of influential Americans to promote the idea of resettling the refugees in Arab lands.*

When these efforts failed to move the White House, the Israelis sent over Weizmann, who, according to Niles, was the only Israeli Truman would listen to. On April 25, Truman met with Weizmann. Afterward, Truman told Acheson that Weizmann had "taken a helpful attitude on all of them."[70] Weizmann asked Truman to lobby actively for Israel's membership at the UN, which was coming up for a vote the next month. It looked like a deal had been made: Israeli concession to the December 11 resolution in return for active American support at the UN.

In a meeting in Washington the next day with Epstein and Abba Eban, Acheson stressed American willingness to lobby at the UN if the Israelis took a conciliatory position on refugees, borders, and Jerusalem. Weizmann wrote Truman thanking him for the visit, but stating that the answer to "the problem of Arab refugees" lies "not in repatriation but in resettlement."[71] That brought Truman up short. When Truman showed the letter to Acheson, he said that Weizmann's "attitude on refugees was not satisfactory."[72] Truman wrote Ethridge that he was "disgusted with the manner in which the Jews are approaching the refugee problem." In a typical display of ex post facto bluster, Truman also wrote that he had told Weizmann "exactly what I thought about it."[73]

Ethridge was assured by the State Department that the administration would maintain its threat not to champion Israel at the UN, but Epstein got "the friends" to intervene with Truman, and at the last moment, Epstein wrote Shertok, "Truman instructed Acheson . . . to support actively our admission [to the] UN." Truman told Clifford that if Israel were in the UN, they would "cooperate better on Arab refugees and Jerusalem."[74] That was pure rationalization. Truman had caved in again. A dispirited Ethridge announced that he would leave his post after the next month's meetings in Lausanne.

*Eliahu Epstein would change his last name to "Elath" (after the port city on the Gulf of Aqaba that Epstein had helped secure for Israel at the UN) in late 1948, but I will continue to refer to him as "Epstein."

———————

In Lausanne, the commission met where the Anglo-American Committee had met earlier—at the five-star Hotel Beau Rivage on the shore of Lac Léman. The commission members met separately with the Arab delegation and with the Israelis, while the Arabs and Israelis met informally. In initial talks, Ethridge found the Arab representatives "increasingly indicating disposition to come to grips with the situation," but he found that the Israeli delegation, led by Walter Eytan from the foreign ministry, "had not modified its position."[75] Eytan reiterated that Israelis were not responsible for the refugees and that "physical return to Israel is impossible socially and physically."[76]

Ethridge and a new assistant secretary of state, George C. McGhee, who had been put in charge of refugee issues, tried to sweeten the agreement with Israelis by promising regional development aid for resettlement and repatriation and by setting a specific number of 200,000 refugees for the Israelis to offer to repatriate. (That would have given Arabs about 20 percent of Israel's population.) But they continued to get nowhere. To make matters worse, Israel advanced new territorial demands on May 20 that included part of southern Lebanon and the Gaza Strip, which Egypt controlled. Eytan also rejected Jordan's right to the West Bank, insisting that "no Arab state has a right to any territory in Palestine."[77]

The Israelis didn't expect to get what they asked for, but they wanted to forestall any demands that they give up what they already had. Eban expressed the basic position in a private letter to Eytan. "Our frontier position therefore boils down to the following: We are entitled to wherever we are."[78] The Israeli territorial demands, coupled with their intransigence on refugees, infuriated Ethridge and Acheson and led the secretary of state to urge Truman to make another effort to sway the Israelis. Truman was further provoked by a memo from Undersecretary of State James Webb that recounted boasts from Israeli officials that they could shape the administration's responses "through means available to them in the United States."[79]

On May 28 an angry Truman wrote Ben-Gurion that "the government of the United States is seriously disturbed by the attitude of Israel with respect to a territorial settlement in Palestine and to the question of

Palestinian refugees, as set forth by the representatives in Lausanne in public and private meetings." If Israel "continues to reject the basic principles" of the December 11 resolution, the letter concluded, "the U.S. government will regretfully be forced to the conclusion that a revision of its attitude toward Israel has become unavoidable."[80] Truman didn't specify exactly what the administration was threatening to do, but he had a list that included suspending half the loan the Export-Import Bank of the United States had granted to Israel.

Niles had probably already warned the Israelis of this threat, and in early June they swung into action. The Israeli embassy in Washington got Isaiah Kenen, who was an American citizen working for the Israelis at the UN in New York, to issue a pamphlet on the refugees. Ben-Horin also sent a memo on the refugees to more than six hundred government officials and journalists. Another AZEC staffer, Hyman Schulson, sent out a memo to the White House and Congress warning that "tendencies hostile to Israel have once more gained the upper hand in the Department of State" and recommending the Hoover plan as a solution to the refugee crisis.[81]

Shertok enlisted McDonald's help. On June 20, McDonald read out to members of Israel's foreign minister the cables, marked personal, that he had sent to the State Department and White House on June 11. In these cables McDonald advised the administration not to issue threats against the Israeli government. He advised Clifford that the Israeli government would make concessions on refugees "if request for these is not again put in form of [a] demand."[82] McDonald's advice was ridiculous and displayed again the degree to which he had become a patsy for the Israeli government.

But the most important steps were taken by the network of "friends." On June 9, Feinberg saw Truman. According to an Israeli embassy official, the wealthy businessman "explained [the] absurd manner [of the way the] Palestine Conciliation Commission [was] handling [the] Lausanne negotiations." Feinberg also suggested a "strong successor" to Ethridge who would "bring Jews, Arabs together." When Feinberg specifically discussed borders and refugees, "Truman seemed impressed . . . and promised to call in Webb. [The] President [was] not critical at all [of] our attitude [in] current negotiations."[83]

This lobbying had its effect, as McGhee discovered when he was enlisted by the State Department to threaten Israel with a cutoff of the Export-Import Bank funds. McGhee told the story of what happened in his memoir, *Envoy to the Middle World*:

> I was advised by the Department that this recommendation had been approved and that I should inform the Israeli Ambassador. I asked the Ambassador to lunch with me at the Metropolitan Club and put our decision to him in the most tactful and objective way I could. The Ambassador looked me straight in the eye and said, in essence, that I wouldn't get by with this move, that he would stop it . . . Within an hour of my return to my office I received a message from the White House that the President wished to dissociate himself from any withholding of the Ex-Im Bank loan. I knew of the President's sympathy for Israel, but I had never before realized how swiftly the supporters of Israel could act if challenged.[84]

Nothing came of Truman's letter to Ben-Gurion. In replying on the prime minister's behalf, Shertok simply reiterated the Israeli government's position. "It was never part of the Israeli design to force Arabs out of the country," he asserted. He dismissed the refugees as "members of an aggressor group defeated in a war of its own making. History does not record any case of large-scale repatriation after such experience."[85]

Israel remained unwilling to budge on refugees, borders, and Jerusalem. Elias Sasson, who had represented Israel in Lausanne, was critical of his government's policy, but he found himself in a minority. Sasson, who shared Goldmann's vision of Israel being part of a Near East federation with its Arab neighbors, summed up the Israeli strategy in a letter to one of his subordinates at the foreign ministry:

> The Jews think that peace can be achieved without paying the price— either maximal or minimal. They want the Arabs to cede the territory occupied by Israel; to absorb all the refugees in the Arab states; to accept frontier modifications favorable to Israel in central Palestine, in the south, and in the Jerusalem area; to waive rights to their property in Israel in return for compensation to be assessed by the Israelis and to be paid over a period of years after agreements have been signed; to institute immediate diplomatic and economic relations with Israel; and so on, and so forth.[86]

That's exactly what Ethridge had observed. The newspaper publisher left Lausanne at the beginning of June, and the conference closed down.[87] In his postmortem, Ethridge wrote Acheson that "Israel must accept primary responsibility . . . for [the] stalemate . . . Her attitude toward refugees is morally reprehensible and politically short-sighted . . . There has never been a time in the life of the commission when a generous and far-sighted attitude on the part of the Jews would not have unlocked peace."[88]

Ethridge was equally disappointed with Truman. Decades later he told an interviewer at the Truman Library that "Truman let me down on two phases of the Palestine thing," citing the president's failure to use the threat of either UN admission or the Export-Import Bank loan to pressure the Israelis. "I didn't have any [leverage]," he said. "That was one reason I said, 'I'm going home.'"[89]

Truman appointed the former New Deal official Paul Porter to succeed Ethridge, and Porter and McGhee tried to revive the peace negotiations; but in August, Acheson pulled the plug. The commission met periodically over the years, but never accomplished anything. In the absence of any peace agreements, what stood up were the armistice agreements that Bunche, who had been reviled by the Israeli press and by *Nation* editor Frieda Kirchwey, had negotiated among the parties. Bunche deservedly won the Nobel Peace Prize for these treaties. The treaties didn't promise lasting peace, however, only a truce until one of the parties decided to break them, as the Israelis did in 1956.

The Catastrophe

Ethridge was too optimistic about what could have happened in Lausanne. Even if Israel had agreed to take 200,000 refugees, it is doubtful that the Arabs could have agreed among themselves about the peace treaty with Israel. The Egyptians feared that recognizing Israel would legitimize Jordan's deal with the Israelis. The Egyptians had a stake in perpetuating the refugee crisis, which would cause further instability in Jordan and Israel.[90]

Each Arab country also contained a restive public that opposed any agreement with the Israelis, including the armistices that Bunche negotiated. The Arab leaders feared that if they were to reach an agreement with the Israelis, they would soon be overthrown. The threat was real both from the greater public and from competing elites. Over the next three years, due partly to dissatisfaction over the outcome of the 1948 war, the rulers in Egypt and Syria were toppled by coups, and Abdullah was assassinated by a Palestinian.

Yet while Israel humiliated the Arab leaders by defeating them in war, the Arab states didn't lose any territory in the conflict. In fact, they gained land. Jordan got the West Bank and Egypt got Gaza. The real losers were the Palestinian Arabs. They lost any chance for the self-determination Wilson had promised colonial peoples in 1917. In April 1950, Transjordan, now called the Kingdom of Jordan, annexed the West Bank. Abdullah ordered the name "Palestine" removed from maps and official declarations. Palestinians had become a stateless people. European Jews, dispersed through often hostile countries for centuries, had created a homeland for themselves in Palestine, but at the cost of depriving its Arab inhabitants of a homeland and of dispersing them throughout the Arab Middle East and later Europe and North and South America.

For Zionists, the war was a triumph; for Palestinian Arabs, the Nakba, or Catastrophe. When Zionists began colonizing Palestine in the late nineteenth century, the Jewish population was somewhere between 6 and 8 percent. When Herzl's first Zionist Congress sent two rabbis from Vienna to investigate Palestine as the site of a Jewish state, they reported back, "The bride is beautiful but she is married to another man."[91] In November 1947, Jews still constituted only a third at best of Palestine's population, but the United Nations partition of November 1947 gave them 56 percent of Palestine. By October 1949, the National Security Council reported that the Jewish state would make up 78 percent of what had been Palestine.[92]

Israel's lands included 475 towns and villages in which Arabs had once dwelled. About a quarter of the buildings in Israel had once been owned by Arabs. About 90 percent of the olive groves and half of the citrus orchards had once belonged to Arabs.[93] There were about 725,000 refugees, most of whom resided in Lebanon, Syria, Jordan and the West Bank, and the Gaza Strip. The great bulk of them were bystanders in the civil war and the war between the Arab states and the Israelis. They were sullen, demoralized, but in the long run a source of instability and rebellion for the Arab states and the Israeli conquerors. The refugees, Ethridge warned Acheson in March 1949, create "a core of [an] irredentist movement that will plague all Arab states and provide [the] basis for continual agitation to [the] point that there will be no possibility of having anything more than [an] armistice in the Middle East."[94]

Truman stopped paying attention to Israel and its neighbors after 1949. He also finally stopped expressing regrets that he and Bevin had failed to get the Jews and Arabs to agree to the proposals of the Anglo-American Committee. If anything, as Israel emerged as a viable and even powerful state in the turbulent Middle East—and as Jews in the United States and in Israel began to bestow honors upon him—Truman basked in the role he had played in Israel's founding.

In November 1953, after leaving the presidency, Truman traveled with Eddie Jacobson to New York to be feted at the Jewish Theological Seminary. When Jacobson introduced him as "the man who helped create the state of Israel," Truman responded, "What do you mean, 'helped to create.' I am Cyrus. I am Cyrus."[95] Truman was referring to Cyrus, the Persian king who overthrew the Babylonians in 593 B.C.E. and helped the Jews, who had been held captive in Babylon, return to Jerusalem and rebuild their temple.

But Truman's first impulses about the Jewish state were more worthy of remembrance. As a Jeffersonian Democrat and the child of a Civil War border state, Truman understood the perils of creating a state based on a single race or people or religion. Europe was filled with the scars of such efforts, and what the Jews were doing in Palestine was bound to create a new gash in a region already scarred by centuries of religious war and conquest justified by sacred texts and apocryphal history. An American scientist, Henry S. Pritchett, had clearly understood that in 1926 after spending only two weeks in Palestine. Ralph Bunche had grasped it. Truman, too, had sensed it and had wanted better for the Jews and Arabs of Palestine.

Jesus, the first Christian, and the last in a line of Hebrew prophets, was reported to have asked, "For what shall it profit a man, if he shall gain the whole world, and lose his own soul?" Israel's Jews had gained a world of their own, but at the expense of another people. History, of course, often works that way. And if the people who are vanquished disappear, or are relatively weak and few in number, the victors can eventually lay aside the memory of what they have done. Few Georgians today remember or regret having driven the peaceful Cherokee Indians off their lands.

Israelis and their supporters spent decades trying to explain away the dark side of their conquest of Palestine. They claimed they were victims and the Palestinian Arabs aggressors. They linked the mufti and his successors to Hitler and the Nazis. They insisted that there was no such thing as Palestinians—a claim that Jordan's rulers were eager to reaffirm. But the Palestinian people have not gone away and have grown in number, and are a living reminder that what was a triumph for Zionism in 1948 has been an enduring catastrophe for them.

The Zionists who emigrated to Palestine treated the Arab inhabitants very much like America's Indians, but Palestine's Arabs are unlikely to suffer the ignominious fate of many Indian tribes. Speaking to a reporter two weeks before his death in 2004, the Palestinian leader Yasir Arafat said, "We have made the Palestinian cause the biggest problem in the world . . . One hundred and seven years after the [founding Zionist] Basel Conference, ninety years after the Sykes-Picot Agreement, Israel has failed to wipe us out. We are here, in Palestine, facing them. We are not red Indians."[96]

After his presidency, Truman gloried in helping to establish a Jewish state, but when all the reasons and rationalizations were put aside— when all the perverse circumstances of history, including the twisted leadership of the Palestinian Arabs, were taken into account, and even when the horrors of the Holocaust were fully acknowledged—Palestine's Arabs had still gotten screwed, and screwed by people who over the centuries had suffered even worse indignities, yet who had always claimed to stand for better.

The Lessons of History

An old professor of mine used to say that history is the sum total of sentences in the past tense. That's a clever formulation, but it fails to capture what the actual writing of history (as opposed to simple con-versation) is about. Even the most anodyne history textbook contains an *argument* about the past. This book is no exception. While it is a narrative of events that took place from the 1880s to 1950, it is also an argument about what those events mean for people today.

Some readers might think that the argument of this book is that Truman should not have recognized Israel in May 1948. That's not, however, what I am suggesting. In the circumstances—and the circum-stances go back at least to 1917 and the Balfour Declaration—Truman had little choice. The only way that Truman and the United States might have created a binational or federated Palestine—or made sure the original partition proposed by the United Nations went into effect— was through credibly threatening and, if necessary, using an American-led force to impose an agreement upon the warring parties. And it might have taken years (as it has in the former Yugoslavia) to get the Jews and Arabs to accept their fates, and it still might not have worked. With the Cold War looming, and with the American public tired of war, Truman was not ready to do that, as he first made clear in August 1945.

It's also not my argument that Ben-Gurion should have been more amenable to compromise. He was, after all, still leading the Zionist movement in the shadow of the Holocaust. While the Nazi defeat dis-credited political anti-Semitism in much of Europe and in the United States, that was by no means evident in 1946. The Jews, as far as Pales-tine's Zionists were concerned, were still engaged in a war of survival. Nor, too, finally, am I suggesting that Palestine's Arabs should have turned their back on the mufti and accepted what they could get from the Zionists in 1947. They, too, were engaged in what they thought was a war of survival—one going back to the 1880s—and, like many move-ments among colonized people, were plagued by misleadership. (At least the mufti recognized that the Palestinians' Arab allies were up to no good.)

The history of Palestine and of Israel's founding cannot be changed, and it is silly to play games of what-if. But it is not silly to draw lessons from the past that are relevant to the present and the future. And the main lesson of this narrative is that whatever wrongs were done to the Jews of Europe and later to those of the Arab Middle East and North Africa—and there were great wrongs inflicted—the Zionists who came to Palestine to establish a state trampled on the rights of the Arabs who already lived there. That wrong has never been adequately addressed, or redressed, and for there to be peace of any kind between the Israelis and Arabs, it must be.

Zionists in Europe, Palestine, and the United States, with the notable exception of Ahad Ha'am and his protégés, refused to acknowledge that any wrong occurred. They advanced one rationalization after another—from the imperial-era argument that they were bringing civilization to savages to the later argument that while the Jews had nowhere but Palestine to go, Palestine's Arabs could comfortably live in any Arab country without sacrificing their right to self-determination. These arguments were put forth by European Socialists and by the foremost American liberals and moralists. And the violent and sometimes senseless reactions by the Palestinian Arabs and by neighboring Arab states to the original wrong inflicted upon Palestine's Arabs lent credibility to the Zionist rationalizations.

After Israel's founding, its supporters continued to grasp at any contention that would counter the idea that the Zionists owed Palestine's Arabs anything. They dismissed the case of the refugees. In 1949 Stephen Wise wrote a letter to an old friend assuring her that Jews had no role in the flight of refugees during the war. "The fullest assurance was given to the Arabs of Palestine after the Arabs of neighboring lands began to war against the State of Israel that they were safe, that their rights would be respected," he wrote. "But the coercion of the Arabs [*sic*] state compelled them to flee, against their own will and judgment."[97]

Eleanor Roosevelt, who had worried earlier about the fate of Palestine's Arabs, had banished any concerns by April 1949. Responding in her column to another writer who had advocated that Israel compensate the refugees driven from their homes during the war, she wrote:

> The writer . . . intimates the Arabs were driven from their homes. It is odd that she did not happen to find in Israel the many counties in which the Arabs remained and are quite happy living side by side with the Jews and even taking part in the government of the community. This fact makes some of us wonder why the Arab refugees ran away from a "danger" which was certainly no worse than the danger they took themselves into . . . The Arab will probably be better off if the funds already in hand are used to resettle them in some of the Arab countries where there are vacant lands that need people to work on them.[98]

One can say of Wise or Roosevelt that they didn't really know what was happening in Israel and Palestine, but I think it is more accurate to say that they didn't want to know what was happening, that they were determined to dismiss any suggestion that the Israelis had done wrong. They were willfully ignorant. That continues to be the case today among people who want to believe that Israel's government can do no wrong.

Americans, and American Jews, cannot finally determine how or even whether the conflict between the Israelis and Palestinians can be resolved. But Americans, and American pro-Israel organizations, have played an outsized role to date in allowing Israelis to overlook what they did and are continuing to do to Palestine's Arabs. If America's policy toward Israel and the Palestinians is to be determined not merely by passing considerations of realpolitik but by our conviction of what is right and wrong, then there are good reasons to make sure that in the future the Palestinians get treated justly and that their demands for full political, social, and economic rights are not dismissed on the basis of biblical exegesis or cultural inferiority. If America has tilted in the past toward Zionism and toward Israel, it is now time to redress that moral balance.

On Wednesday, September 21, 2011, when President Barack Obama gave his annual address at the United Nations, the conflict between Israelis and Palestinians was once again high on the agenda. Earlier that year Mahmoud Abbas, the president of the Palestinian Authority, had requested that the Security Council recognize Palestine as an independent state; but Obama, who had frequently declared his support for Palestine statehood, had promised to veto the request in the Security Council. Obama contended that if the Palestinians wanted a state, they should pursue it through negotiations with the Israelis: "Ultimately, it is the Israelis and the Palestinians who must live side by side. Ultimately, it is the Israelis and the Palestinians—not us—who must reach agreement on the issues that divide them: on borders and on security, on refugees and Jerusalem."[1]

On the surface, Obama's explanation made sense. It would certainly be preferable if the Israelis and Palestinians were to settle their differences in face-to-face talks. But they had tried that, and failed, in Obama's first years, largely because Israel's government, led by Prime Minister Benjamin Netanyahu, had refused to discuss borders and had set conditions for an agreement that he knew the Palestinians would reject. Why not allow the Palestinians the symbolic victory of the UN recognition, which might pressure the Israelis into negotiating?

Obama appeared to be doing exactly the opposite of what Truman had done sixty-four years earlier. In the fall of 1947, Truman had decided to back a Jewish state at the United Nations and the next May he recognized the new state of Israel. In both cases, Truman's State Department had advised him to hold out for negotiations between the Zionists and the Arabs. The British had taken a similar position. But Truman recognized that Palestine's Arabs were unwilling to negotiate with the Zionists, so he acceded to the Zionist request that he recognize their state. Why would Obama deny the Palestinians what Truman had given the Zionists?

In the sixty years between Israel's founding and Obama's election in 2008, Israel had become a prosperous state—twenty-seventh on the International Monetary Fund's list for per capita income, ahead of Spain and Portugal—and the thirteenth-most-powerful and also a nuclear-armed military, well ahead of any other country in the Middle East. But the basic conflict between the Zionists and Palestine's Arabs—now between Israelis and Palestinians—had remained unresolved.

From 1949 to 1967, Arab Palestinians lived under Egyptian rule in the Gaza Strip and under Jordanian rule in the West Bank. After the Six-Day War, Israel occupied both the Gaza Strip and West Bank and annexed East Jerusalem and soon began establishing settlements in violation of UN resolutions and international law, which forbids an occupying power to transfer its own population to the lands it is occupying. The Israeli government justified some of the initial settlements on grounds of military security, but since the mid-1970s settlements have been established on the basis of either commercial convenience or religious Zionism, which posits a greater Israel as a Jewish birthright. About 350,000 settlers now live in the West Bank and almost 300,000 in East Jerusalem in government-protected and -subsidized communities. Their growing numbers threaten to make a mockery of a two-state solution to the conflict.

The early Zionist movement fashioned itself a junior partner of imperial Britain, but Israel today has become one of the world's last colonial powers. The Palestinians in the occupied territories have no political rights, their freedom of movement and trade is sharply constricted, and they are subject to arbitrary arrest and imprisonment and even torture by Israel's military, and to continual harassment and violence from the settlers. That's not an outcome that many of the early Zionists envisaged.

In the 1920s, Labor Zionists tried earnestly to distinguish Zionism from colonialism, and their descendants in Israel's Labor Party and in smaller parties on the left have wanted to return the occupied lands as part of a peace agreement. In 1993 in Oslo, Labor prime minister Yitzhak Rabin did sign an agreement with the Palestine Liberation Organization to move toward a partitioned country, but Rabin was assassinated by a religious Zionist and further efforts at resolving the conflict have floundered. Labor Zionism itself has become marginalized.

In its place are the descendants of Jabotinsky and Ahimeir's Revisionism, along with the religious parties. They advocate a "greater Israel" that would include the West Bank. They espouse a militant Jewish nationalism that overrides a commitment to universal rights. Labor Zionists governed Israel until 1976, but since then the country has been governed for twenty-six of the last thirty-seven years by the descendants of the Revisionist movement, housed primarily in the Likud Party, in coalition with the religious and settler parties. These latter-day Revisionists operate within an existing democratic structure, but their outlook derives from European (including Russian) and Middle Eastern authoritarian movements. Like Jabotinsky, they are first and foremost Jewish nationalists.

About 4 million Palestinians live in the West Bank and Gaza. There are also about 5 million Palestinian refugees who live in Lebanon, Syria, the West Bank, and Jordan under the care of the United Nations Relief and Works Agency for Palestine Refugees in the Near East. The West Bank's per capita income is about one-fifteenth that of Israel. About a third of Gazans are unemployed. Israel finally evacuated Gaza in 2005 but retained control of its airspace, port, and imports and exports. Palestinians on the West Bank and Gaza are cut off from each other, unable to get from one place to the other.

The Palestinians' political leadership reflects that of a people who have been denied self-government for a century by occupying powers. In 1964 the Arab League designated the Palestine Liberation Organization (PLO), a coalition of existing guerrilla groups, the largest of which was Yasir Arafat's Fatah movement, as the official representatives of the

Palestinian people. The PLO conducted guerrilla raids from Israel's neighbors and undertook airplane hijackings and other terrorist acts. In 1988, during the second year of the First Intifada (uprising), it accepted Israel's existence and set as its objective a separate Palestinian state in the West Bank and Gaza with Jerusalem as its capital. But when the PLO and Fatah finally assumed political leadership after the Oslo Accords, they were ill prepared to govern. Arafat, like the mufti, sought to monopolize power for himself and his lieutenants. The Palestinian Authority government was corrupt and inefficient.

Fatah's main rival is Hamas, which was established in 1987 out of the Palestinian branch of the Muslim Brotherhood. The brotherhood had set up an Islamic center in Gaza in 1973 with Israeli encouragement. The Israelis saw the brotherhood's incrementalism and religious inwardness as an alternative to the PLO's secular revolutionism. Just as the British and the Zionists in the 1920s encouraged a division between Muslims and Christians—the Christians being seen as the more militant—the Israelis thought they would benefit from a division between the Muslim Brotherhood and the PLO.

But Hamas turned out to be more militant and less amenable to compromise than the PLO. It opposed Israel's existence; it encouraged armed struggle, including suicide bombing; and it espoused a theocratic politics. If Arafat and Fatah were the heirs to the mufti and his Arab High Command, Hamas was the heir to the Islamic guerrilla groups of the 1930s. Hamas named their rockets Qassam after guerrilla Iman Izz ad-Din al-Qassam, whom the British killed in 1935. Indeed, there were family ties. The father of the Hamas leader Khaled Meshal had fought with Abd al-Qadir al-Husseini and his Army of the Holy War in the 1936 revolt.

During the 1990s, Hamas attempted to subvert the Oslo Accords through terrorist bombings, and in 2001 it became a leader of the Second Intifada. Then, in January 2006, Hamas defeated Fatah in elections for the Palestinian Authority that the United States had encouraged. There were indications that Hamas, faced with having to govern, might prove conciliatory, but the Israelis and Americans refused to recognize the Hamas-led government. The Bush administration cut off aid, and the Israelis, backed by the United States, tried to starve the government out by denying it the tax revenues it collected on its behalf. At American urging, Abbas shifted power over security and finance from the prime minister's office, which was controlled by Hamas, to himself, and encouraged the American and Israeli quarantine of the new government. But, like other Bush administration efforts, this one backfired. Fatah and Abbas couldn't pay their own workers, including their security forces, but Hamas was able to get funding from Iran for its security forces, schools, and clinics.

The United States and Israel pushed Abbas's Fatah-led security forces to counter Hamas in Gaza. When the U.S. Congress balked at providing funds, the administration got Egypt and Jordan to contribute arms. The fighting escalated in Gaza between Hamas and Fatah. At the Saudis' urging, Abbas and Meshal agreed to a new unity government in February 2007, but the United States and Israel opposed it, and the Bush administration continued its efforts to eliminate Hamas from the government. When word of the American plans leaked in a Jordanian magazine, the fighting escalated again, and in mid-June, Hamas drove Fatah security forces out of Gaza, which the Israelis had evacuated, and won sole control of its government.[2]

The movement's split didn't entirely rule out an agreement with Israel. Hamas deferred to Abbas and Fatah when it came to negotiations with Israel, promising to abide by, without formally accepting, an agreement that Abbas might reach if it were accepted by the Palestine National Council or a popular referendum. For their part, Abbas and his prime minister, Salam Fayyad, tried to mimic the Zionist strategy of creating a nation within a nation to prepare for independence. And Fatah and Hamas engaged in periodical unity talks. There was some progress in talks between Abbas and Prime Minister Ehud Olmert, but when Netanyahu succeeded Olmert, the talks broke down, and Abbas went to the United Nations to win recognition of the Palestinian state.

After Truman left office, American governments tried, but failed, to resolve the conflict between the Israelis and the Arab states and between the Israelis and Palestinians. John F. Kennedy failed to get the Israelis to resettle the refugees; Richard Nixon's and Ronald Reagan's secretaries of state both advanced and then withdrew peace plans. Even the successes were underlain by failure. In 1975, Gerald Ford's secretary of state, Henry Kissinger, got the Israelis to talk through him to the Syrians and Egyptians, but at the expense of promising the Israelis that the United States would not talk to the PLO until it recognized Israel's existence. That crippled American diplomacy for years to come.

Jimmy Carter oversaw the Camp David Accords between Israel and Egypt in 1978, but Carter failed to win Begin's agreement to deal with the Palestinians, and left office in disfavor with American supporters of Israel. George H. W. Bush probably went the furthest in pressuring Israel. In 1991 he withheld loan guarantees in order to get the Israelis to attend the Madrid peace conference with Palestinian representatives. Bush's bold move contributed to Israel and the Palestinians undertaking talks at Oslo in 1993, but Bush, like Carter, became widely hated by Israel's supporters, who helped defeat him at the polls in 1992.

Bill Clinton had the good fortune to be president when the Oslo Accords were signed, but after Rabin was assassinated, and after Netanyahu came to power for the first time in 1996, Clinton was less successful in moving the Oslo process forward. On the eve of leaving office, he tried to precipitate an agreement between Israel's new prime minister, Ehud Barak, and Arafat, but he had not laid the groundwork, and these Camp David talks ended in acrimony and finger-pointing, and contributed to the resurgence of the Likud Party under Ariel Sharon and to the Second Intifada.

George W. Bush initially backed Sharon's attempt to destroy the Palestinian Authority. After Arafat died in December 2004, Bush urged elections for president and legislative council; but when Hamas won the January 2006 elections for legislative council, he joined the Israelis in trying to undermine the new Palestinian government. After these efforts resulted in splitting occupied Palestine in two, with Hamas in control of Gaza and Fatah in control of the West Bank, he and Olmert attempted to reinvigorate the peace process, but Olmert blundered into a new war in Gaza and in Lebanon that derailed his government. As Obama was becoming president, Netanyahu's right-wing coalition was returning to power on a promise to gut the negotiations that his predecessor had begun.

Throughout this period, American presidents believed that if they generously funded the Israelis, the Israelis would prove amenable to compromise with the Palestinians. From 1976 to 2004, Israel was the largest recipient of American foreign aid, averaging about $3 billion a year. From 1949 to 2013, Israel received $115 billion, more than half consisting of military aid.[3] But when it came to the peace process, the promise of aid failed to move the Israelis. Much of the military aid went to defraying the military costs of the occupation. And any attempt to use the aid as leverage to promote the peace process, as George H. W. Bush did, was met with sharp protest from a powerful pro-Israel lobby.

The American Zionist movement contracted after Israel won its independence in May 1948. Silver and Neumann lost a battle with Ben-Gurion over control of the funds raised in America for Israel and quit the movement. In 1949 the American Zionist Emergency Council changed its name to the American Zionist Council, and Louis Lipsky succeeded Silver as its head. The new organization remained a coalition of the Zionist groups, but as it had under Silver, it took on a life of its own.

In 1951, Israel wanted an American who was not identified with the embassy or Jewish Agency to lobby on Capitol Hill for foreign assistance. UN Ambassador Abba Eban convinced Lipsky to hire Isaiah Kenen, who had done public relations for Eban at the UN. Lipsky made Kenen the executive director of the American Zionist Council. Even though Kenen was paid partly by the Jewish Agency and the Israeli government, he did not register as a foreign agent with the U.S. government. Kenen and Eban wanted to avoid the stigma and restrictions attached to Kenen being classified as a foreign agent. In 1962 the Justice Department ordered that the council and Kenen would have to register. In response, Kenen split off from the council and reincorporated in January 1963 as the American Israel Public Affairs Committee (AIPAC). AIPAC claimed that it received no funds from the Israeli government.

Most of the older Jewish organizations had become Zionist after World War II, but groups like the American Jewish Committee and the Anti-Defamation League, which is part of B'nai Brith, still devoted the bulk of their activities to domestic American affairs. After the Israeli victory in the Six-Day War and Israel's close call in the 1973 Yom Kippur War with Egypt and Syria, Jewish organizations experienced a surge in contributions and membership, and groups like the American Jewish Committee became more focused on Israel than on civil rights or other domestic issues.

This growing commitment to Israel stemmed partly from pride in

Israel's accomplishments and military victories but also from fear for its survival, which was dramatized, as Peter Novick recounts in *The Holocaust in American Life*, by a renewed and vastly expanded attention to the Nazi genocide. That was evidenced in numerous books and films and in the building of the Holocaust Memorial Museum in Washington, D.C. But there was another more subtle factor at work. By the end of the 1960s, anti-Semitism had largely disappeared from American public life. That made American Jews feel freer to display their public interest in Israel. At the same time, the growing absence of anti-Semitism deprived American Jews of an important source of ethnic identity. The burr of anti-Semitism was replaced by support for Israel. Many synagogues and temples now sported blue-and-white Star of David Israeli flags alongside American flags. Support for Israel even became included in Reform Judaism's liturgy.[4]

Of all lobbying groups, AIPAC became the most powerful. It had a large and very wealthy membership. It didn't directly endorse or fund candidates, but it put out the word which candidate deserved financial support or opposition. AIPAC's model could be a called "a thousand Feinbergs," after Truman's foremost Jewish contributor, Abraham Feinberg. It didn't rely on Jewish votes but on Jewish campaign money. AIPAC first flexed its political muscle in 1984 when it was instrumental in defeating Illinois Republican senator Charles Percy, who as chairman of the Senate Foreign Relations Committee had defied AIPAC by supporting the sale of advanced aircraft to Saudi Arabia. By threatening with defeat candidates who opposed its recommendations, and by funding generously its supporters, AIPAC was able to exert enormous clout in congressional votes on anything pertaining to Israel.

AIPAC was sometimes accused of being, like its predecessor, an agent of the Israeli government, but that seems not to have been the case. AIPAC's positions sometimes diverged from those of the Israeli government. What distinguished AIPAC was that it based its program on what it thought to be in Israel's best interest. It was a lobby *for* Israel that was not run by Israel. AIPAC officials were ready to argue that its policies were in America's best interest, but that was an afterthought. And to be fair, if a huge and obvious difference in interest had appeared—such as, for instance, Israel taking the side of a country at war with the United States—the members of organizations like AIPAC would have been conflicted, to say the least.[5]

In its first decades AIPAC was aligned with American liberals and Democrats, and its main staff were liberal Democrats like the former Ted Kennedy aide Thomas Dine. But as Israel turned to the right, so did AIPAC's orientation. It was often at odds with Rabin and lukewarm on the Oslo Accords. In 1996, just after Netanyahu was elected prime minister, AIPAC appointed Howard Kohr, a former official with a Republican group, the National Jewish Coalition, as its executive director.

AIPAC's rightward shift coincided with increasing Republican support for Israel's conservative governments. Republican support began during the Reagan years, spurred in part by the entry into Republican ranks of neoconservatives who viewed Israel as a key Cold War ally; but support then spiked after the al-Qaeda terrorist attacks on September 11, 2001. Much of the new enthusiasm for Israel came from the religious right.

Fundamentalist Christians, who believed in the Jews' return to Zion and their eventual conversion to Christianity, saw in Israel's founding the confirmation of biblical prophecy. And, like other Restorationists, they believed in a "greater Israel" and viewed Palestinians as interlopers. After September 11, however, conservative Christians also came to identify Israel with opposition to Islamic terrorism.[6] Support for Israel became a hallmark of their foreign policy. In 2006, the Dallas pastor John Hagee brought conservative Christian groups together in a new coalition, Christians United for Israel, that backed the Israeli right wing and the objective of a greater Israel.

Conservative Republicans also came around after September 11. In November 2010, the Virginia Republican Eric Cantor, who was about to become House Majority Leader, met with Netanyahu. Afterward his office issued a statement: "Eric stressed that the new Republican majority will serve as a check on the Administration and what has been, up until this point, one party rule in Washington. He made clear that the Republican majority understands the special relationship between Israel and the United States, and that the security of each nation is reliant upon the other."[7] Cantor, who was one of the few Jewish Republicans in the House, had always been a strong Israel supporter, but his statement, coming from a party leader, was widely taken to mean that the Republicans would block any attempt by Obama to pressure Israel to end the occupation.

There were dissenting voices within the Jewish community and among the liberal intelligentsia with regard to Israel's turn to the right. *The Nation* became a sharp critic of the Israeli occupation, as did the *New York Times* editorial page and *The New York Review of Books*. There were several small organizations, such as Americans for Peace Now, that reflected a growing rift between American liberal Jews and the Revisionist Zionism that increasingly dominated Israeli politics. In April 2008, Jeremy Ben-Ami, who had served as Bill Clinton's deputy policy director, founded J Street as a serious counter-lobby to AIPAC.

Obama himself got his view of Israel from liberal Jews disenchanted with Israel's turn rightward. The Chicago rabbi Arnold Wolf, a critic of the occupation, was a friend and neighbor, and several prominent Chicago Jews who became supporters of J Street oversaw his political rise.[8] Wolf, who described himself as a "religious radical" and a "liberal activist," represented a return to the universalism of nineteenth-century Reform Judaism.[9] He supported Israel's existence, but he wanted the Israelis to pursue policies that fully recognized the rights of the Palestinians. As a founder in 1973 of a dissident group, Breira, he had locked horns repeatedly with AIPAC and other Jewish establishment groups.

The influence of these liberal Jews was evident in Obama's campaign for president. Speaking before Jewish leaders in Cleveland in February 2008, Obama criticized supporters of Israel who demanded that he back whatever government was in power. "There is a strain within the pro-Israel community that says unless you adopt an unwavering pro-Likud approach to Israel that you're anti-Israel," he said.[10] And when he came to office, he began pressing the Israelis to abandon their Revisionist approach toward greater Israel and the Palestinians.

Benjamin Netanyahu, who became prime minister again a month after Obama was inaugurated, had never favored a Palestinian state, and during his campaign he had criticized his predecessor, Ehud Olmert, for offering a peace plan to the Palestinians that would have required Israel to withdraw from some settlements in the West Bank. At Netanyahu's first meeting with Obama in May 2009, the Israeli tried to focus the meeting on Iran's development of a nuclear weapon. Netanyahu and other Israeli officials were worried about the threat that a nuclear Iran might pose, and about the leverage Iran would acquire by ending Israel's nuclear monopoly in the region, but Netanyahu also wanted to divert Obama's attention from the occupation. Obama wouldn't be diverted. He asked Netanyahu to lay the basis for continuing negotiations with the Palestinians. He wanted the Israelis to freeze the growth of settlements, including new building in East Jerusalem.

AIPAC immediately signaled its reservations with Obama's request. The organization rarely issued statements on its own. Instead, it prompted its supporters in Congress to back resolutions. On May 28, it got 329 votes in the House and 76 in the Senate for a resolution calling on the administration "to work closely with our democratic ally . . . The U.S. must be a trusted mediator and a devoted friend to Israel."[11] The resolution, which clearly reflected Netanyahu's unhappiness with Obama, was a message to the president to act as a "devoted friend" (rather than a critic or an enemy) of Israel and its prime minister.

But Obama was determined to revive the peace process between the Israelis and Palestinians. In a long-awaited speech on June 4 in Cairo on America's Middle East policy, Obama showed that he was serious about respecting the moral claims of Palestinians as well as Israelis. He described the Israelis and Palestinians as each having "legitimate aspirations" and a "painful history." Israel's "aspiration for a homeland," Obama explained, was rooted in centuries of persecution that "culminated in an unprecedented holocaust," while the Palestinian people had "endured the pain of dislocation . . . for more than sixty years . . . They endure daily humiliations—large and small—that come with the occupation." Obama called on the Palestinians to "abandon violence" in pursuing their homeland and on Hamas to acknowledge "Israel's right to exist," but he also warned the Israelis that the "United States does not accept the legitimacy of continued Israeli settlements . . . It is time for these settlements to stop."[12]

Obama once again found himself under attack from a major Jewish organization. The ADL's executive director, Abraham Foxman, expressed his disappointment that "the President found the need to balance the suffering of the Jewish people in a genocide to the suffering of the Palestinian people resulting from Arab wars." Foxman also criticized Obama for implying that "Israel's right to exist" was "a result of anti-Semitism and the Holocaust."[13] Foxman didn't say so explicitly, but other critics would make the point more explicit: that the land of Israel belonged to the Jews by biblical birthright. That was an argument that Zionists had made since the 1880s, but it was one based on religious faith rather than legal precedent.

Later that month, Netanyahu, speaking at Bar-Ilan University, responded to Obama. Netanyahu, like Foxman, rejected the view that Israel's right to exist was rooted in the Holocaust. "Our right to build our sovereign state here, in the land of Israel, arises from one simple fact: this is the homeland of the Jewish people, this is where our identity was forged," he declared. "This is the land of our forefathers." But Netanyahu also offered what appeared to be an important concession. Netanyahu said he favored a Palestinian nation with "its own flag, its own national anthem, its own government." That showed that Obama's tough talk had had some effect.

But Netanyahu, who was nothing if not clever, set conditions on the negotiations over a Palestinian state that Palestinians had already rejected. He insisted that they recognize Israel as "the nation state of the Jewish people." That meant, he explained, Palestinians had to reject the right of return, which they had said repeatedly they were unwilling to do at the beginning of negotiations without comparable concessions from the Israelis. He also said Jerusalem must "remain the united capital of Israel," which ruled out its also being the capital of Palestine.[14] And he said Palestine must be entirely demilitarized, without an army or control of its own airspace—a demand that, when later clarified, would also prove unpalatable to the Palestinians.

The next month Obama met with Jewish leaders in the White House to try to tamp down the growing criticism of his initiatives. The Jewish leaders wanted him to favor Israel in the negotiations. "If you want Israel to take risks, then its leaders must know that the United States is right next to them," Malcolm Hoenlein, the executive vice chairman of the Conference of Presidents of Major American Jewish Organizations, told the president. Nahum Goldmann had created the conference in 1956 as a voice of his own liberal Zionism, but under Hoenlein it had drifted to the right.[15]

But Obama was sticking to his guns. "Look at the past eight years," he responded. "During those eight years, there was no space between us and Israel, and what did we get from that? When there is no daylight, Israel just sits on the sidelines, and that erodes our credibility with the Arab states."[16] Foxman followed up on Hoenlein's concerns, complaining that Obama was not being "evenhanded" when he asked for sacrifices from Israelis but not from Palestinians. "Abe, you are absolutely right and we are going to fix that," Obama told him. Turning

Foxman's comment on its head, Obama said that "the sense of even-handedness has to be restored."[17] Obama rejected Foxman's definition of evenhandedness, which implicitly identified the Israelis as the party more deserving of American support, in favor of an evenhandedness that put the moral claims of Palestinians on an equal footing with those of Israelis.

In October, under prodding from George Mitchell, whom Obama had appointed his special envoy for Middle East peace, and the veteran negotiator Dennis Ross, who had joined the White House staff, Netanyahu agreed to freeze settlement construction. But he once again introduced conditions that made it unpalatable to Mahmoud Abbas and the Palestinian Authority, who were already under attack from Hamas and its followers for concessions they had made to Olmert. He exempted East Jerusalem, the projected capital of Palestine, and public buildings from a freeze, as well as dwellings whose construction was under way. The latter was the tricky part. Prior to Netanyahu's announcement, settlers, expecting some kind of freeze, had hurriedly begun building houses. As a result, more new homes would be built during Netanyahu's freeze than in 2008 and only slightly fewer than in 2009. The freeze was a ruse, and while the Obama administration was temporarily taken in, Abbas was not. The Palestinians refused to negotiate.

In September 2010, a month before the freeze was to expire, Obama, Mitchell, and Ross got Netanyahu and Abbas to meet, but the talks quickly broke down. Abbas tried to give Netanyahu the documents detailing the agreements that he and Olmert had reached on territories and land swaps. Netanyahu would not accept the documents. Instead, he insisted that they begin by discussing Israeli security. Abbas had already agreed in his talks with Olmert to stationing an international force in the Jordan Valley, but Netanyahu now insisted that Israeli troops remain there "for decades, many decades."[18] That would have meant Israel continuing to occupy a fourth of the West Bank. Abbas understandably broke off the negotiations.

Obama made one last attempt to spark the negotiations. When it was already too late, Bill Clinton had gotten Palestinian and Israeli negotiators to agree "with reservations" to various land swaps. Obama now thought of introducing his own version of the "Clinton parameters" for what he called "a viable Palestine and a secure Israel." Obama provided very little detail—Mitchell and Ross had disagreed on how much to include—but at a speech on May 19 at the State Department, he did say that an agreement "should be based on the 1967 lines with mutually agreed swaps."[19]

Netanyahu, who was scheduled to arrive in Washington to address AIPAC's annual conference and the House of Representatives (at the invitation of the Republican majority), decided to make a fuss over Obama's seemingly innocuous mention of the 1967 lines. As he was leaving for Washington, Netanyahu issued a statement charging that Obama had put Israel's security in jeopardy by suggesting that Israel would "have to withdraw to the 1967 lines, which are both indefensible and which would leave major population centers in Judea and Samaria beyond those lines."[20] (Revisionists who favor a greater Israel regularly used the biblical names "Judea" and "Samaria" to refer to the West Bank. Netanyahu was sending a coded message to his supporters by using these terms.)

Netanyahu's charges against Obama, which he took the unprecedented step of repeating in what was supposed to be a pro forma press conference with the president in Washington, were sheer demagoguery. Obama had proposed using the 1967 lines as a starting point for making land swaps. Netanyahu conveniently omitted the proposal for land swaps from his account of Obama's proposals. After displaying his disrespect for Obama, Netanyahu received a hero's welcome at AIPAC and at the House of Representatives, where Democrats, intimidated by AIPAC, vied with the Republicans to see who could cheer the loudest. The Israeli prime minister received twenty-nine standing ovations, four more than the president had received for his State of the Union address that year.[21]

Obama was furious with Netanyahu for upstaging him, but the president was beginning to lose support among Jewish Democrats. At the AIPAC meeting, Senate Majority Leader Harry Reid and House Minority Whip Steny Hoyer, both of whom were leading recipients of money from individuals and groups that backed the Israeli government, indicated their opposition to Obama's parameters. "No one should set premature parameters about borders, about building, about anything else," Reid said.[22] Soon after his duel with Netanyahu, Obama abandoned his attempt to resolve the Israeli-Palestinian conflict and, like many of his predecessors, resigned himself to favoring Israel over the Palestinians.

Obama may have decided that he simply couldn't move the Israeli prime minister, although each time he had pressed Netanyahu he had gotten a concession. But there was another factor that came into play that month and during the summer of 2011. Since Truman's win in 1948, the Democrats had become dependent on Jewish campaign money. The veteran Jewish Telegraphic Agency reporter Ron Kampeas wrote of estimates that Jews had contributed between a third and two-thirds of the party's money. Two-thirds seems way too high, but it could be between one-fourth and one-third.[23] Some of that money has reflected Jewish support for liberal domestic policies, but much of it has had to do with support for Israel. One former campaign official said of these latter donors, "If you have money, you have a platform."

During May 2011, the White House had conducted a "listening tour" of Jewish donors and had found dissatisfaction with his policies toward Israel.[24] On May 19, the day of Obama's speech at the State Department, *The Wall Street Journal* reported that "some Jewish donors say Mr. Obama has pushed Israeli leaders too hard to halt construction of housing settlements in disputed territories." In the article, one large donor to Obama's 2008 campaign claimed that Obama had "degraded the Israeli people."[25] A week later, the billionaire Haim Saban, who holds American and Israeli citizenship and has been one of the Democrats' largest donors, announced that he would not contribute to Obama's presidential campaign because the president had not shown sufficient support for Israel.[26]

Saban's statement was a major blow, and it was followed by a very unusual memo from AIPAC that subtly rebuked Obama by echoing the positions that Netanyahu had taken in his speech at the AIPAC meeting. The memo blamed the Palestinians for the breakdown in negotiations, attributing to them the position about the 1967 borders that Netanyahu attributed to Obama. The *Washington Post* blogger Jennifer Rubin, who was close to the lobby, wrote, "While the critique was ostensibly phrased in opposition to the Palestinians' tactics, make no mistake: these were the U.S. positions that AIPAC was criticizing."[27] AIPAC's break with the president would potentially affect Jewish donors.

Over the next month Obama began to conciliate his critics by shifting ground on Israel and the Palestinians. In June, Obama held a meeting in the White House with Jewish leaders. Two years earlier he had claimed to be evenhanded in his dealings with the Israelis and Palestinians. Now he claimed that he was favoring the Israelis. "My administration is not being evenhanded," he said. "We are being decidedly more attentive to Israel's security needs."[28]

AIPAC had opposed the Palestinians' bid for UN recognition and had gotten the House to pass 407–6 and the Senate unanimously a resolution calling on the administration to veto the Palestinian bid and also to withhold funds from the Palestinian Authority if Fatah and Hamas were to sign a unity agreement without Hamas recognizing Israel.[29] Obama hardened his opposition to the Palestinian bid and to the unity government, even though a representative unity government of Palestinians, in which Hamas promised to defer to Abbas on negotiations, would have made the Palestinians more rather than less able to negotiate a credible agreement with the Israelis.

Thus, Obama gave up any attempt to revive the peace process. Mitchell and Ross resigned. The talks between Netanyahu and Abbas broke off because, as Obama knew, Netanyahu laid out blatantly unacceptable conditions for negotiation. Threatening a veto at the UN wouldn't revive the negotiations, but it would pacify and please Obama's critics at AIPAC and among major Jewish donors. Obama's UN stance—so paradoxical on one level if one considers what the United States did in 1947 and 1948—appears in fact to have been shaped, like Truman's, by political concerns.

Obama's speech at the UN that September reflected his abandonment of evenhandedness. In his Cairo speech, he had vividly described the moral basis of Israeli and Palestinian claims for statehood. In this speech he devoted a few abstract sentences to the "aspirations of the Palestinian people" and followed them with a panegyric to Israeli security:

> America's commitment to Israel's security is unshakeable. Our friendship with Israel is deep and enduring. And so we believe that any lasting peace must acknowledge the very real security concerns that Israel faces every single day.
>
> Let us be honest with ourselves: Israel is surrounded by neighbors that have waged repeated wars against it. Israel's citizens have been killed by rockets fired at their houses and suicide bombs on their buses. Israel's children come of age knowing that throughout the region, other children are taught to hate them. Israel, a small country of less than eight million people, looks out at a world where leaders of much

larger nations threaten to wipe it off of the map. The Jewish people carry the burden of centuries of exile and persecution, and fresh memories of knowing that six million people were killed simply because of who they are. Those are facts. They cannot be denied.

In November, Obama held another series of meetings with Jewish leaders and donors. "Obviously, no ally is more important than the state of Israel," he told a fund-raising event on New York's Upper East Side, at the home of the president of the American Jewish Congress.[30] Obama invited Saban for a private Oval Office meeting the following month, from which Saban emerged a supporter. Afterward, Saban gave $1 million to a Democrat super PAC and penned an op-ed, "The Truth About Obama and Israel," in *The New York Times* backing Obama's re-election.[31] Obama appointed Saban's wife to a position at the United Nations.[32]

At the United Nations in 2012, the Palestinians once again made a bid for UN recognition, and once again the United States threatened a veto in the Security Council. In his annual speech to the UN in September, Obama didn't even bother to explain why. He devoted exactly one paragraph of a sixty-paragraph address to Israel and Palestine. In it he portrayed the Palestinians rather than the Israelis as the principal obstacle to peace. "Among Israelis and Palestinians, the future must not belong to those who turn their backs on a prospect of peace. Let us leave behind those who thrive on conflict, those who reject the right of Israel to exist," he said.[33]

In Obama's first term, he replicated almost exactly what happened to Truman in his first term. Like Truman, he began with the understanding that in the clash between Jews and Palestinian Arabs, the United States needed to play a strong role as mediator, and that the Arabs as well as the Jews had a strong claim upon the American sense of justice and fair play. But he found himself facing unyielding opposition in Israel and growing pressure from AIPAC and Jewish donors, as well as a weak and divided Palestinian leadership. Obama, like Truman, backed down and took a position that, by ostentatiously favoring the Israelis, betrayed his own moral understanding. The players were different in 1947 than in 2011, but the script was the same.

Of course, nothing is certain in politics. As Obama, no longer facing reelection, opened his second term, he showed signs of renewed determination to bring the Palestinians and Israelis together. In March, Obama made his first trip to Israel. While much of the trip was devoted to charming the Israeli government and its American supporters, Obama made a strong case for Palestinian rights in a concluding speech in Jerusalem:

> It is not fair that a Palestinian child cannot grow up in a state of their own, living their entire lives with the presence of a foreign army that controls the movements not just of those young people but their parents, their grandparents, every single day. It's not just when settler violence against Palestinians goes unpunished. It's not right to prevent Palestinians from farming their lands or [restrict] a student's ability to move around the West Bank or displace Palestinian families from their homes. Neither occupation nor expulsion is the answer. Just as Israelis built a state in their homeland, Palestinians have a right to be a free people in their own land.[34]

In July, Obama's new secretary of state, John Kerry, using a combination of bribes and threats, cajoled the Israelis and the Palestinians into beginning negotiations. Kerry's effort to pressure the Israelis was aided by the European Union, which announced a ban on contributions from any of its official bodies to Israeli institutions that have ties to the occupied territories.

But an enduring, and not merely partial and fleeting, agreement remains extraordinarily difficult to obtain. On the eve of negotiations, the Netanyahu government announced plans for 1,187 new housing units in East Jerusalem and the West Bank, including in Ariel, a settlement that is well inside the West Bank and was previously considered a prime candidate to be evacuated in any two-state agreement. Mark Regev, a government spokesman, said that the units were in areas "that will remain part of Israel in any future peace agreement."[35] That clearly includes Ariel as well as East Jerusalem, which the Palestinians have contemplated as the capitol of their state. As he was forming the current government, Netanyahu pledged that he would "never divide"

Jerusalem.[36] And the pro-settler Jewish Home party occupies a prominent place in Netanyahu's governing coalition.

If the Israeli government doesn't seem poised to make a deal, neither does the Palestinian, except on terms that its citizens will reject.
Abbas, whose representatives will negotiate with the Netanyahu government, and his Fatah party have become weaker over the years. In
April, Abbas's well-regarded prime minister, Salaam Fayyad, resigned
as a result of a dispute over control of the Palestinian Authority's
finances. Abbas's appointed replacement quit after two weeks then was
convinced to stay on, but, after five months on the job, had still not assembled a government.

Abbas seems to have agreed to resume negotiations partly in order
to obtain $4 billion that Kerry had promised the Palestinian Authority.
Abbas even withdrew his demand that the Israelis freeze settlement
construction as a condition of negotiations. The Palestinian president
could conceivably reach an agreement on Netanyahu's terms by abandoning Jerusalem and agreeing to settlements that would divide the
West Bank, but he would have to buck widespread opposition for such
an agreement. Hamas had edged closer over the last decade to backing
a two-state solution, but it already distanced itself from these negotiations, denouncing Abbas for being willing to "swap Palestinian principles for politicized money."[37] Would Abbas be willing to risk a
rebellion? In 2000, Arafat was unwilling to risk trying to sell a much
more favorable agreement to the Palestinians.

In the current circumstances, perhaps the only way in which the
two sides could reach an equitable and enduring agreement would be if
the United States and the European Union took a strong hand in the
negotiations. They would have to make clear, particularly to the Israelis,
that they would not tolerate any other outcome. Obama might even
have to threaten a cutoff of American aid. Would he be able to ignore
the political uproar in Washington these kind of actions would provoke? Or the unrest they would create in an already troubled region? If
the precedent established by Truman in his first and second terms
holds, Obama will finally back down and avoid the political turmoil
that greeted the last American president who tried to press the Israelis
to make dramatic concessions, George H. W. Bush. But history is full
of surprises, and the time for an end to the irrepressible conflict could
finally come.

NOTES

INTRODUCTION: TRUMAN'S QUALMS

1. Details of the meeting from Abba Hillel Silver to Benjamin Akzin, Sept. 10, 1948, Hyman A. Schulson files; Truman Library presidential schedules; United Press and Jewish Telegraphic Agency reports; *Israel Documents*, May–September 1948 (Israel State Archives, Jerusalem, 1979), 588, and Michael Cohen, *Truman and Israel* (Berkeley: University of California Press, 1990), 242.
2. Paul C. Merkley in *The Politics of Christian Zionism* 1891–1948 (London: Routledge, 1998), Michael T. Benson in *Harry S. Truman and the Founding of Israel* (Westport, CT: Praeger, 1997), and Howard M. Sachar in *A History of Israel: From the Rise of Zionism to Our Time* (New York: Alfred A. Knopf, 2007) portray Truman as a proto-Zionist.
3. Peter Novick, *The Holocaust in American Life* (Boston: Houghton Mifflin, 2000), 93.
4. www.whitehouse.gov/the-press-office/remarks-president-cairo-university-6 -04-09.
5. See Novick on this subject.

PART I EPIGRAPH

Judah L. Magnes, "Toward Peace in Palestine," *Foreign Affairs*, Jan. 1943.

1. THE ORIGINS OF ZIONISM: HERZL, AHAD HA'AM, AND GORDON

1. Justin McCarthy, *The Population of Palestine: Population History and Statistics of the Late Ottoman Period and the Mandate* (New York: Columbia University Press, 1990), 10, 12.

2. Yosef Gorny, *Zionism and the Arabs 1882–1948: A Study of Ideology* (New York: Oxford University Press, 1987). There was an incident of European-type Christian anti-Semitism in Syria in 1840 when French and Syrian Christians invoked the "blood libel" in accusing Damascus Jews of murdering a monk. The French reputedly initiated the libel to curry favor among the region's Christians. There were also incidents of anti-Semitism in Palestine during the Egyptian occupation of the 1830s when Christians were elevated over Muslims. But no similar incidents took place after the Ottomans resumed their rule.

3. Johann Gottlieb Fichte, "To the German Nation," www.fordham.edu/halsall/mod/1806fichte.html, quoted in Sven-Erik Rose, "Lazarus Bendavid's and J. G. Fichte's Kantian Fantasies of Jewish Decapitation in 1793," *Jewish Historical Studies*, March 22, 2007.

4. Robert S. Wistrich, "George von Schoenerer and the Genesis of Modern Austrian Anti-Semitism," in *Hostages of Modernization: Studies on Modern Antisemitism, 1870–1933/39*, ed. Herbert Strauss Walter (Bechin: Walter de Gruyten, 1993).

5. Quoted in Arthur Hertzberg, *The Zionist Idea: A Historical Analysis and Reader* (Philadelphia: Jewish Publication Society, 1997), 180.

6. Leo Pinsker, *Auto-Emancipation . . .* (New York: Maccabaean Publishing Co., 1906), in Hertzberg, 183.

7. Ibid., 184.

8. Moshe Leib Lilienblum, "The Future of Our People," in Hertzberg, 173.

9. Pinsker, in Hertzberg, 185.

10. Ibid., 190.

11. Ibid., 194.

12. Lilienblum, "The Path to Repentance," quoted in Anita Shapira, *Land and Power: The Zionist Resort to Force, 1881–1948* (Palo Alto, CA: Stanford University Press, 1999), 40.

13. On what archaeologists currently know, or think they know, about the period that the Old Testament covers, see Israel Finkelstein and Neil Asher Silberman, *The Bible Unearthed: Archaeology's New Vision of Ancient Israel and the Origin of Its Sacred Texts* (New York: Simon & Schuster, 2001). For a journalistic summary, see Amy Dockser Marcus, *The View from Nebo: How Archeology Is Rewriting the Bible and Reshaping the Middle East* (Boston: Little, Brown, 2000).

14. See McCarthy, "Palestine's Population During the Ottoman and British Mandate Periods," www.palestineremembered.com/Acre/Palestine-Remembered/Story559.html#Table%201.

15. Shapira, 41.

16. See Patricia Seed, "Imagining a Waste Land; or, Why Indians Vanish," in *American Pentimento: The Invention of Indians and the Pursuit of Riches* (Minneapolis: University of Minnesota Press, 2001).

17. Cotton Mather, *Magnalia Christi Americana; or, The Ecclesiastical History of*

New England (Hartford, CT: Silas Andrus & Son, 1858), quoted in Giles B. Gunn, *New World Metaphysics: Readings on the Religious Meaning of the American Experience* (New York: Oxford University Press, 1981), 84.

18. E. Robinson and E. Smith, *Biblical Researches in Palestine and in the Adjacent Regions: A Journal of Travels in the Year 1838*, vol. II (London: John Murray, 1841), 81.

19. Leon Simon, *Ahad Ha'am, Asher Ginzberg: A Biography* (Philadelphia: Jewish Publication Society of America, 1960), 38.

20. Ahad Ha'am, "The Wrong Way," in the Jewish Virtual Library.

21. Ibid.

22. Ahad Ha'am, "An Open Letter to My Brethren in the Spirit," in the Jewish Virtual Library.

23. Letter, Sept. 18, 1910, in Hertzberg.

24. Simon, 64.

25. Ahad Ha'am, "Palestine," in Adam Shatz, ed., *Prophets Outcast: A Century of Dissident Writing About Zionism and Israel* (New York: Nation Books, 2004).

26. Walter Laqueur, *A History of Zionism: From the French Revolution to the Establishment of the State of Israel* (New York: Schocken Books, 1972), 83.

27. Austrian Liberalism was very different from American New Deal liberalism. It was the creed of the rising bourgeoisie/professional class against absolute monarchy, and had nothing in common with socialism or populism.

28. Theodor Herzl, *The Diaries of Theodor Herzl*, ed. Marvin Lowenthal (New York: Grosset & Dunlop, 1962), 4.

29. Moses Hess, *Rome and Jerusalem* (New York: Bloch, 1943), in Hertzberg, 133.

30. Carl E. Schorske, *Fin-de-Siècle Vienna: Politics and Culture* (New York: Vintage, 1981), 146.

31. Herzl, *The Jewish State* (Hales Corners, WI: Voasha Publishing, 2008), 76. Herzl defined nationhood in terms that applied to Jews, but not to many other groups. Testifying before a Royal Commission in 1902, he said that a nation is "a historical group of men of intelligible and visible cohesion held together by a common enemy." In the case of Jews, "the common enemy is anti-Semitism."

32. Ibid., 156.

33. Ibid., 145.

34. Ibid., 145.

35. Schorske, 172.

36. Herzl, *The Complete Diaries of Theodor Herzl*, ed. Raphael Patai (New York: Herzl Press and Thomas Yoseloff, 1960); see letter, Jan. 11, 1902; also July 28, 1901.

37. See John B. Judis, *The Folly of Empire: What George W. Bush Could Learn from Theodore Roosevelt and Woodrow Wilson* (New York: Scribner, 2004), 11–13.

38. See Jeremy Salt, *The Unmaking of the Middle East: A History of Western Disorder in Arab Lands* (Berkeley: University of California Press, 2009), and John A. Hobson, *Imperialism* (London: Allen and Unwin, 1948), for discussion of civilization

as key motif of imperialism. Also Judis, *The Folly of Empire*. In *Imperialism*, Hobson writes, "The moral defense of Imperialism is generally based upon the assertion that . . . the political and economic control forcibly assumed—by 'higher' over 'lower races' does promote at once the civilization of the world and the special good of the subject races."

39. Herzl, *Jewish State*, 96.

40. Tom Segev, *One Palestine, Complete: Jews and Arabs Under the British Mandate* (New York: Henry Holt Metropolitan Books, 2000), 150.

41. Herzl, *Jewish State*, 82.

42. Ibid., 87.

43. Ibid., 95.

44. Ibid.

45. Herzl, *Altneuland*, www.hagshama.org.il/en/resources/view.asp?id=1600.

46. Herzl, *Diaries*, ed. Lowenthal, 220.

47. Ibid., 215.

48. Laqueur, 106.

49. Herzl, *Diaries*, ed. Lowenthal, 224.

50. Simon, 172.

51. Ahad Ha'am, "The Jewish State and Jewish Problem," in the Jewish Virtual Library.

52. Aaron David Gordon, "Some Observations," in Hertzberg.

53. Gordon, "People and Labor," in Hertzberg.

54. Ibid.

55. Gordon, "Our Tasks Ahead," in Hertzberg.

56. Ibid.

57. Gordon, "People and Labor," in Hertzberg.

58. Quoted in Zeev Sternhell, *The Founding Myths of Israel: Nationalism, Socialism, and the Making of the Jewish State* (Princeton, NJ: Princeton University Press, 1998), 72.

59. Quoted in Bernard Avishai, *The Tragedy of Zionism: How Its Revolutionary Past Haunts Israeli Democracy* (New York: Helios Press, 2002), 92.

60. Sternhell, 6.

61. Quoted in Shabtai Teveth, *Ben-Gurion and the Palestinian Arabs: From Peace to War* (Oxford: Oxford University Press, 1985), 145.

62. Quoted in Shapira, 45. On this debate, see also Benny Morris, *Righteous Victims: A History of the Zionist-Arab Conflict, 1881–2001* (New York: Vintage, 2001), 57.

63. Shapira, 46.

64. Ibid., 51.

2. THE ORIGINS OF PALESTINIAN NATIONALISM

1. Alexander Keith, *The Land of Israel According to the Covenant with Abraham, with Isaac, and with Jacob* (New York: Harper & Brothers, 1844), 34.

2. Gudrun Krämer, *A History of Palestine: From the Ottoman Conquest to the Founding of the State of Israel* (Princeton, NJ: Princeton University Press, 2011), 165–66.
3. Interview with Frank Giles, London Sunday *Times*, June 15, 1969.
4. www.politico.com/blogs/bensmith/1211/Gingrich_Palestinians_invented_promises_Netanyahustyle_foreign_policy.html.
5. See Krämer, 2ff.
6. Judges 20:10: "Then all the children of Israel went out, and the congregation was assembled as one man, from Dan even to Beersheba, with the land of Gilead, to Yahweh at Mizpah."
7. See Krämer, 155.
8. See, for instance, *Foreign Relations of the United States* (here in after, *FRUS*) (Washington D.C.: U.S. Government Printing Office, 1867), 1866. "Mr. Morris to Mr. Seward," Nov. 30, 1866, about "the recent arrival and settlement of a colony of American emigrants in Palestine, in the vicinity of Jaffa."
9. See Rashid Khalidi, "Contrasting Narratives of Palestinian Identity," in Patricia Yaeger, ed., *The Geography of Identity* (Ann Arbor: University of Michigan Press, 1996), 215–16.
10. Paul McGeough, *Kill Khalid: The Failed Mossad Assassination of Khalid Mishal and the Rise of Hamas* (New York: New Press, 2009), 407.
11. Krämer, 44.
12. David W. Lesch, *The Arab-Israeli Conflict: A History* (New York: Oxford University Press, 2007), 7.
13. Quoted in Krämer, 85.
14. Lesch, 35–36.
15. Quoted in Rashid Khalidi, *Palestinian Identity* (New York: Columbia University Press, 1997), 75.
16. The letter is included in Walid Khalidi, ed., *From Haven to Conquest: Readings in Zionism and the Palestine Problem Until 1948* (Beirut: Institute for Palestinian Studies, 1987), 91–92.
17. Negib Azoury, *Le Reveil de la Nation Arabe* (Whitefish, MT: Kessinger Publishing, LLC, 2009), v. My translation.
18. Baruch Kimmerling and Joel S. Migdal, *The Palestinian People: A History* (Cambridge, MA: Harvard University Press, 2003), 24.
19. Quoted in Khalidi, *Palestinian Identity*, 32.
20. Ibid., 53.
21. See Abd al-Wahhab Kayyali, *Palestine: A Modern History* (London: Croom Helm, 1978), 24, and Khalidi, *Palestinian Identity*, 129.
22. Figures from Khalidi, *Palestinian Identity*, 126–28.
23. Khalidi, *Palestinian Identity*, 81.
24. Yehoshua Porath, *The Emergence of the Palestinian-Arab National Movement 1918–1929* (London: Frank Cass, 1974) (London, 1995), 25.
25. Ann Mosely Lesch, *Arab Politics in Palestine, 1917–1939: The Frustration of a Nationalist Movement* (Ithaca, NY: Cornell University Press, 1979), 30.
26. Khalidi, *Palestinian Identity*, 155.

3. CHAIM WEIZMANN AND THE BALFOUR DECLARATION

1. Krämer, 138.
2. Quoted in David Fromkin, *A Peace to End All Peace: The Fall of the Ottoman Empire and the Creation of the Modern Middle East* (New York: Henry Holt & Co., 1989), 143.
3. Chaim Weizmann, *Trial and Error: The Autobiography of Chaim Weizmann* (Westport, CT: Greenwood, 1972), 54.
4. Segev, 40.
5. Nahum Goldmann, *The Autobiography of Nahum Goldmann: Sixty Years of Jewish Life* (New York: Holt, Rinehart & Winston, 1969), 110.
6. Introduction to Nahum Sokolow, *History of Zionism: 1690–1918* (London: Longmans, Green & Co., 1919).
7. Weizmann, 109–11.
8. Isaiah Friedman, *The Question of Palestine: British-Jewish-Arab Relations 1914–1918* (New York: Shocken Books, 1973), 283.
9. Ibid., 99.
10. *Palestine: A Study of Jewish, Arab, and British Policies*, vol. I (New Haven, CT: Yale University Press, 1947), 78.
11. Quoted in Jonathan Schneer, *The Balfour Declaration: The Origins of the Arab-Israeli Conflict* (New York: Random House, 2010), 131.
12. Quoted in Friedman, 12.
13. Bernard Wasserstein, *Herbert Samuel: A Political Life* (Oxford: Oxford University Press, 1992), 204.
14. Herbert Samuel, *Memoirs* (London: Cresset Press, 1945), 140–41.
15. Wasserstein, 207.
16. Ibid., 199.
17. Friedman, 336.
18. Ronald Sanders, *The High Walls of Jerusalem: A History of the Balfour Declaration and the Birth of the British Mandate for Palestine* (New York: Holt, Rinehart & Winston, 1984), 108.
19. Quoted in Segev, 36.
20. On Lloyd George's attitude to Jews, see Sanders, 74–76.
21. Segev, 8.
22. Wasserstein, 208.
23. Samuel, 142.
24. Letter from McMahon to Sharif of Mecca, Oct. 24, 1915, in Lesch, 79–80.
25. Quoted in Krämer, 141.
26. Quoted in Fromkin, 185.
27. Sanders, 118.
28. Jason Tomes, *Balfour and Foreign Policy: The International Thought of a Conservative Statesman* (Cambridge: Cambridge University Press, 1997), 201.
29. Segev, 38.
30. Schneer, 344.

31. Harry Defries, *Conservative Party Attitudes Toward Jews 1900–1950* (London: Routledge, 2001), 28.

32. Tomes, 201.

33. Sanders, 90.

34. Quoted in Friedman, 126.

35. Margaret MacMillan, *Paris 1919: Six Months that Changed the World* (New York: Random House, 2003), 420.

36. Segev, 110.

37. Ibid., 95.

38. Friedman, 288.

39. *Palestine*, vol. I, 99.

40. Ibid., 251.

41. Ibid.

42. Leonard Stein, *The Balfour Declaration* (New York: Simon & Schuster, 1961), 545–46.

43. Doreen Ingrams, ed., *Palestine Papers: 1917–1922* (London: Eland Books, 2010), 16 (collection of documents from the British archives).

44. See memorandum of discussion Balfour had with Brandeis and Frankfurter, June 24, 1919. E. L. Woodward and Rohan Butler, eds., *Documents on British Foreign Policy: 1919–1939* (London: H.M. Stationery Office, 1947), 1276–78.

45. Friedman, 265.

46. Laqueur, 196.

47. Weizmann, 260.

48. Ingrams, 13.

49. Quoted in Avishai, 105.

50. Ingrams, 19.

51. Quoted in Porath, 35.

52. Ingrams, 74.

4. HERBERT SAMUEL AND THE BRITISH MANDATE

1. MacMillan, 424; Ingrams, 73.

2. See Judis.

3. Ingrams, 61.

4. Ibid., 53.

5. Ibid., 96.

6. Ibid., 24.

7. David Ben-Gurion, *My Talks with Arab Leaders* (Jerusalem: Keter Books, 1972), 6.

8. Ingrams, 25.

9. The proposal from the conference, written in English and Hebrew, is included in the appendix of Neil Caplan, *Palestine Jewry and the Arab Question, 1917–1925* (New York: Frank Cass & Co., 1978).

10. Caplan, 25.

11. Ibid., 28.

12. Ibid., 29.

13. Ingrams, 66.

14. Ibid., 68.

15. Quoted in *Palestine*, vol. I, 163.

16. Lesch, 205.

17. Ingrams, 47.

18. Segev, 106.

19. Walter Francis Stirling, *Safety Last* (London: Hollis & Carter, 1953), 115.

20. Ingrams, 67–68.

21. Ingrams, 81.

22. Ibid., 138.

23. See Khalidi, *Palestinian Identity*, 166.

24. George Antonius, *The Arab Awakening: The Story of the Arab National Movement* (London: Hamish Hamilton, 1938), 352.

25. In Lesch, 87–88.

26. Krämer, 209.

27. Philip Mattar, *The Mufti of Jerusalem* (New York: Columbia University Press, 1988), 15.

28. Ingrams, 89.

29. Lesch, 70.

30. Khalidi, *Palestinian Identity*, 170.

31. Ibid., 173.

32. Bernard Wasserstein, *The British in Palestine: The Mandatory Government and the Arab-Jewish Conflict, 1917–1929* (Oxford: Basil Blackwell, 1978), 65; Segev, 137.

33. Segev, 143.

34. Caplan, 66.

35. Wasserstein, *The British in Palestine*, 87–88.

36. *Palestine*, vol. I, 261.

37. *Palestine*, vol. I, 149.

38. Zangwill summarizes his article in Israel Zangwill, *The Voice of Jerusalem* (London: Kessinger Publishing, 1921), 105–106.

39. Caplan, 28.

40. Wasserstein, *Herbert Samuel*, 240.

41. Samuel, 168.

42. Wasserstein, *Herbert Samuel*, 255.

43. Ibid., 255.

44. Statement included in Aaron S. Klieman, ed., *The Rise of Israel: Great Britain and Palestine, 1920–1925* (New York: Garland Publishing, 1987), 239ff.

45. In a magazine interview in 1920, Churchill had said, "If as may happen, there should be created in our own lifetime by the banks of the Jordan a Jewish State under the protection of the British Crown which might comprise three or four millions of Jews, an event will have occurred in the history of the world which

would from every point of view be beneficial and would be especially in harmony with the truest interests of the British Empire." *Palestine*, vol. I, 266.

46. Ingrams, 119.
47. Caplan, 83.
48. Ingrams, 123.
49. State Department Records, The National Archives at College Park, MD, 353, roll 79.
50. Ibid.
51. Segev, 179.
52. Ingrams, 128.
53. Klieman, 261.
54. *Palestine*, vol. I, 282–83.
55. www.mideastweb.org/Middle-East-Encyclopedia/muhammad_rashid_rida .htm.
56. Wasserstein, *Herbert Samuel*, 257.
57. Wasserstein, *British in Palestine*, 116.
58. Segev, 190.
59. Caplan, 89.
60. Caplan, 91.
61. Caplan, 97.
62. Wasserstein, *Herbert Samuel*, 268.
63. Segev, 187.
64. Ingrams, 123.
65. C. R. Ashbee, *A Palestinian Notebook 1918–1923* (New York: Doubleday, Page & Co., 1923), 267.
66. www.jewishvirtuallibrary.org/jsource/History/haycraft.html.
67. Ingrams, 146 (memo from John Shuckburgh, Assistant Secretary for Colonies in Charge of the Middle East, Nov. 7, 1921). The conversation is also recounted in Richard Minertzhagen, *Middle East Diary 1917–1956* (London: Cresset Press, 1960), 103–6. The meeting is described in Segev, 194–95.
68. John Quigley, *The Case for Palestine: An International Law Perspective* (Durham, NC: Duke University Press, 2005), 18.
69. *Ha'aretz*, July 15, 1923.

5. THE FAILURE OF THE "DOUBLE UNDERTAKING"

1. *Palestine*, vol. I, 416.
2. Shapira, 120–33.
3. Quoted in Avishai, 106.
4. Quoted in Sternhell, 105.
5. Sachar, 181.
6. Shapira, 165.
7. Ibid., 170.
8. *The Maccabean*, June 1920. State Department Records, 353, roll 79.

9. Laqueur, 344.

10. Eran Kaplan, *The Jewish Radical Right: Revisionist Zionism and Its Ideological Legacy* (Madison, WI: University of Wisconsin Press, 2005), 14.

11. Published in Russian in *Razsvyet*, Nov. 4, 1923, translation by Jabotinsky Institute.

12. Ibid.

13. Shapira, 198.

14. Jabotinsky, "The Ethics of the Iron Wall," *Razsviet*, Nov. 11, 1923. Translation by Jabotinsky Institute (with minor grammatical revisions).

15. Kaplan, Chapter 1.

16. Ibid., 20.

17. Rashid Khalidi emphasizes this point in *The Iron Cage: The Story of the Palestinian Struggle for Statehood* (Boston: Beacon Press, 2006).

18. Lesch, 97.

19. State Department Records, roll 83.

20. Ibid.

21. Mattar, 38, 45.

22. State Department Records, roll 83, report of consulate in Jerusalem.

23. Teveth, 173.

24. Ibid., 93–96.

25. Judah Magnes, "Like all the Nations," pamphlet, in Hertzberg.

26. *The New York Times*, Nov. 24, 1929.

27. Magnes.

28. Naomi Shepherd, *Ploughing Sand: British Rule in Palestine, 1917–1948* (New Brunswick, NJ: Rutgers University Press, 2000), 179.

29. Segev, 332.

30. Shaw Report. See *Palestine*, vol II, 621ff.

31. Ibid., 629.

32. Ibid., 637.

33. All citations from white paper are from www.jewishvirtuallibrary.org/jsource/History/passfield.html.

34. Ibid., 128.

35. *Palestine*, vol. II, 648.

36. Ibid.

37. Brandeis Papers, Library of Congress, reel 90.

38. Ibid., 651.

39. Ibid., 651–52.

40. On the role of Laski, Bevin, and the Whitechapel election, see Kingsley Martin, *Harold Laski (1893–1950): A Biographical Memoir* (New York: Viking Press, 1953), 208–10, and Alan Bullock, *The Life and Times of Ernest Bevin* (London: Heinemann, 1967), 455–57.

41. *Palestine*, vol. II, 657–59.

42. Ibid., 659.

43. See Porath, *The Palestinian Arab National Movement: From Riots to Rebellion, 1929–1939* (London: Frank Cass, 1974), 102.
44. Lesch, 104.

6. THE IRREPRESSIBLE CONFLICT

1. Quoted in Lucy S. Dawidowicz, *The War Against the Jews, 1933–1945* (New York: Bantam Books, 1975), 11.
2. Aristide Zolberg, *A Nation by Design: Immigration Policy in the Fashioning of America* (Cambridge: Harvard University Press, 2006), 273.
3. Sachar, 198.
4. Kimmerling and Migdal, 105.
5. Porath, 125.
6. Khalidi, *The Iron Cage.*
7. In 1933, Rashid Rida wrote, "Whoever sells a piece of Palestinian soil and its surroundings to the Jews or the English acts like someone who sells them the Aqsa Mosque and the homeland at large." Krämer, 251.
8. Kimmerling and Migdal, 62.
9. Krämer, 262.
10. Shapira, 214.
11. Tom Segev, *The Seventh Million: The Israelis and the Holocaust* (New York: Picador, 2000), 23.
12. Teveth, 124.
13. Ibid.
14. Teveth, 153.
15. Teveth, 157.
16. Ben-Gurion, 15. Similar account in Teveth and in Sir Geoffrey Furlonge, *Palestine Is My Country: The Story of Musa Alami* (London: John Murray Publishers, 1969), 102–105.
17. Teveth, 155.
18. Simha Flapan, *Zionism and the Palestinians* (London: Croom Helm, 1979), 143.
19. Shepherd, 186.
20. Quotations from Peel Commission Report, http://domino.un.org/unispal.nsf/0 /08e38a718201458b052565700072b358?OpenDocument.
21. Ibid.
22. Ibid.
23. *Palestine*, vol. II, 817.
24. Antonius, 411.
25. Benny Morris, *Righteous Victims: A History of the Zionist-Arab Conflict, 1881–2001* (New York: Vintage, 2001), 143.
26. *Palestine*, vol. II, 854.
27. Flapan, 242.

28. Quoted in Benny Morris, *The Birth of the Palestine Refugee Problem Revisited* (Cambridge: Cambridge University Press, 2004), 47. Morris's book is the authoritative source on the subject of transfer.

29. Morris, *The Birth Revisited*, 48.

30. Wise Papers, Center for Jewish History, New York, NY, box 100.

31. See report of the American delegation on Ben-Gurion's plea to them in Brandeis Papers.

32. Mattar, 73.

33. Teveth, 151.

34. Teveth, 166.

35. Segev, *One Palestine*, 367.

36. Teveth, 165.

37. Flapan, 141.

38. See Segev, *One Palestine*, 414.

39. Khalidi, *The Iron Cage*, 107.

40. Ibid., 109.

41. Cohen, "Appeasement in the Middle East: The British White Paper on Palestine, May 1939," *Historical Journal* 16, no. 3 (Sept. 1973), 572.

42. Cohen, "British Strategy and the Palestine Question 1936–1939," *Journal of Contemporary History* 7, nos. 3/4 (July–Oct., 1972), 168.

43. Segev, *One Palestine*, 436.

44. Gabriel Sheffer, "Appeasement and the Problem of Palestine," *International Journal of Middle East Studies* 11, no. 3 (May 1980), 391.

45. Segev, *One Palestine*, 440.

46. *Palestine*, vol. II, 909–10.

47. *Palestine*, vol. II, 908.

48. Khalidi, *The Iron Cage*, 116.

49. Cohen, "British Strategy," 182.

50. Charles L. Geddes, ed., *A Documentary History of the Arab-Israeli Conflict* (New York: Praeger, 1991), 188.

51. Ibid.

52. Ilan Pappe, *The Rise & Fall of a Palestinian Dynasty: The Husaynis, 1700–1948* (Berkeley: University of California Press, 2010), 148.

53. Kimmerling and Migdal, 60.

54. Ibid., 131.

55. Sachar, 230; Krämer, 240.

56. Krämer, 294.

57. Ibid., 299.

58. Shapira, 238.

59. Ibid., 232.

60. Ibid., 232.

61. Ibid., 226.

62. Jabotinsky, "Evidence Submitted to the Palestine Royal Commission," 1937, in Hertzberg, 565.

63. Hannah Arendt, "Anti-Semitism," *The Jewish Writings*, eds. Jerome Kohn and Ron H. Feldman (New York: Schocken Books, 2007), 58, and "Zionism Reconsidered," 343ff.

64. Teveth, 681.

PART II EPIGRAPH

Brandeis Papers, reel 89.

7. THE ORIGINS OF AMERICAN ZIONISM

1. Quoted in Michael B. Oren, *Power, Faith and Fantasy: America in the Middle East 1776 to the Present* (New York: Norton, 2007), 143.

2. Melvin I. Urofsky, *American Zionism from Herzl to the Holocaust* (Lincoln: University of Nebraska Press, 1975), 46.

3. Jonathan D. Sarna, *American Judaism: A History* (New Haven, CT: Yale University Press, 2004), 202.

4. Hertzberg, *The Jews in America: Four Centuries of an Uneasy Encounter* (New York: Columbia University Press, 1989), 229.

5. Nathan Glazer, *American Judaism* (Chicago: University of Chicago Press, 1972), 82.

6. Ibid., 85.

7. Ibid., 120.

8. Stephen Wise, *Challenging Years: The Autobiography of Stephen Wise* (New York: Putnam & Sons, 1949), 10.

9. Hertzberg, *The Jews in America*, 187.

10. Sarna, 149.

11. The text of the Pittsburgh platform is available at www.jewishvirtuallibrary.org /jsource/Judaism/pittsburgh_program.html.

12. Naomi Cohen, *The Americanization of Zionism, 1897–1948* (Waltham, MA: Brandeis University Press, 2003), 42.

13. Ibid., 44.

14. Wise, 9.

15. Urofsky, 97.

16. From *Servant of the People: Selected Letters of Stephen S. Wise*, ed. Carl Hermann Voss (Philadelphia: Jewish Publication Society of America, 1969). Letter to Otto Wise, March 15, 1904: "I am an ultra-liberal."

17. See Urofsky, *A Voice that Spoke for Justice: The Life and Times of Stephen S. Wise* (Albany: State University of New York, 1982), 8–9.

18. Letter to Mrs. Walter Rauschenbusch, Jan. 16, 1928.

19. Letter to Maximilian Heller, Dec. 4, 1899.

20. Glazer, 55.

21. Wise Papers, box 1.

22. Glazer, 50.

23. Cohen, *Americanization of Zionism*, 18.

24. Ibid.

25. Urofsky, *American Zionism*, 128.

26. Mark Twain, *Innocents Abroad* (New York: Harper & Brothers, 1911), 261.

27. Kathleen Christison, *Perceptions of Palestine: Their Influence on U.S. Middle East Policy* (Berkeley: University of California Press, 2001), 21.

28. Rafael Medoff, *Zionism and the Arabs: An American Jewish Dilemma, 1898–1948* (Westport, CT: Praeger, 1997), 11.

29. *The Maccabean*, July 1902.

30. Medoff, 10.

31. See discussion here and demographer Justin McCarthy's figure on Arabs for 1893 (553,000) and 1912–14 (738,000) and on Jews (2 percent in 1893 and 6 percent in 1912) at www.mideastweb.org/palpop.htm.

32. Medoff, 10.

33. Medoff, 17.

34. Leah Asher, "What Has Zionism Accomplished?" *The Maccabean*, Jan. 1903.

35. Urofsky, 104.

36. Evyatar Friesel, "Brandeis' Role in American Zionism Historically Reconsidered," *American Jewish History*, Sept. 1979, 92–124.

37. Urofsky, 107.

38. Friesel.

39. Ibid.

8. ZIONISM AND AMERICAN LIBERALISM: BRANDEIS AND HIS CIRCLE

1. Urofsky, *Louis D. Brandeis: A Life* (New York: Schocken Books, 2009), 19.

2. Ibid., 31.

3. Emanuel Neumann, *In the Arena: An Autobiographical Memoir* (New York: Herzl Press, 1976), 33.

4. Ben Halpern, *A Clash of Heroes: Brandeis, Weizmann, and American Zionism* (New York: Oxford University Press, 1987), 96.

5. Brandeis Papers, a draft for a speech, "Zionism and Patriotism." Brandeis crossed out the paragraph about the importance of the strike to him, partly, I suppose, because it wouldn't have been important to his listeners.

6. Urofsky, *Brandeis*, 399.

7. Alton Gal, "In Search of a New Zion," *American Jewish History*, Sept. 1978.

8. *Brandeis on Zionism* (Washington, D.C.: Zionist Organization of America, 1942), 40.

9. Urofsky, *American Zionism*, 128.

10. Ibid., 28.

11. *Brandeis on Zionism*, 132.

12. Louis D. Brandeis, "The Jewish Problem and How to Solve It," at www.law.louisville.edu/librabry/collections/brandeis/node/234.

13. Urofsky, *Brandeis*, 153.

14. Goldmann, 208.
15. Urofsky, *Brandeis*, 730.
16. Irving Howe, *World of Our Fathers* (New York: Schocken Books, 1989), 208.
17. Brandeis.
18. Ibid.
19. Horace Kallen, "Democracy Versus the Melting Pot," *The Nation*, Feb. 25, 1915.
20. Brandeis.
21. Ibid.
22. Ibid.
23. Ibid.
24. Ingrams, 72.
25. *The Papers of Woodrow Wilson*, vol. 59, ed. Arthur Stanley Link (Princeton: Princeton University Press, 1988), 609.
26. State Department Records.
27. *Letters of Louis D. Brandeis, 1916–1921*, eds. Urofsky and David Levy (Albany: State University of New York Press, 1975), 495.
28. Brandeis Papers, reel 89.
29. Medoff, 79.
30. Peter Grose, *Israel in the Mind of America* (New York: Schocken Books, 1984), 81.
31. *Brandeis on Zionism*, 147–48.
32. Ibid., 152–53.
33. Brandeis Papers, reel 89.
34. Ibid.
35. Medoff, Chapter Six.
36. Brandeis Papers, reel 91.
37. *Letters of Louis D. Brandeis*, vol. 5, 603.
38. Medoff, 85.
39. Ibid., 39.
40. Ibid., 52.
41. Urofsky, *American Zionism*, 139.
42. State Department Records, 353, Reel 79.
43. Felix Frankfurter, "The Palestine Situation Restated," *Foreign Affairs*, April 1931.
44. Ibid.
45. *Servant of the People*, 60.
46. Henry S. Pritchett, "Observations in Egypt, Palestine, and Greece," *International Conciliation*, November 1926.
47. *The New York Times*, Nov. 30, 1926.
48. Wise, Introduction to Wise and Jacob de Haas, *The Great Betrayal* (New York: Brentano's, 1930), xvii, xix, xx.
49. Medoff, 65.
50. Wise Papers, box 102. See also Medoff, *Militant Zionism in America: The Rise and Impact of the Jabotinsky Movement in the United States, 1926–1948* (Tuscaloosa: University of Alabama Press, 2002), 18.

51. Medoff, *Militant Zionism*, 21.
52. Medoff, *Zionism and the Arabs*, 73.
53. Ibid., 81.
54. Ibid., 44.
55. Ibid., 61.
56. Ibid., 80.
57. Ibid., 59.
58. Neumann, 70.
59. Ibid., 4.
60. Brandeis Papers, reel 89.
61. Quoted in Richard Slotkin, *Gunfighter Nation: The Myth of the Frontier in Twentieth-Century America* (New York: Atheneum, 1992), 48.
62. Urofsky, *Brandeis*, 731–32.
63. Jewish Telegraphic Agency, Dec. 13, 1929. The speech is reprinted in *Brandeis on Zionism*, but the passage on the Indians is not included.
64. John Haynes Holmes, *Palestine Today and Tomorrow: A Gentile's Survey of Zionism* (New York: Macmillan, 1930), 89, 248.

9. ABBA HILLEL SILVER AND THE ZIONIST LOBBY

1. Marc Lee Raphael, *Abba Hillel Silver: A Profile in American Judaism* (New York: Holmes & Meier, 1989), 113.
2. Michael Meyer, "Abba Hillel Silver as Zionist Within the Camp of Reform Judaism," in *Abba Hillel Silver and American Zionism*, eds. Mark Raider, Jonathan D. Sarna, and Ronald W. Zweig (London: Frank Cass Publishers, 1977).
3. Raphael, 20–21.
4. Leon Feuer, "Abba Hillel Silver: A Personal Memoir," *American Jewish Archives*, Nov. 1967.
5. On Wise: Urofsky, *American Zionism*, 126. On Silver: Raphael, 20.
6. Neumann, *Abba Hillel Silver: Militant Zionist* (New York: B'rith Rishonim of U.S., 1967), 6.
7. Quoted in Meyer, 14.
8. *Servant of the People*, 79.
9. Mark A. Raider, "Where American Zionism Differed: Abba Hillel Silver Reconsidered," in *Abba Hillel Silver and American Zionism*, 87.
10. Meyer, 15.
11. Abba Hillel Silver, *Therefore Choose Life: Selected Sermons, Addresses, and Writings*, vol. I (Cleveland: World Publishing Co., 1967), 216.
12. Meyer, 19–20.
13. Silver, 217.
14. Ibid., 218.
15. Hans Diner, "Zion and America: The Formative Visions of Abba Hillel Silver," in *Abba Hillel Silver and American Zionism*, 68. JTA, Sept. 9, 1927.
16. Medoff, *Zionism and the Arabs*, 71.

17. Raphael, 73.
18. Aaron Berman, "American Zionism and the Rescue of European Jewry: An Ideological Perspective," *American Jewish History*, March 1981.
19. Silver, 420.
20. Ibid., 426.
21. Silver, "Toward American Jewish Unity," in Hertzberg, *The Zionist Idea*, 598.
22. JTA, May 14, 1933.
23. JTA, Jan. 7, 1934.
24. JTA, Aug. 26, 1935.
25. Raider, 99.
26. Medoff, 96.
27. *Refugees and Rescue: The Diaries and Papers of James G. McDonald 1935–1945*, ed., Richard Breitman, Barbara McDonald Stewart, and Severin Hochberg (Bloomington, IN: Indiana University Press, 2009), 176.
28. Neumann, *In the Arena*, 147.
29. Urofsky, *American Zionism*, 426.
30. Ibid.
31. Raider, 110.
32. Urofsky, *American Zionism*, 426.
33. Urofsky, *American Zionism*, 427.
34. Raphael, 81.
35. Feuer, 109.
36. Goldmann, 227.
37. Urofsky, *A Voice*, 338.
38. Ibid., 339.
39. Neumann, *In the Arena*, 192.
40. From Silver, "Toward American Jewish Unity," in Hertzberg, *The Zionist Idea*, 592–600.
41. Raphael, 89.
42. Ibid.
43. Silver, "Toward American Jewish Unity," 592–600.
44. Silver Papers, reel 102.
45. Irwin Oder, "American Zionism and the Resolution of 1922 on Palestine," *American Jewish Historical Society*, 1956.
46. State Department Files, roll 83.
47. On this subject, see Lawrence Davidson, *America's Palestine: Popular and Official Perceptions from Balfour to Israeli Statehood* (Gainesville, FL: University Press of Florida, 2001). I have also read the State Department and consular records from this period and from 1936–37, and apart from some ranting about Jewish Bolshevism from one junior official in Jerusalem, I could find no evidence of anti-Semitism.
48. On the chronology, see Cohen, *Americanization of Zionism*, 144ff.
49. *FRUS*, 1936, vol. III, 444.
50. Davidson, 124.

51. Silver Papers, reel 102.
52. Ibid., reel 103.
53. Numbers from Doreen Bierbrier, "The American Zionist Emergency Council: An Analysis of a Pressure Group," *American Jewish Historical Quarterly*, Sept. 1970.
54. Silver Papers, reel 102.
55. Ibid.
56. Zvi Ganin, "The Silver-Wise Conflict in the 1940s," *Studies in Zionism* 5, no. 1.
57. Grose, 145.
58. Raphael, 129.
59. Ibid., 128.
60. Ganin.
61. Raphael, 128.
62. Ibid., 120.
63. Ibid., 122.
64. Silver Papers, reel 103.
65. Silver Papers, reel 104 (*The Day*, Dec. 31, 1944).
66. Urofsky, *A Voice*, 346.
67. Ibid., 228.
68. Ganin.

PART III EPIGRAPH

Brian Urquhart, *Ralph Bunche: An American Life* (New York: W. W. Norton & Company, 1993), 146.

10. HARRY TRUMAN AND THE $64 QUESTION

1. Segev, *The Seventh Million*, 97.
2. W. K. Hancock and M. M. Gowing, *British War Economy* (London: H.M. Stationery Office, 1949), Chapter XIX.
3. Kimmerling and Migdal, 138.
4. Segev, *One Palestine*, 84. Morris, *1948: A History of the First Arab-Israeli War* (New Haven, CT: Yale University Press, 2008), 29, estimates "over 26,000."
5. Dan Tschirgi, *The Politics of Indecision: Origins and Implications of American Involvement with the Palestine Problem* (New York: Praeger, 1983), 154.
6. A. Sargent, *The British Labour Party and Palestine, 1917–1949* (Ph.D. thesis, University of Nottingham, 1980), 26.
7. Bartley C. Crum, *Behind the Silken Curtain* (New York: Simon & Schuster, 1947), 51.
8. David McCullough, *Truman* (New York: Simon & Schuster, 1992), 448.
9. Bullock, *Ernest Bevin: Foreign Secretary, 1945–1951* (New York: W. W. Norton & Co., 1983), 167.
10. Amikam Nachmani, *Great Power Discord in Palestine: The Anglo-American*

Committee of Inquiry into the Problems of European Jewry and Palestine 1945–46 (London: Routledge, 1987), 144.

11. Bullock, *Ernest Bevin*, 168.

12. Ritchie Ovendale, *British Defence Policy Since 1945* (Manchester: Manchester University Press, 1994), 20–21.

13. *FRUS*, 1944, vol. V, 616; *FRUS*, 1945, vol. VIII, 2.

14. For biographers and historians who suggest that Truman was a Christian Zionist, see Benson; Sacher, 255; and Michael Beschloss, "Truman and the Birth of Israel," *Presidential Courage: Brave Leaders and How They Changed America, 1789–1989* (New York: Simon & Schuster, 2007). Also, Truman contributed to the legend in his later interview with Merle Miller, recounted in Miller's *Plain Speaking: An Oral Biography of Harry S. Truman* (New York: Black Dog & Leventhal Publishers, 1973), 213–15. My own view of Truman is probably closest to that of Zvi Ganin in *Truman, American Jewry, and Israel, 1945–1958* (New York: Holmes & Meyer Publishing, 1979) and Michael Cohen in *Truman and Israel*, and to that of the superb biographer Alonzo L. Hamby in *Man of the People: A Life of Harry Truman* (New York: Oxford University Press, 1995). On the progress of Truman's policy toward Palestine and Zionism, Allis Radosh and Ronald Radosh, *A Safe Haven: Harry S. Truman and the Founding of Israel* (New York: Harper Perennial, 2009), is the latest and most complete blow-by-blow account of what happened.

15. Hamby, 474.

16. Truman Papers.

17. Truman Papers.

18. Cohen, *Truman and Israel*, 7.

19. Ibid., 8, 9.

20. Truman Papers.

21. Hamby, 30.

22. Tschirgi, 145.

23. Urofsky, *American Zionism*, 396.

24. Dean Acheson, *Present at the Creation: My Years in the State Department* (New York: W. W. Norton & Co., 1969), 169.

25. Cohen, *Truman and Israel*, 36–37.

26. Ibid., 46.

27. Ganin, *Truman, American Jewry, and Israel*, xiii.

28. Mitchell Bard, *The Water's Edge and Beyond: Defining the Limit of Domestic Influence on U.S. Middle East Policy* (New Brunswick, NJ: Transaction Publishers, 1991), 141.

29. Sachar, 592.

30. Feuer, 123.

31. Ganin, 37.

32. See Sonja Schoepf Wentling and Medoff, *Herbert Hoover and the Jews: The Origins of the "Jewish Vote" and Bipartisan Support for Israel* (Washington, D.C.: Create Space Independent Publishing Platform, 2012), 145.

33. Chaim Simons, *A Historical Survey of Proposals to Transfer Arabs from Palestine, 1895–1947*, 2004 at www.preterhuman.net/texts/unsorted/arabtransfer.rtf.

34. Besides his papers, which are limited because he preferred the telephone, the best source on Niles may be the extensive notes that the writer Alfred Steinberg kept for a profile of Niles he produced for *The Saturday Evening Post* in 1949. Niles seems to have cooperated with Steinberg. These notes are in Niles's file at the Truman Library. The only longer profile of Niles is an extraordinary honors thesis on Niles, "David K. Niles and the United States Policy Toward Palestine," by then Harvard undergraduate David B. Sachar that was submitted in March 1959.

35. Oscar Ewing Oral History, Truman Library (online).

36. Oder.

37. Peter L. Hahn, *Caught in the Middle East: U.S. Policy Toward the Arab-Israeli Conflict, 1945–1961* (Chapel Hill, NC: University of North Carolina Press, 2004), 21–22.

38. *FRUS*, 1945, vol. VIII, 695.

39. Clark Clifford, whose memoirs ring with self-justification and vilification of his foes, writes, "I had no firsthand evidence of it, but I know Henderson was among a group of Mideast experts in the State Department who were widely regarded as anti-Semitic." See Clark Clifford, *Counsel to the President: A Memoir* (New York: Random House, 1991), 4. For a contrary view, see the extensive study of Henderson and his beliefs by Allen H. Podet, "Anti-Zionism in a U.S. Official," that appeared in *American Jewish Archives*, Nov. 1978. Podet, who is critical of Henderson as a foe of Zionism, rejects the view that he was an anti-Semite. "Anti-Semitism is not supported by the evidence," he concludes.

40. Harry S. Truman, *Memoirs*, vol. I (New York: Signet, 1955), 84. Truman's memoirs are useful for their account of conversations based on diaries or minutes and for learning how Truman viewed his actions toward Palestine and Israel *after* his presidency and after he decided to recognize the new state, but Truman tends to downplay his own confusion and indecision during the first years of his administration.

41. Ganin, *Truman, American Jewry, and Israel*, 30.

42. JTA, May 10, 1945.

43. JTA, August 3, 1945.

44. Truman Papers.

45. *FRUS*, 1945, vol. I, 973.

46. See Evan M. Wilson, *A Calculated Risk: The U.S. Decision to Recognize Israel* (Cincinnati: Clerisy Press, 2008), 131. Wilson was an NEA official during the Truman years.

47. Truman Papers.

48. Truman Papers (online).

49. *FRUS*, 1945, vol. VIII, 742.

50. JTA, August 22, 1945.

51. *Political Documents of the Jewish Agency: May 1945–December 1946* (hereafter, *PDJA: '45–'46*), 73.

52. Radosh and Radosh, 92.
53. Truman Papers.
54. Truman Papers.
55. *FRUS*, 1945, vol. VIII, 747.
56. Ibid., 739.
57. Ibid., 741.
58. Raphael, 138.
59. Silver Papers.
60. Margaret Truman, *Harry S. Truman* (New York: William Morrow & Co., 1973), 299.
61. Silver Papers.
62. Ganin, 40, 197.
63. On this point, see Nachmani, Chapter Two.
64. Victoria Honeyman, "Britain, Palestine, and the Creation of Israel," POLIS Working Papers from the Institute for Public Policy and Public Choice, 2011–12.
65. Truman Papers (Rosenman file).
66. Truman Papers.
67. JTA, November 19, 1945.
68. Ganin, *Truman, American Jewry, and Israel*, 55–56.
69. See *FRUS*, 1945, vol. 1, 16, 18. I have put some of the statements in quotes because, according to Henderson, the record was verbatim. The statement about "hundreds of thousands" comes from William A. Eddy, *FDR Meets Ibn Saud* (New York: American Friends of the Middle East, 1954), 36–37. Eddy was a participant in the meeting.
70. Truman Papers (online).
71. JTA, December 5, 1945. Stern was actually close to the Revisionists, which made his report of Truman's position more credible, since it did not mirror his own.
72. *PDJA: '45–'46*, 225–26.

11. THE SEARCH FOR AN ANGLO-AMERICAN CONSENSUS

1. The list can be found in Truman's Secretary Papers, Truman Library.
2. I. F. Stone, "Zionists Tell Committee Their Story," *PM*, Jan. 9, 1946. From the Wise Papers.
3. Nachmani, 141–42.
4. Richard Crossman, *Palestine Mission: A Personal Record* (New York: Harper & Brothers, 1947), 33.
5. Crum, 21–22.
6. Quoted in Nachmani, 123.
7. See Nachmani, 164–65.
8. Ibid., 165.
9. JTA, March 11, 1946.
10. Nachmani, 191.
11. Ibid.

12. *JTA*, Sept. 3, 1942.
13. *Dissenter in Zion: From the Writings of Judah L. Magnes*, ed. Arthur A. Goren (Cambridge, MA: Harvard University Press, 1982), 46.
14. Testimony, March 14, 1946, Magnes Papers.
15. Nachmani, 171.
16. Ibid.
17. Testimony.
18. Wilson, 166.
19. *PDJA: '45-'46*, 315.
20. Walid Khalidi, "On Albert Hourani, the Arab Office, and the Anglo-American Committee of 1946," *Journal of Palestine Studies*, Autumn 2005.
21. Quoted in Issa Khalaf, *Politics in Palestine: Arab Factionalism and Social Disintegration, 1939–1948* (Albany: State University of New York Press, 1991), 118.
22. Wilson, 172.
23. JTA, March 25, 1946.
24. Nachmani, 168.
25. Ibid.
26. Ibid., 169.
27. Flapan, *The Birth of Israel: Myths and Realities* (New York: Pantheon Books, 1987), 67.
28. Radosh and Radosh, 141.
29. Nachmani, 189–91.
30. http://avalon.law.yale.edu/twentieth_century/angch01.asp.
31. *PDJA: '45-'46*, 1946, 370. The diary entry was originally supposed to be a letter to Silver and Wise, but Ben-Gurion decided not to send it.
32. Ibid., 371.
33. Nachmani, 210.
34. *PDJA: '45-'46*, 1946, 376–77.
35. Silver Papers.
36. Truman Library, Niles Papers.
37. Truman Library.
38. Francis Williams, *Ernest Bevin: Portrait of a Great Englishman* (London: Hutchinson, 1952), 260.
39. Tschirgi, 178.
40. JTA, May 18, 1946.
41. Wise Papers.
42. JTA, June 13, 1946.
43. *Opinion*, April 1945.
44. JTA, July 13, 1946.
45. Quoted in Raphael, 144.
46. Sachar, 265.
47. *FRUS*, 1946, vol. VII, 80.
48. Henry A. Wallace, *The Price of Vision: The Diary of Henry A. Wallace, 1942–1946* (Boston: Houghton Mifflin, 1973), 604.

49. Acheson, 175.
50. JTA, July 28, 1946.
51. Wise Papers.
52. Robert J. Donovan, *Conflict and Crisis: The Presidency of Harry S. Truman, 1945–1948* (New York: W. W. Norton & Co., 1977), 319.
53. Truman Library, Clifford Papers.
54. Cohen, 134.
55. Ibid.
56. McDonald Papers, Columbia University.
57. Truman Library, Clifford Papers.
58. Wallace, 606–607.
59. *FRUS*, 1946, vol. VII, 673–74.
60. James Forrestal, *The Forrestal Diaries* (New York: Viking, 1951), 347.
61. Ganin, *Truman, American Jewry, and Israel*, 92. Hutcheson also objected to the report's support for autonomous provinces, not because it didn't go far enough but because it went too far toward encouraging separate states. Crum and Niles convinced him, however, to confine his objections to other differences between the Morrison-Grady plan and the committee's report. See *PDJA, '45–'46*, 514.

12. NAHUM GOLDMANN AND THE ROAD TO PARTITION

1. Raphael Patai, *Nahum Goldmann: His Mission to the Gentiles* (Tuscaloosa: University of Alabama Press, 1987), 96. Goldmann himself wrote two excellent autobiographies and left current accounts of his conversations that are in his papers, but there are considerable inconsistencies in detail among these different accounts, particularly in Goldmann's accounts of his fractious relations with Silver, but in this case on the question of whether Niles called Goldmann or whether Epstein relayed his message. Patai, who had Goldmann's cooperation but was not under his supervision, does an excellent job in adjudicating among the conflicting accounts.
2. Goldmann, 12.
3. *Nahum Goldmann: Statesman Without a State*, ed. Mark A. Raider (Albany: State University of New York Press, 2009), 44.
4. Patai, 62.
5. *Statesman Without a State*, 39.
6. *PDJA, '45–'46*, vol. VII, 281–83.
7. Raphael, 149.
8. *The New York Times*, July 11, 1946.
9. *The New York Times*, July 12, 1946.
10. Hadassah Papers, Center for Jewish History.
11. Ibid.
12. Ganin, *Truman, American Jewry, and Israel*, 86.
13. *PDJA, '45–'46*, 496.
14. Ibid., 500.

15. Patai, 105.

16. Patai quoting from the minutes of Rabbi Leon Feuer, the AZEC representative in Washington, page 109.

17. *PDJA*, '45–'46, 515. Sources for what happened are Goldmann's report to the Jewish Agency, included in *PDJA*, Acheson's memorandum, which is in the Truman Library, and Goldmann's *Autobiography*, which contains some materials not in his report to the Jewish Agency but alluded to in Acheson's memorandum.

18. Truman Papers.

19. Patai, 113.

20. See Naomi Cohen, *Not Free to Desist: The American Jewish Committee, 1906–1966* (Philadelphia: Jewish Publication Society of America, 1972), 293ff.

21. Goldmann, *The Jewish Paradox* (New York: Grosset & Dunlap, 1978), 35. The version here is a composite of Proskauer's memoirs and letters; Goldmann's books and reports; Patai's and Ganin's accounts, based on interviews with Goldmann; and Cohen's interview with Proskauer. Like my account of the clash with Silver, it is not a definitive version but merely what strikes me as the most plausible account.

22. Ganin, *Truman, American Jewry, and Israel*, 92.

23. Cohen, *Not Free to Desist*, 299.

24. Ganin, *Truman, American Jewry, and Israel*, 93.

25. *PDJA:* '45–'46, 518.

26. Wise wrote in a letter to an old friend that transfer was "beyond where he dared to go but not beyond where we wished to go." Medoff, *Zionism and the Arabs*, 141.

27. *FRUS*, 1946, vol. VII, 681–82.

28. *PDJA:* '45–'46, 593.

29. Ibid., 558.

30. Ibid., 511.

31. Hadassah Papers, Center for Jewish History.

32. *Time*, Oct. 14, 1946.

33. Hadassah Papers.

34. Truman Library, Niles Papers.

35. *PDJA:* '45–'46, 564.

36. Truman Library.

37. Truman Library, Oral Interview with Abraham Feinberg. Also Radosh and Radosh, 189. The only trouble with this anecdote is that there is no record in September or October 1946 on the president's calendar of a meeting with Feinberg. Feinberg might have seen the president on the evening of September 26 during a visit of the executive committee of the Democratic National Committee to the Oval Office. DNC chairman Hannegan had originally introduced Feinberg to Truman and cultivated him as a Democratic supporter.

38. *FRUS*, 1946, vol. VII, 699.

39. Truman Papers.

40. *PDJA:* '45–'46, 677.

41. Ibid., 682.
42. JTA, Oct. 6, 1946.
43. Robert Ferrell, *Harry S. Truman: A Life* (Columbia, MO: University of Missouri Press, 1994), 307.
44. Truman Papers.
45. *FRUS*, 1947, vol. V, 1057.
46. Bullock, 511.
47. Wise Papers.
48. Silver Papers.
49. Patai, 161.
50. *PDJA: '45–'46*, 719.
51. JTA, Oct. 28, 1946.
52. Raphael, 154.
53. JTA, Dec. 24, 1946.
54. See Neumann, *In the Arena*, 232. Other reports had Neumann calling Weizmann a "demagogue" for his attacks on Silver and Neumann.
55. Silver Papers.
56. Wise Papers.
57. Khalaf, 131.
58. J. C. Hurewitz, *The Struggle for Palestine* (New York: Norton, 1950), 171–72.
59. *FRUS*, 1947, vol. V, 1046.
60. *PDJA*, 1947, 147.
61. *FRUS*, 1947, vol. V, 1045.
62. *PDJA*, 1947, 201, 205–209.
63. *PDJA*, 1947, 245.
64. Ferrell, 307.
65. *FRUS*, 1947, vol. V, 1050.

13. PASSING THE BUCK

1. *FRUS*, vol. V, 1049.
2. See Michael Ottolengi, "Harry Truman's Recognition of Israel," *The Historical Journal*, Dec. 2004.
3. FRUS, vol. V, 1049.
4. Ibid., 1051–52.
5. Ibid., 1070.
6. *PDJA*, vol. V, 1104.
7. Silver Papers.
8. See Cohen, *Truman and Israel*, 67.
9. Truman Papers.
10. *PDJA*, 1947, 310.
11. JTA, May 15, 1947.
12. UN Transcript: http://unispal.un.org/UNISPAL.NSF/0/D41260F1132AD6BE0 52566190059E5F0.

13. See Sachar, page 286, for a summary of memo. There is also an analysis of the Soviet action in *PDJA*, 1947, Editorial Note, pages 368–69, which cites a recounting of the events, based on Soviet sources, by Yuri Strizhov, "The USSR and the Establishment of the State of Israel," in *International Affairs*, Dec. 1995.

14. UN Transcript: http://unispal.un.org/UNISPAL.NSF/0/D41260F1132AD6BE0 52566190059E5F0.

15. *PDJA*, 1947, 469.

16. *FRUS*, vol. V, 1089.

17. JTA, May 15, 1947.

18. *PDJA*, 1947, 623.

19. Ibid., 375–76.

20. David Horowitz, *State in the Making* (New York: Knopf, 1953), 158.

21. *FRUS*, vol. V, 1115.

22. Ibid., 1118.

23. Radosh and Radosh, 238.

24. Morris, *1948*, 45.

25. Horowitz, 207.

26. Brian Urquhart, *Ralph Bunche: An American Odyssey* (New York: Norton, 1993), 146.

27. Ibid., 146.

28. Ibid., 140.

29. Wilson, 222.

30. Urquhart, 150.

31. Morris, *1948*, 50.

32. Wise Papers.

33. *PDJA*, 1947, 619.

34. As quoted in *The Day*, Sept. 3, 1947.

35. Horowitz, 213.

36. *PDJA*, 1947, 423.

37. Truman Papers.

38. Ibid. The Wadsworth memo, labeled "Strictly Confidential," is included in Niles Papers at the library.

39. *PDJA*, 1947, 414.

40. Loy Henderson Oral History, Truman Library.

41. *FRUS*, vol. V, 1147.

42. Ibid., 1148.

43. Ibid., 1149.

44. See Henderson.

45. *FRUS*, vol. V, 1151.

46. Ibid., 1156.

47. Ibid., 1158.

48. Bullock, 583.

49. Henderson.

50. Silver Papers.

51. JTA, Oct. 7, 1947.
52. *The Nation*, Jan. 25, 1947.
53. Ibid., May 17, 1947.
54. Ibid.
55. Morris, *1948*, 62.
56. *The Nation*, May 17, 1947.
57. Silver Papers.
58. Radosh and Radosh, "Righteous Among the Editors: When the Left Loved Israel," *World Affairs Journal*, Summer 2008. On Kirchwey, see also Sara Alpern, *Freda Kirchwey: A Woman of the Nation* (Cambridge, MA: Harvard University Press, 1987).
59. Ganin, *Truman, American Jewry, and Israel*, 156.
60. Forrestal, 323.
61. Jacobson Papers, Truman Library.
62. Forrestal, 323.
63. Jacobson Papers, Truman Library.
64. Ganin, *Truman, American Jewry, and Israel*, 75.
65. *PDJA*, 1947, 738.
66. http://avalon.law.yale.edu/twentieth_century/decad164.asp.
67. *FRUS*, vol. V, 1180.
68. Ibid., 1182.
69. *FTA*, Oct. 14, 1947.
70. Truman Papers.
71. *FRUS*, vol. V, 1174.
72. Ibid., 1255.
73. *PDJA*, 1947, 861.
74. Silver Papers.
75. *FRUS*, vol. V, 1267.
76. Weizmann, 458.
77. Margaret Truman, *Sarasota Journal*, Dec. 14, 1972.
78. www.hks.harvard.edu/case/3pt/rowe.html.
79. *FRUS*, vol. V, 1271.
80. Ibid., 1272.
81. Morris, *1948*, 52.
82. *FRUS*, vol. V, 1282.
83. Truman Papers.
84. Morris, *Righteous Victims*, 186.
85. Transcript of UN debate available at http://unispal.un.org/unispal.nsf/udc.htm.
86. Central Zionist Archives.
87. *FRUS*, vol. V, 1284.
88. Forrestal, 346.
89. Truman Papers.
90. Henderson.
91. *PDJA*, Dec. 1947–May 1948, 6.

92. McCullough, 602.
93. Truman Papers.
94. Truman, *Memoirs*, vol. II, 187.
95. Ganin, *Truman, American Jewry, and Israel*, 145.
96. *The Nation*, Dec. 20, 1947.
97. Wilson, 251.
98. Urquhart, 155.
99. Ibid., 154.
100. Truman, *Harry S. Truman*, 385.

14. UNMATCHED INEPTNESS

1. UNISPAL document.
2. *FRUS*, 1947, vol. V, 1293.
3. See Khalaf, Chapter Eight.
4. On Zionist military strategy, see Morris, *1948*.
5. Goldmann, *Jewish Paradox*, 94.
6. *Israel Documents: December 1947–May 1948* (hereinafter, *ID48*), Jerusalem, 1979, companion volume, 18.
7. Green Papers, Hoover Institution.
8. Wilson, 255.
9. Green Papers.
10. *ID48*, 86.
11. *FRUS*, 1948, vol. V, 546–54.
12. Townsend Hoopes and Douglas G. Brinkley, *Driven Patriot: The Life and Times of James Forrestal* (New York: Knopf, 1992), 397.
13. JTA, Feb. 20, 1948.
14. *Department of State Bulletin*, March 7, 1948, 295.
15. *New York Post*, Jan. 16, 1948.
16. Silver Papers. (What is recounted here is based on the AZEC official Abraham Tuvin's report to Eliahu Ben-Horin of what Thackrey told him of the editor's conversation with the president.)
17. Donovan, 371–72.
18. *FRUS*, 1948, vol. V, 593.
19. Ibid., 632.
20. Ibid., 640.
21. Ibid., 645.
22. *ID48*, 448.
23. *FRUS*, 1948, 750.
24. Hahn, 40.
25. Schulson Papers, New York Public Library.
26. Hannah Arendt, "To Save the Jewish Homeland," *Commentary*, May 1948, in *The Jewish Writings*, 389.

27. Medoff, *Jewish Americans and Political Participation: A Reference Handbook*, (Santa Barbara, CA: ABC-CLIO, 2002), 294.

28. Jack Ross, *Rabbi Outcast: Elmer Berger and American Jewish Anti-Zionism* (Washington, D.C.: Potomac Books, 2011), 85.

29. Silver Papers, minutes from March 23, 1948, meeting.

30. Cohen describes these groupings in *Truman and Israel*, Chapter Five.

31. Communications with both men pop up repeatedly in the diaries that Lowenthal kept. See Lowenthal Papers at the University of Minnesota Library, Minneapolis.

32. On Wahl, see John Earl Haynes, Harvey Klehr, and Alexander Vassiliev, *Spies: The Rise and Fall of the KGB in America* (New Haven, CT: Yale University Press, 2009), 207–11.

33. *ID48*, 294–95.

34. Truman Papers, Jacobson File.

35. Truman Papers.

36. Lowenthal Papers.

37. In his later accounts of the administration's policies on Zionism and the recognition of Israel, Clifford insisted that politics played no role in his or the president's deliberations. (See Clifford, "Recognizing Israel," *American Heritage*, April 1977, and *Counsel to the President* or Clifford's oral history at the Truman Library.) But Clifford, like Truman in his memoirs, protests too much on this score. While some historians may have overstated the role of politics in Truman's decision making, there is no question it was there. Clifford's recollections of decision making on Palestine are also self-serving and not entirely trustworthy. In a 1975 interview with the historian Alan Podet, for instance, he denigrated the role of Niles in influencing Truman's policy on Palestine in the course of elevating his own importance. "David Niles was a staff member of the White House functioning in the field of minorities," Clifford told Podet: "He was one of perhaps ten such staff members and was not very important. People on the White House staff might very well have difficulty remembering who he was, or in recalling him at all" (Podet, "Oral History Interview with Clark Clifford," American Jewish Archives). This quotation says much more about Clifford than it does about Niles, and is a warning to be wary of Clifford's recollections.

38. On the origins of the memoranda, see Cohen, *Truman and Israel*, 189. The memos are in the Lowenthal Papers in Minneapolis.

39. Clifford's first memorandum from March 6, 1948 is in *FRUS*, 1948, vol. V, 687–88, and his second from March 8 is in *FRUS*, 1948, vol. V, 690–724.

40. JTA, March 4, 1948, and March 5, 1948.

41. This account is based on Jacobson's recollection of what happened, which he wrote out in a letter to Weizmann's associate Josef Cohn. Truman Papers, Jacobson File. Jacobson's account of his visit accords with Truman's own recollection in *Memoirs*, vol. II, 189.

42. Truman, *Memoirs*, vol. II, 190.

43. Weizmann, 472.
44. *ID48*, companion volume, 109.
45. UNISPAL documents.
46. *FRUS*, 1948, vol. V, 742–43.
47. *ID48*, 476.
48. Silver Papers.
49. *The New York Times*, March 22, 1948.
50. Radosh and Radosh, 307.
51. *The New York Times*, March 21, 1948.
52. Truman, *Harry S. Truman*, 388.
53. McCullough, 611. Clark Clifford, "Recognizing Israel."
54. George Elsey, *An Unplanned Life: A Memoir* (Columbia, MO: University of Missouri Press, 2005), 161.
55. *FRUS*, 1948, vol. V, 750.
56. Hamby, 413.
57. Cohen, *Truman and Israel*, 178.
58. *Time*, April 5, 1948.
59. Truman Papers.
60. Silver Papers.
61. *ID48*, 606.
62. *FRUS*, 1948, vol. V, 832.
63. Ibid., 833.
64. Quoted in *Dissenter in Zion*, 494–97. There were no minutes taken of Magnes's visit with Truman. I am quoting from Magnes's journal, but based on an entry on his visit with Marshall, which corresponds closely with the U.S. government report on his visit, I am assuming that his report is reasonably accurate in this case as well.
65. *FRUS*, 1948, vol. V, 756.
66. *ID48*, companion volume, 22.
67. Morris, *1948*, 121. Much of the war narrative relies on Morris, *Righteous Victims* and *1948*; Mark Tessler, *A History of the Israeli-Palestinian Conflict* (Bloomington: University of Indiana Press, 1994), and *The War for Palestine: Rewriting the History of 1948*, eds. Eugene L. Rogan and Avid Shlaim (Cambridge: Cambridge University Press, 2001). For estimates about refugees, my principal source is Morris, *The Birth Revisited*. Many of the files from Israel's State Archives that Morris used are no longer available to researchers. See Shay Hazkani, "Catastrophic Thinking," *Haaretz*, May 16, 2013.
68. Menachem Begin, *The Revolt: Story of the Irgun* (New York: Steimatzky Agency, Ltd., 1977), 163.
69. Morris, *Righteous Victims*, 209.
70. *ID48*, companion volume, 25.
71. Ibid.
72. *FRUS*, 1948, vol. V, 889.
73. Lowenthal Papers. Lowenthal kept a diary during May 1948 of his White House and Zionist activities.

74. Quoted in Cohen, *Truman and Israel*, 208.
75. *FRUS*, 1948, vol. V, 898.
76. Ibid.
77. *FRUS*, 1948, vol. V, 878.
78. Clifford, *Counsel to the President*, 5.
79. Ibid., 6.
80. Like all the key incidents in the administration's debate over Palestine, the details of what actually happened are shrouded in controversy. You can get a different narrative depending on whose recollections you trust most. My own narrative draws from Marshall's memorandum (*FRUS*, 1948, vol. V, 972–76), Elsey's notes (*FRUS*, 1948, vol. V, 946), Clifford's *Counsel to the President*, Lowenthal's diary entries from his papers, and John Acacia, *Clark Clifford: The Wise Man of Washington* (Lexington: University Press of Kentucky, 2009).
81. Clifford, *Counsel to the President*, 12.
82. Quotations from Marshall Memorandum, 975.
83. Clifford, *Counsel to the President*, 13.
84. Ibid., 15.
85. *FRUS*, 1948, vol. V, 1005 (from Lovett's memorandum of a conversation with Clifford).
86. Lowenthal Papers, Diary for May 13.
87. Ibid., Diary for May 12.
88. Ibid., Diary for May 14.
89. Ibid., Diary for May 15, Lowenthal's report of what Clifford told him, which conforms to what Lovett himself wrote up immediately afterward, takes precedence over Clifford's later insistence that politics and political pressure never entered the discussion.
90. Lowenthal Papers, May 15, 1948.
91. Ibid.
92. Ibid.
93. Cohen, *Truman and Israel*, 222.
94. Truman Papers.

15. TRIUMPH AND CATASTROPHE

1. See Ganin, *Truman, American Jewry, and Israel*; Benson (with a brief afterword); and Radosh and Radosh, *Safe Haven*.
2. *FRUS*, 1948, vol. V, 1037.
3. Lowenthal Papers.
4. Ibid.
5. Shlaim, "Israel and the Arab Coalition in 1948," in *The War for Palestine*, 88–89.
6. Morris, *1948*, 195.
7. *Israel Documents: May–September 1948* (hereinafter, *IDMaySep48*), Jerusalem, 1981, 162. In 1948, Moshe Shertok became Moshe Sharett. Since my narrative ends in 1949, I decided to continue calling him Shertok.

8. *FRUS*, 1948, 994–95.
9. Urquhart, 159.
10. *FRUS*, 1948, vol. V, 1152–54.
11. *IDMaySep48*, 162.
12. John Bagot Glubb, *A Soldier with the Arabs* (London: Hodder & Stoughton, 1957), 149.
13. Urquhart, 168.
14. Morris, *1948*, 290–91.
15. *FRUS*, 1948, vol. V, 1325.
16. See Morris, *1948*, 301–309.
17. *IDMaySept48*, 364.
18. Ibid., 374.
19. Silver Papers.
20. *Palestine*, Summer 1948.
21. *FRUS*, 1948, vol. V, 1398.
22. UNISPAL, "Progress Report of the United Nations Mediator" (Paris, 1948).
23. *FRUS*, 1948, vol. V, 1415.
24. JTA, Sept. 23, 1948. For platform, www.presidency.ucsb.edu/ws/index.php?pid=29599.
25. Cohen, *Truman and Israel*, 243.
26. JTA, Sept. 24, 1948.
27. Cohen, *Truman and Israel*, 244.
28. *IDMay48*, 637.
29. Truman Papers. Handwritten chronology by Jacobson.
30. The telegram is in Truman's papers.
31. Details of the phone conversation: *FRUS*, 1948, vol. V, 1431–32 and 1437–38.
32. *FRUS*, 1948, vol. V, 1490.
33. *New York Herald Tribune*, Oct. 23, 1948.
34. Clifford Papers, Truman Library.
35. *FRUS*, 1948, vol. V, 1513.
36. See Cohen, *Truman and Israel*, 253, on Taft's statement.
37. *Israel Documents: October 1948* (hereinafter *IDOct48*), 54.
38. Wise papers.
39. See Morris, *1948*, 323.
40. *FRUS*, 1948, vol. V, 1476.
41. Ibid., 1493.
42. Morris, *The Birth Revisited*, 492.
43. Truman Papers. Handwritten chronology by Jacobson.
44. *IDOct48*, 106.
45. *FRUS*, 1948, vol. V, 1527.
46. Ibid., 1535.
47. *IDOct48*, 111.
48. *FRUS*, 1948, vol. V, 1528.
49. *IDOct48*, companion volume, 29 (translation from Hebrew).

50. Lowenthal Papers. Diary for November 7.
51. *FRUS*, 1948, vol. V, 1567.
52. Lowenthal Papers.
53. *FRUS*, 1948, vol. V, 1582n.
54. See Lowenthal Papers.
55. *FRUS*, 1948, vol. V, 1611–12.
56. UNISPAL document.
57. Ibid.
58. G. E. Bishart, "Land, Law, and Legitimacy in Israel," *The American University Law Review* 43, no. 467 (1994), 514.
59. *FRUS*, 1949, vol. VI, 738.
60. *Israel Documents: October 1948–April 1949* (hereinafter *IDOct48Apr49*), 445.
61. *FRUS*, 1949, vol. VI, 806.
62. Ibid., 876.
63. *IDOct48Apr49*, 92 in companion volume (translated from Hebrew).
64. *FRUS*, 1949, vol. VI, 905.
65. Ibid., 925.
66. *Israel Documents: May–December 1949* (hereinafter, *IDMay49Dec49*), 261.
67. *FRUS*, 1949, vol, VI, 863.
68. *IDOct48Apr49*, 605.
69. See Medoff, *Zionism and the Arabs*, 151.
70. *FRUS*, 1949, vol. VI, 943.
71. Ibid., 948.
72. Ibid., 954.
73. Ibid., 957.
74. *Israel Documents: May 1949*, 38.
75. *FRUS*, 1949, vol. VI, 975.
76. Ibid., 976.
77. Ibid., 1037.
78. *IDMay49Dec49*, 109.
79. *FRUS*, 1949, vol. VI, 1061.
80. Ibid., vol. V, 1072, 1074.
81. Niles Papers, Truman Library.
82. On McDonald's meeting with Foreign Ministry officials, see *IDMay49Dec49*, 145, and on cables, see *FRUS*, 1949, vol. VI, 1115.
83. *IDMay49Dec49*, 112.
84. George McGhee, *Envoy to the Middle World: Adventures in Diplomacy* (New York: Joanna Cotter Books, 1983), 37.
85. *FRUS*, 1949, vol. VI, 1105.
86. *IDMay49Dec49*, 48 companion volume (translated from Hebrew).
87. For still another tale of intrigue by the Zionist network in Washington during this period, see Hahn, 105–6.
88. *FRUS*, 1949, vol. VI, 1124–25.
89. Truman Library oral history.

90. Sasson makes some of these observations in his memo from Lausanne. *IDMay49Dec49*, 49, companion volume (translated from Hebrew).

91. Quoted in Shlaim, *The Iron Wall: Israel and the Arab World* (New York: W. W. Norton, 2001), 3.

92. *FRUS*, 1949, vol. VI, 1431.

93. Figures from Donald Neff, *Fallen Pillars: U.S. Policy Towards Palestine and Israel Since 1945* (Washington, D.C.: Institute for Palestine Studies, 1995), 93.

94. *FRUS*, 1949, vol. VI, 877.

95. www.christianitytoday.com/ch/2008/issue99/7.30.html.

96. Graham Usher, *Al-Ahram Weekly*, Nov. 4–10, 2004.

97. *Servant of the People*, 289.

98. American Zionist Council papers. Roosevelt was probably put up to writing this by Epstein and the AZEC during the debate taking place over Truman administration policy in the spring of 1949.

AFTERWORD: OBAMA AND THE TRUMAN PRECEDENT

1. www.whitehouse.gov/the-press-office/2011/09/21/remarks-president-obama-address-united-nations-general-assembly.

2. See Judis, "Clueless in Gaza," *New Republic*, February 19, 2013.

3. See Jim Zanotti, "Israel: Background and U.S. Relations," *Congressional Research Service*, Nov. 7, 2012.

4. Sarna, 335–36.

5. For a plausible interpretation of AIPAC's role, see Dan Fleshler, *Transforming America's Israel Lobby: The Limits of Its Power and the Potential for Change* (Washington, D.C.: Potomac Books, 2009).

6. In his book *The Right Man: The Surprise Presidency of George W. Bush, An Inside Account* (New York: Random House, 2003, 259), the former Bush speechwriter David Frum recounts how George W. Bush, trying to decide what position to take on the Israeli-Palestinian conflict, asked his aide Karl Rove, "What do our folks think of the Israeli-Palestinian conflict?" Rove, who understood that Bush was referring to his evangelical supporters, replied, "They think it's part of your war on terror."

7. *Huffington Post*, Nov. 12, 2010.

8. On the links between Obama and Chicago's Jewish community, see Peter Beinart, *The Crisis of Zionism* (New York: Times Books, 2012), Chapter Five.

9. Many of Arnold Wolf's writings can be found here: www.bjpa.org/Publications/results.cfm?Authored=Arnold-Jacob-Wolf&AuthorID=4953#.

10. Ron Kampeas, "Obama: Don't Equate 'Pro-Israel' and 'Pro-Likud,'" JTA, Feb. 24, 2008.

11. JTA, May 28, 2009.

12. www.nytimes.com/2009/06/04/us/politics/04obama.text.html?pagewanted=all.

13. JTA, June 4, 2009.

14. www.haaretz.com/news/full-text-of-netanyahu-s-foreign-policy-speech-at-bar
    -ilan-1.277922.
15. Michael Massing, "Deal Breakers," *American Prospect*, March 2002.
16. Scott Wilson, "Where Obama Failed," *Washington Post*, July 14, 2012.
17. Ibid.
18. Kenneth G. Lieberthal, Martin S. Indyk, and Michael E. O'Hanlon, *Bending History: Barack Obama's Foreign Policy* (Washington, D.C.: Brookings Institution Press, 2012), 128.
19. Daniel C. Kurtzer, Scott B. Lasensky, William B. Quandt, Steven L. Spiegel, and Shibley Z. Telhami, *The Peace Puzzle: America's Quest for Arab-Israeli Peace, 1989–2011* (Ithaca, NY: Cornell University Press, 2013), 262–63.
20. *The New York Times*, May 19, 2011.
21. www.salon.com/2011/05/24/netanyahu_standing_ovations/.
22. Alana Goodman, "Top Democrats," *Commentary*, May 24, 2011.
23. Ron Kampeas, "Democrats Launch Pro-Obama Pushback among Jews," May 24, 2011.
24. *The Forward*, June 29, 2011.
25. Laura Meckler, "Jewish Donors Warn," *The Wall Street Journal*, May 19, 2011.
26. Goodman, "Key Donor," *Commentary*, May 25, 2011.
27. Jennifer Rubin, "AIPAC Weighs In," *Washington Post*, June 15, 2011.
28. Wilson, "Where Obama Failed."
29. House Resolution 268, July 7, 2011.
30. Associated Press, Nov. 30, 2011.
31. *The New York Times*, Sept. 4, 2012.
32. *Politico*, Sept. 20, 2012.
33. www.nytimes.com/2012/09/26/world/obamas-speech-to-the-united-nations
    -general-assembly-text.html?pagewanted=all.
34. Transcript, *The New York Times*, March 21, 2013.
35. Isabel Kershner, "Timing of Israeli Housing Plans May Be Part of a Political Calculation," *The New York Times*, Aug. 12, 2013.
36. *The Times of Israel*, Jan. 8, 2013.
37. *The Times of Israel*, Aug. 13, 2013.

ACKNOWLEDGMENTS

The Carnegie Endownment for International Peace has a small library, but it has borrowing privileges everywhere, and its librarians—Kathleen Higgs, Keigh Hammond, Christopher Scott, and Christopher Henley—were able to get me books, papers, and documents that I wouldn't have been able to see without going to Jerusalem or London. I could not have done this book without their help.

When I finished my first draft, Richard Just, Jordan Smith, Peter Beinart, William Burr, and Mary Edsall read and commented on it. They acted out of friendship and curiosity—none of them, nor anyone else I am about to thank, should be blamed for my mistakes or tied to the argument that the book makes. Eli Zaretsky, Nancy Fraser, and Dan Lewis read specific chapters and helped me figure out what the book was about. I got help on what books to read and archives to consult and on stray facts from Walter Laqueur, Philip Mattar, Jonathan Cohn, Rashid Khalidi, Adam Shatz, Charles Manekin, Sidney Blumenthal, Eric Alterman, Gershom Gorenberg, and Juan Cole.

This book is based, wherever possible, on archival research. I want to thank Michael Devine, Randy Sowell, and Liz Safly at the Truman Library (which also provided me with a travel grant); Susan Woodland and Melanie Meyers at the American Jewish Historical Society in New York; Tal Nadan of the Manuscripts and Archives Division of the New York Public Library; Thomas J. McCutchon at the Columbia University Rare Book and Manuscript Library; Katherine Strickland of the University of Texas Libraries, and the staff at the U.S. Library of Congress Manuscript Reading Room for their help, advice, and kindness.

During the many weeks I spent in New York at libraries, I enjoyed the hospitality of Tom and Mary Edsall. Tom also allowed me to try out some of the ideas in this book on his classes. Ira Forman, who was then the executive director of the National Jewish Democratic Council, invited me to accompany his group on a trip to Israel, which allowed me to stay over several weeks to do research at the Central Zionist Archives. Bernard Avishai and Sidra DeKoven Ezrahi made my time in Jerusalem less lonely. When I was at Carnegie, Rebecca Weiner tried to teach me Hebrew.

While I relied wherever possible on original documents and papers, I learned about their existence from reading books and articles and sometimes from consulting the authors themselves. I've tried to indicate these books in the footnotes, but I want to single out Rafael Medoff, whose *Zionism and the Arabs* was an inspiration to me, and who told me, when I was at a loss, where to find various papers I wanted to consult. My old friend Daniel Ben-Horin, the son of Eliahu Ben-Horin, shared his father's scrapbooks and manuscripts with me.

Rafael Sagalyn guided me in proposing the book and negotiated my contract. At various times over the next six years, as the book's initial deadline faded into the distance, and as the book itself changed shape, I felt certain that Eric Chinski, my editor at Farrar, Straus and Giroux, would tell me to get lost, but Eric was always encouraging and, when I finally finished a draft, gave me excellent advice about improving it. I am also grateful for the editorial advice and assistance with photos and maps I got from his assistant, Gabriella Doob. David Chesanow improved my grammar, Jane Elias spotted errors, and Lenni Wolff and Abby Kagan helped turn the text into a book.

My daugters, Hilary and Eleanor, had the good sense to leave home before I started this book, but my wife, Susan, suffered through it all, including our vacations that I spent closeted in a motel room writing while she had to fend for herself. I can't thank her enough.

INDEX